AFTERMATH OF WAR

AMERICAN DIPLOMATIC HISTORY
Lawrence S. Kaplan, *Editor*

Aftermath of War: Americans and the Remaking of Japan, 1945–1952
Howard B. Schonberger

*The Twilight of Amateur Diplomacy: The American
Foreign Service and Its Senior Officers in the 1890s*
Henry E. Mattox

THE EAST ASIAN INSTITUTE OF COLUMBIA UNIVERSITY
The East Asian Institute is Columbia University's center for research, education, and publication on modern East Asia. The Studies of the East Asian Institute were inaugurated in 1962 to bring to a wider public the results of significant new research on modern and contemporary East Asia.

AFTERMATH OF WAR

Americans and the Remaking of Japan, 1945–1952

Howard B. Schonberger

THE KENT STATE UNIVERSITY PRESS
Kent, Ohio, and London, England

© 1989 by The Kent State University Press, Kent, Ohio 44242
All rights reserved
Library of Congress Catalog Card Number 88-30585
ISBN 0-87338-369-9 (cloth)
ISBN 0-87338-382-6 (paper)
Manufactured in the United States of America

Second paperback printing, 1992

Library of Congress Cataloging-in-Publication Data

Schonberger, Howard B.
    Aftermath of war : Americans and the remaking of Japan, 1945–1952
/ Howard B. Schonberger.
        p.   cm. — (American diplomatic history)
    Bibliography: p.
    Includes index.
    ISBN 0-87338-369-9 (alk. paper). ISBN 0-87338-382-6 (pbk.: alk. paper) ∞
    1. Japan—History—Allied occupation, 1945–1952. 2. United States—Foreign
relations—Japan. 3. Japan—Foreign relations—United States. 4. United
States—Officials and employees—Biography. I. Title. II. Series.
DS889.16.S36 1989
327.73052—dc19   88-30585
                                                 CIP

British Library Cataloging-in-Publication data are available.

This book is
dedicated
In love and gratitude
to my parents
Sidney and Rebecca Schonberger

国際交流基金 寄贈

CONTENTS

ACKNOWLEDGMENTS

The first research for this book began by accident nearly twenty years ago. I had recently finished my graduate work at the University of Wisconsin under the direction of William Appleman Williams. My revised dissertation on the late nineteenth-century linkage of American farmers, food processors, and transportation interests in expanding markets for exports and constructing an informal overseas empire had been accepted for publication. I was absorbed in teaching at Hampton Institute in Hampton, Virginia, doing organizing against the Vietnam War, and gaining insight into the civil rights struggle of black Americans. Then one afternoon my colleague in the Department of History, Lawrence S. Wittner, reminded me of my scholarly calling. He invited me to join him in an exploratory research trip to the newly opened MacArthur Archives in nearby Norfolk.

The most interesting materials in the MacArthur collection I found covered the years the general spent as head of the Occupation of Japan. I plunged into my new work with naive gusto. I had no idea of the many frustrating delays and lengthy detours that lay ahead for me on the research path from these first visits to the MacArthur collection to the completion of this book. But what kept me going were the many friends I made along the way. It was they, more than anything else, who sustained my original fascination with the U.S.-Japanese connection.

John W. Dower deserves special thanks. He set for me the highest standard of excellence in the wide net he casts for his own research, the analytical incisiveness of his writing, and his commitment to E. H. Norman's vision of history as an essential feature of a community which is genuinely civilized.

He has been unstintingly generous in sharing with me his vast and well-organized collection of documents, articles, and books on the Occupation of Japan. Finally, he has given me many hours of sage advice, reassuring encouragement, and careful readings of my work.

I am indebted to many other friends as well. Lawrence S. Wittner and Michael Schaller shared with me their wealth of knowledge of postwar American foreign policy and scrutinized the first draft of my entire manuscript. Roger Dingman, William S. Borden, Joe B. Moore, Laura E. Hein, and Herbert Bix have educated me by the high quality of their own scholarship on the Occupation of Japan and their stimulating exchange of ideas. John Roberts, a journalist resident in Japan, provided invaluable advice and documentation for my work on the Japan Lobby.

During the academic year 1975-76 I was a Fulbright Lecturer at Hiroshima University and had my first opportunity to meet many of the most renowned and active Japanese scholars of the Occupation. I am deeply grateful for all the scholarly and personal assistance I received in Japan and subsequently from Ikuhiko Hata, Takeshi Igarashi, Shoichi Koseki, Eiichi Shindo, Rinjiro Sodei, Eiji Takemae, and Yoko Yasuhara.

Numerous archivists and librarians provided me with critical help. At the National Archives John Taylor deserves special mention for his willingness to direct me to records relevant to my research. The professional staffs of the MacArthur Archives, Princeton University Library, Herbert Hoover Presidential Library, Wisconsin State Historical Society, and British Public Record Office were always encouraging during my research visits.

Some of the chapters in this book, or portions of chapters, appeared earlier as articles. They have been revised to incorporate recent scholarship and eliminate duplication. I thank the journals and publishers for granting me permission to use previously printed materials.

The University of Maine has been my academic home since 1971. The administration, faculty colleagues, and staff have been unfailingly supportive of my work. I have received three University of Maine Faculty Research Fund awards. Members of the administration assisted me in preparing successful grant applications to the American Philosophical Society and the National Endowment for the Humanities. My colleagues David C. Smith, Douglas Allen, and Ngo Vinh Long have been a constant source of encouragement and offered many helpful suggestions and ideas for improving my analysis of world affairs. Tom Patterson and Paul Schroeder of the Fogler Library reference department have conscientiously responded to my numerous queries. Finally, Department of History secretaries Carole Gardner and Carol Rickards cheerfully typed the many drafts of the chapters of my book.

This book is dedicated to my parents Sidney and Rebecca Schonberger.

They have provided me with a model of dedication to social justice and international peace which I have tried to emulate in all my work. Over the years they followed the ups and downs of my research and the seemingly endless writing with a proper mixture of interest and skepticism. The faith they have shown in me has been one of the finest rewards of working on this book.

Finally, thanks go to my wife Ann, and my children, Lisa and Benjamin. They have lived with this book for longer than they care to remember. They endured my many hours of hiding in my office, my frequent despairs, and my occasional raucous excitement at discovering important documents. They grudgingly traveled to research libraries with me during family vacations. Yet they remained supportive and interested. Without them, in all candor, I would never have finished this book.

With the exception of these acknowledgments, Japanese personal names are rendered in Japanese order throughout the text, that is, family name followed by given name.

INTRODUCTION

With the fighting in World War II over in mid-August 1945, more than one-half million American troops moved to occupy Japan. Much of the country was ruined, buried under the rubble and debris of saturation bombing and the atomic bombings of Hiroshima and Nagasaki. The rulers of Japan were stunned by defeat; the people feared what the victors might impose upon them. With breathtaking audacity, General Douglas MacArthur, Supreme Commander for the Allied Powers, set out to remake an ancient and highly sophisticated society of some eighty million people.

Only in the first four months after the war did the Occupation of Japan receive any widespread attention by the American public. With hatred of the Japanese aroused by the bloody military campaigns in the Pacific in 1944 and 1945, Americans closely watched to see that SCAP—an acronym applied to both MacArthur and Occupation headquarters—demilitarized Japan and carried out a program to democratize the country in line with directives from Washington. Once satisfied by news that General MacArthur had the Japanese in hand, Americans who thought at all about foreign affairs during the early Cold War era concentrated on the crises in Europe, the Middle East, or China and tended to forget about Japan altogether. That tendency went largely unchecked for almost twenty-five years after the Japanese peace and security treaties of 1951 ended the Occupation.

However, over the last decade there has been a growing fascination by Americans with Japan which oscillates between awe and fear. Those on the left are worried about gathering evidence of a resurgence of Japanese militarism and ultranationalism. Japanese economic expansion, they argue, has led to the revival of Japanese imperialism. More conservative observers find in Japan's celebrated economic growth a model for the United States to follow. Ezra Vogel in his popular *Japan as Number One* extols the success of Japanese educational, business, and governmental institutions in creating the new economic "miracle."[1]

But most mainstream comment is stridently critical of Japan. Japan is reproached for failing to contribute more to the defense of the "free world" and for not following the American lead in the ongoing redistribution of power in Asia since the end of the Vietnam War. Most of all, Japan's strong economic competition in world markets, symbolized by the enormous trade surplus Japan has developed with the United States, is seen as cause for alarm. Pulitzer Prize winning journalist Theodore White, in a controversial 1985 *New York Times* magazine article, analyzed the "Danger of Japan" in language eerily reminiscent of the 1930s. Japanese business and government officials were "on the move again" in a brilliant global commercial offensive, "as they go about dismantling American industry." For the big Japanese companies "the whole world has become the 'Greater Co-Prosperity Sphere.' " Quoting high Reagan administration officials, angry industrialists, and several congressmen, White warned of a full-scale trade war between the United States and Japan—or even worse. It would be well for the Japanese to remember, he concluded, that "if peace is paramount they need us to keep the peace more than we need them."[2]

Most recent commentary in the United States on Japan asks what role the American government and American corporations played during the Occupation in making Japan, for good or ill, the great world power it has now become. Theodore White laid out the conventional wisdom on the subject. He ascribed the current commercial success of the Japanese to the "mercy and generosity" of the United States during the Occupation. American economic aid, directives to MacArthur "cut from the cloth of American good-will," and the protection of American military forces saved the Japanese from ruin after the war and "allowed their industry, their universities, their ingenuity to flourish." The Americans allowed the Japanese to "pick and choose" from amongst the directives and arranged for a generous peace treaty. Once the Americans pulled out, White concluded, the Japanese launched a program to catch up to and overtake the United States in the commercial field by fair means and foul.[3]

Virtually all scholars of Japan reject the use by White and the "Japan bashers" of the racist idiom of Japanese economic supermen using unfair tactics to outperform other countries. Nor do these scholars accept the protectionist and other policy conclusions of such writers. But, wittingly or not, White and his followers draw their interpretation of the Occupation from the scholarship of the Conservative School of Japanese studies that has been dominant in the United States since World War II. It may be useful to briefly review the background and salient arguments of this school in the context of American scholarship on the Occupation more generally In so doing, the significance of the arguments presented in this book and the limitations of popular interpretations of the Occupation and its legacy become clearer.

American scholarly views of the Occupation can be considered in three main schools—the Conservative, Progressive, and New Left. Most of the senior scholars of the Conservative School such as Edwin O. Reischauer, Robert E. Ward, and Herbert Passin were trained for wartime intelligence or participation in the Occupation. Aided by government and foundation support, they introduced Japanese studies programs to American universities in the 1950s and established the paradigm concepts in the field.[4] They have emphasized in all their work the success aspects of prewar and postwar Japanese history. In their view Japan's experience of a militarist takeover and aggressive imperialism in the 1930s was an aberration. Until that time Japan was modernizing toward a more prosperous and less authoritarian state system as well as working in peaceful cooperation with the Western capitalist powers. From their analysis of Japan's prewar history, the Conservative School scholars concluded that under the direction of SCAP the purge of the military and a few fascist intriguers, accompanied by modest reforms of Japanese institutions, was sufficient to put Japan back on the path of modernization from which it had strayed. They placed emphasis in their studies on the generosity of the Americans and the cooperation of the Japanese in the "massive experiment in 'planned' or 'directed' political change." They also argued that the Occupation laid the groundwork for what was once almost universally considered the desirable economic miracle of the 1950s and 1960s. Finally, the Conservative scholars defended the Japanese peace and security treaties of 1951 for insuring Japan's participation in the "free world."[5]

A small group of mostly forgotten scholars in the Progressive School of Japanese studies attempted for a short time after the war to challenge the Conservative scholarship on the Occupation. Like their ideological rivals, Owen Lattimore, T. A. Bisson, and Miriam Farley were also participants in the planning for or implementation of the Occupation. Drawing heavily on the historical writings of Canadian diplomat E. Herbert Norman, they stressed that the roots of Japanese aggression in Asia in the 1930s could be found in the complex nature of the authoritarian state that developed under the Meiji Restoration after 1868. Moreover, all the dominant sections of the ruling oligarchy—the court, army, Zaibatsu businesses, and state bureaucracy—were agreed on the goal, if not the methods or timing, of conquering an Asian empire at least from the 1880s. Consequently, the problem for SCAP was not a mild housecleaning of a few militarists or ultranationalists, as the Conservative School scholars propounded, but a series of thoroughgoing reforms which would destroy the prewar ruling oligarchy and elevate the truly democratic and anti-imperialist elements in Japan who could be found primarily in the trade union movement, peasant associations, universities, and moderately left-wing parties.

But as early as 1948, these Progressive scholars became disillusioned with the Occupation. Convinced that the intervention of the American business community and conservative Washington policymakers resulted in a sharp swing to the right in Occupation policy, they focused their writing on the persistence of prewar power centers in Japan. Finally, Progressive scholars, hopeful that Japan would remain neutral in the Cold War, criticized the American peace and security treaty plans which forced Japan to rearm, keep American bases, and limit contact with the Chinese mainland.[6]

The anti-Communist hysteria that developed in the United States over the triumph of the Chinese Communist revolution and the Korean War led to the demise of the Progressive School and the ascendancy of the Conservative School of Japanese studies. Owen Lattimore, T. A. Bisson and other Progressives were hauled before witch-hunting investigative committees, pushed out of their jobs, and denied outlets for publication. In addition, Conservative School scholars, whose work buttressed the policy views of American ruling circles after 1947, explicitly took on the task of developing a countertheory to that of the Progressives and influential Marxists in Japan as well. Reischauer, for example, emphasized Japan as a model capitalist state—rational, industrially prosperous, and politically democratic—in order to challenge the "historical illusions" behind Marxism and the blurred vision of Japan and Asia as seen through Marxist glasses.[7] With the Progressive scholars so heavily assaulted politically and ideologically, Conservative School scholarship became the unchallenged orthodoxy on the Occupation for over two decades.

The Vietnam War and social upheaval in America during the 1960s created the climate in which benign assessments of the American Occupation of Japan would be questioned. A group of Japanese historians and American diplomatic historians led by John Dower turned to the forgotten Progressive School of Japanese studies and "New Left historians" William A. Williams and Gabriel Kolko for inspiration. They pointed out how the decision of the Truman administration to keep the emperor institution intact and work through the existing Japanese government seriously compromised all efforts at democratization before the first American soldier set foot on Japan. They focused attention on what Conservative School scholars slighted or denied even occurred, namely the "reverse course," a unilateral and politically reactionary "shift of emphasis" from reform to economic recovery. The political crisis in China and the threat of a global economic collapse after 1947, these scholars argued, led the Truman administration to try to make Japan the dominant economic and political power in Asia and to begin a limited rearmament program as well. To the New Left Scholars these international objectives of American policy explicitly entailed gutting major early reforms and restoring key elements of the prewar oligarchy. The outbreak of the Korean War accelerated all these trends and culminated in the peace and security treaties that linked Japan as an ally of the United States in the restoration of capitalism and the suppression of left-wing nationalism and revolution in Asia. In short, New Left scholars, while acknowledging important changes wrought by the Occupation, emphasized the continuities in the class structure, ruling personnel, domestic and foreign policies, institutions, and attitudes between prewar and postwar Japan.[8]

This book attempts to grapple with the complex arguments of each of the three schools of Occupation scholarship through the novel approach of collective biography. It discusses eight Americans who were significant figures in the major stages of the Occupation. Five of these Americans were official architects of Japan policy; the three remaining men functioned at lower levels in the American policy-making community or outside of it altogether. All recognized that the tasks of any occupation were temporary. The ultimate goal was peace with sovereign Japan in a world polarized by war and politics, want and plenty, capitalism and socialism. Inevitably sharp differences emerged among these men as they attempted to remake the Old Japan into a New Japan.

For too long the Occupation on the American side has been viewed as the personal monopoly of General Douglas MacArthur. Voluminous documentary materials recently available to scholars belie such a simplistic interpretation. To begin with, some of the most critical decisions affecting the Occupation were taken before MacArthur became supreme commander and without ever consulting him. Reflecting three years of debate by wartime planners, the final directives to MacArthur were replete with ambiguous compromises. Yet, as argued in the first chapter on Ambassador Joseph Grew, the decision to keep the Japanese governmental structure in place, including the emperor institution, critically affected all else. It imposed severe limits on the "demilitarization and democratization" program MacArthur sought to implement and preserved the option, which Grew considered vital, of making Japan, rather than China, the anchor of American policy in Asia.

There was a puzzling paradox in having a military officer renowned for his hatred of Franklin D. Roosevelt enthusiastically implementing a reform program for Japan akin to the New Deal. In fact for a short time MacArthur proved its staunchest defender against those in Washington after 1947 who sought to dismantle many of the early reforms. The key to resolving the paradox, as chapter two on MacArthur argues, is the central importance to the general of winning the Republican presidential nomination and election in 1948. His every word and action in Japan was taken with an eye to supplementing his war-hero status in the United States with a reputation as a peacemaker and competent administrator over a civilian government.

Even though he recognized that the Japanese elites opposed the far-reaching reform program, MacArthur saw no acceptable alternative but to rely on them for the day-to-day administration of the country. To do otherwise, he feared, was to invite chaos, mass misery, communism, and the demise of his presidential aspirations. From the opening months of the Occupation MacArthur's fervent press corps conveyed the message across America that Japan, unlike Germany and other nations in which the United States was deeply involved, was successfully achieving the goal of a peaceful and stable democracy and thwarting Russian aims as well. The complete failure of MacArthur's presidential bid and his subsequent claim to have been a reluctant participant in the political arena do not gainsay the significance of the supreme commander's political opportunism for understanding the many contradictions in his handling of the Occupation.

Though rarely heard in the United States, many civilians serving in SCAP headquarters questioned how successful a policy of democratization could be when Washington and MacArthur were so evidently committed to preserving the emperor institution and supporting conservative Japanese governments. T. A. Bisson, a member of Government Section of SCAP in 1946 and 1947, was more impressed with the continuities than the discontinuities between prewar and postwar Japanese life. Heavily involved in programs for the democratization of the business system, Bisson repeatedly met overt opposition from his Japanese counterparts. He complained without effect to his superiors within SCAP that the deliberately inflationary economic policy of the Japanese government was undermining his own work and other critical American reform programs. Even before the "reverse course" in American policy after 1947, Bisson considered the prospects for a truly democratic Japan dim. Disillusioned by his experience, Bisson returned home to become one of the most trenchant left-wing critics of the American Occupation.

To American wartime planners of the Occupation the development of a strong bread-and-butter trade union movement was to be a principal bulwark of a new democratic Japan, checking the unrestrained power of Japanese business and conservative politicians alike. But even before the end of 1945 the upsurge of labor activism and the close ties of the trade unions to the left-wing opposition parties alarmed many American officials in Tokyo and Washington who soon defined the Japanese Left as a greater threat to a democratic Japan than the prewar oligarchy. James S. Killen, an officer in the papermakers union of the militantly anti-Communist American Federation of Labor, took over as chief of Labor Division in the spring of 1947, and as chapter four argues, devoted the bulk of his energies to strengthening the nonpolitical bread-and-butter trade unionists against the Communist activists.

But like the more radical Bisson, Killen was also appalled by the uncooperativeness and antilabor practices of Japanese business and government. He quickly concluded that as long as SCAP failed to dampen the inflationary spiral undermining the Japanese worker's real wages, strikes and political action against conservative Japanese governments were unavoidable. To Killen's dismay inflation went unchecked. In addition, in July 1948 MacArthur decided—in accord with the new emphasis in American policy on economic recovery in Japan—to remove the militant government workers, comprising about one-third of the trade union movement, from the protections of the SCAP-sponsored Trade Union Law of December 1945. For months Killen had fought against those in SCAP recommending such a change in policy. He argued correctly, as subsequent developments showed, that the revision in labor policy was not so much an anti-Communist program as one which undermined the strength of the entire Japanese labor movement. In the wake of MacArthur's decision, a disillusioned Killen resigned and returned home to mobilize the leaders of the American labor movement against what all agreed was a reactionary labor policy in Occupied Japan.

Unlike such left-wing and liberal critics of the Occupation as Bisson and Killen, those who considered the original democratic reform program and MacArthur's implementation of it too radical were increasingly successful in influencing Washington policy. The most notable of these conservative critics was Harry F. Kern, foreign affairs editor of *Newsweek* magazine and the subject of chapter five. Kern organized in 1947 and 1948 a Japan Lobby which, in essence, represented the interests of American corporations having or seeking investments in Japan and influential Japanese conservatives opposed to the "demilitarization and democratization program." What impressed Kern and his friends most about the Japan of 1947 was the stagnation of the Japanese economy, the social and political activism of Japanese workers and the Left, and the threat which SCAP-sponsored legislation in the business field represented to American corporate interests.

Aided by Secretary of Commerce W. Averell Harriman and other powerful figures in the Truman administration, Kern and the Japan Lobby became the catalyst for a major shift in American policy from emphasis on democratic reform to economic reconstruction and the gradual restoration of unfettered conservative rule in Japan. By 1949 Kern and the Japan Lobby took on the role of watchdog over any attempt by MacArthur to thwart the new policy direction and provided a vital informal communication linkage between conservative

Japanese and Washington policymakers designing the economic and military terms of the Cold War alliance.

The key figure in the shift of American policy for Japan that occurred in 1947 and 1948 was Under Secretary of the Army William H. Draper, whose office was most directly responsible for the Occupation. A Wall Street investment banker before the war, General Draper was especially sympathetic to the criticisms of Japanese economic policies offered by Kern and the Japan Lobby. He also shared the geopolitical analysis developed by George Kennan and the State Department Policy Planning Staff in mid-1947. They argued that with China falling into the hands of the Communists, Japan was the most important element in a new balance of power in Asia and, therefore, had to be denied to the Soviet bloc.

It was Draper's singular contribution to take a proposed four-year economic recovery program for Japan analogous to the Marshall Plan for Europe and attach to it, over the strenuous objections of key figures in the State Department and SCAP, conditions which ensured the subversion of the original demilitarization and democratization program. Only the full restoration of the Japanese business class and conservative politicians offered hope to Draper for securing American interests (which he defined primarily as the interests of American business) in Japan and the rest of Asia against the threat of nationalism and communism. When MacArthur refused to implement his new directives in early 1948, it was Draper who successfully organized the Washington bureaucracy, Congress, and the American business community to bring SCAP back into line.

Ironically, Japanese conservatives and businessmen found it politically impossible or economically unprofitable to fully implement the austerity measures required by the recovery program to increase Japanese exports and thereby make American aid imports eventually unnecessary. Facing another battle with Congress over funding for the Japanese program, Draper persuaded Joseph Dodge, president of the Detroit Bank and probably the most important overseas economic troubleshooter of the Truman administration, to go to Japan to implement a December 1948 National Security Council (NSC) directive calling for an economic stablization program and establishment of a single dollar/yen exchange rate which would assure the integration of Japan with world markets.

Dodge became the financial czar of Japan in 1949 and early 1950. The economic impact of his wide-ranging policies is still a matter of great debate today. Unquestionably the Dodge Plan caused wrenching economic dislocations and generated enormous political opposition by all sectors within Japan, especially the trade union movement and the very large class of small businessmen. Though not questioning the objectives of the Dodge Plan, even large industrialists and bankers and the conservative ruling party found Dodge's orthodox economic philosophy too rigid and his program too drastic.

Despite all the objections, Dodge, as chapter seven emphasizes, persisted in seeing his program as the only means by which to assure the multiple objectives of the integration of Japanese and Southeast Asian markets, the creation of Japan as a bulwark of anti-Communist containment throughout Asia, and continued funding by Congress for the remainder of the Japanese recovery program. American purchases of supplies from Japan for United Nations forces in Korea after July 1950 rescued the economy from the doldrums suffered during the year of the Dodge Plan. Dodge's personal influence waned thereafter but was nevertheless considerable. Working with his friends in the Economic and Scientific Section of SCAP, Dodge was instrumental in the development in 1951 of the "U.S.-Japan economic cooperation" program. By that program Dodge sought to guarantee Japanese economic growth, the participation of Japanese industry in the U.S.-sponsored global rearmament program begun in the wake of the Korean War, and finally the establishment of a nexus of aid and trade between the United States, Japan, and Southeast Asia which was necessary to U.S. containment policy for Asia.

No one was more responsible for completing the breathtaking transformation of Japan from bitter enemy to Cold War ally than John Foster Dulles, a seasoned diplomat and top foreign policy advisor to the Republican Party. Dulles was brought into the State Department in April 1950 to work on the Japanese peace treaty. By that time the Pentagon and the State Department were in agreement that Japan ought to play a more active role in U.S. anti-Communist containment policy in Asia and that to do so required Japan both to rearm and to allow U.S. military bases to remain for the indefinite future. But the two departments quarreled over whether these objectives were best accomplished by prolonging the Occupation or granting an early peace treaty. In September 1950 Dulles finally resolved the dispute and proceeded to negotiate specific terms of peace between the Japanese and the United States and its World War II allies.

The key to the whole enterprise for Dulles was a Japanese commitment to a separate bilateral security treaty with the United States. The pact provided for unrestricted American base rights and commitment by Japan to rearmament beyond the 75,000-man National Police Reserve created soon after the outbreak of war in Korea. Japanese conservatives were willing to concede base rights to the American military establishment. But they strenuously balked at Dulles's demand to create a ground force of between 300,000 and 325,000. Reluctantly they counteroffered with a vague promise to organize a new 50,000-man force. Though disappointed, Dulles and the Pentagon nevertheless considered that satisfactory. By linking the peace treaty granting Japan its political independence to the bilateral security pact on bases and rearmament, Dulles insured the military integration of Japan into the great arc of anti-Communist containment running from Alaska to the Philippines. Moreover, contrary to the wishes of the Japanese leadership, Dulles successfully insisted that the new alliance required Japan's economic isolation from the People's Republic of China and accommodation with the rump Nationalist regime on Taiwan. Though serious objections to both the peace and security treaties were raised, not only by the Russians and the Communist Chinese but by most American allies as well, Dulles ignored them or made only minor concessions more of form than substance. Having succeeded by April 1952 in enrolling Japan into the American sphere of influence in the Pacific, Dulles stood on the threshold of achieving his lifelong ambition, the job of secretary of state.

Six major themes cut across the boundaries of the individual chapters in this book. They are stated here merely as propositions and elaborated on more fully in the conclusion. First, American policy for Occupied Japan rested primarily on enlightened self-interest more than generosity or goodwill. Secondly, throughout the eighty months of the Occupation the Japanese oligarchy that held power after the war managed remarkably well to thwart American policies not to their liking and achieve key objectives of their own. Thirdly, evidence for an American sponsored ''reverse course'' away from reform in Japan after 1947 is unmistakable. Fourth, the ''reverse course'' within Japan had an external dynamic. The reconstruction of Japan under the aegis of conservative politicians and business leaders required, in George Kennan's famous phrase, that Japan seek an ''empire to the south.'' Fifth, American businessmen played a crucial role in defining the ''reverse course'' and subsequent Occupation policies. Finally, American policymakers treated Japan not as an isolated experiment in social engineering but primarily within the framework of global economic concerns and Cold War fears of the Soviet Union and communism.

This book makes no pretense at offering a history of the Occupation of Japan. Such a history would have to give detailed attention to the Japanese side of the Occupation and to draw upon Japanese sources. I have not. In addition, such a study would treat the role of U.S. allies in the Occupation more fully than I have done. By contrast, I have sought to focus upon key Americans and their program for postwar Japan. How these Americans thought, and how they rationalized and explained the actions they took is crucial to an understanding of the transformation of a defeated enemy into the most important Pacific ally of the United States in the Cold War. More broadly, this study also may help to explain the roots of present-day conflicts within the Japanese-American alliance.

1 JOSEPH C. GREW

The Emperor of Japan and Planning the Occupation

No question caused greater difficulty for American policymakers responsible for winning the war against Japan and preparing for the Occupation than how to treat Emperor Hirohito. Some shared the predominant public view in the last months of the Pacific war that the emperor had approved the Japanese attack on Pearl Harbor and bore responsibility for a war of aggression against the United States. Adherents of this opinion argued that no modification of "unconditional surrender" terms permitting the retention of the imperial institution should be made; the throne was the foundation of power for militaristic and ultranationalistic groups directing the Japanese war effort. Furthermore, Hirohito himself should be tried as a war criminal. A Gallup poll taken in June 1945 indicated the depth of American support for severe treatment of the emperor. It showed that 33 percent of respondents favored hanging Hirohito, another 37 percent favored putting him on trial as a war criminal, imprisoning him for life, or exiling him, and only 7 percent thought the emperor should be left alone or used as a puppet under United Nations supervision.[1]

Among the many high-placed critics of such public opinion, the most notable was Joseph Grew. A proponent of modifying "unconditional surrender" to permit the retention of the imperial institution and of using Hirohito's authority for at least the first phase of the Occupation, Grew was the former U.S. ambassador to Japan and, during 1944–45, under secretary of state. He firmly advocated the monarchy be used to unify "liberal" elements in Japan willing to cooperate with the global postwar objectives of the United States.

And Grew was a key participant in the development of plans for the Occupation of Japan, especially the treatment of the emperor.

The Making of a Diplomat

Born in 1880 into a wealthy and socially prominent Boston family, Joseph C. Grew attended Groton prep school and Harvard College. Shortly after graduating from Harvard in 1902, he decided on a career in the U.S. diplomatic service. Starting as a consular clerk in Cairo, the young diplomat and his new wife, daughter of a "Boston Brahmin," jumped from post to post over the world until settling down for almost nine years in Berlin prior to American entry into World War I. His work as secretary to the U.S. Commission to the Paris Peace Conference attracted the favorable attention of President Woodrow Wilson's advisor, Colonel Edward M. House, and others, and Grew was promoted to ministerial rank in 1920. Grew served as minister to Denmark and Switzerland and then as delegate to the Conference on Near Eastern Affairs in Lausanne during 1922 and 1923. Lausanne established Grew's reputation as a skilful diplomat and he was chosen by Secretary of State Charles Evans Hughes as under secretary, theoretically the number two position in the department. But Hughes gave Grew trivial duties, as did his successor, Secretary of State Frank Kellogg. Grew became increasingly isolated from the policy-making circles of the department. His plans for developing a professional Foreign Service met with mounting congressional and public criticism, and in the spring of 1927 a humiliated under secretary welcomed his appointment as ambassador to Turkey, a post he proudly held for the next five years.[2]

With his appointment as ambassador to Japan in 1932 Grew moved into a storm of domestic and international conflict. The world depression profoundly shook each of the five major groups or cliques that formed the oligarchy ruling Japan since the Meiji Restoration of 1868. The army and navy leaders, the top government bureaucrats, the leaders of the political parties, the Zaibatsu families who controlled the financial and industrial nexus, and the large landholders—all jockeyed to hold or increase power within the ruling coalition under the stress of economic disaster. But all were committed to strengthening the emperor system as the keystone to maintaining their rule over the Japanese people. Using every method of propaganda known, the oligarchy had created by the 1930s an emperor perceived as the personification of the whole nation. He was said to be descended from a supernatural being and therefore to be revered as a religious figure and unquestionably obeyed as the father of all Japanese.

The depression did not undermine the authority of the emperor system. It did prompt more intense government repression of dissenting groups and political parties. Extreme right-wing organizations gained large followings and influence, especially in the military. The day the Grews left Washington for the Orient, a band of young naval officers and army cadets assassinated Prime Minister Inukai Ki, the third prominent victim of nationalist agitation that year. In the aftermath, the war minister backed the demand of the army for an end to governments headed by leaders of the political parties and thus retracted a concession made by the oligarchy to popular unrest after World War I. When Grew took up his mission a nonparty regime headed by a retired admiral was in place and the military had clearly assumed a more important role in the ruling coalition.[3]

As Grew quickly discovered, the growing military involvement of Japan on the Asian mainland helped entrench the military cabinets of the 1930s. Military incidents in Manchuria in 1931 prompted a Japanese occupation of the area and the establishment of the puppet state of Manchukuo (Manzhouguo). This move, which shattered the agreements of the Western Powers and Japan for dealing with China reached at the Washington Conference of 1921 and 1922, was a predictable outcome of the expansionist foreign policy supported by the ruling oligarchy since 1890. Japanese leaders believed that, for Japan to successfully industrialize and become a great power, it was necessary to secure markets and raw materials from overseas. Manchuria, Northern China, and Korea played the most prominent role in the evolving plans for empire. Both the Sino-Japanese War of 1894–95 and the Russo-Japanese War of 1904–05 were fought to secure and protect Japan's economic and security interests in the area. The withdrawal of European military power from China during World War I prompted greater Japanese expansion on the mainland. The Washington Conference agreements ended the immediate threat of war with the West but encouraged the rise of Chinese nationalism and the beginning of the unification of China under Generalissimo Chiang Kai-shek (Jiang Jieshi). As the decade of the 1920s drew to a close, Japanese efforts to expand in northern China met stiff resistance from the Chinese. The depression intensified the oligarchy's interest in the raw materials and markets of the Asian mainland and lit the fuse that exploded in the Manchurian incident.[4] Defying Western demands to adhere to the Washington Conference treaties and the League of Nations, Japan had become an openly predatory nation in the eyes of most of the world when Grew arrived in Tokyo.

Sensitive to the vigorous protests and threats of military action by Secretary of State Henry Stimson and the policy of nonrecognition of Manzhouguo by President Herbert Hoover, a stream of high court officials, Foreign Office bureaucrats, and naval officers visited Grew within a few months of his arrival to express their strong misgivings about the Manchurian venture. Variously called by Grew the "thoughtful," "liberal," "moderate," or "saner" Japanese, these men were the type Grew knew and understood. Almost all of them were from wealthy and socially prominent families, had studied in the West, spoke English, and shared a disposition for Western concepts of peace and order. Grew held out hope that they would be able to regain control over the militarists and put Japan back on the path taken during the 1920s.

Grew idealized the Japan of the 1920s, describing it with glowing simplicity in terms of constitutional party government and peaceful diplomacy. In so doing he ignored the fact that, even after passage of universal manhood suffrage in 1925, no party represented any significant proportion of peasants and workers. The oligarchy, including the "moderates," carried out a program of active repression against the militant labor and tenant farmer unions as well as against socialist and anarchist organization. The gains of the two major parties were made through often corrupt collaboration with key bureaucrats, military leaders, and the Zaibatsu. Although the governments of the 1920s tolerated limited union organization and moderate leftist parties and passed some social legislation, Japan's experiment with party government was far from a triumph of popular democracy. Similarly, Japanese diplomacy of the 1920s, while based on peaceful cooperation with the West, still remained committed to plans for empire in China as the highest priority. Those who Grew considered extremists differed from his moderate friends not so much in their diplomatic objectives as in their tactics and the timing of Japan's expansionist moves.[5]

In any case, members of the Imperial Court had an especially strong influence on Grew. Count Kabayama Aisuke of the House of Peers linked Grew to a network of aristocrats including Imperial Household Minister Matsudaira Tsuneo, Prince Tokugawa Iyeseto, heir of the last of the Shoguns, Prince Chichibu, the emperor's brother and an Oxford graduate, and Prince Konoye Fumimaro, a nobleman of extraordinary wealth who, as premier, became Grew's hope at the end of the 1930s for avoiding a clash between Japan and the United States. Yoshida Shigeru, then ambassador to Italy, served as one of Grew's most important liaisons to Japanese political circles in the 1930s. Yoshida and his father-in-law, Count Makino Nobuaki, sought to convince Grew that the forces of moderation, backed by the emperor himself, were on the upswing. Kabayama, Yoshida, Makino, Matsudaira, former foreign minister Baron Shidehara Kijuro, whose diplomacy of the previous decade rested on commitment to the Washington treaties, and a few others persuaded Grew of the "pendulum theory" of Japanese development. "Japanese history shows that the country has passed through periodical cycles of intense nationalism attended by anti-foreign sentiment, but these periods have always been followed by other periods of international conciliation and cooperation," Grew maintained, "and there will be a similar outcome in the present situation."[6]

Through his acquaintance with this small coterie of aristocrats and internationalists, Grew also derived his view of the emperor as the cornerstone of a great culture and civilization temporarily derailed by militarists and ultranationalists. According to this line of thinking, Japan's actions in the 1930s did not stem from any structural flaws in the oligarchic state system, headed by the emperor, that was established in the Meiji Restoration. In fact, Grew shared the belief of Count Makino that the danger of both fascism and communism in Japan was not real as long as the emperor remained supreme. Even after the outbreak of war with China and in the Pacific, Grew held firmly to the view that the emperor was the key to a moderate and internationally peaceful Japan.

Though by 1934 Grew came to see Japanese expansionism in China as a fixed policy because the military "was firmly in the saddle and will continue to be there," he remained hopeful that "painfully and by slow degrees" the moderates could regain control and restrain the militarists. He believed that American policy toward Japan should avoid recriminations and be conducted in a spirit of conciliation which would assist the Japanese moderates. The outbreak of the Sino-Japanese War in 1937 did not alter Grew's conviction that the United States should refrain from meddling in the conflict. Secretary of State Cordell Hull and most of the State Department agreed with Grew, but unlike him, sympathized with the plight of the Chinese and considered it futile to talk of improving relations with Japan until its violations of the peace structure in China ceased.[7]

Grew remained sympathetic to the Japanese position in China even after more than two years of war. He considered that "Japan in China has a good case and strong case if she knew how to present it, but her stupidity in publicity and progaganda is only exceeded by her stupidity in methods." Grew had nothing but praise for Minister to China John V. A. MacMurray's celebrated 1935 memorandum in which "Chinese intransigence" was contrasted with the patient efforts of Japan to preserve the Washington Treaty system before the Manchurian incident. "Japan in China has behaved like a bull in a china shop," Grew wrote to a former ambassador to Japan in February 1940. "That means largely the military. They have injured if not ruined their own reasonably sound cause by their ruthless methods. Apart from breach of treaty commitments they have set out to bomb our American property out of existence and to crowd legitimate American business and trade out of China by monopolies, trade restrictions, and a hundred other methods of discriminating interference."[8]

With the announcement in July 1939 of its intention to terminate the U.S.-

Japan commercial treaty, the State Department embarked on a course of pressuring Japan to respect American interests in China. Grew was not even consulted, no doubt because of his repeated admonitions against any sanctions that were not backed by a willingness to go to war. In the aftermath of the unexpected Nazi-Soviet pact and the outbreak of war in Europe, the Japanese sought to improve relations with the United States and avoid abrogation of the commercial treaty in January 1940. Grew saw his task as informing the Japanese people, especially the moderates, that they were deluding themselves if they believed there could be a Japanese-American rapprochement and a continuation of Japanese policies in China. Ever the optimist, Grew considered his efforts by February 1940 to have helped "liberal minded Japanese . . . to see where the tactics of the military are leading the country so far as relations with the United States were concerned . . . . A patient effort is developing to conciliate and play the game along saner lines. The extremists in the army have been taken out of controlling positions and have been replaced by officers of broader vision. . . . The bombings of American property and the indignities to American citizens have almost but not quite stopped."[9]

Though Grew's efforts were appreciated by the moderates, he did not reorient their thinking or shake their complacency. After all, such moderates as Prime Minister Konoye and Foreign Minister Hirota Koki had led the hardliners in Japan after the outbreak of war in China in 1937 in seeking a "fundamental solution of Sino-Japanese relations" through aggressive military campaigns. Leaders of Japanese business and industry, also moderates in Grew's view, publicly supported after 1937 a military government for all of China. The emperor himself refused in 1938 to grant an audience to the Army General Staff which, at that point, opposed military and political activities in China.[10] Yet in the spring of 1940 Grew was still inclined to believe that these same moderates had finally come to see the fallacy of Japan's quest for autarky and welcomed encouragement from the United States.

Events quickly overwhelmed Grew's controversial policy that he called—in answer to those who dubbed him an appeaser—"constructive conciliation." Throughout the summer of 1940 Grew made repeated pleas to Japanese leaders not to join with Germany and Italy in an Axis alliance but to adjust relations with the United States. He got nowhere. In his famous "green-light" cable of 12 September 1940, sent two weeks before Japan formally joined the Tripartite Pact, Grew confessed the failure of his diplomacy. With his confidence lost in the independent strength of the moderates and in their policies Grew recommended the implementation of sanctions by the United States and preparation for war against Japan.[11]

The formation of the Axis alliance and the creation of new authoritarian institutions by the second Konoye cabinet deepened Grew's pessimism. Occasionally during 1941 Grew had recurrent hopes that an agreement might be reached which would take the two governments off their collision course. Grew favored taking up the Japanese initiative of August for a meeting somewhere in the Pacific between Premier Konoye and President Roosevelt. But by then Japanese armies had already occupied French Indochina and operational plans were hastened for an invasion of Malaya, the Netherlands East Indies, and the Philippines. The Imperial Navy had begun preparations for an attack on Pearl Harbor. On the American side, Roosevelt responded to Japan's southward advance by freezing all Japanese assets in the United States and embargoing oil. Though his prognosis was generally gloomy, Grew again and again urged the State Department not to insist on detailed commitments as a condition for the meeting of the two heads of state. Secretary of State Cordell Hull disagreed. On his advice, the president informed Japanese Ambassador Nomura Kichisaburo that Japan must first stop its military advances, withdraw troops from China, resolve problems of trade discrimination, and give a clearer statement of its position in regard to the European war. With that the Konoye cabinet resigned.[12] In short, the Japanese government sought both hegemony over China and Southeast Asia and friendly relations with the United States. When Roosevelt and Hull confronted the Japanese with a choice between those two objectives, the attack upon Pearl Harbor was the tragic answer.

For months Grew had warned Washington that time was running out and war was unavoidable without a relaxation in the American negotiating position. But the boldness and success of the attack on Pearl Harbor took him, like almost all Americans, by bitter surprise. He and his staff were interned in the American embassy from 8 December 1941 to 25 June 1942. Two months later, he arrived in New York and went directly to Washington to report to Secretary Hull. At age sixty-two, Grew viewed his career as coming to an end. His advice and the work of the embassy had been largely ignored. Little did he forsee that the next three years would be his most significant in shaping the course of American policy in the Far East.

Propagandist for Victory

Grew's first assignment as special assistant to the secretary of state was a speaking tour coordinated by the Office of War Information. Though he had no Japanese language competency, a superficial understanding of Japanese history, and little acquaintance with the Japanese people outside of the elites, Grew thought of himself, and was regarded publicly, as the leading American authority on Japanese affairs. In more than two hundred speeches during his first year back home he attempted to capitalize on that reputation and help OWI's campaign against the "unfounded optimism and smug complacency" of the American people toward defeating Japan. He made repeated references to his six-month internment in solitary confinement in small and bitterly cold quarters and offered descriptions of the water cure and other atrocities inflicted on American missionaries held with him. He drew a grim picture of the brutal enslavement of the peoples of Asia under Japanese rule and warned —into the spring of 1943—of Japanese plans for an attack on the West Coast. He repeatedly criticized the public myth of Japanese weakness and exhorted his audiences to aid in war production.[13]

Newspaper headlines of his speeches from across the country illustrate his explicit purpose of sending people "home in an angry and fighting mood." "Grew Bids U.S. Buckle Down to Tough War Job, Calls on Public to Wake Up, Stop Groping"; " 'Japs Tougher than Nazis,' says Grew"; "Grew Inspecting Detroit. Visits War Plants. Says 'Defeat Japan's Might Quickly Or It Will Rule The World.' " The enemy was always defined in these speeches as the Japanese military machine which had ruthlessly plotted conquest since 1931 and exercised control over a docile and regimented people ready to sacrifice their lives for the emperor and the homeland. Even after the American success in stopping further Japanese conquests by 1943, Grew warned against being taken in by peace offensives of presumably liberal cabinets which were still controlled by the military. The military machine had to be completely smashed, and that entailed sacrifice and hard work from the American people.[14]

While emphasizing the bestiality and cruelty of the Japanese military machine in these early wartime speeches, Grew faithfully carried out OWI's injunction against criticism of the emperor. One of his off-the-record talks was titled "Liberal Elements in Japan" in which he specifically mentioned Admiral Nomura, Ambassador Kurusu Saburo, and Japanese businessmen who had lived abroad. But Grew implied that the emperor too was one of the "great many Japanese who did not want this war and did nothing to bring it about. These elements are powerless at present and will have to fight the war through to the bitter end, but once the Japanese military machine is completely defeated, these liberal elements may form a nucleus around which some authority with which the United States and the United Nations can deal."[15] Only in mid-1943 did Grew think it appropriate to shift the emphasis of his on-the-record speeches to this topic and not until December 1943 did he publicly touch on the emperor question per se.

The central importance Grew attached to the emergence of "liberal elements" in Japan after the defeat of the military is explained not only by personal friendships and a shared antipathy towards communism, but by his

Former Ambassador to Japan Joseph C. Grew warns the American
people not to underestimate the strength of the Japanese enemy.
Life, 7 December 1942; Keystone Press Service.

perception of their commitment to American economic war aims. Like Secretary of State Hull, Grew saw high tariffs, import quotas, exchange restrictions, and barter agreements as restricting international trade in the 1930s and a key factor in the coming of the war.

The Japanese militarists turned from one kind of economic system—the honest kind, based on a real exchange of goods, in which we and they had lived and dealt for more than 80 years—to another kind of economic system devised, and developed by their Axis partners in Europe. This other kind is fundamentally dishonest, since it requires that the conquering power import without exporting. The economics of totalitarianism is wholesale robbery.

Japanese liberals, including big businessmen who had been "cajoled, bribed, or blackmailed" into acquiescence with the militarists, understood the necessity of ending excessive trade barriers as the foundation for a world economic order most conducive to peace. They would need food, cotton, and other goods to rebuild and the United States would have those goods in abundance to sell after the war.[16] Generally speaking, Grew favored a program of dollar loans abroad and a reduction everywhere of barriers to international trade to enable the United States to serve its own interests and humanity at the same time.[17]

As American forces took the offensive in the Southwest Pacific, Grew and other American policymakers began serious consideration of the future of Japan in a territorial sense and, more broadly, in terms of U.S. requirements in the Pacific. Ritual disclaimers of selfish aims and the rhetoric of international cooperation notwithstanding, Grew's correspondence with William Howard Gardiner illustrates his belief in the Pacific as an American lake after the war. Gardiner, former president of the Navy League, praised Grew's speaking campaign on behalf of utterly crushing Japanese militarism in a lengthy letter of March 1943 and then offered the argument that to protect its industrial and worldwide trading base, the United States had to develop naval and air power capable of being projected across the Pacific, Atlantic, and the Caribbean. The United States would have no rivals in the Pacific, Gardiner insisted, if the war against Japan was carried out with only secondary help from the British, Russians, and Chinese. "Let the recovery of the Netherlands East Indies, the Philippines, and all other islands in the Pacific, as well as removal of the Japanese from Singapore and all Southeast Asia, follow as the manifest results of American naval and aerial operations . . . . For such a procedure would improve immeasurably the peace settlement we would be able to make in the regions of the Pacific, and our future political standing and commercial opportunities in Asia." Grew thanked Gardiner for his "admirable exposition" and promised to "keep the picture as you present it much in mind."[18] Grew considered the letter to be of such importance that he and other State Department officers had it shown to Admiral William Leahy, Franklin Roosevelt's chief of staff, who discussed it with the president. Though he disagreed with the Navy Department's unilateral approach to postwar security planning in the Pacific, Grew wrote Hull in July 1944 that it was "fundamentally essential we control certain strategic islands in the Pacific'' and that this control should be established within the framework of the United Nations.[19] In short, Grew favored depriving Japan of its overseas colonies and territories and making the Pacific an American sphere of influence. In time, Japan would be permitted access to the raw materials and markets of the region but only within the framework of multilateral economic policies and American strategic hegemony.

Beginning in the summer of 1943, Grew began to tone down his rhetoric about Japanese military ruthlessness and bestiality and to openly suggest that there were "liberal elements" with whom the United States could deal in reaching a postwar settlement. In a radio broadcast on 28 August 1943, Grew declared that if "an ancient tree is torn up by the roots and remodeled it will not live, but if the healthy trunk and roots remain, the branches and foliage can with care achieve regeneration. Whatever is found to be healthy in the Japanese body politic should be preserved; the rotten branches must be ruthlessly cut away." Grew did not publicly reveal that he considered the monarchy as part of the healthy trunk and root system of the Japanese politic until December, but astute observers and many of Grew's correspondents recognized the centrality of the emperor to Grew's thinking about a peace settlement.[20] Privately, Grew told friends that it was foolish to contemplate a full-fledged democratic system for Japan. "The Imperial Throne is the only substantial cornerstone on which something healthy can be built in the future," he wrote in July 1943. "Very likely the present Emperor will have to go but I am not at all convinced that the institution of the Throne should be scrapped."[21]

That the State Department's advisory committee on postwar foreign policy headed by Hugh Borton (formerly a professor of Japanese history at Columbia University) shared this analysis of the emperor problem as it developed concrete plans for postwar Japan in 1943 was especially gratifying to Grew. He was kept apprised of their work and offered general comments on it. Borton specifically mentioned Matsudaira Tsuneo, Kido Koichi, and Prince Konoye, old court friends of Grew, as candidates for leading a reformed government and argued that the emperor institution was "likely to be one of the more stable elements of postwar Japan. As such, it may be a valuable factor in the establishment of a stable and moderate postwar government." Praising Borton's work in a letter to Stanley Hornbeck, Hull's chief advisor on the Far East, Grew reiterated his conception of the emperor as a bulwark against the chaos of the right or left and the "cornerstone for healthy and peaceful growth."[22]

At the meeting of the Illinois Education Association in Chicago on 29

Joseph C. Grew speaks on "Our Ramparts We Watch" at the Pentagon, 5 May 1943. Signal Corps Photo, National Archives.

December 1943, Grew clearly revealed what he meant by the healthy trunk and roots of Japanese society. At one point he declared, "I knew that many of the highest statesmen of Japan, including the emperor himself, were laboring earnestly but futilely to control the military in order to avoid war with the United States and Britain . . . ." Elsewhere he remarked that "Shintoism involves Emperor worship . . . and when once Japan is under the aegis of a peace-keeping ruler not controlled by the military that phase of Shintoism can be an asset, not a liability, in a reconstructed nation." In general, Grew pleaded for tolerance and recognition that there were indigenous forces for a reformed government within Japan. Quoting his good friend and leading

Western authority on Japan, Sir George Sansom, Grew concluded that under favorable conditions Japan could become a "more modern and democratic type of constitutional monarchy."[23]

Though he emphasized that his speech did not reflect the official view of the government, Grew had circulated the text in the Far Eastern Division of the State Department where several paragraphs praising the emperor and the "moderates" aroused strong objections and were deleted in a clumsy last minute maneuver. The incident indicated that Stanley Hornbeck, leader of the pro-Kuomintang (Guomindang) wing of the so-called China Crowd, was still the dominant force in the State Department and that Grew and his allies working on postwar Japan policy were obliged to move with great caution. The president, the China Crowd, most American businessmen, and public opinion assumed that with the military defeat of Japan, China would emerge as the leading power of East Asia. China was touted as a politically independent nation and an equal with the other members of the "Big Four" in the struggle against the Axis. While junior, more progressive diplomats in the China Crowd considered the government of Jiang Jieshi beyond salvation, Hornbeck and the conservative China hands maintained that American influence and economic assistance could remedy the problems.[24] But all strongly opposed Grew and the so-called Japan Crowd for projecting a politically reliable and economically strong Japan as the dominant nation of the Far East and principal American ally in the region.

Even in its final toned-down version, Grew's Chicago speech provoked harsh public criticism across the country. The attacks reflected, on the one hand, a racist vindictiveness towards the Japanese as the war dragged on and American casualties mounted and, on the other, an attachment to a sentimental vision of a united, progressive, and strong China. The *Sacramento Bee* wondered if Grew was becoming too soft on Japan. To maintain the throne with Hirohito on it "is a goal the Japanese, not the United Nations, are fighting for. He is the individual who has been pinning medals on the killers of American soldiers and the executioners of American airmen." Speaking for a large body of congressional and military opinion, the *New York Times* considered Grew's advocacy of "an autocratic theocracy incapable of developing a real democracy" contrary to previous American statements of war aims and "out of place" while American forces in the Pacific were fighting against everything the emperor symbolized.[25]

The liberal and left-wing press was also irate at the new note Grew was sounding in American policy. In an editorial for the Foreign Policy Association *Bulletin* titled "People not Emperor—Hold Key to Peaceful Japan," Laurence K. Rosinger argued that to prevent a resurgence of militarism in

Japan required a genuine popular voice in Japanese government. Young journalist I. F. Stone wrote in *PM* that Grew's avowal of faith in the emperor and the Japanese upper class was the "same line of hooey fed to us from the beginning of Japan's attack on Manchuria in 1931 . . . . The Japan Grew would save is essentially the same Japan that ravages China and stabbed us in the back at Pearl Harbor."[26]

As Waldo Heinrichs, Grew's judicious biographer, suggests, Grew's shift from war to peace themes in his speeches may have been as much directed at the Japanese "moderates" as the American public. Many of Grew's speeches were published in the Department of State *Bulletin,* and thus easily available to the Japanese. By 1943 a loose "peace party" was developing amongst former Japanese prime ministers and palace advisors who saw the continuation of the war as disastrous and were devising approaches to terminate it that would leave some of Japan's conquest in Asia intact, and, above all, preserve the imperial institution. Against the backdrop of the American conquest of the Marshall Islands and the fall of Saipan in July 1944 (which allowed B-29 bombers to raid the home islands), the peace conspiracy in the inner circles of the oligarchy grew and succeeded in ousting General Tojo Hideki, prime minister at the time of the Pearl Harbor attack. But fearing that an immediate surrender would not be accepted by a people so indoctrinated in the idea of Japanese invincibility, the interim government of General Koiso Kunichi attempted to improve the military situation. The "peace party" in 1944 was not yet ready to respond to Grew and end the war.[27]

Grew was disappointed and chastened by the reactions to his Chicago speech. Clearly, open support of the emperor was anathema to the American people and in a presidential election year, impolitic as well. In "preparing public opinion for a sane peace" Grew learned to be more circumspect while making sure to express a burning rage at reports of new Japanese atrocities in the Philippines and elsewhere. For example, in *Ten Years in Japan,* published in the spring of 1944, Grew carefully selected and extensively edited materials from his diary, correspondence, and speeches which balanced the ruthlessness and brutality of the Japanese military with the alleged basic childlike goodness of the Japanese people who had intense loyalty and love for the emperor. The book suggested the emperor's interest in peaceful relations with the United States and the sincere but futile efforts of his moderate aristocratic friends to halt the drift to war. Grew avoided drawing any direct conclusions from his experience in Japan for the postwar settlement, though the book was clearly meant to help lay the groundwork for an American deal with the moderates including the emperor. By contrast with the Chicago speech, most reviewers of *Ten Years in Japan* were favorable to Grew and the book rose to second on the *New York Times* best-seller list in June and July 1944.[28]

The Japan Crowd

A major reorganization at the State Department in early 1944 gave Grew and the Japan Crowd an unexpected opportunity to promote their school of postwar planning. The frequently abused subordinates of Dr. Stanley Horn- beck, fed up with his optimistic reports of Jiang Jieshi's political and military progress in face of overwhelming evidence to the contrary, rebelled and suc- ceeded in convincing Hull to remove him as director of the newly created Office of Far Eastern Affairs (FE). Not only were the China specialists who were critical of the Guomindang given a new chance to play a role in policy- making but, more importantly, on 1 May Grew became director of FE. There, as he modestly put it to a British friend, "some of my views concerning postwar developments in the Far East may register."[29]

In addition to Grew's appointment, Joseph Ballantine, a former counselor of the American embassy in Tokyo, was made deputy director of FE. A core of Japan specialists from the foreign service, including Eugene Dooman, Grew's chief aide as counselor to the embassy in Tokyo, Robert Fearey, Grew's private secretary in Japan, and Earle Dickover, a former first secretary in Tokyo, were members of the recently created Inter-Divisional Area Com- mittee on the Far East (IDACFE) whose numerous papers on a comprehensive range of Occupation problems became the basis of most State Department policy. These changes were generally taken to mean that the direction of Far Eastern policy had been transferred from the China Crowd to the Japan Crowd centered around Grew and that Japan, rather than China, would play a more important, if not dominant role, in American plans for postwar Asia.[30]

Grew was especially interested in the papers drafted in the spring of 1944 by the IDACFE for consideration by the Post-War Programs Committee (PWC), then the highest organ of State Department post-surrender planning. He was no doubt pleased with the results. Among the most important recommenda- tions of these papers was that United Nations forces in Japan not be given distinct zones of occupation such as were planned for Germany. Instead there would be a centralized administration of the whole country by military gov- ernment. The explicit assumption behind the recommendation was a minor role in the Occupation by American allies. The "geographic position of the United States in relation to Japan and the military and financial resources of the United States as well as events leading to the Pacific War," the planners argued, "operate to place on the United States a primary responsibility for assuring the fulfilment of the terms of surrender and the operation of military government."[31]

A number of papers indicated the mild nature of the Occupation which was projected. The first phase of "stern discipline" would be brief and the Japanese people would not be needlessly humiliated. After the punishment of the war criminals, a second and longer phase of the Occupation would create the conditions for the "emergence of a liberal government" by preventing any resurgence of militarism and gradually relaxing the restrictions of the first phase. Hugh Borton specifically identified the liberal forces in Japan as the statesmen of the 1920s Anglo-American school, among them personal advisors of the emperor, business leaders whose prosperity was based on world trade rather than the Greater East Asia Co-Prosperity Sphere, Christian leaders, and some educators and reformers. The papers anticipated that a liberal government would not uproot such venerable institutions as Shinto worship. In a paper drafted by Eugene Dooman it was recommended that only the national Shinto shrines be closed for Shintoism was a "harmless, primitive, animism" not injurious to American interests once Japanese militarism had been destroyed. In the third and final stage of the Occupation, Japan would be integrated into the world economic system and prepared to take its place in the United Nations.[32]

Though this conception of the Occupation implied lenient treatment of the emperor after surrender, the State Department Japan specialists toiled over the answers to the War and Navy department questions on the explicit status of the emperor. "Will he be removed both as an individual and as an institution . . . ? Will both remain? If so under what measure of control?" Two opposing position papers were prepared. Hugh Borton personally favored suspending none of the emperor's functions but recognized that this implied permanent retention of the throne, a position which the Allies would not find acceptable. Instead he recommended the Occupation regime permit the emperor only the authority to delegate administrative duties to subordinate officials in order to "assure the good behavior of the Japanese people and to keep in office the maximum number of Japanese officials who would be willing to serve directly under the supervision of [Allied] civil affairs officers." Borton added that the emperor and his family should be placed in protective custody and then removed from Tokyo to an easily guarded place. If there developed a substantial movement among the Japanese for the abolition of the emperor institution, "the military authorities should take no action against that movement . . . and should cease to utilize the emperor as a political instrument."[33]

Earle Dickover, perhaps playing the devil's advocate, presented a memorandum looking to the abolition of the emperor institution. To retain and make use of the emperor in administering Japan would contribute toward the perpetuation of an undemocratic institution, Dickover argued, and since democracies were the best guarantee of peace and security, the most prudent course was "to work toward the discrediting of the institution in Japanese eyes and toward its eventual destruction." It was doubtful "if democracy can gain a firm foothold in the country unless and until a more or less clean break with the past is made. For our own security, therefore, it would seem desirable that we assist liberal minded Japanese to rid themselves of some of the relics of the past including the institution of the emperor."[34]

Significantly, Dickover and Borton shared in the consensus that there were liberal elements in Japan's traditional oligarchy upon which American policy should be based. American policymakers ignored or rejected the more radical perspective that not only argued for the eventual destruction of the emperor institution but emphasized strengthening trade union and other popular forces outside the oligarchy. To radical critics like T. A. Bisson, the liberal elements within the oligarchy were compromised by their past record in the Pacific war and repression at home and would resist the far-reaching reforms needed to make Japan truly democratic.[35]

Having just been appointed director of FE, Grew prepared a lengthy letter for the PWC which was charged with resolving the contrasting positions of Borton and Dickover. Grew's influence may have been a factor in PWC's lopsided twelve-to-one vote in favor of adopting Borton's memorandum. Grew admitted there were many imponderable factors in trying to find elements in Japan who would help to establish order and prevent the resurgence of military aggression. The enlistment of those Japanese civilian leaders who had opposed war with the United States and had not changed their views during the war was crucial to avoiding a long and expensive Occupation. Since the Japanese were "somewhat like sheep following leaders," Grew felt that a change to liberal leadership would change the entire political climate of the country. It was only common sense to have the throne as a symbol of the new leadership. It would "offer a measure for the constructive development of Japan in the ways of peace and for the regeneration of the Japanese people in a direction which would conduce to the security of the United States." Grew was convinced that the emperor institution had been used in the 1920s to promote peaceful cooperation and this would happen again. "The cult of manifest destiny and military aggression has been artificially developed and the Emperor has quite simply been used as a convenient facade to justify and to consecrate that cult in the eyes of the people. I therefore say, without qualification, that the Emperor can be used equally well—indeed far more easily—as a facade to justify and to consecrate a new order of peaceful international cooperation." Grew predicted that Hirohito himself would accept responsibility for the war and abdicate, turning over the throne to his brother Prince Chichibu or his minor son, the Crown Prince Akihito.[36]

The final revised memorandum of 9 May reflected the united stand of Grew and most other Japan specialists in the State Department against harsh treatment of the emperor. The emperor would be placed under protective custody but permitted to delegate administrative responsibilities. In a small concession to Dickover's position, the committee opposed any action by Occupation authorities that implied "recognition of or support for the Japanese concept that the Japanese emperor is different from and superior to other temporal rulers, that he is of divine origin and capacities, that he is sacrosanct or that he is indispensable."[37] These recommendations indicated that the question of the permanent status of the emperor was not completely closed. The Japanese might change their attitude from devotion to the throne to favoring its abolition. Nor could the impact of Allied governments and the hardening of American public opinion in favor of severe treatment of the emperor be gauged. But the IDACFE recommendation to use the emperor institution to maintain peace and stability during the Occupation, as Grew and others understood, would certainly weight the scales of later policy debates on the side of retaining the monarchy on a permanent basis.

The Undersecretary of State

Leaving the question of the permanent status of the emperor formally undecided proved advantageous to Grew and the State Department in deflecting mounting public criticism against a "soft peace" for Japan. Following the resignation of Cordell Hull on 21 November 1944 and the elevation of Edward Stettinius as secretary of state, Grew was nominated as under secretary of state. In this context, a group of liberal and independent congressmen decided to make an issue of the evident "soft peace" thrust of American planning for postwar Japan. Senator Joseph Guffey, a Democrat from Pennsylvania, read into the *Congressional Record* on 6 December an editorial from the *Philadelphia Record* attacking Grew for his aristocratic connections in Japan and for frequently advocating a policy of "doing business with Emperor Hirohito after the war. He says we must preserve the Mikado as a Japanese symbol around which a stable, peaceful government can be built." Guffey and a few others succeeded in having Grew's nomination, together with a slate of assistant secretaries, recommitted.[38]

Appearing before the Senate Foreign Relations Committee, Grew struck back. As in his private correspondence, Grew contended that his views were being distorted and improperly reported. He claimed never to have advocated either retention or elimination of the emperor after the war. "I believe that the problem should be left fluid until we get to Tokyo." The Allies should wait and see about dealing with the emperor, Grew equivocated, for keeping Hirohito on the throne might obviate the need for thousands of American troops to maintain indefinite control over seventy million Japanese. Though the nomination sailed through the Senate sixty-six to seven on 19 December the debate must have impressed Grew again with how sensitive the whole question of peace with Japan, particularly the status of the emperor, had become.[39]

Grew now held a job of staggering responsibilities. The priorities in the department called for Stettinius to be away from Washington when necessary to handle the launching of the United Nations and that left Grew in charge much of the time as acting secretary of state. His memorandam of conversations on Trieste, the French Resistance, Yugoslavia, and many others indicate the scope of Grew's day-to-day concerns. Nevertheless, he took special interest in the Japanese surrender and in Occupation planning. The spade work on these issues took place in 1945 in the newest and most important planning organ during the war, the State-War-Navy Coordinating Committee (SWNCC), consisting of the assistant secretaries from each of the participating departments. Eugene Dooman, who functioned as a surrogate for Grew, headed SWNCC's Sub-Committee on the Far East (SFE) after February 1945 and sought to gain SWNCC acceptance of the State Department's planning papers of 1943 and 1944 on which he and other Japan hands had worked.[40]

Before SFE completed a draft early in June of a comprehensive post-surrender policy document known as SWNCC 150, Grew called upon Dooman to draft closely related position papers on surrender terms and a proposed public statement of them to the Japanese. Grew made his own views on the subject widely known in the State Department beginning in late 1944 when American military strategists prepared for taking Iwo Jima and Okinawa and planned the invasion of the Japanese home islands. Theoretically he was bound by the formula adopted at the Casablanca Conference in January 1943 for an "unconditional surrender" of all the Axis powers. Intended to solidify the alliance against threats of a separate peace, "unconditional surrender" implied profound economic and social change in the Allied-occupied Axis countries so as to eliminate aggressive forces from the world. But Grew, like many other conservatives, was always lukewarm in support of unconditional surrender. He feared that no Japanese government would ever surrender unconditionally. Not only did he believe that the war would be prolonged and cost unnecessary loss of life, but he thought extensive changes in the Japanese political economy were not required to achieve a stable and peaceful nation.[41] Of course, formally revising the Casablanca agreement was out of the question. What Grew sought was a public statement to the Japanese which "conditionalized" unconditional surrender so as to induce a quick capitulation.

The key issue for Washington planners in considering surrender terms for Japan was how to treat the emperor. In the meetings of Secretary of State Stettinius's new Staff Committee which Grew chaired, the under secretary argued forcefully for concessions to the Japanese government's position for retention of the emperor institution. He told Stettinius early in January that Admiral Chester Nimitz and other naval officers with whom he had recently talked had agreed that the emperor should be "let alone, as he might be found to be an important, if not essential asset" in saving thousands of American lives.[42] The one thing that might prevent Japanese troops all over Asia from continuing to fight, Grew reiterated to Stettinius in April, would be an imperial rescript considered sacred by the Japanese. No such rescript was likely if Hirohito and his advisors believed that the throne was to be abolished.[43]

With the end of fighting in Europe on 8 May, Grew felt an even greater urgency in finalizing surrender terms and announcing them to Japan. Just as he had predicted, the cost in lives and property to both the United States and Japan climbed drastically as the war continued. The Okinawa campaign then underway indicated that the planned invasion of the home islands scheduled for November would be met by stiff and well-directed Japanese resistance. Before Okinawa fell, Americans suffered nearly fifty thousand casualties and lost 350 ships. At the same time American planes were bombing almost every major city in Japan. Two raids on Tokyo at the end of May killed over one hundred thousand Japanese and reduced the capital to rubble and ashes.[44]

Grew also thought the moment finally had come to give encouragement to the "peace party" in Japan. When the Koiso government fell in early April 1945, Admiral Suzuki Kantaro—whose credentials as a moderate were known to Grew—became premier. Reports through the Office of Strategic Services in Switzerland and elsewhere indicated a new interest by the Japanese in making peace. The militarists might still be in control, but Grew felt "certain that the issue of surrender or destruction will sooner or later be debated, if it is not now being debated, within the innermost recesses of the Japanese political structure."[45]

Grew was correct. Key figures in the peace party led by Prince Konoye were growing desperate to quickly reach a settlement. They were confident on the basis of what they had already heard, that the United States "would not go so far as to reform Japan's kokutai [national polity] or abolish the imperial house." In a meeting with the emperor in February, Konoye spelled out the dangers of a "communist revolution" which might accompany a war fought to the bitter end. By starting negotiations with the U.S., Konoye argued, the monarchy would be saved, the war would be brought to a quick conclusion, and a potential revolution aborted.[46]

A final concern for Grew in seeking immediate action on Japanese surrender terms was geopolitical. At the Yalta Conference in February 1945, President Roosevelt and Premier Joseph Stalin laid out the basis of American and Soviet cooperation in Asia. Stalin agreed that the Soviets would enter the war against Japan approximately three months after the surrender of Germany, a point that all U.S. military and civilian planners considered vital to victory in the Pacific. In return, Roosevelt promised to pressure Jiang Jieshi to accept Russian demands for rights and concessions in China which the Japanese had gained in 1905 in the aftermath of the Russo-Japanese War, including South Sakhalin and the Kurile Islands, a lease to Port Arthur, and preponderant interest in Manchurian railroads. In the context of growing tensions between the American and Soviet diplomats over European issues that followed so soon after Roosevelt's death, Grew became gloomy and developed pronounced reservations about the Yalta accords on the Far East. He saw the Soviet Union as an aggressive power which "will constitute in [the] future as grave a danger to us as did the Axis." He predicted that Russia would use its entry into the war against Japan to force both China and Japan into its totalitarian orbit. "A future war with Soviet Russia is as certain as anything in this world can be certain," Grew told colleagues in the department.[47]

After a meeting on 12 May 1945 with Secretary of the Navy James Forrestal, Assistant Secretary of War John McCloy, and ambassador to Russia, Averell Harriman—all of whom shared a deep distrust of the Russians—Grew openly questioned whether the United States should support what had been agreed to at Yalta. "Is the entry of the Soviet Union into the Pacific War at the earliest possible moment of such vital interest to the United States," Grew asked Secretary of War Henry Stimson, "as to preclude any attempt . . . to obtain Soviet agreement to certain desired political objectives in the Far East prior to such entry?" Specifically Grew thought it advisable for the new president, Harry Truman, to go the Big Three meeting at Potsdam and obtain Stalin's promise to influence the Chinese Communists to bring about a unified China under Nationalist rule; to return Manchuria to China; and to respect the independence of Korea. In addition Grew feared, as did Konoye and Yoshida in Tokyo, that once the Soviets entered the war they would demand a role in the Occupation of Japan. He asked Stimson whether such a Soviet occupation would "adversely affect our long term policy for the future treatment of Japan?"[48] Though there is no direct evidence linking Grew's antipathy towards the Soviets and his policy on surrender, it seems reasonable to conclude that Grew wanted an end to the war before the Russians entered in order to avoid paying them the political price agreed to at Yalta.

Saving lives, responding to the peace party in Japan, and thwarting Soviet ambitions in the Far East impelled Grew to take the issue of Japanese surrender directly to the president. Truman's statement on the day of German surrender had assured the Japanese that unconditional surrender did not mean "extermination or enslavement" but opened the way for participation in "the fellowship of peace-loving and law-abiding nations." That was a positive step,

Grew thought, but the Japanese had not responded. In a meeting on 28 May Grew argued passionately for the president to make another statement in a forthcoming speech before Congress that the Japanese "will be permitted to determine their own political structure." That language, Grew believed, would overcome "the greatest obstacle to unconditional surrender by the Japanese . . . their belief that this would entail the destruction or permanent removal of the Emperor and institution of the Throne." Coming so soon after the devastation of Tokyo, a statement by the president would have the maximum psychological impact and most likely prospect for success. The surrender of Japan as soon as possible was necessary to the accomplishment of American objectives in the Far East with the least possible loss of American lives. According to Grew's account of the meeting, the president was extremely appreciative of his advice and said his "own thoughts had been following the same line."[49] But Truman wanted Grew to consult with his top military aides and report back on the matter.

At a Pentagon meeting on 29 May with Stimson, Forrestal, Army Chief of Staff General George Marshall, and three others, Grew presented a draft of a statement for inclusion in the president's speech to Congress. By assuring the Japanese they would be able to determine their own political structure, Grew contended, the president might make it easier for them to "surrender unconditionally instead of fighting fanatically for their Emperor." According to Grew's record, Stimson, Forrestal, and Marshall were "all in accord with the principle, but for certain military reasons, not divulged, it was considered inadvisable . . . now."[50]

The question of timing was the nub of the whole matter according to the views of those present. Grew apparently thought that Marshall and others were concerned about the effect of the announcement on the fighting on Okinawa. Actually, as Stimson explained in his diary, the secretary of war could not discuss his view that the warning to Japan be made *after* an atomic bombing but before the scheduled invasion of the home islands. Several of the participants did not know of the bomb or its expected availability for combat use in August and were not cleared to have this information.[51] Grew knew of the bomb but there is no contemporary evidence that his anxiety for an early surrender statement ever stemmed from a desire to avoid its use. In any event, the disappointed Grew reported to Truman the results of the meeting and vigorously continued to try to persuade him not to postpone issuing a surrender statement.[52]

In early June Grew forwarded a memorandum by former president Herbert Hoover to Truman that urged a statement to the Japanese with reference to maintaining the emperor system. Grew underscored Hoover's point by warning that the Japanese "are prepared for prolonged resistance if it be the intention of the United Nations to try the present emperor as a war criminal or to abolish the imperial institution.'' Finally on 18 June Grew, along with the Joint Chiefs of Staff, went to see the president. With the imminent fall of Okinawa, another opportune time had come for a clarification of the American position on the emperor, Grew argued. The president told Grew that he liked the idea of such an announcement but he had decided to wait until he met with Stalin and Winston Churchill at the scheduled Big Three meeting at Potsdam in mid-July. Grew responded that the United States had borne the brunt of the fighting against the Japanese and hence need not consult its allies. Moreover, from Grew's perspective, a delay until Potsdam might harden Japanese attitudes. But the Joint Chiefs of Staff argued that any modification of unconditional surrender would be taken by the Japanese as a sign of weakness, and Truman went along with them.[53]

For the moment, the president prepared for a full scale invasion of the home islands and welcomed Soviet assurances of help on the Asian mainland as a way of reducing American losses in that operation. While the atomic bomb potentially could force a surrender from the Japanese and reduce the importance of early Soviet entry into the war, making American political concessions to them unnecessary, there were still too many unknowns about the bomb and Japan. At this stage of its development, there was no assurance that the bomb would work, that its explosive power would be impressive, or that its impact on the Japanese would be any different from conventional bombing raids. The administration, contrary to Grew, believed that additional military force was required to force surrender with or without the bomb.[54]

Having the president's promise to take up with the Allies some kind of public statement on surrender at the Potsdam Conference, Grew cooperated in the initiative of Stimson in the work of a joint State and War department committee created to draft the document. Knowing of the strong opposition within his own department to revision of the unconditional surrender formula, Grew was eminently pleased with the resulting draft submitted to the president on 2 July. After declaring that the United Nations would "prosecute the war against Japan until her unconditional capitulation,'' the statement then laid out conditions for surrender. These were based largely on the first version of what became known as the "U.S. Initial Post-Surrender Policy for Japan," SWNCC 150. Japanese military forces would be disarmed and the authority of the military eliminated; the Japanese empire would be dismantled and the home islands occupied until war-making potential was destroyed; and Japanese war criminals would be treated sternly while democratic tendencies amongst the people would be encouraged within a framework of freedom of speech and respect for human rights. The key paragraph of the document promised Japanese industrial recovery with access to world markets and raw materials and the withdrawal of Occupation forces with the establishment of a "peacefully inclined, responsible government of a character representative of the Japanese people. This may include a constitutional monarchy under the present dynasty if it be shown to the complete satisfaction of the world that such a government shall never again aspire to aggression."[55]

Convinced that moderate Japanese would find these terms generous and acceptable, Grew took the initiative in seeing that the draft statement survived the further scrutiny of the administration and the president intact. The military services, which only a few weeks before had opposed anything but a firm unconditional surrender policy, were apparently satisfied after the conquest of Okinawa that an offer of a political settlement of the war would not be taken by the Japanese as a sign of Allied weakness. At the State Department, however, Grew encountered serious difficulty over the explicit assurances on the retention of the emperor institution.

As in earlier discussions, Assistant Secretaries Archibald MacLeish and Dean Acheson doubted whether there should be any modification of unconditional surrender, especially on the emperor question. The throne, Acheson argued, was a dangerous, anachronistic, feudal institution. He challenged Grew to explain "why, if the Emperor had no importance in Japanese war-making capacity, the military element in Japan should be so insistent on retaining the Emperor." To MacLeish what made Japan "dangerous in the past and will make her dangerous in the future if we permit it, is, in large part, the Japanese cult of emperor worship which gives ruling groups in Japan . . . their control over the Japanese people." Bolstered by opinion polls indicating that most Americans wanted harsh treatment for the emperor after the war, MacLeish dared proponents of the draft statement to make their position public.[56]

But for Grew the critical audience was James F. Byrnes who became secretary of state on 3 July. Byrnes refused to commit himself to the draft proclamation before his departure for Potsdam on 6 July. He had consulted with Cordell Hull who told him that the concession to Japan's emperor institution seemed "too much like appeasement" and warned him of "terrible political repercussions" in the United States from it.[57]

By the time the Potsdam Conference began on 17 July, Truman had just received word that the atomic bomb had been successfully tested in New Mexico. Some analysts have argued that the deletion of all references to the emperor institution from the final 26 July proclamation, replacing them with the promise of a withdrawal of Occupation forces after "there has been established in accordance with the freely expressed will of the Japanese people a peacefully inclined and responsible government," was made because Byrnes and others consciously wanted to use the bomb. But as Barton Bernstein has demonstrated, the evidence indicates that Byrnes, and apparently Truman, were fearful that concessions might strengthen the Japanese military and thereby prolong the war and that failure of the Japanese to accept these modifications could be politically injurious at home. Had Grew and Stimson been more powerful and closer to Truman, the president might have been willing to take these risks. But Grew was headed for retirement and was not even at Potsdam. Stimson was also ready to retire and was shunted aside at the Big Three conference. Even without the explicit assurances on the emperor institution, the Potsdam Proclamation, Truman hoped, would be sufficient inducement for Japanese surrender. If not, the bomb offered the possibility of ending the war without an invasion or concessions to the Soviet Union for their participation.[58]

While some Japanese diplomats correctly interpreted the Potsdam terms to mean that the Japanese people could "freely" express their will to retain the emperor and that the government should not delay in accepting the document as the basis for surrender, Prime Minister Suzuki and Foreign Minister Togo feared the military and others would strenuously resist such a course. They believed that more time was needed to persuade the potential opposition of the acceptability of the Potsdam terms. The Suzuki cabinet chose not to respond to the statement and gave the impression, inadvertently, of rejecting it. The "prompt and utter destruction" promised the Japanese nation if the Potsdam ultimatum was not accepted became a shocking reality with the dropping of the atomic bombs on Hiroshima and Nagasaki on 6 and 9 August. Coupled with the Soviet declaration of war on 8 August, the bombs finally induced the Suzuki cabinet to begin direct negotiations with the United States to end the war. The emperor himself entered the decision making process and the cabinet agreed on 10 August to accept the Potsdam terms on the one condition that they did not "compromise any demand which prejudices the prerogatives of His Majesty as a Sovereign Ruler."[59]

Secretary Byrnes began consideration of a reply immediately. According to Herbert Feis, who was in the State Department at the time, Byrnes did not invite Grew, Dooman, or other Japan experts into the discussion. "Grew, mastering his personal pride, opened the door between his office and Byrnes' and said, 'Mr. Secretary, if you are working on the Japanese note I believe I and some others could be helpful.' He and Dooman were then reluctantly admitted into the discussion." They advised against humiliating the emperor by making him sign the surrender document, a suggestion that was rejected at the time, but later adopted at the insistence of the British. In the end, the American reply stated that the emperor's authority would be subject to the Allied Supreme Commander. The note was vague enough to permit the peace party centered around Prince Konoye to argue that the throne would not be eradicated. Following another intervention by the emperor, the Suzuki cabinet accepted the Potsdam Proclamation and the American note as the basis for surrender on 14 August and resigned the following day.[60] The Pacific war had finally ended.

Aftermath

The day after surrender Grew submitted his resignation and the president accepted it immediately. Suffering from a gallstone condition, Grew had resolved in late 1944 to stay in government service only until the war ended. He was sixty-five years old and had served as a diplomat for forty-one years. Nevertheless, press speculation that Grew's resignation also resulted from his unpopular reputation as an advocate of a soft peace and incompatibility with Secretary of State Byrnes was accurate. "My resignation was entirely on my own initiative," Grew wrote his old friend William R. Castle, "but I saw the handwriting on the wall and I would not and could not have stayed."[61]

Soon after Grew's retirement other members of the Japan Crowd were eased out of the State Department. Men who hoped China might still emerge as the anchor of American policy in the Far East and who favored a punitive and thoroughgoing reform program for Occupied Japan took their place. Grew was replaced as under secretary by his erstwhile opponent on the emperor question, Dean Acheson. John Carter Vincent, a China specialist who favored the arrest of Hirohito as a war criminal, took over from Dooman at SWNCC's Sub-Committee on the Far East and from Joseph Ballantine as director of the Far East Division. After Grew declined a perfunctory offer to serve as State Department advisor to General MacArthur, Byrnes appointed George Atcheson, Jr., another China hand, rather than Dooman, whom Grew had strongly recommended.[62] Ironically, the triumph of the China Crowd at the State Department occurred as the United States lost almost all control over the political situation in China and gained almost complete control over the political situation in Japan.[63]

Before the new leadership at the State Department firmly grasped the reins of power, the intimate circle of court officials, high-level bureaucrats, and business leaders which Grew and the Japan Crowd had helped coax to power over the military, united to defend the throne and capitalism. The threat of revolution appeared from ultrarightists, Communists, and the working class within Japan and possibly from the occupying powers as well. At Prince Konoye's urging, the old guard civilians organized a government around Prince Higashikuni, the emperor's uncle, and launched a major campaign to encourage the people to find comfort in the emperor's benevolence. The real cause of Japan's suffering, the new regime claimed, was not the emperor nor any other particular person or group but a "lowering of national morality."[64]

The Higashikuni cabinet harkened back to its Meiji era roots by also agreeing to give a greater voice to the business class. It continued to honor accounts due on war production contracts and to pay indemnity claims for war damage. These measures protected the major business firms from bankruptcy and, by contributing to rampant postwar inflation, brought the urban masses near to starvation. Most importantly, for a full two weeks after surrender, the cabinet opened the back doors of its arsenals to favored businesses and individuals, as well as public bodies, and destroyed all records of the transactions. Violating direct American orders, Japanese officials deprived the incoming occupiers of a vast military storehouse of everything from machine tools and copper wire to uniforms and foodstuffs. No American at the time recognized the true dimensions or implications of the so-called hoarded goods scandal. The liquidations substantially exceeded the $2.2 billion of American aid for Japan during the more than six years of the Occupation, exacerbated the early inflationary cycle by keeping vitally needed foodstuffs and raw materials out of production, and provided enormous political leverage to Japanese conservatives.[65]

Probably Grew would not have sanctioned all the measures taken by the Japanese moderates in the immediate post-surrender period. But in a general way he hoped the American government and SCAP would support the position of the Japanese bureaucracy and business class. The instructions to Supreme Commander of Allied Powers Douglas MacArthur which were contained in the final initial Post-Surrender Policy for Japan document, SWNCC 150/4/A, of 6 September appeared to have that effect in the first months of the Occupation. From Grew's perspective SWNCC 150 had undergone significant improvement right after surrender at the hands of Assistant Secretary of War John J. McCloy, a Republican from Wall Street.[66] Instead of a military government for Japan, which Grew and other officials had assumed from the outset of the planning process, McCloy won assent for MacArthur to exercise his authority through the Japanese governmental machinery, including the emperor. This was an extremely important change made possible by the surrender of the Japanese government intact and the cooperation of the emperor with American authorities. Indirect government, as progressive SCAP officials soon discovered to their dismay, provided key elements of the ruling oligarchy the means to delay or subvert those reform directives of the occupiers which were not to their liking.[67]

In addition, as Grew understood, the decision to have SCAP exercise his authority through the Japanese government, including the emperor, weighted the ambiguous language in SWNCC 150 on the emperor question in favor of permanent retention of the throne. Attempting to reconcile the contrary views of the Japan Crowd and its adversaries, McCloy held that SCAP was not committed to support the emperor if he opposed the attainment of American objectives. Changes in the form of government initiated by the Japanese people or government "in the direction of modifying its feudal and authoritarian tendencies are to be permitted and favored." If such changes involved the use of force by the Japanese people, SCAP would decide whether or not to intervene. Theoretically the door remained open for the arrest, trial, and punishment of Hirohito as a war criminal and ultimately even the abolition of the monarchy. In October 1945 Acheson, Vincent, and several other State Department officials advocated that position.[68]

In practice, as public attention turned away from Japan, policymakers accepted MacArthur's pronouncements that the cooperation of the emperor was critical to the continuation of an orderly and peaceful Occupation as well as long-range friendly relations with Japan. By January 1946, as Grew had hoped, the issue in Washington was no longer whether to preserve the emperor institution or try Hirohito as a war criminal but the necessary constitutional framework for the monarchy.[69] Outright democracy in Japan, Grew reiterated, would lead to chaos and "leave [the] field wide open for would be dictators." In these early months of the Occupation, Grew praised the work of General MacArthur and implicitly criticized his own successors in the State Department who were calling for immediate and thoroughgoing democratic reforms. MacArthur "must govern from the top down, not from the bottom up," Grew wrote in October 1945, "and that is precisely what he appears to be doing. I knew [Prime Minister] Shidehara and [Foreign Minister] Yoshida and some of the other members of the present Cabinet very well . . . . [They] were bitterly opposed to militarism and all its works. I am not anxious about the future of Japan as long as the Communists don't get control."[70]

But by 1947 Grew made known his growing anxiety at the way in which Washington policymakers and General MacArthur were interpreting the basic directives for the Occupation, particularly those dealing with the Japanese economy. Somehow in April 1945 New Deal economist Edwin Martin convinced Grew's alter ego on SWNCC's Sub-Committee on the Far East, Eugene Dooman, to split up responsibilities at the State Department so that Dooman handled the political aspects of postwar planning while Martin gained control over economic reforms. Overwhelmed with work on the politics of surrender and pressured by radical reformers in and out of the department, Dooman may have felt that protecting the emperor institution and the civilian moderates in power would ultimately undermine any radical economic programs proposed by Martin. In any event, contrary to the philosophy of the Japan Crowd, Martin succeeded in including in the original and subsequent drafts of SWNCC 150 provisions for promotion of democratic organizations in labor, industry, and agriculture, and a "wider distribution of ownership, management and control of the Japanese economic system." A purge in the economic field and a program for the dissolution of large industrial and banking combines was specifically added in the final initial Post-Surrender Policy document written under McCloy's supervision.[71]

Aroused by published and private reports of plans to implement these programs, especially purges of businessmen, Grew warned Under Secretary of State for Economic Affairs William Clayton in January 1947 that breaking up the Zaibatsu should not be carried "so far as to penalize all Japanese businessmen merely because they have a little money as this would lead directly to communism and render impossible individual initiative in getting the country on its feet." The Japanese people, Grew concluded, could not "be driven to democracy by mandate and artificially created hardships. If such a policy is followed it will have precisely the reverse effect of that intended and will drive Japan . . . straight into the Russian orbit."[72]

In 1948 Grew became the honorary cochairman of the American Council on Japan, the principal postwar conservative lobby group on Japan issues. The intensification of the Cold War, the collapse of the Nationalists in China, the rising costs of the Occupation, and the covert opposition of Japanese officials to key reform programs made Washington policymakers increasingly receptive to the long held ideas of Grew and Japan Lobby members for a restoration of a strong capitalist order in Japan led by moderates and united under a constitutional monarchy. When, in defiance of new orders from Washington, SCAP continued to implement the economic reform program, the Japan Lobby under Grew evolved into an anti-MacArthur organization. [73]

Initially Grew and his friends were puzzled at their conflict with MacArthur, so renowned for his outspoken conservative politics. But Grew and a few others began to suspect the explanation for the general's behavior lay in MacArthur's ambition to be the Republican party nominee for president in 1948 rather than any change in his conservative political ideology. Those suspicions, which recent historical research indicates were well-founded, prompted Grew and the Japan Lobby to work more strenuously to limit MacArthur's freedom of action in Japan and support Washington's efforts for the restoration of Japan as America's key ally in the Pacific.

2 DOUGLAS MACARTHUR

The Peacemaker
and the Presidency

To most Americans the Occupation of Japan is still personified by General Douglas MacArthur. His legend has eclipsed the major policymakers in Washington and the middle-echelon figures in the Occupation bureaucracy who proved instrumental in the building of the New Japan. More recent historical evaluations of the Occupation have reduced the general from Olympian to more human proportions. Many policies for which MacArthur claimed exclusive credit are now shown to have originated in Washington. Criticisms of MacArthur's handling of Occupation affairs, once largely suppressed by rigorous censorship, are now easily revealed to scholars working in numerous archival collections. Yet even these valuable new studies have failed to focus on or give careful attention to how MacArthur's political ambitions influenced every aspect of the Occupation and contributed to the MacArthur legend.[1] The eventual outcome of idolatry is iconoclasm. Only by shattering the illusion of MacArthur's omnipotence and giving full weight to the general's political opportunism can his impact on the Occupation be comprehended.

The Making of the Supreme Commander

Soon after the devastating explosion of the atomic bomb over Hiroshima, President Harry Truman, after much hesitation, decided to appoint General Douglas MacArthur, then head of American forces in the Pacific, as the Supreme Commander for the Allied Powers in Japan. With the approval of the heads of state of Great Britain, China, and Russia, the president sent Mac-

Arthur his first directive as SCAP on 15 August 1945. The general was to require the emperor, through his representatives, to sign an instrument of surrender. From the moment of the surrender of Japanese armed forces, "the authority of the Emperor and the Japanese Government to rule the state will be subject to you . . . . You will exercise supreme command over all land, sea and air forces which may be allocated for enforcement in Japan of the surrender terms by the Allied Powers concerned." MacArthur promptly acknowledged the honor of having been chosen for such a challenging position. "The entire eastern world is inexpressibly thrilled and stirred by the termination of the war," he cabled the president. "I shall do everything possible to capitalize [upon] the situation along the magnificently constructive lines you have conceived for the peace of the world."[2]

A brief review of his career is important in understanding MacArthur's new role as head of the Occupation of Japan. Douglas MacArthur was born in the Arsenal Barracks of Little Rock, Arkansas in early 1880. His father, Arthur MacArthur, had been a colonel in the 24th Wisconsin Volunteers during the Civil War, a captain on the Indian frontier, and the military governor of the Philippines who helped crush the insurrection against American colonial rule. Spurred by family tradition, his mother's ambitions, and his own interest, MacArthur enrolled at West Point in 1899. After graduating first in his class he received his first military assignment in the Philippines. In 1905 the young lieutenant joined his father's staff in Japan as aide-de-camp and accompanied him on an extensive nine-month tour of the Far East. MacArthur always believed that "the experience was without doubt the most important factor of preparation in my entire life." That the Pacific frontier was vital to American interests now became a matter of faith to him. "Here lived almost half the population of the world, and probably more than half of the raw products to sustain future generations. Here was western civilization's last earth frontier. It was crystal clear to me that the future and indeed, the very existence of America, was irrevocably entwined with Asia and its island outposts." In addition MacArthur was impressed with the "boldness and courage" of the Japanese soldiers. As a result of victories in the Russo-Japanese War, the island nation would never again be satisfied with a secondary position in world affairs.[3]

Sixteen years passed before MacArthur returned again to the Orient. Duty as military aide to President Theodore Roosevelt, action in the American occupation of Vera Cruz, and, above all, outstanding leadership of the "Rainbow Division" during World War I marked MacArthur as one of the most ambitious and promising young officers in the American military establishment. After the war Brigadier General MacArthur became superintendent of West Point but was exiled to the Philippines in 1922 for his efforts to reform and revitalize the tradition-bound U.S. Military Academy. With the help of Governor General Leonard Wood and the extraordinary intercession of Mary MacArthur, the general's mother (who shared living quarters with her son almost continuously until her death in 1935), MacArthur was elevated to the rank of major general in 1925. As the youngest major general in the army, MacArthur looked forward to further advancement. He left the Philippines in 1930 to become army chief of staff with the temporary rank of four star general.[4]

MacArthur displayed unusual political partisanship in his new post. Deeply resentful of the severe retrenchments imposed on the armed forces by the depression-minded Congress, he lashed out at pacifists and Communists. His handling of the Bonus March of 1932 did more to tarnish his public reputation than any other incident of his career. More than twenty thousand World War I veterans and their families had massed in Washington to petition Congress for early payment of their service bonuses. Convinced that they were a mob animated by Communist revolutionaries, MacArthur interpreted his orders from President Herbert Hoover to clear the veterans' encampments with reck-lessness and brutality. At his command, cavalry with sabers drawn, six tanks, and a column of infantry routed the peaceful marchers. Harshly criticized by most of the American press, MacArthur became a symbol of dangerous militarism to Franklin D. Roosevelt and other liberals who always suspected that he harbored presidential ambitions. Conservatives, on the other hand, considered the general a defender of fundamental American principles under attack from Communist and criminal elements.[5]

By the spring of 1933, MacArthur's position as chief of staff had become precarious. He had outspokenly supported Hoover's reelection bid and was appalled by New Deal programs. When Roosevelt tried to cut the military budget for 1934, MacArthur became incensed and exchanged heated words with the president. Roosevelt determined to find a suitable new post for MacArthur, preferably far from Washington where he could not exert influence on domestic politics.

No doubt MacArthur himself, although only fifty-five years old, was eager for a respite from the harsh political spotlight and relieved to return to the Philippines in late 1935 as military advisor to the new Commonwealth created to prepare the islands for independence. The next year MacArthur accepted the position of field marshall of the small, barefoot, peasant Philippine Army. With his young new second wife, Jean, MacArthur lived in air-conditioned comfort atop the luxurious Manila Hotel and earned a salary higher than his old friend Manuel Quezon y Molina, president of the Commonwealth. Although most military experts considered his task a hopeless one, he tried to prepare for the defense of the Philippines against attack, most likely from the increasingly belligerent Japanese. For personal and strategic reasons, he regarded the Philippines as the most significant American outpost in the Far East.[6]

Despite limited support from Washington, MacArthur became confident of the success of his plans for defense of the islands, predicting at every occasion that the Japanese would be afraid to pay the price for an assault on the Philippines. His prophetic powers were wanting, as only a few hours after the devastatingly successful attack on Pearl Harbor, the Japanese began their onslaught of the Philippines. Two waves of Japanese bombers and fighter planes quickly destroyed the carefully husbanded B-17 fleet on the runways at Clark Field near Manila. Recalled to active service in the U.S. Army in July 1941 (he had retired at the end of 1937 in order to remain in Manila), MacArthur had been warned of a possible Japanese attack. Like his colleagues in Hawaii, however, he was unprepared for the skill and daring of the enemy. After the Japanese swept his defenders from the beaches of Luzon, Mac-Arthur executed a difficult retreat of American and Filipino troops to the Bataan peninsula and appealed to Washington for reinforcements. But the loss of the air defenses and the crushing blows to the Pacific Fleet at Pearl Harbor virtually assured defeat. MacArthur directed the hopeless military operation on Bataan from the island fortress of Corregidor at the mouth of Manila Bay.[7]

In one of history's many ironies, the general succeeded in turning defeat in the Philippines into a personal triumph. The American press devoted an extraordinary amount of coverage to the brave and agonizing defense of Bataan and MacArthur's efforts at cheering on his troops. After his dramatic escape from Corregidor through the Japanese blockade in a PT boat convoy with his family and a small group of officers, MacArthur landed in Australia to organize the Allied counteroffensive. He told the American people, who now regarded him as a genuine war hero, "I came through and I shall return." The Office of War Information suggested changing the phrase to "we shall return." But cultivating public attention upon his personal exploits, MacArthur refused to hear of it.[8]

Throughout the war, MacArthur's reputation as a great military leader grew, aided by a tightly organized public relations staff and the general's own flair for publicity. In New Guinea and throughout the Pacific MacArthur's forces engaged in a series of successful amphibious operations that pushed back the boundaries of the Japanese empire in the Southwest Pacific. Although he denied ever holding any personal political ambitions, MacArthur did not object when the first serious "MacArthur for President" drive began to develop in mid-1943. Bolstered by the Hearst press, the Scripps-Howard papers, and other conservative organs, MacArthur's opposition to the New Deal and complaints that the Roosevelt administration was deliberately weakening his command gained wide publicity. Senator Arthur Vandenberg of Michigan assumed informal charge of the MacArthur campaign for the Republican party nomination, contacting the general through MacArthur's intelligence chief, General Charles Willoughby.[9]

But by the spring of 1944 MacArthur's clumsy political foray had collapsed. By winning the early primaries, Governor Thomas Dewey narrowed the chances of a deadlocked convention in which MacArthur might emerge as the darkhorse candidate. The coup de grace to the MacArthur presidential boom came in April 1944, with the untimely public release by Congressman A. L. Miller of his correspondence with the general. "Unless the New Deal can be stopped this time, our American way of life is forever doomed," the well-intentioned Nebraska Republican maintained. MacArthur replied, "I do unreservedly agree with the complete wisdom and statesmanship of your comments." The furor over the Miller correspondence finally forced an embittered MacArthur to withdraw his name from the presidential race and return his full attention to winning support for his strategy of taking the Philippines.[10]

At a conference at Pearl Harbor in July 1944, MacArthur succeeded in convincing Roosevelt not to bypass the Philippines in selecting the final route for the invasion of the Japanese home islands. D. Clayton James, MacArthur's biographer, argues that the two men reached an informal deal at Pearl Harbor. In exchange for using his influence with the Joint Chiefs of Staff on behalf of an invasion of the Philippines to take place in the weeks just prior to the 1944 presidential election, the president gained MacArthur's assurances that great battlefield successes in the islands would be portrayed by Pacific theater public relations officers as stemming from increased Washington support. Whatever scheming did take place, the joint chiefs approved the Philippine invasion plan shortly after the Pearl Harbor meeting. To an expectant press corps, MacArthur carefully stage-managed his entry with the third wave of troops at Leyte beach in the Philippines in October 1944, proclaiming to the people of the islands, "I have returned."[11]

The return was neither as simple nor as glorious as MacArthur expected, however. The Japanese put up stiff resistance, especially in Manila. Furthermore, his administration of civil affairs through well-known collaborators came under increasing criticism in both Manila and Washington, and rumors spread that MacArthur had large business interests in association with the Filipino oligarchy which influenced his handling of political affairs.[12]

The opportunity afforded by President Roosevelt's decision in April 1945, after intense interservice rivalry, to give MacArthur control over all American army and army air forces in the Pacific for the invasion of Japan undoubtedly appeared as a welcome escape from his troubles in the Philippines. In the next four months MacArthur was preoccupied with plans for the Allied invasion scheduled for the fall. With unexpected suddenness the atomic bombs on Hiroshima and Nagasaki and the Russian declaration of war forced a Japanese surrender. Instead of leading the invasion, MacArthur became supreme commander with responsibility for presiding at the surrender ceremonies and directing the occupation of Japan. It was an inviting role for the sixty-five-year-old general. General Robert Eichelberger, commander of the Eighth Army, recorded in his diary that MacArthur, on receiving the news of his appointment, ''was quite happy and said, 'They haven't got my scalp yet, have they Bob?' ''[13]

The Proconsul of Japan

In the first months following his dramatic unarmed landing at Atsugi airfield near Yokohama and acceptance of the Japanese surrender on the battleship *Missouri* on 2 September, MacArthur worked to establish his authority as proconsul of Japan. The planning documents produced at the end of the war by the State-War-Navy Coordinating Committee all assumed that the preponderance of military forces in the Occupation would be American, that Japan would not be divided up into zones of occupation as in Germany, that there would be a single, American supreme commander, and that the United States would exercise preeminent influence in any international control commission that might be established.[14] Great Britain, China, and Russia balked at the nominal role which the Americans planned for them. Responding to this pressure the State Department on 21 August requested that the eleven nations who had fought against Japan join a Far Eastern Advisory Council (FEAC) to consult with and advise but in no sense control the actions of the supreme commander.

The Russians refused to participate in the FEAC. Ambassador to Russia Averell Harriman sympathized with their position. He told Secretary of State Byrnes that by failing to respond to Soviet demands for some kind of four-power Allied Control Commission in Tokyo, similar to those established throughout Europe, the United States was needlessly slighting Soviet prestige.[15] Harriman was rightly convinced that Stalin did not want to challenge the dominant position of the United States in Japan and the Pacific. He had accepted with hardly a protest Truman's rejection of his request for a joint U.S.-Soviet command in Japan and a Soviet zone of occupation in the northernmost island of Hokkaido. Stalin also declined to send a Soviet military contingent to Japan on the grounds that this could inconvenience MacArthur. But Harriman warned Byrnes that the Soviets would raise the issue of control

General Douglas MacArthur, Supreme Commander of Allied Powers, leaves his headquarters in the Dai Ichi Building, Tokyo, Japan, with his aide-de-camp, Colonel Laurence E. Bunker. 2 April 1948. Signal Corps Photo, National Archives.

of Japan at the London Foreign Ministers Conference in September.

When Byrnes tried to brush off the Soviets on the Japanese issue in London, the whole conference became deadlocked. Back in Washington the secretary of state tried to break the logjam with the Russians by a compromise proposal for an Allied Military Council in Tokyo under the supreme commander. But MacArthur strenuously objected, fearing that such a body would diminish his authority and raise economic and political questions which should be settled elsewhere. He told Truman emissary Edwin A. Locke in October that control policy for Japan "should for the most part be made in Tokyo rather than in Washington." MacArthur spoke strongly of the "problems created for him by policy pronouncements made in Washington without prior consultation with him," Locke wrote Truman.[16]

Over MacArthur's grousing, the State Department struggled until early 1946 to create an essentially tokenistic international supervisory structure which would not interfere with de facto unilateral U.S. control of the Occupation. Harriman suggested acceptance of a Soviet proposal for a control commission in Japan similar to those in Hungary, Rumania, and Bulgaria. Since those commisssions were basically powerless, the Russians were clearly less interested in the substance of control than in protecting their prestige as a great power and establishing the comparability of the spheres of influence of both nations. Knowing that MacArthur had threatened to quit as supreme commander if there was any Allied infringment on his authority, the State Department resisted the word "control" in the title of the international body it sought to organize in Tokyo. After lengthy negotiations a compromise was finally reached at the Moscow Conference of Foreign Ministers in late December. An Allied Council for Japan of the Big Four powers to consult with MacArthur was established in Tokyo and a Far Eastern Commission (FEC) of all eleven allies in Washington would replace the FEAC and nominally formulate broad policy and approve fundamental changes in Japan.[17]

MacArthur and the State Department publicly clashed over the Moscow agreement. Byrnes hailed the accord as one that safeguarded the "outstanding and efficient administration set up and executed by General MacArthur." The same day a State Department press officer said that MacArthur had been kept informed of the negotiations in Moscow and had not objected to the new control plan for Japan. But MacArthur quickly issued a statement contradicting the State Department claim. He insisted that he had "no iota of responsibility for the decisions which were made" at Moscow.[18]

In practice MacArthur had few problems with either control body. The general made a lengthy speech at the opening session of the Allied Council for Japan in April 1946 at which he emphasized its strictly advisory role. Thereafter, his staff followed orders from headquarters to "talk the Council to death." Similarly, by the time the FEC held its first meeting on 26 February 1946 the U.S. had already set broad policy for Japan. MacArthur told Major General Frank R. McCoy, the American chairman of the FEC, that the new body by its terms of reference had "no executive powers, functions or responsibilities" and could not require approval of the actions of the supreme commander or the Japanese government in advance.[19] Certainly the international control arrangement for Japan was never a serious problem to MacArthur, for it left his authority unhampered, even if subject to more public challenge than he would have wished.

Given the preponderence of American power in the Pacific after the war, the crucial issue concerning MacArthur's proconsular authority in Japan was not Allied control but how closely Washington policymakers directed his activities. From very early in his military career MacArthur had displayed a penchant for repeated conflicts with his superiors, especially civilians. That pattern reemerged almost immediately as the Occupation began. Upon receiving a draft of SWNCC 150, U.S. Initial Post-Surrender Policy for Japan, MacArthur objected to several sections he found "unwise, rigid, too detailed and unnecessary."[20] Though approved by the president on 6 September essentially unchanged, the initial Post-Surrender Policy did not restrict MacArthur so much as allow him wide leeway of interpretation. MacArthur's guidelines, including the detailed JCS 1380/15 approved 3 November, reflected the unresolved contradictions at the end of the war between conservative political planners and liberal economic planners for the Occupation. On the one hand, these basic directives called for a remarkably progressive set of reforms of Japan's entire social structure but, on the other hand, directed that these reforms be implemented through the emperor of Japan and officials of the Japanese government whose interest was generally opposed to the democratization program.[21] In essence, whether he pushed the reform agenda or supported the conservative Japanese government, MacArthur could rightly claim his actions were consistent with Washington policy.

The contradictions in the Initial Post-Surrender Policy provided the backdrop for the first open challenge MacArthur made of Washington's authority over him. On 17 September, less than three weeks after the surrender ceremony, MacArthur publicly announced that the conservative government of Prince Higashikuni, an uncle of the emperor, had been so cooperative in carrying out the directives of his headquarters that U.S. military forces could be reduced from his August estimate of as high as 500,000 to 200,000 within six months. The Joint Chiefs of Staff, State Department, and the White House were infuriated on several counts with the uncleared statement. First, MacArthur's language left the impression that the supreme commander rather than the U.S. or any foreign government was the author and arbiter of the basic directive for Japan. Secondly, there were considerable doubts that the Japanese government was as cooperative as MacArthur suggested. Most importantly, a reduction in troop strength in Japan was contrary to global efforts to slow the pace of postwar demobilization and maintain the draft in order to meet vastly increased American military requirements.[22]

When the *Washington Post* accused MacArthur of "mixing politics with statesmanship" by his statement it was not far off the mark. General Robert E. Wood, the Republican leader who became head of the MacArthur-for-President movement in the 1948 election, had warned MacArthur two weeks earlier that the Truman administration, by talk of an extended Occupation of

Japan under a large army, sought to put the burden on him for maintaining the unpopular draft. "It would appear to me that once Japan is disarmed it would require a relatively small force, perhaps 200,000 to 300,000 men," Wood wrote. "The commander who demands an exorbitant army will later be pilloried, in my opinion, in the eyes of the public." According to General Bonner Fellers, secretary to the supreme commander, MacArthur shared Wood's views and launched his 17 September bombshell as a preemptive strike against political enemies in Washington.[23]

Outraged as Truman and his aides were at MacArthur, challenging his growing power as SCAP proved very difficult. After telephoning the president, Acting Secretary of State Dean Acheson issued a statement that the number of troops required in Japan was purely a military matter, but in carrying out policy for Japan, "the occupation forces are the instruments of policy and not the determinants of policy." Senators Kenneth Wherry of Nebraska and A. B. Happy Chandler of Kentucky jumped to MacArthur's defense and charged that Acheson had insulted and blighted the name of the supreme commander. Acheson responded to Wherry's question about who made policy for Japan by sending him a copy of the Potsdam Proclamation and releasing the heretofore secret Initial Post-Surrender Policy for Japan document.[24]

The flap over MacArthur's statement finally ended with an exchange of messages between Army Chief of Staff George C. Marshall and SCAP. With the concurrence of Truman, Marshall demanded that MacArthur "coordinate" all future statements on troop strength or demobilization prior to release with the War Department. Though MacArthur apologized for any embarrassment he had caused, he insisted he had acted "in complete conformity with the War Department's announced policy of demobilizing just as rapidly as conditions permitted."[25] Truman took no further action against the recalcitrant general.

MacArthur believed that Acheson's attack on him was "directed by the President [who was] starting out to fool the people just like Roosevelt did."[26] Such a view of the president's intentions led to more clashes between MacArthur and Washington policymakers, especially representatives of the State Department. Diplomat George Atcheson, who headed the Office of the Political Advisor (POLAD) until his accidental death in May 1947, complained to Dean Acheson that, on matters of substance, "General MacArthur or his Chief of Staff and other members of the Bataan Club who act as his Privy Council or *genro* wish if possible to keep the State Department out." MacArthur simply refused to recognize that foreign "policy is made at home."[27]

MacArthur responded to such allegations, which often surfaced in the press, by arguing that he was confident of success in Japan if there was not "too much back seat driving. During the fighting I had great difficulty in obtaining Washington's interest. Now that it is over I have equal difficulty with its too great interference."[28] Such an attitude, repeatedly conveyed, made Washington policymakers reluctant to issue orders to the supreme commander during the early years of the Occupation.

Appointments by MacArthur of close friends in the military to key positions in SCAP further assured the general's domination of the Tokyo scene in the opening phase of the Occupation. The high-ranking military officers of the four general staff sections and nine special staff sections in charge of the nonmilitary aspects of the Occupation reported directly to MacArthur. By 1948 General Headquarters, SCAP had evolved into a bureaucracy of over five thousand mostly civilian staff members. Major General Courtney Whitney, a Manila lawyer, headed the powerful Government Section (GS) of SCAP, which operated with the Japanese government to draft legislation and implement reforms in such areas as civil liberties, the purge, and antitrust. Though a conservative, Whitney supported the major reform directives from Washington and worked well with many of the young civilian specialists under him who were genuinely committed to building a democratic Japan. Major General William Marquat, a bomber pilot, took over in early 1946 as head of the Economic, Scientific Section (ESS). Marquat exercised authority until the end of the Occupation in such areas as taxation, exchange rates, and trade regulations. Major General Charles Willoughby headed Military Intelligence (G-2). Established to watch Japanese ultranationalists, G-2 focused its surveillance on Japanese leftists and American reformers in GS and ESS. Often MacArthur had to exercise his supreme authority to settle the factional wars within SCAP. Usually he sided with General Whitney of GS who had his own door to the supreme commander's office through which he could enter at any time.[29] Within SCAP, at any rate, no one ever openly challenged the prerogatives of MacArthur.

In the Public Eye

From the outset of the Occupation, the American press assumed that MacArthur had political aspirations. MacArthur vehemently denied that he did. "I have never entered politics, and I never intend to do so," he told the president of the United Press three weeks after the surrender ceremony. "I am on my last public assignment, which when concluded will mark the definite end of my service."[30]

But whether intended or not, MacArthur's clashes with Washington over Allied control of Japan and his authority to make policy there heightened speculation about his political ambitions for the presidency. The general's most avid supporters from the 1944 campaign were convinced he would run and that his chances for success in 1948 would be much improved. Roy Howard, head of the Scripps-Howard newspapers and a Republican party activist, advised MacArthur on 20 November 1945 that he should try "functioning in a sort of political limbo" to let rumors of his interest in the presidency subside. "I believe that the spread of these rumors at this time would certainly work havoc with the hopes of any who may be looking to you for action in 1948." Lyle Wilson of the United Press put his finger on a key element of any presidential bid by MacArthur. He predicted after MacArthur's fracas with the State Department over the Moscow agreement on international control of Japan that, sooner or later, the general would "break with the [Truman] Administration on the Russian issue and be a logical candidate for President."[31]

To MacArthur loyalists, a short Occupation in which the general established his credentials as a successful statesman was crucial to prospects for the 1948 election. Surveys during the war had consistently shown that MacArthur was considered one of the most admired military figures in the nation. But as pollster Elmo Roper had put it, "only a small segment [of people] had faith in his abilities as a civilian leader." The problem remained much the same after the war. In a Gallup poll conducted in April 1946, MacArthur topped General Eisenhower, President Truman, Winston Churchill, Governor Thomas Dewey, Governor Harold Stassen, and others as the most admired person in the world. Yet in every Gallup poll conducted in 1946 and 1947 in which Republicans were asked their choice of a presidential nominee, MacArthur received under 10 percent of the vote. Reflecting the tradition of the separation of civilian and military authority, the overwhelming majority of those polled did not think that General Dwight Eisenhower, MacArthur, or any other war hero would become a candidate for president.[32]

More candid than the American press, the London *Economist* in January 1946 laid out the problem of a MacArthur presidential bid and its impact on his handling of the Occupation. The fundamental difficulty with American policy in Japan was that the victors expected to carry through far-reaching social reforms to convert Japan into a peace-loving democratic state "while at the same time relying on the old civil servants and politicians for the day-to-day administration of Japan." That problem was aggravated by the presence of MacArthur as supreme commander for he was

not a mere soldier. He is also a factor in the struggle for power in America. Even if he himself does not consider the possibility of running for the presidency in 1948, there are many men who are considering it for him and the period of supreme authority in Japan is clearly the testing time of his career. He cannot afford to make mistakes, he cannot afford to let chaos develop with mass misery and starvation. His record must be one of efficiency. At the same time he is faced with the acute problem of finding an administration [in Japan] able to cope with possible collapse. He cannot keep a large army of occupation. The American soldier must go home. No officials or experts must be retained once they are anxious to leave. The only alternative is to use the existing Japanese administration.[33]

While there is no direct evidence of MacArthur's personal planning for the presidency until the fall of 1947, the general's behavior over the first two years of the Occupation did follow the script laid out by the *Economist*. He constantly sought to prove both his faith in the American liberal tradition of democratic capitalism and his ability to work through a Japanese state system which had no historical commitment to that goal. Using public relations strategies, he and his aides strove to create the appearance of a successful Occupation guided by the supreme commander. Moreover, throughout the postwar years, MacArthur was always ambiguous enough about his interest in the presidency to encourage his supporters and arouse the fears of Democratic and Republican rivals. Following a trip to Tokyo, Eisenhower warned Truman that MacArthur would return to the United States before the 1948 election to make a presidential bid. Later Truman told Secretary of Defense James Forrestal that both Eisenhower and MacArthur, the nation's two greatest war heroes, seemed to suffer from either ''Potomac fever'' or ''brass infection.''[34]

MacArthur seemed to think that his success in democratizing Japan and establishing his political credentials at home required that he act as a sovereign head of state, casting an image of unapproachable authority. During his more than five years in Japan, MacArthur never spoke to any Japanese other than the emperor and a handful of the highest ranking officials. (By contrast, almost any American visitor of stature whom MacArthur wished to impress was welcome at headquarters.) His isolation from the lives of ordinary Japanese extended even to his travels. Except for his initial trip from Atsugi airbase and Yokohama to Tokyo, all MacArthur ever saw of Japan was through the window of his limousine along the route between his home at the American Embassy and General Headquarters at the Dai Ichi Insurance building near the Imperial Palace. ''MacArthur's attitude toward the Japanese,'' one correspondent observed, ''is that of father toward child.''[35] That attitude reflected the racism respectable at the time. At a congressional hearing after his firing by Truman in 1951, MacArthur gave this evaluation of the Japanese:

If the Anglo-Saxon was say forty-five years of age in his development in the sciences, the arts, divinity, culture, the Germans were quite as mature. The Japanese, however, in spite of their antiquity measured by time, were in a very tuitionary condition. Measured by the standards of modern civilization, they would be like a boy of twelve as compared with our development of forty-five years.

Like any tuitionary period, they were susceptible to following new models, new ideas. You can implant basic concepts there. They were still close enough to origin to be elastic and acceptable to new concepts.[36]

Sharing this outlook, most Americans, one prominent diplomat observed, found it admirable that MacArthur should have untrammeled power to raise the wayward Japanese to the democratic maturity of the United States. As long as American democratic principles were affirmed, MacArthur's imperiousness towards the Japanese appears to have only added to his political stock at home.[37]

Throughout the early fall of 1945, the Occupation functioned in an unremitting glare of publicity. Angered at the Japanese enemy by the ferocious fighting and heavy casualties at the end of the war, Americans watched to see that the supreme commander eradicated all vestiges of Japanese militarism. With the exception of a few radical critics who questioned the wisdom of keeping the existing Japanese government intact, the American press found the basic Occupation guidelines for demilitarizing and democratizing Japan reassuring. The issue was how MacArthur interpreted these directives and the skill with which they were administered. In general, MacArthur failed to meet immediate post-surrender public demands for a punitive approach toward the Japanese. A Gallup poll conducted during the week of 21 September 1945 indicated 61 percent of the respondents thought the Occupation was "not tough enough" on the Japanese while only 32 percent thought that the "treatment is just right."[38]

In defending himself against widespread accusations that he was too soft on the Japanese, MacArthur pointed out the need to move slowly until the demilitarization program was completed. More importantly, beginning with the published reports of headquarters' Civil Liberties directive of 4 October 1945, MacArthur placed his prestige and political prospects at home behind a series of reform measures which sharply defused criticism of his handling of the Japanese. Under the terms of the directive over two thousand political prisoners were released, limits on freedom of speech and assembly were abrogated, and the Home Ministry which directed the feared thought police was abolished. The logic of the directive, not MacArthur's political preference, called for the legalization of the Japanese Communist party as well.[39]

When the Higashikuni cabinet resigned rather than carry out the directive, MacArthur insisted that the new ministry of Baron Shidehara Kijuro take immediate action. The general then made a public statement on 9 October on other "required reforms." The statement appeared to be an additional attempt by MacArthur to win popular approval at home by indicating his full-fledged acceptance of the stern but progressive agenda of his Washington guidelines. Japan's "traditional social order" would have to be changed, its constitution liberalized. He expected the new government to first of all emancipate the women of Japan for "the well-being of the Home." Then it was to encourage unionization of labor, end the exploitation of children, open up schools to more liberal education, and democratize the economy.[40]

But only a short time later, MacArthur astounded presidential envoy Edwin A. Locke in a meeting in Tokyo by debunking many of the same democratic reforms called for in his 9 October statement. MacArthur and his economic advisor, Colonel Raymond C. Kramer, openly defended their unwillingness to press forward more vigorously with the directives on the dissolution of the Zaibatsu companies, the purge, and reparations. MacArthur emphasized to Locke his own concern with keeping a tight lid on Japanese politics and preventing "so-called liberals," who were really Soviet agents, from instigating a Communist revolution.[41] Though MacArthur often talked of uprooting feudalism and planting capitalist democracy in Japan, his interest in reform, it seemed, flowed more from political opportunism than any ideological commitment.

For MacArthur the most delicate political issue of the early months of the Occupation was the emperor institution. Many in Japan and back home considered the emperor at the apex of the Japanese system of feudalism and regarded his abdication or trial as a war criminal as critical to the realization of a democratized Japan. MacArthur did not. He first met the emperor on 27 September at his embassy home in a move to underscore the authority of the Supreme Commander over the Son of Heaven. *Life* magazine's photograph of the tall American general (without a tie) and the small Japanese emperor (in formal dress) taken before their half hour talk dramatically captured the relationship. The meeting was shrouded in secrecy. But it was made clear afterwards that MacArthur refused to accept the emperor's own assessment of his responsibility for Japan's decision for and conduct of the war in the Pacific. The meeting offered the first public indication that MacArthur intended to ignore calls to depose the emperor and instead use him to carry out policy in Japan.[42]

Life accurately predicted how MacArthur hoped to reconcile keeping the emperor institution with his vision of a democratic revolution in Japan. A proposed reform of the Japanese constitution under MacArthur's aegis would "probably demote the emperor from the status of god and make him a constitutional monarch scarcely more powerful than the British." Privately MacArthur warned the War Department that to indict the emperor as a war criminal and remove him from the throne would lead to the disintegration of the Japanese nation and would require he be given a minimum of one million troops for an indefinite period.[43]

The emperor's 1946 New Year's Day rescript strengthened MacArthur's reputation as a tough-minded reformer in Japan. Obviously issued in anticipation of a revision of the Meiji constitution, the major points of the rescript were a denial of the emperor's divinity, a bulwark in the dominant presurrender ideology of Japan, and a denial that "the Japanese people are superior to other races and fated to rule the world." But in the midst of massive demonstrations for food, calls for the resignation of the Shidehara cabinet, and a wave of strikes precipitated by desperate living conditions, the emperor also attacked "radical tendencies in excess." MacArthur praised the rescript to press reporters. The emperor had undertaken "a leading part in the democratization of his people. He squarely takes his stand for the future along liberal lines."[44]

Throughout the fall of 1945 the Occupation rounded up the leading suspected war criminals and preparations were made for the Tokyo War Crimes Trials. Then on 4 January 1946, headquarters, in accordance with Washington policy, launched the first in a series of purge orders. It destroyed the right-wing of the Progressive party, eliminated key leadership of the conservative Liberal party, and covered bureaucrats, police, and military officers as well. The purge precipitated a major crisis in the Shidehara cabinet and shocked Japanese conservatives by its scope. In justifying the purge order, MacArthur had General Whitney blast the "inertia, if not active opposition" within the Japanese government to cleaning "its own stable. Centuries of feudal submission and the complete, untrammelled and irresponsible freedom of the executive proved obstacles too great to be overcome by the people themselves."[45]

By mid-January 1946 praise for MacArthur's handling of the Occupation in the American press cut across nearly the entire political spectrum. The *Nation,* which only a few months earlier had damned MacArthur's "soft peace" policy, focused comment on how the purge orders were crippling right-wing political organizers throughout Japan and giving "great encouragement to the liberated progressive forces now preparing for the coming elections . . . . The result of the purge may be a left majority in the next Diet." *Time* magazine, which had consistently supported MacArthur from the outset of the Occupation, contended in January that while sometimes principles had outrun performance, "General MacArthur had done a bang-up job of occupying Japan." Paul Manning, a CBS war correspondent, wrote in *Reader's Digest* in January 1946 that MacArthur was doing brilliantly in administering "neither a 'soft' peace nor a 'hard' peace. The distinction does not interest him. He is determined to administer a peace which shall guarantee that never again in our lifetime shall Japan be a threat to the world." *Life* magazine, like many others, contrasted the "sensationally successful" Occupation of Japan under MacArthur, to the failures and problems of the United States in Germany and elsewhere. Only reports from the Left in the *U.S. News* and *Amerasia* evidenced significant skepticism about a revolutionary change in Japan from a feudal dictatorship to a modern democracy. But even these magazines avoided any criticism of MacArthur directly.[46]

Certainly MacArthur, his staff, and his political supporters at home must have been pleased with the generally favorable reviews of the Occupation and lack of criticism of the general himself. In a survey by pollster Elmo Roper that appeared in January 1946, more than 71 percent of respondents were well satisfied with the "way the occupation of Japan is going" while only 15 percent were not satisfied. (By comparison 60.7 percent were well satisfied that the occupation of Germany was going well and 24 percent were not satisfied.) Approval of Japanese Occupation policies was up twenty points from the previous month while approval of German occupation policies remained the same. The same poll showed MacArthur only slightly behind General Eisenhower as the most admired military man in America.[47]

Pushing the Reform Agenda

For MacArthur the most important step in the peaceful transformation of Japan from a feudal system to a capitalist democracy, one which his aides if not the general himself regarded as crucial for his political prospects at home as well, was the revision of Japan's Meiji constitution of 1889. The general received no specific directives from Washington on the question, only a broad mandate to proceed along lines laid out in SWNCC 228, "The Reform of the Japanese Governmental System," dated 9 January 1946. It was assumed that the Japanese government would take the initiative in making constitutional revisions in accord with the democratic principles of SWNCC 228. Moreover, MacArthur believed until the end of January that under the terms of the Moscow agreement revision of the Japanese constitution was the responsibility of the new Far Eastern Commission, not SCAP. The Shidehara cabinet had appointed Matsumoto Joji, a distinguished Tokyo legal scholar, in October 1945 to head a constitutional revision committee. As the primary objective of the Matsumoto committee was to preempt any action by SCAP which tampered with the imperial institution, officers of SCAP's Government Section were dismayed by the proposed revisions of the constitution presented in February 1946. The emperor would be a "supreme and inviolable" sovereign rather than "sacred and inviolable." Furthermore, the committee proposed no significant provisions for parliamentary control of the government. Mac-

Arthur concluded that Matsumoto was "an extreme reactionary" whose revisions were "nothing more than a rewording of the old Meiji Constitution."[48]

Consequently, on 3 February MacArthur directed Government Section to draft a constitution to guide the Shidehara cabinet in the formulation of its own fundamental legal document. In the new constitution, MacArthur insisted, the emperor would be "at the head of state" but his powers would be "exercised according to the will of the people." Moreover, Japan would have to renounce war and the taking up of arms, "even for preserving its own security." Under the leadership of Charles Kades, a New Deal lawyer, a committee of Government Section officials hurriedly prepared their own draft of an acceptable constitution. Speed was important, for MacArthur feared that the Matsumoto draft played into the hands of the FEC, many of whose members were on record in favor of abolishing the throne and having Hirohito tried as a war criminal. To forestall any FEC plans for a republican form of government, the new constitution had to be so innovative that the FEC could not object to it. In addition, MacArthur was determined that Japan's first general elections, only two months away, would also constitute an unofficial plebiscite on a revised constitution.[49]

In a dramatic meeting held 13 February, Chief of Government Section Courtney Whitney presented the American draft constitution to the Japanese cabinet. Among other provisions, it guaranteed civil liberties, deprived the peerage of its privileges, made the cabinet fully answerable to the Diet, and renounced armies and war.[50] But it shocked the Japanese primarily because it appeared to deprive the emperor of his political authority. Foreign Minister Yoshida Shigeru characterized it as "revolutionary" and "outrageous," and others expressed dismay. But Whitney was not sympathetic and announced that unless the cabinet approved the document as representing its own views, MacArthur could not "guarantee the person of the Emperor." Finally, on 6 March the Japanese cabinet, in accord with the emperor's own view, bowed to American pressure.[51] After more than three months of Diet debate that was dominated by the parties on the Right—which emphasized that, in essence, the new constitution in no way altered the character of the national polity (kokutai)— the "MacArthur Constitution" was ratified and came into effect in May 1947.

MacArthur regarded the new constitution, particularly the articles on the emperor institution and the "no-war" article, as the key to the democratization of Japan. He always believed that he had prevented the demise of the emperor institution by reducing the emperor to a mere "symbol of state" within a democratic framework. In practice, the emperor was considerably more than that, playing a behind-the-scenes role in some of the most crucial decisions of the Occupation period and remaining a key to the perpetuation of conservative elite authority. Yet MacArthur never wavered in his commitment to the emperor, meeting him twice each year during the course of the Occupation. The general recalled that the emperor had "played a major role in the spiritual regeneration of Japan and his loyal cooperation and influence had much to do with the success of the occupation."[52]

MacArthur took justified pride in the most unique and ultimately the most significant section of the "MacArthur Constitution," the famous "no-war" Article 9. In its final form, it read as follows:

> Aspiring sincerely to an international peace based on justice and order, the Japanese people forever renounce war as a sovereign right of the nation and the threat or use of force as means of settling international disputes.
>
> In order to accomplish the aim of the preceding paragraph, land, sea, and air forces, as well as other war potential will never be maintained. The right of belligerency of the state will not be recognized.[53]

The origin of Article 9 is still in dispute amongst scholars in both the United States and Japan. Some have held that it was forced upon the Japanese government by MacArthur's personal fiat. Others contend that either Charles Kades or Courtney Whitney of Government Section were responsible. Still others agree with MacArthur that the idea of a no-war clause to the consitution was proposed by Prime Minister Shidehara at a meeting with him held on 24 January 1946, even before Government Section had begun its work on a draft constitution.[54] Whatever the case, it is certain that Article 9 originated in Tokyo rather than Washington and would not have been adopted without MacArthur's support. During the war the "permanent and complete" disarmament of Germany and Japan was a major goal of American policy. The hatred and fear of Japan made such a prospect a very popular one, and the Initial Post-Surrender Policy for Japan document sent to Tokyo to guide MacArthur explicitly stated the objective of "complete and permanent" disarmament. But in SWNCC 228 the demilitarization concept was hedged by reference to the future prerogatives of the civilian branch of the Japanese government.[55] In view of these ambiguous instructions, MacArthur's own thoughts on war and his political ambitions became the key to the resolution of this critical issue.

After 1945 MacArthur's thinking on war underwent a fundamental change. Some combination of fear of the destructive power of the atomic bombs, a sense that atomic weapons had made the army's role in any future war obsolete, a more pronounced religious feeling, and an appreciation of the war-weariness of the American people prompted him to declare after the Japanese surrender ceremony that "if we do not now devise some greater and more equitable system, Armageddon will be at our door." While he would rely on the military might of the United States temporarily, MacArthur repeatedly suggested that a new spiritual order was the only alternative to global destruction. "Force has failed," MacArthur cabled a memorial service at the University of Southern California, "and force alone will continue to fail to save mankind from destruction. For our own salvation we must turn to the things of the spirit."[56]

MacArthur gave evidence of his new thoughts on war in his first public endorsement of the proposed new constitution. He singled out Article 9 as the foremost of its provisions. "The cynic may view such action as demonstrating but a childlike faith in a visionary ideal, but the realist sees in it far deeper significance. The proposal of the Japanese government . . . in effect but recognizes one further step in the evolution of mankind, under which nations would develop, for mutual protection against war, a yet higher law of international social and political morality." MacArthur went on to recommend the no-war clause be adopted by the United Nations, for the alternative to universal disarmament, he concluded, was the yawning abyss of another war which might "blast mankind to perdition."[57]

Any plans by MacArthur and his aides to use the new constitution in Japan to strengthen the general's political credentials at home were tempered by the need to avoid playing into the hands of Japanese critics of the constitution who insisted it was illegitimately imposed upon their nation. Officials had to maintain the fiction of the wholly Japanese origins of the new constitution. Yet virtually every American commentator detected the hand of the supreme commander behind the principal articles of the new charter, especially the no-war article.

Though confounding both his conservative friends and liberal critics, MacArthur gained favorable press reviews for his defense of the no-war clause as a first step towards universal disarmament. MacArthur's position, the *Christian Century* noted, stood in sharp contrast to Truman's calls for an extension of the draft, rearmament, and readiness for imminent hostilities.[58] The *Saturday Evening Post*'s foreign editor, Martin Sommers, praised the new Japanese constitution for creating "a model state without an army or navy, dedicated to progress through peaceful pursuits alone." Many Americans privately approved of MacArthur's statements on war and his administration of the Occupation, Sommers asserted, but were reluctant to speak up for fear that such approval "might be interpreted as endorsement of MacArthur's alleged presidential ambitions." Sommers returned from Tokyo mistakenly convinced that MacArthur was wholly devoted to fashioning a peaceful and democratic Japan and had no interest in being a presidential candidate. Doubts did persist, especially in left-wing journals, that the constitution had changed the substance of power retained by the old order.[59] But for MacArthur and his aides, the new charter represented the most important reform in Japan and a most valuable one for political purposes at home.

With crises erupting in Europe, the Middle East, and China throughout 1946 and 1947 and the new constitution for Japan in place, the American press gave only sporadic attention in its foreign news reporting to MacArthur and the remainder of the agenda for reform in Japan. Nevertheless, the supreme commander sought to build a record in Japan that substantiated his conversion from warrior to peacemaker. He took a keen interest in the elimination from public life of Japanese militarists and ultranationalists through war crimes trials for the most prominent figures and purge proceedings for the rest. MacArthur established the rules of evidence for the Manila War Crimes Trials of his adversaries in the Philippines, Generals Homma Masuhara and Yamashita Tomoyuki, and repeatedly goaded regular military officers answerable to him to move swiftly on these cases. Not surprisingly the defendants were found guilty and sentenced to death. In his final judgment MacArthur fully supported the Manila proceeding despite nagging questions that were raised about its fairness.[60]

By contrast to the Manila trials, MacArthur and the American public gave little attention to the Tokyo War Crimes Trials that followed the precedent established at Nuremberg. Former Prime Minister Tojo Hideki and twenty-six other prominent Japanese men were accused of participating in a conspiracy to wage aggressive war. (The emperor was conspicuously absent from the list.) After a trial lasting for more than two years, all were found guilty. Seven were hanged and the rest received lengthy prison sentences.[61]

The first purge order from MacArthur's headquarters on 4 January 1946 fell heavily on the leadership of the right-wing political parties and, as already mentioned, reassured critics of the Occupation at home that MacArthur did not favor a soft peace. MacArthur must have anticipated similar approval for the second and third purge orders of late 1946 and early 1947. These orders removed or barred more politicians from public life and many leaders of business, the mass media, and the military as well. Angered at the planned extension of the purge, newly elected Prime Minister Yoshida Shigeru wrote MacArthur in October 1946 that the result might well be "anarchy, chaos, and communism."[62] Though MacArthur ignored Yoshida's charges they were echoed in January 1947 in *Newsweek* magazine in the first public indication of the erosion of support for the reform agenda at home.[63]

The impact of the purge in Japan, in fact, was considerably less pervasive than Japanese conservatives and their American friends feared or later claimed since MacArthur relied on the Japanese government to administer the purge and never intended it to "lose the services of many able governmental individuals who would be difficult to replace in the organization of a new Japan." Compared to the U.S. Occupation zone in Germany, where 2.5 percent of the population was purged, the figure for Japan was .29 percent. Moreover, of the 210,000 Japanese eventually purged, 80 percent were officers in the military.[64] The purge of the political elite resulted in a major reshuffling of political party alignments but did not undermine the control of the cabinet or Diet by the conservative parties throughout virtually the entire Occupation. MacArthur dismissed the recommendation of the FEC that the first general election called for in April 1946 be postponed until the purge was completed. The FEC accurately predicted that the old guard politicians with their money and influence would easily get themselves elected. Even when many of these politicians were purged they were able to name their own replacements. In addition the political purge had the effect of strengthening the state bureaucracy upon whom the Americans relied to administer the country. Despite the clear roots of the bureaucracy in Japan's prewar program of aggression and repression, it was virtually untouched by the purge. Similarly the business and media elite were little affected by the purge orders.[65]

While MacArthur personally focused attention on demobilizing the Japanese military machine and the political reforms in the early months of the Occupation, economic conditions rapidly deteriorated in Japan. "My chief concern is that you should be well supplied with a good economic and fiscal man," Assistant Secretary of War John J. McCloy wrote MacArthur in November 1945. "Economics determines politics and there are problems of tremendous economic significance." Though McCloy did not spell out the problems he had in mind they certainly included the destruction of most of Japan's major cities during the firebomb raids at the end of the war, idle factories, spiraling inflation, raging black market, and millions of homeless, unemployed, and hungry. MacArthur's directives did specify that the Japanese government was solely responsible for economic reconstruction. But many in SCAP quickly concluded that the policies of the conservative cabinets were deliberately inflationary and contributed to rather than ameliorated the situation. Apparently confident until 1947 that the political reforms would eventually solve the problem, MacArthur dismissed their appeals to intervene in Japanese economic affairs. At the same time, Washington officials, preoccupied with European problems, ignored the festering economic crisis in Japan. Secretary of War Robert Patterson told a friend in July 1946 that MacArthur's administration of Japan was "the one bright spot in post-war accomplishments [and the] spirit of the War Department was to let [SCAP] alone."[66]

But the response of Japanese workers to the economic crisis in Japan threatened to damage MacArthur's projection of Japan as an island of stability in a sea of Asian turmoil. Using their new political rights, hungry and angry workers quickly organized left-wing unions, conducted strikes, and held large and militant protest rallies against the conservative postwar cabinets. Mac-Arthur was shocked by the militancy of the protests and concerned about "underground communist agitation." At first he emphasized the need for legislation, like the Trade Union Law of December 1945, that sought to channel union activities into the collective bargaining framework familiar in the United States. He also sought more relief aid from Washington. He warned his old friend Herbert Hoover, who visited Tokyo as chairman of the Famine Emergency Committee in May 1946, that unless more food was sent he could not ensure against "mass starvation and civil disobedience."[67]

But MacArthur soon resorted to repression of the burgeoning trade union movement by attacks on its left-wing leadership. The spread of production control strikes in which workers challenged management prerogatives by taking over operation, though not ownership, of a plant particularly alarmed SCAP. When these strikes were coupled with six major Communist-led mass demonstrations in two months against food shortages MacArthur issued a stern warning against "mob disorder and violence." The violence "which undisciplined elements are now beginning to practice will not be permitted to continue," MacArthur stated on 20 May. "They constitute a menace not only to orderly government but to the basic purposes and security of the occupation itself." Japanese management seized the initiative to thwart further production control strikes and the Left suffered a temporary setback.[68]

When economic conditions deteriorated still further by the end of 1946, a new and more dramatic confrontation between the labor movement and Mac-Arthur developed. Achieving nothing through collective bargaining for increased wages with the Yoshida government, officials of the well-organized government workers unions called for a general strike to take place 1 February 1947. It was expected that nearly four million trade unionists and sympathizers would participate. Despite promises from the unions to maintain vital services, SCAP officials feared a collapse of the transportation, communication, and food distribution system. After warnings made privately by SCAP officials to call off the strike were ignored, MacArthur reluctantly intervened on 31 January with orders to the trade union leaders to call off the strike. "I will not permit the use of so deadly a social weapon in the present impoverished and emaciated condition of Japan," he said. The unions involved in the threatened strike, he claimed, represented a small minority who might plunge the nation into a disaster similar to that which the right-wing minority had produced before the war.[69]

The arrival in Tokyo on 26 January of a high-powered group of newspaper publishers and editors, including Roy Howard, owner of the Scripps-Howard chain of twenty-six dailies and head of the United Press, had increased Mac-Arthur's anxiety to avoid a politically damaging intervention against the general strike. Intervention might be construed at home as strikebreaking or, at the least, a tacit admission that democracy in Japan was faltering. But the mainstream American press either ignored the labor strife or provided Mac-Arthur favorable coverage. *Time* magazine praised SCAP's intervention against "adolescent trade unions" groping to learn democracy. Miles Vaughn, United Press bureau chief in Tokyo and an "old Japan hand" from before the war, filed stories blaming the strike on Japanese Communists.[70]

MacArthur managed to avoid damaging fallout at home from the abortive general strike but his presidential ambitions played a significant role in the labor policies he followed thereafter. Shortly after 1 February, Roy Howard—who fancied himself a Republican kingmaker—visited MacArthur and told him that radicals in SCAP, most prominently Chief of Labor Division Theodore Cohen, were primarily responsible for the national crisis that had just occurred. Howard told MacArthur that as long as Cohen and other radicals remained in their posts, "the General could not hope to get the support of the Scripps-Howard newspapers for the presidency."[71] After a wait of a few months, MacArthur quietly kicked Cohen upstairs to a new post as economic advisor to General Marquat and chose James Killen of the American Federation of Labor as the new chief of Labor Division. In so doing MacArthur appeased Howard and conservative critics of his labor program and gained a political asset with the American labor movement.

Once clearly defeated for the 1948 Republican presidential nomination and no longer concerned about the liberal press or the vote of American labor, MacArthur consistently intervened against the Japanese labor movement. The most dramatic confrontation occurred in late July 1948 when government workers comprising about one-third of the Japanese labor force engaged in numerous dispute tactics to demand higher wages in line with those of workers in the private sector. Fearing once again a general strike, MacArthur supported legislation removing government workers from the protections of the Trade Union Law. As discussed more fully in chapter four, Killen resigned in protest and launched a successful campaign to obtain the endorsement by the AFL-CIO for a resolution calling on the Army Department to order MacArthur to "discontinue repressive action that is being carried out under the guise of anti-Communism against legitimate trade union objectives." But MacArthur, with Washington's tacit support, refused to make any concessions to Japanese or American labor demands. Critical as he remained of the Japanese feudal system and Japanese monopolies, MacArthur most feared a socialist alternative. He proclaimed the Left the number one enemy in Japan in a speech on 2 September 1946 on the anniversary of the Japanese surrender.[72]

Usually MacArthur's partisan political ambitions merged successfully with his interpretation of the democratic reform agenda for Japan. But political opportunism gained the upper hand in the case of one of the most potentially consequential reforms of the Occupation. For at least the first eighteen months of the Occupation the breakup of the Zaibatsu holding companies and enormous combines that exerted effective control over the Japanese economy and had profited immensely from the war was regarded in Washington as critical to the demilitarization and democratization of Japan. Yet MacArthur hastily approved a plan submitted by the Yasuda combine in late October 1945 as satisfying the dissolution requirements of his basic policy guidelines. A scheme to avert more drastic action, the Yasuda plan dissolved the Yasuda holding company but was full of loopholes that allowed the huge operating companies to remain intact under indirect family control. Other major Zaibatsu firms quickly agreed to dissolution on the same terms as the Yasuda plan.[73]

Amidst some press criticism of MacArthur's leniency towards the Zaibatsu and agitation by liberal economists in the State Department, Washington sent Corwin D. Edwards of Northwestern University to Japan early in 1946 to study the situation. The Edwards mission sharply criticized the Yasuda plan as wholly inadequate and recommended sweeping measures for structural changes in the Japanese business system. MacArthur clearly did not like the Edwards report. He sent Washington a critique prepared by Economic and Scientific Section complaining that various of the report's provisions were "too liberal" and "unworkable." MacArthur expressed fear that some of the changes called for would create chaos in the Japanese economy and "instead of creating free enterprise . . . place business in a strait-jacket of governmental controls." In spite of MacArthur's objections, the Edwards report became the basis for U.S. policy on the Zaibatsu, known by its Far Eastern Commission number FEC-230.[74]

In a remarkable reversal of positions, MacArthur became in 1947 and 1948 the leading defender of the FEC-230 program against Washington policymakers now opposed to economic reform. Suffice it to say here that MacArthur read the administration's new position on the Zaibatsu as a personal attack against him and may have anticipated political advantage by adopting the image of reformer and trustbuster. Whatever his motivation, MacArthur used tactics during the FEC-230 struggle that proved politically embarrassing. He was forced to capitulate and allow the dismantling of the dissolution program. Very soon Japan's industrial and financial elites consolidated their position as the dominant element in postwar Japan, exercising control in 1952 over a more concentrated and interconnected system of corporations than before the war.[75]

One of the most dramatic and important reforms carried out in the early democratization period, the sweeping land reform of 1946-47, was given a more radical edge by SCAP headquarters than Washington apparently intended. Although no evidence has been found linking MacArthur's land reform policies directly to his partisan political ambitions, he surely saw it within the framework of his vision of a democratic Japan and the strengthening of his reputation at home as a tough-minded reform statesman. On the one hand, land reform would strike at the landlords who were a bulwark of the feudalistic and militaristic Japan of the past. On the other hand, land reform would help demobilize and prevent radical agrarian movements amongst the miserably poor tenant farmers and small landowners. Approximately 70 percent of Japan's farmers rented part of the land they cultivated and about 50 percent rented more than half of what they worked. After paying for their tools and supplies, they had barely enough income for subsistence.[76]

On the advice of Wolf Ladejinsky, an anti-Communist Russian émigré and advisor to SCAP on land reform, MacArthur rejected the land reform legislation passed by the conservative controlled Diet in December 1945 as wholly inadequate. The SCAP-sponsored bill passed in October 1946 was the major land reform legislation of the Occupation. Among other provisions, absentee landlords had to sell all their land to the government and land was to be bought at a fixed price with tenants allowed to pay in installments over thirty years at a low rate of interest.[77] The new legislation, MacArthur wrote his friend and political ally, John Callan O'Laughlin, publisher of the *Army-Navy Times,* would transform "several million tenant farmers, traditionally vassals of feudalistic landlords, into 'capitalistic' owners of the land they long have worked. This will raise the status of the individual and create in them a powerful bulwark against the creation of radical ideology which seeks to suppress just such private enterprise."[78]

Rhetorically the leadership of the ruling Liberal party opposed the American sponsored land reform. But Prime Minister Yoshida accepted the counter-revolutionary premises of land reform where he had not in the case of the American proposed Zaibatsu dissolution program. His appointments to the Ministry of Agriculture and other actions indicated support by the ruling Liberal party for land reform in practice. In addition, the depression and the war had weakened the landlord class so that their elimination under the Occupation carried less political risk and even helped consolidate the power of the industrialists over political affairs. Under these circumstances the actual redistribution of land took place in 1947 and 1948 with little incident except for understandable complaints from landlord committees that land reform was confiscation of private property. The percentage of owner operated land rose from 54 percent of all cultivated land in 1947 to 90 percent in 1950. Farmers owning their own land increased from 38 percent of the total to 70 percent in the same period.[79]

In accord with his basic directives, MacArthur sought to go beyond the political and economic reform of Japan to create a "grassroots democracy" in such areas as education, local government, law enforcement, and religion.[80] But important as he believed all of these reforms to be, the general only gave close personal attention to the reform of Japanese religious life. Washington planners had decided that Shinto, the Japanese state religion, was an instrument of aggression. Laws and regulations which discriminated on the basis of religion would be abolished and freedom of religious worship proclaimed. In line with these directives MacArthur ordered on 15 December 1945 the abolition of state Shinto. The "MacArthur Constitution" guaranteed religious freedom and met the issue of church and state separation directly. "No religious organization shall receive any privileges from the state nor exercise any political authority."[81]

Convinced the Japanese "needed spiritual leadership as well as material administration" and, no doubt, alert to political possibilities at home, MacArthur awkwardly interpreted religious freedom in Japan as a green light for SCAP authorities to actively support Christian missionary work and the small community of about 300,000 Japanese Christians. In a well-publicized letter to the president of the Southern Baptist Convention in November 1946 he wrote of "an opportunity without counterpart since the birth of Christ for the spread of Christianity among the peoples of the Far East." Though not a churchgoer, MacArthur issued calls for a thousand missionaries to come to Japan and wrote letters to missionary boards for more Christian volunteers. MacArthur gave permission to church personnel to enter Japan before he did educators and businessmen. Despite scarcity of resources, MacArthur permitted the first full-time missionaries to return to Japan in December 1945 and their numbers increased gradually so that in 1949 over nine hundred new missionaries were cleared for entry.[82]

MacArthur used his administrative powers to assist the missionary effort to the fullest. Frequently, Japanese Christians received special permission to use public school buildings. For fear of undercutting the Protestant evangelical movement his headquarters dropped an investigation into allegations that Japan's most prominent Christian, Dr. Kagawa Toyohiko, had supported the war effort. MacArthur praised the selection of right-wing Socialist Katayama Tetsu, a lifelong Presbyterian, to head a coalition cabinet in May 1947 as part of a ''steady advance of the Christian faith in the East'' which would provide an invincible spiritual barrier against totalitarian ideologies.[83]

Probably the best known example of MacArthur's commitment to the Christian cause in Japan was his aid to the American Bible Society. Declaring a plan to ship 125,000 Bibles to Japan in 1948 inadequate, MacArthur helped the society reach the fantastic goal of distributing ten million Bibles throughout the country. Christian missionaries were delighted with MacArthur's support for their crusade. Many actively urged their congregations at home to support MacArthur's presidential bid in 1948; all were encouraged to work more vigorously at converting the Japanese.[84]

In the end, the dream of MacArthur and the missionaries of a more Christian Japan remained just that. By 1951 there were about 200,000 Protestants in Japan, the same as before the war, and 157,000 Catholics, a slight increase over 1941. In the last year of the Occupation there were fewer than one-half of 1 percent Christians in the Japanese population compared to the 55 percent who were Buddhist. No wonder the missionaries and MacArthur preferred to measure their success in Japan by vague concepts of spiritual influence rather than by the number of Christian converts.[85]

Public Relations and the Hero of Japan

For those closest to MacArthur and in all likelihood for the general himself, a corps of friendly foreign correspondents in Japan was critical to any plans for a 1948 presidential bid. They would have to establish in the public mind a record for MacArthur of statesmanship and efficiency. Conversely, MacArthur could not afford reports of chaos, mass misery, starvation, and political unrest, a point Japanese conservatives played on with relentless skill to obtain more relief supplies through SCAP headquarters. While American policy dictated the destruction of the centralized and state-controlled press of Japan, from the outset of the Occupation SCAP headquarters attempted with considerable success to control the flow of news out of Japan in a manner consistent with a 1948 election bid for General MacArthur.

The first wave of American correspondents in Japan were mostly veterans of the Pacific theater fighting. Thus, they were no strangers to insolent and uncooperative treatment by MacArthur's public relations staff, headed by General LeGrande A. Diller, a member of the Bataan group closest to MacArthur. During the war, Diller had censored reports of high casualities in the Pacific and any criticisms of MacArthur and helped to see to it that MacArthur's name appeared regularly in the headlines of American newspapers recounting the approaching victory over Japan. Though security provisions were somewhat relaxed after surrender, foreign correspondents still found themselves severely restricted. Diller rebuffed correspondents who complained of his censorship. "We are getting tough. And we are going to get tougher. We are not going to let you give MacArthur's critics in the States any ammunition. Furthermore, when we do lift the censorship, we will still have control over what you write about MacArthur. Don't forget," he warned, "the Army controls the food here."[86]

Diller's was no idle threat. Following lifting of censorship on Allied correspondents by order of the War Department on 6 October 1945, Diller announced that MacArthur had set up a "quota system" which would sharply reduce the number of correspondents and change their status to civilians who would be eligible for food, housing, and transportation only if available. Under these regulations, General Headquarters had greater control over foreign correspondents than it ever possessed during the war. American publishers protested to the War Department against the quota system and MacArthur was forced to rescind the measure. Within a month MacArthur relieved Diller and appointed General Frayne Baker as his new press officer.[87]

Accurate reporting of the news from Japan remained as difficult under Baker as before. *Chicago Sun* reporter Mark Gayn repeatedly got into trouble with SCAP officials for digging behind the sterile and optimistic press handouts. At a Press Club dinner in April 1946, Gayn led a group of newsmen in pointing out that the president of the Liberal party, Hatoyama Ichiro, the largest vote-getter in the just concluded election and a certain bet to become the prime minister, had written a book before the war praising the methods of Hitler and Mussolini. The embarrassing publicity about Hatoyama's record forced SCAP to carry through with a purge proceeding that had been aborted earlier. Later in the year Gayn was threatened with a court-martial for writing about a supposedly secret conference of SCAP officials concerning the purge of Japanese businessmen. The *Sun* protested to the War Department while twenty correspondents in Tokyo met with General Baker to demand an explanation of their rights. The court-martial against Gayn was soon dropped but security regulations were immediately tightened and orders were issued that all conversations at headquarters were to be considered official.[88]

In the view of Gayn and numerous other correspondents, insistence by headquarters that the Occupation be reported as an unparalleled success in social engineering and that those who dug up evidence to the contrary were dishonest and hostile to MacArthur was closely related to the 1948 election. "[T]hough few Americans have known it, the Inner Circle [around MacArthur] has functioned as a tight political machine with a 'favorite son' and with intimate bonds with the solid, conservative, isolationist core of the

Republican Party," Gayn recorded in his diary for 10 October 1946. In Gayn's estimate, General Bonner Fellers, a friend of Herbert Hoover, and General Robert E. Wood, chairman of the board of directors of Sears, Roebuck and founder of the America First Committee, played the key role in the political machine. Fellers and others were looking to the next election, for MacArthur's chances were much improved over 1944. They could sell MacArthur not only as a military hero but also as "an administrator, who in a year has transformed an aggressor nation into a democracy." One colonel told Gayn that at age sixty-six MacArthur was showing his age. "He knows this is the last election he can enter or influence. We all think he will make a try at one or the other."[89]

With the election of the Republican controlled Eightieth Congress, the growing unpopularity of President Truman, and repeated encouragement from MacArthur's friends at home for a run at the GOP nomination, the sensitivity of Tokyo headquarters to press criticism reached new heights. MacArthur himself suspected with considerable justification that his political rivals at home lay behind such critical stories as did appear. When the War Department insisted on a press tour of Japan in 1946, MacArthur conceded on the condition that the list of newsmen represented "not include those connected with papers of known hostility to the Occupation. Such papers as the *Christian Science Monitor, Herald-Tribune, Chicago Sun, San Francisco Chronicle, PM, Daily Worker,* and others of this stamp whose articles have approached downright quackery and dishonesty."[90]

To one of his political confidants, John Callan O'Laughlin, MacArthur was more blunt. He complained about the "unrelenting gigging" of a small section of the press whose criticisms of the Occupation "more than coincidentally [were] timed and attuned to the propaganda offensives launched in Moscow."[91] In 1947 MacArthur increased his power over the accreditation of correspondents to his theater and used it to keep unfriendly reporters from entering Japan and to prevent their reentry after they left.

The most dramatic and most publicized attempt by MacArthur to control the news from Japan through his accreditation power was clearly linked to the presidential election. The chief of *Newsweek*'s Tokyo bureau, Compton Pakenham, had friends in the Imperial Palace and the Japanese government who strenuously opposed the reform programs being implemented from MacArthur's headquarters. They linked up with Pakenham in order to reach conservative sympathizers in Washington who shared their doubts about the initial democratization policies of the Occupation. Aided by *Newsweek*'s editor for foreign affairs, Harry F. Kern, Pakenham's dispatches criticizing the purge of Japanese businessmen and attributing economic difficulties to reformist zealots in MacArthur's headquarters rankled the general and his aides.[92] On 12 February 1947, MacArthur told Robert Wood, a key organizer of his 1944 and 1948 presidential campaigns, that Pakenham's articles were a smear and a "link in the campaign which is being so assiduously pressed in the east to discredit me."[93] In August Pakenham took a leave from his post in Japan, but when he sought to return in January 1948, headquarters refused to reaccredit him.

For MacArthur, that proved a politically costly mistake. As discussed more fully in chapter six, during the six months of Pakenham's leave, Kern and *Newsweek* became the major source of public criticism of Occupation policy, SCAP personnel, and particularly MacArthur's handling of economic affairs. In not reaccrediting Pakenham MacArthur misjudged the powerful forces behind *Newsweek* and the damage the fight over Pakenham might deal to his political fortunes. Harry Kern immediately complained to the Army Department which requested an explanation from Tokyo. MacArthur replied that Pakenham's association with "reactionary Japanese" and his "marked antipathy" to the Occupation made reaccreditation inadvisable. When MacArthur refused to be any more specific, Kern saw the sympathetic Secretary of Defense James Forrestal. MacArthur denied to Forrestal that he had been motivated by the negative coverage of the Occupation in *Newsweek*. Once again *Newsweek* and the Truman administration collaborated to embarrass MacArthur into submission. MacArthur's exchange of letters with Forrestal, a rebuttal by Pakenham, and a vigorous protest by the Tokyo Correspondent's Club were published in *Newsweek*.[94]

When the Pakenham case was seized upon by MacArthur's opponents in the critical Wisconsin presidential primary, the general was ready for a compromise. Secretary of the Army Kenneth Royall issued a circular on 23 March affirming the right of newsmen in zones of U.S. occupation to report and criticize without fear of being disaccredited. Pakenham quietly returned to Japan. When *Newsweek* made no further mention of the incident, some observers suggested that the army had insisted that that was the price for insuring MacArthur would allow Pakenham to return.[95]

The Pakenham case emboldened other correspondents to publicize incidents of intimidation, coercion, and censorship by SCAP officials and at least temporarily shattered the facade of MacArthur's invulnerability to criticism. MacArthur still operated on the military principle, as Keyes Beech of the *Chicago Daily News* put it, "that the American people are entitled to know only what the military wants them to." But as the pressures created by the presidential race ended after the summer of 1948 and MacArthur's own importance in the Occupation receded, formal complaints against SCAP by the press corps diminished and its morale improved.[96]

The Peace Treaty of 1947 and the Birth of the
MacArthur-for-President Campaign

Without consulting Washington, General Douglas MacArthur met with reporters at the Foreign Press Club in Tokyo on 19 March 1947 to argue that the time had come for an American withdrawal from Japan. The Occupation had successfully demilitarized Japan and laid the groundwork for political democracy. But the final phase of the Occupation, the economic recovery of Japan, could not be achieved because U.S. and Allied policy remained one of continuing trade restrictions. "If we keep this economic blockade up, more and more we will have to support this country. It is an expensive luxury. But we will pay for it or let the people [of Japan] die by millions." The only alternative, MacArthur suggested, was for the United States to "initiate at this time peace talks with Japan." He was fully confident that Japan was capable of assuming a sovereign role in world affairs following a temporary United Nations regime of control. America's problem in Asia, he concluded, was "to keep Japan up" and that was best done through a peace treaty "as soon as possible." After his formal statement William Costello reported in the *New Republic,* "MacArthur laughed heartily when asked to name his favorite song. He said unhesitatingly, 'You can say my favorite tune is "Home, Sweet Home." ' " [97]

MacArthur's press conference remarks triggered a flurry of debate over Japan policy within the Truman administration. Only a few days before, the president had proclaimed in the Truman Doctrine that the United States faced a global Communist threat. The immediate need was for aid to Greece and Turkey. But a much greater program of building up Western Europe and Japan as anti-Communist bastions was clearly envisioned. Led by Secretary of Defense James Forrestal, a new group of planners, many of whom had earlier been preoccupied with European policy, challenged MacArthur's statements about economic recovery and an early peace. The general, they concluded, was surrounded by incompetents who had failed to prepare Japan for independence and risked a complete economic collapse once American forces withdrew. [98] An early peace treaty with Japan was out of the question, whatever the claims MacArthur might make about the spiritual revolution or political democratization of Japan.

With public sentiment in Japan and amongst Far Eastern Commission members strongly supportive of MacArthur's initiative, however, the State Department adopted a policy of publicly planning for a peace conference while in fact trying to avert it. In July 1947 the department invited all eleven members of the FEC to a preliminary peace treaty conference that was scheduled at a time that was "utterly impractical" for Britain and the Commonwealth nations and was predictably unacceptable to the Soviet Union, as it ignored earlier agreements that the four power Council of Foreign Ministers, representing the United States, Britain, China, and the Soviet Union, first consider the matter before it was submitted to a larger international conference.[99] While singling out the Soviets for delaying the peacemaking process and ignoring the complaints of the other Allies, the State Department made a major reevaluation of Japan policy and determined that the achievement of its objectives required the continuation of the Occupation regime, not a peace treaty.

By mid-October 1947, George F. Kennan of the department's Policy Planning Staff had hammered out a draft proposal of a document that became the basis for the National Security Council's NSC 13 series that governed Japan policy in 1948 and 1949. According to this "reverse course" document, Japan's economic instability greatly increased the threat of Communist penetration. Implementation of an economic recovery program planned by the State Department was therefore the highest priority next to preventing Japan from falling into the Soviet sphere of influence. The reform programs needed to be reexamined in light of whether they contributed to economic recovery and reparations should be terminated quickly to encourage capital investment. U.S. military control of Okinawa and other small islands near Japan was necessary to U.S. security. But whether a similar long-term presence of U.S. forces on the four main islands of Japan was required would be determined when peace treaty terms were finalized at a later date.[100]

Blind to these dramatic changes in American policy for Japan that were triggered by his 19 March news conference, MacArthur accepted the State Department's peace treaty proposal as a good faith effort, assumed that a peace conference ending the Occupation would occur prior to the 1948 election, and fanned the political fires of his friends at home. When MacArthur announced in July that after the peace conference he would return to Milwaukee, where he had spent part of his youth, the *New York Times* reported "zeal and optimism" at the recently organized MacArthur-for-President Club of Wisconsin, the first such organization in the country. By early fall, speculation was rife that MacArthur would soon be coming home to a politically potent groundswell of public support. "Everytime I go near the [National] Press Club," wrote a former press aide to the supreme commander, "they are after me with 'when is General MacArthur coming home.' " General MacArthur "is coming home," *New York Times* editorialist Arthur Krock asserted in September, and "don't think for a minute every move of that trip isn't being carefully planned."[101]

Krock was correct in assessing the thinking of MacArthur and his political supporters. On 13 September in a lengthy meeting with General Eichelberger devoted wholly to domestic politics, MacArthur finally confided that he would make an active run for the presidential nomination. A month later he told Colonel Harold E. Eastwood, who served as confidential liaison between the supreme commander and MacArthur's political strategists at home, that he would not only accept the nomination but would do so with the full understanding of the possibilities of the campaign to follow. "[I have] never been known to shy from a fight," Eastwood quoted MacArthur as saying. At the same time, MacArthur confidentially wrote to General Hanford Mac-Nider, a decorated war hero, wealthy Iowa cement manufacturer, and longtime activist in conservative Republican politics, that while he did not covet nor actively seek the nomination for president, "should such a movement gain widespread popular support there would be no other course open to me but to accept it as a mandate and risk the hazards and responsibilities involved." The supreme commander wanted a frank appraisal from MacNider of the leadership of the MacArthur campaign in Wisconsin and said he would not make a public announcement of his availability for the nomination until he saw whether the presidential boom on his behalf was "limited to a few good friends and well-wishers or has a real substantial popular basis." MacArthur sent virtually an identical letter to Robert Wood, his trusted political advisor in 1944, the next day.[102]

MacArthur regarded MacNider and Wood as "invincibly honest" and the "strongmen" of his 1948 campaign. Together the two men developed the basic strategy of the campaign. Chances for the nomination hinged on a persistent deadlock at the June 1948 Republican convention between the leading contenders for the nomination, New York Governor Thomas Dewey and Ohio Senator Robert Taft. MacArthur would have to appear as the strongest compromise candidate, winning delegate support as the balloting proceeded. Some MacArthur strategists favored a national campaign in which MacArthur would seek to win as many convention delegates in the primaries as possible. But MacNider and Wood opted for focusing limited resources on winning a clear-cut victory in the 6 April 1948 Wisconsin primary in which MacArthur appeared to hold a significant and exploitable advantage as the "native son" candidate in the race. A Wisconsin primary victory, regarded as at least a majority of the twenty-seven delegate votes, would be used at the convention to show popular support for the general. With the exception of former Governor Philip La Follette of Wisconsin, the only career politician in the MacArthur-for-President leadership circle, all who attended the 25 November

1947 strategy meeting in Chicago were convinced that MacArthur had to return home sometime before April 1948 and campaign for the nomination.[103]

Virtually coinciding with MacArthur's green light to his campaign supporters, all prospects for an early peace treaty ended in October 1947 and Washington embarked on a program to make Japan an economically self-supporting, politically stable American ally in the struggle against communism in Asia. This new "reverse course" policy for Japan created profound difficulties for the MacArthur presidential strategy. MacArthur would still be supreme commander in the spring, and to return home and campaign for the presidency while still in uniform would be construed by many as a breach in the tradition of military subordination to civilian authority. MacArthur fully understood the dilemma he now confronted. If he accepted the advice of his political supporters for a return home in the spring, he risked an open breach with the administration and retirement from his post as supreme commander; but if he ignored their advice, he seriously jeopardized his chances for the GOP nomination and a shot at the presidency. MacArthur carefully weighed his options and on 16 November gave Wood his definitive answer to the question of his return.

> I feel that it is extremely debatable as to whether I should return to the United States prior to the Republican National Convention. There is now no likelihood . . . of a peace settlement with Japan by that time . . . and there are many other considerations which point to my earlier return as unwise. . . . The national interest requires my continued presence in Japan [until] a peace settlement, and obviously I could not withdraw actively to enter a political campaign without reverting to an inactive military status and yielding my responsibility as [supreme commander]. It has been publicly predicted . . . , in many quarters, generally hostile, that strategy would dictate my return about March or April for the purpose of gaining the political captial inherent in the welcome [home]. The idea is repugnant to me. It would subject the culmination of my military career to the charge, rightly or wrongly, that my purpose was shrewdly and coldly to turn the symbolic gratitude of the American people for our Pacific victories and post-war occupational accomplishments to personal political advantage. It would be indulging in the cheapest form of theatricals [and] . . . crystallize bitterness in other Republican camps where, as far as I know, only a friendly feeling toward me now exists.[104]

MacArthur did assure the disappointed Wood that, if nominated at the convention as the presidential standard-bearer, he would retire from the military and actively campaign for election "unless the international situation has blown up to so menacing a degree as to render the prospect of field service imminent." In short, the general could hardly have been firmer in his resolve not to return home before the convention, despite the nearly unanimous advice to the contrary of his political supporters in the United States.

Battling Washington and the Election Campaign Fiasco

Not only did the new policy for Japan keep MacArthur from returning home to campaign for the nomination, but it soon threatened the reputation he and his political supporters had crafted of a successful reformer and farsighted world statesman. To Washington policymakers, the demise of the FEC-230 Zaibatsu dissolution program became the critical test of the "reverse course" policy in which emphasis was placed on economic recovery under strengthened conservative rule. But MacArthur had been strongly lobbying the Japanese to implement FEC-230 and did not want to make an awkward change in his position. He aroused Under Secretary of the Army William Draper's worst fears by refusing to delay or revise a deconcentration of industry bill, a key part of the FEC-230 program, which had reached the final stages of passage in the Diet.

Draper leaked information on FEC-230 for *Newsweek*'s 1 December 1947 issue that was clearly meant to embarrass MacArthur into submission and bolster Japanese opposition to the pending SCAP sponsored deconcentration bill. MacArthur refused to budge, however, and pushed the Diet into passage of the legislation. According to an informant of Draper, just before the House of Peers met to consider the deconcentration bill, a colonel from Economic and Scientific Section passed a warning to Prime Minister Katayama that the bill must "be passed so as not to embarrass [MacArthur who] expected to be nominated for president." The supreme commander cared little about how the law was enforced, according to the colonel, as long as there was "no sign to the world of dissension in Japan." That would tarnish his image and "prejudice the future of Japan when the Supreme Commander became President."[105] The stage for another politically controversial showdown between MacArthur and civilian planners in Washington was set, but the stakes for Japan policy and MacArthur's reputation were never so high.

The supreme commander interpreted the negative publicity on FEC-230 as a "definite smear campaign" by those seeking to undercut his presidential bid. The "slightest slip" on his part, he told Colonel Eastwood, would be used by Army Department officials to "stage a necktie party." Hence, MacArthur simply ignored the public pleas of Secretary of the Army Royall on 6 January 1948 that he recognize that new conditions in world politics, the increasing cost of the Occupation, the need for political stability, and a self-supporting economy required a modification of the Zaibatsu dissolution and other reform programs. When the U.S. Senate took up the question, Mac-

Arthur attacked the Zaibatsu system as a form of "socialism in private hands" which, if not replaced with a free enterprise system, would be toppled through a "bloodbath of revolutionary violence."[106] Worst of all from Washington's perspective, in February MacArthur attempted to enforce the new deconcentration law by designating 325 companies representing 75 percent of Japanese industry as possible "excessive concentrations of economic power" subject to the law.

At the same time he was battling Washington on Zaibatsu policy, MacArthur was preoccupied with domestic politics. He constantly dwelled on the weaknesses of other candidates. Front-runner Dewey, he argued, "had been licked once and couldn't win." Taft's lackluster personality and numerous enemies within the party made him a doubtful candidate. Stassen was "too New Dealish." Arthur Vandenberg had serious heart trouble.[107]

But MacArthur understood that his chances for the GOP nomination hinged on more than a deadlock at the convention between Dewey and Taft or on the weaknesses of the other dark horse candidates. He also needed to convince Republican wheelhorses that their best prospect for beating Truman was not a lackluster party insider, but a popular, vote-getting military hero. Even in these circumstances, however, General Dwight Eisenhower might be the party's first choice. But MacArthur, who considered Ike nothing but a "good-time Charlie and a New Dealer," assumed correctly that his former aide-de-camp would withdraw from the race. When Eisenhower did withdraw in January by emphasizing that no military man was qualified to be president under the conditions that then prevailed, MacArthur and his supporters' worst fears were aroused. The action reaffirmed their strong conviction that the eastern, internationalist wing of the GOP, with which Eisenhower was identified, was in tacit collusion with the Democrats to undercut MacArthur's presidential prospects. Once the initial shock wore off, however, MacArthur actually felt "encouraged" by Eisenhower's withdrawal, for it "clear[ed] the way" for his own candidacy as the only military figure in the field.[108]

In the context of these political preoccupations, MacArthur must have anticipated advantages at home in his stubborn determination to proceed with the Zaibatsu dissolution program. Standing up to the Truman administration in Japan as a proponent of small business interests and economic democracy might increase his popularity and defuse those who criticized him as a political reactionary outside of the Republican party mainstream. Whatever the political assumptions behind MacArthur's stance on Zaibatsu dissolution, the strategy backfired. The *Chicago Tribune, Washington Times-Herald, San Francisco Chronicle,* and other conservative newspapers which generally stood behind MacArthur attempted to focus their attack on "New Deal socialists or semi-socialists" in the Truman administration who had framed the dissolution policy.[109] But MacArthur's defense of that policy against Washington's effort to change it undercut such red-baiting tactics. Even more damaging to MacArthur's political fortunes, Washington sent two high-level missions led by staunchly anti-MacArthur forces in March 1948 to redirect the Occupation from reform to economic recovery and integrate Japan into an emerging global cold war security system in Asia.

Accompanied by newspaper headlines heralding drastic changes in U.S.-Japan policy, George F. Kennan became the first important State Department official to visit Japan. Kennan claimed that he was able to persuade Mac-Arthur not to feel bound by earlier American interpretations of the terms of surrender or concerned about world reaction to unilateral changes in U.S. policy. The concept behind FEC-230, he contended, bore "so close a resemblance to Soviet views about the evils of 'capitalist monopolies' that the measures themselves could only have been eminently agreeable to anyone interested in the further communization of Japan." MacArthur denied that his support for the purge of businessmen or other reforms caused economic difficulties in Japan, denounced policies which "had been influenced by academic theorizers of a left-wing variety at home and in Tokyo," and, most importantly, hinted he would administer the deconcentration law as Washington desired. He told Kennan that the program was neither as radical nor as "extreme" as the critics claimed and that it had proceeded as far as necessary. Kennan was not impressed and wrote a stinging rebuke of the whole range of Occupation programs and MacArthur's implementation of them.[110]

To further underscore changed American policy and symbolically demonstrate Washington's authority over the recalcitrant supreme commander, Under Secretary of the Army Draper returned to Japan in late March as head of an impressive mission of American corporate executives. The Draper Mission coincided with the last two weeks of the critical Wisconsin primary campaign, and MacArthur was not happy with the publicity that attended the visit. He told British diplomat Sir Alvary Gascoigne that "American tycoons" like Draper were opposed to the purge and dissolution programs because these reforms "would conflict with their own business interests." MacArthur even asserted that Draper had no right to come to Japan and he would refuse "to accept orders from Draper concerning active items of policy. . . ."[111]

At their first meeting together, on 21 March, conflict erupted immediately when Draper indicated that opinion in Washington favored the "early establishment of a small defensive force for Japan." MacArthur denounced the idea, pointing out that rearmament would delay economic recovery, weaken American prestige in Japan, and provoke hostile reactions in Asia. Though MacArthur and Draper agreed on the need for major cuts in Japanese reparations, on the key question of Zaibatsu dissolution policy the differences remained sharp. Throughout their visit, members of the mission met with Zaibatsu businessmen and other known opponents of MacArthur's views and issued public statements that emphasized that the breakup of the Zaibatsu firms would be harmful to the broad policy objectives of the United States. Finally, MacArthur indicated that he opposed any plans that the Army Department might have for changing to a civilian regime of control for the remainder of the Occupation.[112]

While Kennan, Draper, and other Washington planners certainly held the upper hand in the struggle over Japan policy with MacArthur, the final outcome turned in some measure on the results of the presidential nominating process at home. If MacArthur were to win the Wisconsin primary and enter the Republican convention in June as a serious dark horse candidate he would be stronger in defending his position in Japan. The converse was also true. Political setbacks at home would undermine his authority as supreme commander in Japan. Clearly the stakes in the presidential race were very high for MacArthur as he and his supporters prepared to leap the first and most important hurdle on the road to the Philadelphia nominating convention, the 6 April 1948 Wisconsin primary.

More than MacArthur could realize, his political fortunes rested in the hands of Philip La Follette. Leading light of the once powerful Progressive party of Wisconsin, the former governor's break with the Roosevelt administration in 1937 over foreign policy triggered a rapid decline in his political fortunes. La Follette became a close friend of General Wood in the isolationist America First Committee. With Wood's help, Colonel La Follette secured a post as a public relations officer on MacArthur's staff in the Southwest Pacific. He quickly developed a profound and abiding admiration for MacArthur and became a booster of the general's political fortunes as soon as the war ended.[113]

In consultation with Wood and MacNider, La Follette had organized by January 1948 a delegate slate for MacArthur of a handful of renegade stalwart Republicans along side of former members of the defunct Progressive party like himself. However, the state Republican party machine, led by "Boss" Tom Coleman of Madison, was not so impartially backing Minnesota Governor Harold Stassen for the nomination. Bedeviled by rumors from the Stassen camp that MacArthur would not accept the nomination if offered and that his candidacy was merely a "stalking horse" for Senator Robert Taft, who had not entered the Wisconsin primary, La Follette's campaign for MacArthur began very slowly. By the end of February, Robert Wood issued an ultimatum to MacArthur that he announce his availability for political office or face defeat in the Wisconsin primary. To front-page stories across the nation, MacArthur finally announced on 9 March that he would be "recreant to all my concepts of good citizenship were I to shirk . . . accepting any public duty to which I might be called by the American people."[114]

For the next four weeks General MacArthur's campaign in Wisconsin drew the attention of the entire nation. Inasmuch as he was on active duty in Japan, MacArthur decided not to issue any public statements. The old Wisconsin Progressives pointed to MacArthur's "liberal philosophy and progressive record" in Japan. The general had constructed a democracy for Japan in which cooperatives "have been encouraged, monopolies smashed, labor unions given new impetus, land reform launched, and civil and religious liberties safeguarded," La Follette claimed. The main theme of the former Progressives was the need to "transfer the efficiency and competence of the Japanese occupation regime to the federal government in Washington." In addition they lauded MacArthur as a "pilot of peace" who in Japan had shown that disputes with Russia could be settled without resort to war. "The Russians are not happy," La Follette pronounced on a radio show. "They have met their masters [in Japan]."[115]

The stalwart Republicans of the MacArthur campaign, however, emphasized MacArthur as warrior, the man best suited by his military record to handle the world Communist threat. The only newspaper in Wisconsin supporting MacArthur, the Hearst chain's *Milwaukee Sentinel,* trumpeted that the general alone among American leaders had met "the challenge of Red Facism with courage and success. His destined place is no longer in Japan . . . but in Washington as President." Colonel Robert McCormick's *Chicago Tribune,* which circulated widely in southern Wisconsin, preferred Taft but touted MacArthur as the "Man of the Hour" at a time of genuine fear of another world war.[116]

Immediately after MacArthur announced his availability, the front-runner in the Wisconsin race, Harold Stassen, backed by Senator Joseph McCarthy and the Coleman machine, sharply assailed MacArthur. Stassen argued that MacArthur would involve America too deeply in Japan, China, and Asia, when the "greatest danger [was] from the Communist menace in Europe." He suggested that MacArthur's absence from the United States for eleven years disqualified him from dealing with domestic problems. Stassen's forces also questioned the "native son" theme of the MacArthur campaign, raised the issue of MacArthur's physical fitness at age sixty-eight to be president, and flooded the state with a letter a week before the primary which alluded to MacArthur's divorce and remarriage.

But the most important issue of the primary to the Stassen camp was not MacArthur at all, but Philip La Follette and his delegate slate. The Wisconsin *State Journal* of Madison, which reflected the thinking of the Coleman machine, repeatedly warned that the MacArthur candidacy was merely an attempt by the "La Follette dynasty" to avenge earlier defeats by the stalwart Republicans. If MacArthur won, La Follette would leave them "completely in the cold. . . . He'll call the signals for Wisconsin Republican affairs. The old Progressive gang will be back in power." Whether or not Coleman exaggerated the threat of the MacArthur candidacy to the regular party organization, he turned the primary into a referendum on control of the Wisconsin Republican party.[117]

Despite the energetic campaigning of Stassen, an appearance by Dewey, harsh criticism of MacArthur by some Democrats, and rallies by Veterans-Against-MacArthur groups, most commentators gave MacArthur a substantial lead in the race. "M'Arthur Victory Due in Wisconsin," read the *New York Times* headline of 29 March. The Gallup poll measured substantial gains for MacArthur nationally during March. Dewey was still the favorite of Republicans for the nomination by a substantial margin, but MacArthur had jumped into second place ahead of Stassen, Vandenberg, Taft, and Earl Warren. In a presidential trial heat conducted in mid-March, the Gallup poll showed MacArthur with 44 percent to Truman's 41 percent of the vote.[118] Virtually every leader of the MacArthur-for-President movement shared the conviction of Robert Wood that MacArthur had to be ready for a host of new problems in the wake of victory in Wisconsin.

The results of the Wisconsin race astounded political observers, most crushingly MacArthur himself. In the crucial delegate column, Stassen won 19, MacArthur 8, and Dewey 0. Only the popular vote—40 percent for Stassen, 36 percent for MacArthur, and 24 percent for Dewey—provided any consolation to the MacArthur forces. But that was hardly enough to offset the knowledge that the Wisconsin primary had seriously damaged, if not totally destroyed, MacArthur's chances for nomination. "The General is low as a rug and very disappointed," Ambassador William Sebald was told by MacArthur's chief of staff the day after the primary. "I'm very disappointed," La Follette told the press. "Wisconsin voters muffed the ball." After a few days of reflection, MacArthur strategists agreed that the key to Stassens's upset victory was the Coleman machine. "The primary very clearly showed me," Wood wrote to MacArthur, "that organization is just as important in politics as it is in war or in business. I sent $30,000 into the state, and while it bought us radio time, newspaper ads and other publicity, it was not enough to create an organization to work in the precincts which is the root of all vote getting." Others suggested, though not to MacArthur, that the nation was not ready for a military man as president and that MacArthur's failure to return to campaign insured his defeat.[119]

Despite their own analysis of the Wisconsin debacle, MacArthur's chief political operatives indulged the general's ego and urged him to remain in the running. They still hoped that the delegates to the convention might turn to MacArthur in the event of a deadlock between the front-runners Dewey and Taft. Even after MacArthur was dealt another crushing defeat in the Nebraska primary in mid-April, the polls showed a sharp erosion in his support, and some or his most prominent supporters deserted the campaign, the general himself persisted in believing that he could still win the nomination at the "Big Show" in Philadelphia. The situation called for a new strategy, Mac-Arthur wrote Wood, which centered "around developing and maintaining a friendly beachhead within each of the various delegations to the convention and friendly contacts with the major Republican leaders." Unshaken by the defeatist attitude of Wood and La Follette throughout May and June and still refusing to come home and enter the political fray, MacArthur relied heavily on the guardedly optimistic reports of MacNider. In what surely stands as the measure of MacArthur's wishful thinking and desperation to leave Japan in triumph, the supreme commander outlined for Colonel Eastwood a few days before the convention a complex scenario by which the "big show will have to go about ten ballots for [me] to have a chance." As it turned out, with the lone exception of Hanford MacNider's vote for MacArthur, Dewey was unanimously chosen for the GOP presidential nomination on the third ballot.[120]

Hanging on in Japan

The humiliating collapse of MacArthur's 1948 presidential campaign not only reduced the general's importance on the American political landscape but weakened his authority in Japan. The first indication of that was the capitulation of MacArthur to Washington planners on the Zaibatsu dissolution issue. Even before the official release of the Draper Mission report at the end of April, Japanese businessmen whose companies had been listed in February by SCAP as possible targets for deconcentration were hopeful, as the *New York Times* put it, that they would not be "obliged to go to extremes." With the reluctant cooperation of MacArthur, a Deconcentration Review Board whose members were selected by Draper arrived in Japan in May and whittled down the number of Japanese corporations facing deconcentration from the original 325 to thirty, and finally by December 1948, when only nine combine subsidiaries had been reorganized under the law, SCAP headquarters announced the satisfactory completion of the program.[121]

Though not publicly known, the success of Kennan and Draper in winning National Security Council approval of the paper on U.S. policy for Japan over the objections of MacArthur was even clearer evidence that MacArthur was being pushed to the periphery of Occupation policy after the failure of his presidential bid. Responding on 12 June to the draft paper, MacArthur exhibited a tone of irritation and impatience. He opposed any further reduction in the "dangerously low level" of U.S. forces in Japan. He considered that the threat of the Japanese Communists was greatly exaggerated, and so opposed the recommendation that Japanese police forces be expanded. He protested that his implementation of the purge directives was "as mild as action of this sort conceivably could be" and to weaken the program further would invite even sharper international criticism of the Occupation. The implication in the paper that the burden of the Occupation on the Japanese economy was excessive, MacArthur insisted, was "entirely fallacious and devoid of factual basis." Finally, MacArthur objected to any diminution in his power as SCAP, such as the requirement that he consult with Washington before issuing directives. That would "so hamper the Supreme Commander as to render impossible the orderly and effective exercise of his executive authority." Similarly, an independent State Department representative reporting directly to Washington, MacArthur stridently claimed, would introduce a divided command responsibility causing friction between U.S. agencies and allowing the Japanese to "play the ambassador against the Supreme Commander and vice versa." When the National Security Council approved the paper as NSC 13/2 in October 1948, all of MacArthur's objections were ignored except those concerning an independent State Department representative alongside the supreme commander.[122]

Initially the Truman administration believed it could implement NSC 13/2 without a confrontation with SCAP. In the critical economic sphere that proved true. MacArthur and SCAP officials virtually surrendered their authority over the Japanese economy to a host of high-powered experts sent to Japan by the Department of the Army. A report in July 1948 by a special mission on the Japanese exchange rate headed by Ralph Young had sharply criticized the failure of SCAP efforts to halt inflation and boost production and exports and recommended enforcement of a new austerity program. When MacArthur raised objections to the Young report, Washington officials decided to incorporate its recommendations into a separate National Security Council policy and ordered MacArthur to carry them out. Then Joseph Dodge, president of the Detroit Bank, and a host of other economic experts were sent to Japan during 1949 and early 1950 with high enough rank to prevent MacArthur from evading or defying the NSC-mandated austerity program.[123]

Illustrating both the political opportunism of his early commitment to reform and the heightening of the Cold War, MacArthur never objected to the recommendation in NSC 13/2 that SCAP should relax pressure steadily but unobtrusively on the Japanese government in the implementation of ongoing reform programs and should not press for further reform legislation. To the plaudits of Washington planners and most of the American press, MacArthur, after his election bid failure, became increasingly and openly hostile to the Japanese labor movement and the Left. On 22 July 1948 MacArthur personally settled the rift in headquarters over revising the National Public Service Law in favor of the conservative opponents of allowing government employees to strike or bargain collectively. MacArthur's statement was immediately seized upon by the private sector as a warning against all strike activity and led to sharply constricted labor union activities.[124]

No doubt seeking one way to reestablish his bona fides with the core of his conservative supporters at home, early in 1949 MacArthur reversed his position that the Communist threat to Japan had become merely "a nuisance factor" and actively collaborated with the Japanese government in repression of the Left.[125] Coinciding with the labor unrest precipitated by the Dodge austerity plan, SCAP officials advocated a purge of Communists from the public payroll and raised no objection to Diet restrictions on labor union rights. In his 1949 Fourth of July message, MacArthur first made the suggestion that the Japanese Communist party might be outlawed. When Prime Minister Yoshida submitted a draft of a September speech for review by MacArthur, the general noted in the margin, "Entirely unobjectionable," to the section which read "we must combat communism, which under alien instigation seeks to create confusion and destroy social order by deceit and intimidation. We should boldly confront and overcome this sinister force."[126]

Paralleling the rise of Senator Joseph McCarthy and his Republican allies to prominence in the United States, MacArthur and the Japanese government followed up on the idea of overcoming the sinister force of communism in the months just before and after the Korean War. The main Korean organization in Japan, where the Korean population was overwhelmingly left-wing, was forced to dissolve. In May 1950 MacArthur ordered the Yoshida cabinet to purge the entire Central Committee of the Japanese Communist party and seventeen editors of the party daily, *Akahata*. The start of the Korean War triggered even more severe repression. Instigated by Government Section, the Japanese government's Red Purge resulted in about 22,000 Japanese being removed from public life.[127]

Much to the consternation of Washington policymakers, MacArthur resisted NSC 13/2 policy in two areas, the expansion of the national police organization and the return of purged individuals to public life. He considered that the program for reinforcement, training, and reequipment of the Japanese police which was underway was adequate. The Japanese police, he told his critics, were capable of handling any anticipated internal disturbance without intervention of Occupation forces. Even more importantly, MacArthur objected to the NSC 13/2 policy for screening persons for depurging. With justification MacArthur considered the completed purge program he had supervised quite limited and argued that the new NSC 13/2 purge policy required changes which were in conflict with his basic directive, JCS 1380/15. Even after the pertinent paragraphs of the JCS directive were revised, MacArthur continued to move with what the State Department considered exasperating slowness in permitting purgees to be reinstated.[128]

While his authority as SCAP had sharply eroded after the debacle of the Wisconsin primary, the failure of MacArthur to fully implement the police and purge sections of NSC 13/2 prompted a campaign by his critics in the spring and summer of 1949 to force his resignation. *Newsweek* and *Fortune* published articles on the theme "What's wrong with Japan?" and "SCAPitalism Marches On: Japan's Economy Will Be Better Off When It Comes Marching Home." More seriously, Max Bishop and Maxwell Hamilton of the State Department's Far Eastern Office prepared a draft plan in March which called for State Department control of the Occupation. Under it, all "nongarrison aspects" of the Occupation would be handled by a newly appointed American ambassador, and SCAP civil sections would be discontinued. The Far East Command, which MacArthur held in addition to his post as SCAP, would likely be moved to Hawaii. This audacious scheme never gained approval within the State Department. But on 3 June 1949 General Omar Bradley, the Army Chief of Staff and an ally of MacArthur foe General George Marshall, notified SCAP that the "trend of thought" in Washington was to get the State Department to proceed in Japan as it had done in Germany and appoint a civilian High Commissioner. [129]

MacArthur was deeply angered by all the criticisms of the Occupation and vigorously fought the schemes for removing him as SCAP. He published a long article in *Fortune* in the June 1949 issue defending the political and economic progress in Japan. To Bradley, Acheson, and others MacArthur argued that a change in regime of control would destroy the prestige of the United States and be regarded as "a decisive step toward yielding in the face of communist successes in China." By the second week in September the threats to his position as SCAP ended. For reasons not clear from the record, Dean Acheson, with the concurrence of Secretary of Defense Louis Johnson and the approval of the president, wrote MacArthur to assure him that no plans were being made to change the SCAP regime of control and to ask his advice on what had become the highest priority item on the Washington agenda for Japan, a peace treaty ending the Occupation.[130]

On the Comeback Trail

Perhaps the State Department dropped its efforts at removing MacArthur from Japan in the expectation that he would prove a useful ally against the Pentagon in winning presidential approval for its own peace treaty recommendations. Diplomat William Sebald suggested as much when, during the midst of the fight over civilianizing the Occupation, he "sensed a new willingness by MacArthur to 'play ball', an attitude which contrasts favorably with his former criticism of the [State] Department." As discussed more fully in chapter eight, MacArthur and the State Department objected to the controversial Joint Chiefs of Staff NSC 49 document of June 1949 which projected the Japanese home islands as part of an active forward base area for launching attacks against the Soviet Union in the event of a global war and proposed the creation of a Japanese military which, in a war, could be used to tie down the Russians on their eastern front. The military leaders argued for continuing the Occupation until after the creation of Japanese armed forces and on an agreement which permitted American bases to remain in Japan indefinitely.[131]

The State Department, by contrast, still favored a defensive policy that emphasized denying Japan to the Soviets and removing the Communist "conspiracy from within." It urged rapid conclusion of a peace treaty which provided for the development of American military bases in the Ryukyus and limited rearmament for self-defense. The State Department feared that a vast network of bases indefinitely maintained in Japan proper would have an "irritating and not a stabilizing influence on the Japanese population."[132]

At the outset of the renewed debate over Japan's role in America's strategic policy in the spring of 1949, MacArthur's position conflicted with both the Pentagon and the State Department, a factor which probably contributed to the momentum for a change in the SCAP regime of control. The general continued as vigorously as ever to advocate making Japan a symbol of peace in the modern world, "the Switzerland of Asia." To do so required United Nations supervision of restrictions of post-treaty Japan's economic, military, and foreign policies. Japan's "disarmed neutrality," he contended, would be protected by positioning United Nations forces in Okinawa, the Philippines, and other Pacific islands. For MacArthur, a negotiated peace settlement that included the Soviets was the only way to insure that American forces could safely leave Japan. Japanese security could be guaranteed by exacting a pledge from the Soviets to respect Japanese neutrality. The Soviets were difficult, he admitted, but "in his experience he had found that the Soviet Government always endeavored to keep its plighted word."[133]

By late September 1949, however, MacArthur admitted to Sebald that he "had completely changed his views regarding post-treaty controls for Japan." The peace treaty should avoid restrictions on Japan and be as "simple as possible and phrased in general terminology." He now agreed with Acheson's plans for a speedy end to the Occupation—if necessary even without the agreement of the Soviet Union. In the event that the Soviets would not pledge to guarantee Japanese security, he was now prepared to permit an increase in personnel and light arms for Japanese police forces. He also favored the continuation of some American military forces in Japan for the indefinite future. Arrangements for these forces, he advised, should not be part of the multilateral peace treaty but be in a separate bilateral security treaty between the U.S. and Japan. Finally, and perhaps the most important explanation for his change of views, MacArthur recommended that Tokyo be the site of the peace conference at which he should be "nominated as a neutral chairman."[134] What better way to arrange a graceful and historically significant retirement from military service.

The State Department had clearly won an important convert to its version of a rapid peace settlement with Japan. The appointment of Republican John Foster Dulles as special advisor to the State Department on the Japanese peace treaty in April 1950 strengthened the strange alliance of MacArthur and the diplomats. In mid-June 1950, Dulles met with MacArthur and a party headed by Secretary of Defense Louis Johnson and the Chairman of the Joint Chiefs of Staff General Omar Bradley. MacArthur proved most helpful to Dulles in preventing the Pentagon from halting treaty preparations. The two men developed a solid and politically useful friendship which contributed to overcoming the bureaucratic impasse over security arrangements in September 1950. Though he sided with Prime Minister Yoshida in opposing the State Department on a rapid and large-scale Japanese rearmament, MacArthur and Dulles shared similar views about other treaty issues. Dulles wrote the general following his visit to Tokyo in early 1951 to thank him for his indispensable cooperation and wise counsel in laying the foundation for the treaties that ended the Occupation in April 1952.[135]

While MacArthur and Dulles successfully kept the Japanese peace and security treaties from becoming a partisan issue, both men participated in the swelling Republican attack on the Truman administration's China policies that began in the summer of 1949. Long known as a staunch supporter of General Jiang Jieshi and the Nationalists, MacArthur campaigned publicly and privately for some form of American intervention which would thwart the last stage of the Chinese Communist revolution by aiding the Nationalists who had fled to Taiwan. In his view, if "Formosa went to the Chinese Communists, our whole defense position in the Far East was definitely lost [and] could only result eventually in putting our defensive line back to the west coast of the continental United States." MacArthur urged a declaration of American support for Jiang and a resumption of military aid, including the transfer of American ships to the Nationalist navy "sufficient to blockade and destroy China's coastal cities."[136]

Though the highest circles in the state and defense departments seriously contemplated proposals as extreme as those of MacArthur, Secretary of State Acheson convinced the president by the end of 1949 that any intervention on behalf of Jiang would be of doubtful success. At that point, MacArthur joined the military establishment and key State Department figures led by Assistant Secretary of State Dean Rusk and John Foster Dulles, as well as Republican congressmen, in chipping away at Acheson's position.[137] Increasingly it appeared that MacArthur, his authority in Japan as supreme commander weakened, sought to enhance his political fortunes at home by aiding the Republican assault on the administration's failures in China.

The attack by North Korean forces across the 38th parallel on 25 June 1950 resolved a host of problems in American policy throughout Asia and rescued the seventy-year-old MacArthur from the growing obscurity of his command in Japan. By 30 June, President Truman had ordered MacArthur and his forces in Japan to defend South Korea, committed American airpower to the battle, interposed the Seventh Fleet in the waters of Taiwan to "neutralize" the island, and provided for additional military assistance to the French in their struggle against Communist Vietminh in Indochina. The Korean War also eased the way for John Foster Dulles to reach a set of peace and security treaties with Japan and U.S. allies in the Pacific.

Meanwhile, MacArthur once again made headlines across America. While slowly retreating in the face of the invasion from North Korea, the general won time for the addition of United Nations forces to his command. Then in September he launched a daring amphibious landing behind enemy lines at Inchon and, authorized by the president, invaded North Korea as well. By the end of October MacArthur's forces controlled all of South Korea and much of North Korea. During the much-publicized Wake Island conference that month MacArthur assured Truman that there was "very little" chance of intervention by Chinese Communist forces. Misinterpreting a series of attacks by Chinese units that began on 25 October MacArthur ordered his troops on 24 November to the Yalu River in a final offensive he expected would end the war, reunify Korea, and allow for the complete withdrawal of United Nations forces.[138]

Disaster in Korea, Dismissal, and the Election of 1952

The intervention of over 300,000 Chinese troops over the next few days turned MacArthur's anticipated victory into a rout, laying the groundwork for his dramatic removal from command and a subsequent burst of partisan political activity. Caught by surprise by the Chinese maneuvers, MacArthur and his forces beat a bloody and disorderly retreat. By January 1951 they were driven below the 38th parallel. Humiliated and angry, MacArthur demanded that American bombing missions attack the "privileged sanctuary" of China, American naval vessels blockade the China coast, and the Nationalist army of Jiang Jieshi be used to extend the war into China. The Truman administration, however, feared igniting a full-scale war with China and the Soviet Union and sought to silence MacArthur's public statements. When at the end of March MacArthur openly tried to sabotage State Department initiatives for talks with the Chinese, Truman decided he had had enough. A telegram from Mac-Arthur to House Republican leader Joseph W. Martin, Jr., which the legislator read on the floor of Congress, proved the last straw. MacArthur again called for the use of Chinese Nationalist troops and suggested that the administration did not understand the tactics of global communism. An exasperated president, backed by the Joint Chiefs of Staff, relieved him on 11 April of all his commands.[139]

"Destiny is sending me home to tell the people the truth," MacArthur declared as he set out to expose the administration's policy of appeasement and rally the people to his side. A crowd estimated at over five hundred thousand greeted him in San Francisco on 17 April, his first return in fourteen years. The wave of public exultation for MacArthur and the angry denunciations of the president prompted the general the next day to quiet rumors he had presidential aspirations. "The only politics I have is contained in a simple phrase known to all of you—'God Bless America.' " In the most dramatic speech of his career, MacArthur told a joint session of Congress and millions of television viewers on 19 April that he did not advocate any partisan cause but rather love of his country. MacArthur argued that only his policies for Korea would produce victory while those of the administration would mean a continuation of a long and inconclusive war. The address unleashed a new round of Republican attacks on Truman and helped draw millions of sympathizers to parades to see and hear the general in Washington, New York, Chicago, and Milwaukee over the next week.[140]

Hoping to exploit MacArthur's sudden popularity, Republican leaders sought a Senate inquiry, conducted in open sessions with radio and television coverage, into the military situation in Korea and the causes of MacArthur's relief. But the strategy backfired. The Democratic majority that controlled the MacArthur Hearings kept closed sessions and censored transcripts before their release to the press. More importantly, MacArthur's three days of testimony in early May was overshadowed by twenty-eight days of testimony from administration witnesses offering sharp critiques of the general's position. In fact, contrary to the hopes of Republicans, the MacArthur Hearings ended the uproar over the general's recall.[141]

In his farewell speech to Congress in April MacArthur predicted he would "just fade away." But in a series of appearances that lasted until the Republican National Convention in Chicago in July 1952 MacArthur remained in the public spotlight by making vicious and partisan attacks on the Truman administration. MacArthur's supporters claimed that the general (whose travel expenses were covered by such ultraconservatives as oil men H. L. Hunt and Clint Murchison) was merely on a crusade aimed at exposing the failures and weaknesses of the Democrats and "revitalizing the nation." But many of his critics were convinced that MacArthur once again sought the Republican presidential nomination, especially after some of the groups that had backed MacArthur for president in 1948 resumed activity again in the winter of 1952. When Senator Robert Taft did poorly against the moderate front-runner Eisenhower in the Minnesota primary in March MacArthur encouraged his supporters by telling the press in vague terms that he would accept the nomination if drafted at the convention. But MacArthur's forces were even more disorganized, short of funds, and lacking in party influence than in 1948. As Eisenhower's support grew, Robert Wood and other onetime MacArthur backers shifted allegiance to Taft. In all probability the main purpose of MacArthur's slashing attacks on Truman and his slaps at Eisenhower's candidacy was not to promote his own candidacy but to strengthen the right-wing of the Republican party and the chances of Robert Taft's nomination.[142]

The Republican nomination of Eisenhower at the convention and his election in November finally ended MacArthur's long career as presidential aspirant and one of the most partisan military officers in American history. He accepted a post as chairman of the board of the Remington Rand Corporation in August 1952 and emerged as a spokesman for conservative economic interests. In the years before his death on 5 April 1964, a sick and haggard MacArthur spent most of his time at his suite in New York's Waldorf Towers.

In his *Reminiscences* written shortly before his death, MacArthur mused that he wished to be remembered most for his contributions to peace, particularly in Japan. His most recent biographer has granted the general his wish.[143] But even during the Occupation era some American scholars questioned just how serious MacArthur was in remaking Japan into a peaceful democracy or whether MacArthur ever bore the major responsibility for the Occupation he claimed. One of those scholars, T. A. Bisson, served in SCAP Government Section in 1946 and 1947. His firsthand experience of the Occupation, his training as an expert on the Far East, and his left-wing political outlook, led him to challenge MacArthur's interpretation of his initial directives as well as Washington's "reverse course" policies after 1947. To Bisson and many others, General MacArthur's chief historical significance always remained the glories and defeats of his forces in three major wars, not his tenure as supreme commander in Japan.

3   T. A. BISSON

The Limits of Reform in Occupied Japan

In his memoirs, former Prime Minister Yoshida Shigeru identified a group within the American Occupation bureaucracy as "radical elements—what might be called 'New Dealers'—who sought to utilize occupied Japan as an experimental ground for testing out their theories of progress and reform." He claimed that such "mistakes of the Occupation" as the decentralization of the police, the Labor Standards Law, the purge, and the antimonopoly program, resulted from the literal and overzealous interpretation of Washington directives by the "New Dealers." Government Section of SCAP, the prime minister recalled, housed more than its share of officials who had little understanding of actual conditions in postwar Japan or the practical needs of government. Thomas Arthur Bisson, "an enthusiastic New Dealer with advanced views regarding ways and means of democratizing our financial world," for example, had helped draft a purge plan for Japanese business which, had it been enforced, "would have played havoc with our national economy." Working with the "realists" in SCAP, Yoshida boasted he "never lost an opportunity to demand the revision and readjustment" of key Occupation-sponsored reforms and had been able "to temper the, at times, rigorous demands made by the Government Section."[1]

That Yoshida singled out Bisson for special criticism reflected not only Bisson's prominence as a SCAP "New Dealer," but his subsequent importance as a left-wing critic of the "New Japan." From April 1947, when he left Japan, until 1954, when his publishing career came to an abrupt end, Bisson authored two books and numerous articles which emphasized the failure of the Occupation to achieve the announced democratic aims of its initial post-surrender policy toward Japan. By the late 1940s, that interpretation of the Occupation undercut efforts of American and Japanese policymakers to have Japan serve as a model of stable capitalist development for an Asia in revolution. It also clashed with the dominant historiography on Japan emerging in the United States which, not surprisingly, was congruent with the outlook of American policymakers.

Without using Bisson's name but having him prominently in mind, Harvard's Edwin O. Reischauer, the dean of American historians of Japan, was among the first to take issue with "those of leftist sympathies" who argued during and after the Occupation that the "reform of Japan must be thorough-going—even ruthless if necessary." For Reischauer, who had worked on Japan problems for the State Department after the war, the "pessimistic" left-wing view that the Occupation failed to achieve democracy in Japan rested on the misconception that "everything about pre-surrender Japan was bad." The "slight readjustment of the rules and temporary weighing of the scales in favor of the peaceful and democratic forces over the militaristic and authoritarian forces," accomplished by the Americans during the Occupation, Reischauer concluded, was all that was necessary for "reversing the history of the 1930s" and restoring a democratic polity in Japan.[2] Today Bisson's career and writings are still largely forgotten or distorted by such politically inspired stereotypes that developed during the early Cold War.

The Making of a Concerned Scholar

When he joined SCAP in 1946, T. A. Bisson, as he generally signed his publications, was recognized as one of the leading American authorities on East Asia. Born in New York City in 1900 and raised in Englewood, New Jersey, Bisson received a B.A. at Rutgers in 1923 and an M.A. in theology at Columbia University the next year. He then joined the stream of Presbyterian missionaries to China. Bisson did little religious proselytizing. He taught English and Classics for two years at a middle school in Anhwei (Anhui) Province and for one year at Yenching (Yanjing) University in Beijing (then known as Peiping). While in China, Bisson also studied the language intensively for a year and traveled widely through the country. He was charmed by China, its people, its history, its culture, and inexorably Bisson was drawn into the vortex of the politics of the Chinese Nationalist revolution.[3]

"To a man," Bisson recalled, his students had been "enthusiastic supporters of the Kuomintang." The Guomindang (KMT) appeared to them as the only hope of freeing China of the twin evils of warlordism and the infamous unequal treaties imposed by the Western and Japanese powers since the 1840s.

But in the spring of 1927 General Jiang Jieshi, after a triumphal march of his Nationalist troops into Shanghai and Nanking (Nanjing), initiated a campaign of arrests and murders of hundreds of Communists, labor leaders, students, and suspected radicals once allied with the KMT. By his actions Jiang gained the support of the landlord class and many of the foreign powers, allowing him to concentrate on crushing the Communists who had fled into the hills of Kiangsi (Jiangxi) Province.[4] To Bisson and his students KMT's sudden right-wing turn and the onset of what proved to be ten years of civil war between the KMT and the Communists was disheartening. The long struggle to free China from foreign imperialism and internal disunity was once again sidetracked.

Escaping the chaos and repression of the Nationalist Revolution, Bisson returned to the United States in 1928. He determined to pursue an academic career in Chinese studies. At Columbia University Bisson threw himself into his graduate studies and nearly finished the doctoral program. But an offer of the post of Research Associate on the Far East from the prestigious Foreign Policy Association (FPA) in 1929 at $3,000 a year proved irresistable. Soon the Great Depression, marriage, and the birth of two children combined to forever end Bisson's "dream fantasy" of becoming an academic Sinologist. "I went into politics to make a living," Bisson recalled with a twinge of regret.[5] It would be politics that would provide this scholar with his most satisfying moments—and his most painful.

In more than a decade with the FPA, Bisson wrote over a hundred scholarly and popular articles and two books on contemporary developments in China and Japan. His writings rested on a foundation of careful study of newspapers and government documents, as well as firsthand observations made during 1937 in Japan, Korea, and China, including four days of meetings with Chinese Communist leaders in Yenan (Yanan). Though often suffering from an excessive empiricism, Bisson's scholarship in the 1930s was of the highest standard and usually won him praise from scholars and statesmen alike, even those who disagreed with his evident commitment to the success of the Chinese revolution against Western and Japanese imperialism.[6]

Primarily out of his personal experience and professional interest in East Asia, Bisson became actively associated with the American Left during the 1930s. The founding of the American Friends of the Chinese People (AFCP) appears to have provided him with the initial focus for his growing radicalism. Although the AFCP embraced participants of any political stripe who subscribed to its program of support for "the Chinese People's fight for national liberation [and] resistance to Japanese invasion," it was probably controlled by the United States Communist party (CP). Philip J. Jaffe, managing editor of the AFCP's official organ, China Today, and a self-described "very close fellow traveler," invited Bisson to serve on the magazine's editorial board.

T. A. Bisson (left) with Owen Lattimore on trip to Yenan, China in May 1937. T. A. Bisson Papers, University of Maine Library, Orono.

Using the pseudonym Frederick Spencer from 1934 to 1937 for his articles in *China Today,* Bisson lambasted the Nanjing government, lauded the leadership of the Chinese Communists, and demanded that Japan and the United States surrender their imperialist privileges in China.[7]

The outbreak of the Sino-Japanese War in July 1937 prompted Jaffe and others in the AFCP to launch a less "partisan" and more academically respectable journal than *China Today*. As an editor and contributor to the new but still decidedly left-wing journal *Amerasia* from 1937 until 1941, Bisson muted criticism of the Nationalists, promoted U.S. aid to the united front government of China, and sharply attacked Japanese imperialism and its roots in a fascist state system. He advocated the cutoff of trade in war materials to Japan from the United States and pushed for a collective security arrangement of all the nonfascist powers against Japanese imperialism.[8]

As was the case with thousands of other Americans, Bisson's life was changed by the United States entry into World War II. By the end of January 1942, Bisson was ensconsed in the Washington offices of the Board of Economic Warfare (BEW) headed by Vice-President Henry Wallace. Drawing on his research skills and vast knowledge acquired at the FPA, Bisson plunged into a major study of the most effective strategy for blocking the flow of essential war supplies to Japan and disrupting the Japanese economy. But Bisson was constantly distracted from his work. Wallace and the BEW were immediately embroiled in a round of debilitating fights over the scope of the BEW mandate with Harry Hopkins at Lend-Lease, Secretary of State Cordell Hull, and Commerce Secretary Jesse Jones. As chairman of the House Un-American Activities Committee, Representative Martin Dies cast even greater confusion over BEW by sending a public letter to Wallace charging the BEW with being a refuge for Communist dupes and assorted left-wingers. The letter accused thirty-five employees of having been members of fellow traveler organizations, naming ten of them including Bisson.[9]

Bisson remembered his year at BEW with bitterness and frustration. Even after all ten persons named in Dies's letter were cleared by the FBI, Dies relentlessly pursued the BEW. Bisson was subpoenaed to testify in April 1943 before the Dies Committee. Testimonials from his many prominent friends notwithstanding, Bisson's loyalty to the United States was repeatedly questioned by the committee's research director, J. B. Matthews. Matthews zeroed in on two articles Bisson had written for the CP-linked *Soviet Russia Today* and an open letter Bisson had signed in that magazine which advocated closer American relations with Russia to curb German fascism. Bisson vigorously defended himself by stressing that even American military leaders now shared his long-held conviction on the necessity for a collective security agreement with Russia against German and Japanese fascism. It was as a "loyal American citizen," Bisson told the committee, that he had moved his family from New York to Washington at great financial sacrifice to put his abilities at the "full disposal of the Government and its war enterprise."[10]

By the time he testified, Bisson recognized that the BEW was crumbling away, a victim of the political wars within the Democratic party. He decided to return to New York to work for the Institute of Pacific Relations, the primary scholarly organization in the Asian field from its founding in 1925 until its virtual demise in 1953 under the attack of the China Lobby and congressional investigators. Supported with funds from the Rockefeller and Carnegie foundations, IPR by 1943 had become an international organization with national councils throughout the world. The IPR attempted to influence policymakers and public opinion through analyses of issues in the Far East at regular IPR international conferences and through *Pacific Affairs,* the journal of the IPR, and the *Far Eastern Survey,* the journal of the American Council of IPR. Under the leadership of Edward C. Carter, Frederick Field, William Holland, Owen Lattimore, and others, the IPR attracted young, idealistic liberals and radicals to its staff who were united in their deep sympathy for China's plight as a victim of Japanese aggression.[11]

The opportunity to become active in IPR as an associate editor of *Pacific Affairs* was exhilarating for Bisson on several counts. Besides going back to his quiet home on Long Island he would be working with close friends who were the foremost authorities in his field. As an editor of *Pacific Affairs* at this critical juncture of the war, Bisson would have one of the most distinguished platforms in the country upon which to project his own views. At the same time, he was promised the time and facilities to complete two book-length manuscripts—a study of Japan's wartime economy based on his BEW research and an updated version of his study of U.S.-Far Eastern policy.[12]

In the outpouring of reviews, articles, and books from Bisson's pen during his two-year stint with the IPR, one theme predominated, namely that American policymakers, through a combination of ignorance and malevolence, would thwart the legitimate aspirations for self-determination of Asian peoples. In the case of China those aspirations appeared more and more closely tied to the ultimate success of the Chinese Communists. In an article for the *Far Eastern Survey* in July 1943, Bisson posited the thesis of two Chinas, a "feudal" China under the KMT and a "democratic" China under the Communists. The united front had not led in six years of war against Japan to Chinese unity. Instead, the KMT had reimposed a military blockade against the Communists with the result being the emergence of Nationalist-held areas dominated by the feudal landlord-usurer system and Communist-held areas in which agrarian programs were akin to "bourgeois democracy." It followed from Bisson's analysis that American policymakers needed to demand fundamental reforms of the Nationalists and seek to cooperate with the Communists in the anti-Japanese struggle.[13]

Bisson's article created a storm of controversy. It greatly disturbed the Nationalist government officials who suggested Bisson was "completely misinformed or had malicious intent toward China." Friends of the Nationalists in the U.S. opened a decade-long attack on the IPR with a slashing critique of

Bisson's article for its "openly pro-Communist position." Though some American policymakers hoped the article would have a "salutory effect" on the Nationalists, Stanley Hornbeck, the State Department's top advisor on East Asia, strongly objected to Bisson's use of "feudal" in describing the Nationalists and predicted the article would only "confuse Occidental readers and irritate Chinese readers." Not surprisingly, Bisson's coworkers at IPR were more positive. Secretary-General Edward Carter successfully fended off KMT demands that IPR disown Bisson's article and reassured Bisson that he had "rendered a great service to China, the United Nations cause, and to the IPR." William Holland, research director of IPR and editor of *Pacific Affairs*, thought Bisson's argument "fundamentally sound" and told Sinologist Owen Lattimore, a friend of Bisson since their 1937 trip to Yanan together, that Bisson had said "a lot of things that many people feel ought to have been said before this."[14]

But the principal focus of Bisson's writings at IPR was not China but Japan. He warned repeatedly that American policy as designed by Joseph Grew and his State Department friends would thwart the legitimate democratic aspirations of the Japanese people. Though Owen Lattimore's *Solution in Asia* and Andrew Roth's *Dilemma in Japan* were the most popular critiques of U.S. planning for the surrender and the Occupation, and were considered by the Japan Crowd as the ideological fount for the disastrous reform policies in postwar Japan, Bisson's work was perhaps the most sophisticated and thoroughly documented, and was a major influence on Lattimore, Roth, and other dissenters.[15]

Bisson began with an analysis of what he considered the Japan Crowd's simplistic notion that Japanese imperialism was the result of a militarist takeover of the Japanese state beginning in 1931. Drawing heavily from the work of his friend and renowned Japanologist, E. Herbert Norman, Bisson traced the authoritarian imperialist Japanese state system back to the Meiji Restoration of 1868. That state system embraced continuing shifts in power of the business interests, party leaders, the military, bureaucrats, and the landlords. "Neither the absolute supremacy nor the final liquidation" of any of these groups was tolerated, Bisson wrote in *Pacific Affairs* in 1944. Instead, the coalition strove as a whole to "buttress its dictatorship at home," primarily through the theology surrounding the emperor, and by pressing "Japan's 'manifest destiny' overseas." Consequently, for Bisson, no one of these groups was inherently moderate or extremist. When Japan moved to fascism and imperialist aggression in the 1930s, Bisson argued, "the decisive elements in all of the groups [were] in agreement on the program and . . . the steps to be taken." Grew and the Japan Crowd were fostering—perhaps willfully, Bisson suggested—the delusion that the United States had "allies within the gates of the Japanese regime amongst the 'moderates' when in fact these moderates were, in their foreign policy, cautious imperialists willing to move [their] pins forward on the map when additional territory had been occupied."[16]

One of the principal tenets of the Japan Crowd's thesis was the need to preserve the emperor system and use it to serve American objectives in the Occupation. For Bisson, however, the emperor was the staunchest bulwark of the ruling coalition's dictatorship, supplying the master race ideology for Japan's aggression and sanctioning full-blooded repression at home. For Grew to pass off the emperor "as a puppet without political responsibility of any kind" was a gross misreading of history and threatened to undermine the prospects for democracy in Japan.[17]

The sharpest difference between Bisson and the Japan Crowd was over their reading of the role of the Zaibatsu in Japan's ruling coalition. From research for his FPA *Reports* and for the BEW, Bisson became convinced that even at the height of the influence of the military, Japanese cabinets were largely under the control of the Zaibatsu and that the industrial capitalists bore primary responsibility for leading Japan down the road to war. In his third book, *Japan's War Economy,* published in 1945, Bisson carefully documented the increasing size of Japanese companies and new ways Zaibatsu leaders used state power to dominate all facets of Japanese economic and political life. In the preface he let loose with biting sarcasm against the Japan Crowd's "lush mythological growth" and "strange tales" of Zaibatsu executives as men of peace, mortal enemies of the militarists, and friends of the United States. To look to the Zaibatsu to rule Japan in a peaceful, democratic manner for American benefit was, for Bisson, a "grand delusion." He wrote: "The epitome of modern Japan is not the 'militarists,' but the Zaibatsu. If the latter is permitted to control the restoration of Japan's economy, his buddy, the 'militarist,' will be found trotting at his heels again when the job is finished."[18]

Bisson wanted a new and democratic Japan after surrender. That meant a "totally new set of government organs, staffed by totally new personnel, encouraged to develop by the United Nations if the 'revolutionary overthrow' of the old system was not carried through by the Japanese people first," Bisson wrote in *Pacific Affairs* in 1944. To effect real and lasting results, Occupation policy would have to exclude the "moderates" so favored by the Japan Crowd because by definition they were cautious supporters of the Old Japan. Instead the United Nations must seek authentic "liberals" with a history of total opposition to the old regime or at least noncooperation. The new leaders, Bisson wrote, must be men and women in Japan "who led political parties, trade unions, or peasant organizations that were suppressed prior to 1941;

[who] have spoken publicly and unequivocally against the war, and have perhaps languished in jail for their temerity." After listing a few distinguished names like Kato Kanju, Ozaki Yukio, Nosaka Sanzo, and Baroness Ishimoto (among them several Communists), Bisson concluded that only such Japanese could establish a political order in Japan "based on the will of the people and dedicated to democracy and peace."[19]

The immediate aftermath of the end of the war in the Pacific fed Bisson's worst fears regarding American policy in Asia, particularly Japan. Occupation authorities seemed to be carrying out the Japan Crowd's program of preserving the emperor system, defining war criminals so narrowly as to absolve the Zaibatsu and civilian bureaucrats, and in general placing more emphasis on stability and order than democratic reform. But in an October 1945 article in the *New Republic,* Bisson suggested that the departure of Grew and other Japan Crowd figures at the end of the war had prompted the State Department to make a "tardy revision" of Occupation policy which, if implemented, could secure real democracy for Japan. The basic directive of the Occupation sent to General Douglas MacArthur in September included not only limiting Japanese sovereignty to the main islands and the destruction of Japan's military establishment but promotion of policies which would encourage the wider distribution of income and wealth, the development of labor unions, the revamping of the educational system, the purge of economic and political leaders associated with militaristic policies, and so on.[20]

Above all, the basic directive seemed to leave open the possibility, in Bisson's view, for reversal of the most serious mistake of the Occupation, namely, the attempt to carry out reform through the emperor and his bureaucracy. "Only Hirohito's enforced abdication and trial will be sufficient to drive home to the Japanese people," Bisson wrote, "the realization of defeat which is so patently absent." And once Hirohito was off the scene, Bisson insisted, the more difficult task of uprooting the emperor system would have to follow. Without that the democratic forces in Japan would not survive the withdrawal of Occupation troops.[21] In brief, American Occupation policy was still in flux. Much depended on who was in Japan and how they interpreted their somewhat vague directives.

Occupationaire

Whatever his reservations about American policy towards Japan, Bisson left the IPR in October 1945 and spent the better part of the next two years—first as a member of the United States Strategic Bombing Survey mission and then as a top economic analyst for Government Section of SCAP—attempting to realize his vision of a new and democratic Japan.

Bisson's first months in Japan in the fall of 1945 for the Bombing Survey provided him with insight into the scramble of the Old Guard of Japan to maintain power, the political awakening of the Japanese people, and the increasingly conservative role of Occupation officials in the sharpening struggle between the Old Guard and the people. In interviews with several of the Zaibatsu leaders about whom he had written in *Japan's War Economy,* Bisson observed their repeated attempts to blame the military for the war, their raising of the specter of communism, and their parrying of questions linking them to the emperor and control of Japan's war economy. Outside his Tokyo office, Bisson witnessed the intense popular reaction against the Old Guard and its policies. Nothing was being done for the thousands of students and the unemployed who were marching in the streets demanding government food relief, Bisson wrote home to his wife, "yet billions of yen [are] being shoveled out to Zaibatsu concerns in contract cancellation payment—and MacArthur [is] refusing to recognize it as a problem." The air was electric with strikes, demonstrations for food, and protests against the government, and wittingly or not, Occupation authorities were siding with the Old Guard. "The Konoye-Kido clique [the emperor's close aides] is getting in soft at HQ," he wrote.[22]

Before returning to the United States with the Bombing Survey team to celebrate Christmas with his family and complete the draft of his report, Bisson agreed to join SCAP's powerful Government Section (GS). On 1 March he rejoined friends in Tokyo for what he thought was a three-month assignment but which eventually lengthened to fifteen months. During his hectic tenure with GS, Bisson was primarily involved in three major reform areas—the Zaibatsu dissolution program, engineering the passage of the "MacArthur Constitution" through the Diet, and an abortive plan to get SCAP to enforce a workable, anti-inflationary economic stabilization plan.

The political and bureaucratic context in which he had to work on these reforms became distressingly clear to Bisson in his first weeks back in Tokyo. The old-line political parties, as he had predicted, had swept the first general election and an ultraconservative cabinet, including many whom Bisson regarded as war criminals, was established under Prime Minister Yoshida Shigeru. Even worse, in Bisson's opinion, indirect rather than direct rule by the Occupation gave enormous leverage to the bureaucrats in the Japanese government ministries to resist or ignore the whole reform program. In addition, as the administration and enforcement of the American sponsored legislation was in the hands of the Japanese, unless the Americans had a rigorous surveillance system, even those measures that passed the Diet intact could easily be subverted. In charge of surveillance, however, was Major General Charles Willoughby, head of G-2, an admirer of fascist General Francisco

Franco, and more concerned about left-wing infiltration of the Occupation by people like Bisson than about eliminating the reactionaries of Japan. Not surprisingly, the most "indelible impression" Bisson had of the Occupation was the day-in, day-out noncooperation he met by Japanese conservatives and their allies within SCAP.[23]

Given his recognized expertise in the machinations of the Zaibatsu, Bisson's first assignment was to devise an economic purge directive, a key part of the broader program for breaking up concentrations of economic power known as Zaibatsu dissolution. Bisson immediately became embroiled in a squabble with Economic and Scientific Section (ESS) which had been initially assigned the job of writing the economic purge but had not proceeded on the grounds that a purge of Japan's most experienced business personnel would delay vital economic recovery. In Bisson's view, however, the reason for ESS delay was that its staff had too many representatives from American big business with close ties to the financial and industrial elite of Japan.[24]

In any case, under pressure from the GS initiative, ESS worked up its own economic purge proposal that was considerably less sweeping than Bisson's. At first Bisson was encouraged by what he thought was the strong support he received both from his chief, General Courtney Whitney, and from Mac-Arthur for the GS economic purge. But as spring passed into summer without any action, Bisson realized that the real problem lay less with ESS and more with MacArthur. MacArthur, he believed, knew that to approve any economic purge would lead to a fight with the Yoshida cabinet and that would delay passage of SCAP's pet project, the new constitution, then wending its way through the Diet. "The job here is sort of stymied now," Bisson wrote to his wife on 3 July 1946, "with most of the real things crying to be done stalled until the Constitution gets through and lest we upset the reactionary Yoshida Cabinet."[25]

The constitution question, which increasingly occupied Bisson in the summer and fall, fully reinforced Bisson's long-standing suspicions of the Japanese Old Guard. He had mistakenly thought that the GS draft of the Japanese constitution imposed on the Shidehara cabinet in February had settled the matter. But careful study by GS language officers of the phrasings of the Japanese text indicated considerable deviation from the intent of the Americans. Bisson was appalled by the effrontery of the Japanese cabinet negotiators. For example, in the preamble to the constitution and in the first article defining the status of the emperor were several references in the English language text to the "sovereignty of the people's will." The Japanese had translated people as "kokumin." In a lengthy memo to General Whitney in mid-July, Bisson and two other GS staffers argued that the proper translation of people in that context was "jinmin," for "kokumin" meant in English "nation" rather than people and carried with it the connotation that the emperor's will was melted into the will of the people. To Bisson the concept of democracy required that the people have a separate will from the emperor's will. He could not imagine the use of the word "kokumin" in the constitution being acceptable to SCAP.

Similarly, the Japanese had translated the English word "sovereignty" to a Japanese word meaning "supremacy." By these two seemingly inconsequential changes (people into nation and sovereignty into supremacy), Bisson explained, "sovereignty is not located in the people as the basis of the state, but has been shifted to kokumin comprising the people, the Emperor and the government." That paved the way, he feared, for the emperor to exercise a part of the sovereign power rather than exist, as intended by GS, as merely a symbol of state carrying out ceremonial functions. The final compromise accepted by GS did not please Bisson: though people remained kokumin, supremacy was changed back to the original sovereignty.[26] In fact, the whole struggle over the constitution—and there were some thirty similar word changes or amendments by the Japanese to the American draft—was an illustration for Bisson of the "continuing stranglehold over the machinery of government which the predominantly reactionary bureaucrats" exercised. And even the largely successful defense of the American draft of the constitution did not end Bisson's doubts. The constitution, he told his wife, was "blemished" from the outset by its "permanent entrenchment of the Tenno [emperor] system, even though modified in some respects."[27]

By October 1946, with the constitution finally passed by the Diet, Bisson thought he would be able to devote his full efforts to pushing through the long delayed economic purge, and other aspects of the Zaibatsu dissolution program. It was not to be. The inflationary crisis in the economy overshadowed everything. In a remarkable memorandum to General Whitney at the end of October, he argued that monthly inflation rates of 70 and 80 percent were the result of conscious and deliberate policies of the Zaibatsu and government leaders. He noted,

> Whenever possible the Japanese authorities . . . are attempting to maximize government outgo. Virtually every section in SCAP . . . can produce examples of padded budgetary allotments for which approval has been sought. These authorities are at the same time attempting to minimize income, [for example] permitting normal taxes to be paid from relatively worthless restricted deposits. Price rises for commodities are not only permitted by the Japanese authorities whenever possible but are actually fostered by them. The most recent example is the case of rice. . . .

Finally, and despite expressed policy, the Japanese government was sharing scarce raw materials among all users rather than channeling supplies to plants which were essential. As a result, the favored companies were seeking larger profits by remaining idle, speculating in raw materials, and concentrating on rehabilitating their plants to build up their equity. Although there were SCAP directives and Japanese laws and ordinances prohibiting all of these corrupt and inflationary practices, none of them was enforced.[28]

Bisson linked the government's deliberate inflationary policies to a campaign by the Old Guard to sabotage the democratic objectives of the Occupation. Unless SCAP acted quickly, he warned, one of the first casualties of the inflation would be the Zaibatsu dissolution program. The various tax levies and indemnities against the big stockholders in the Zaibatsu companies that were part of the dissolution program had become practically meaningless as businessmen simply paid the government in increasingly devalued yen. Holders of these Zaibatsu stock were also reaping additional gain by the upward valuation of their assets as the inflation progressed. And economic conditions in general were causing the liquidation or absorption of numerous small firms. "In the aftermath of an inflationary bout," Bisson concluded, "the largest and strongest" firms, namely, the Zaibatsu combines, would emerge as powerful as they ever were, SCAP dissolution program or not.[29]

Other SCAP reform efforts were also being undermined by the inflation, Bisson felt. "For the wage and salary earner, the effects of the present inflation are already serious: they would be disastrous if it became a runaway inflation." He accurately predicted a wave of labor disputes and strikes. In short, as inflation weakened labor and generated unrest while strengthening the economic power of the old ruling elements, it was necessarily thwarting the proclaimed SCAP objective of establishing a stable and popularly controlled government.[30]

Although Bisson gained the support of many within SCAP for a detailed and carefully integrated economic stabilization program with provisions for adequate enforcement, a month of meetings and discussion with General Courtney Whitney and MacArthur proved fruitless. SCAP recognized the seriousness of the inflationary problem, Whitney wrote in a curt statement, but it was "thought that the Japanese government should have exclusive responsibility for the necessary stabilization measures."[31]

Just as Bisson had predicted, the inflationary crisis quickly grew worse and spilled over into the most serious political confrontation of the Occupation. A broad coalition of labor unionists, socialists, and Communists—four million strong—called for a general strike to be held on 1 February 1947, as the culmination of a campaign against the Yoshida cabinet and its economic policies. On his own initiative, Bisson argued within SCAP "in favor of permitting the general strike," recalled Chief of Labor Division Theodore

Cohen. Cohen resented the advice. "I told him [Bisson] he was crazy. It was impossible to have a general strike and still have a continuing government." At the eleventh hour, MacArthur intervened to forbid the strike, defending his action on the grounds that the strike would have damaged the economy. But such an argument, Bisson felt, "blandly ignored the more basic fact that the source of the economy's trouble lay primarily in the Yoshida cabinet's reckless spending policies."[32]

One of the fallouts of the aborted general strike was MacArthur's announcement that there would be another national election in April. For Bisson, that would be his last remaining hope for a government committed to democratizing Japan. "With luck," he wrote home, the effects of the purge laws and the unpopularity of the Yoshida cabinet, "could produce a liberal Diet and in turn a decently progressive Cabinet. This is the sine qua non. If the present Cabinet, or one like it continues to hang on, most of our reforms will be vitiated. If a liberal Cabinet comes in, much may yet be salvaged." Bisson hoped for the election of the Social Democrats, the only moderately left-wing party with enough popular strength to win power. A combination of factors seemed to give the Social Democrats an edge in the forthcoming election. Popular resentment against the conservatives was still strong, the Old Guard parties were split into two competing parties, and the Social Democrats under Katayama Tetsu were united.[33]

But SCAP actions two weeks before the election, Bisson argued at the time and later, had the net effect of staving off the worst for the old-line political leaders. Incredibly, MacArthur granted Yoshida permission to revise the very election law SCAP had earlier sponsored in a way that allowed for a small constituency single-ballot voting in which rich party coffers had the maximum effect. SCAP officials were fully aware of the consequences for the upcoming election of Yoshida's proposal, noting that it was "in comparison to the existing system, definitely advantageous to the parties now in power, and unfavorable to minority representation and to women." According to Japanese newsmen, the revision of the election law alone cost the Social Democrats an estimated fifty seats in the lower House of the Diet and meant that they lost the possibility of forming their own cabinet.[34] The result was that Socialist Prime Minister Katayama led a weak and squabbling coalition cabinet for eight months, wrestling throughout with the worst phase of the inflationary spiral, and then surrendering to the conservative rule that has continued uninterrupted in Japan to this day.

Even before the April election which he observed in Kanazawa, the birthplace of his wife, Bisson was personally and politically anxious to leave Japan. The solid friendships he had developed in Tokyo with Canadian diplomat and Japan scholar E. Herbert Norman and others no longer compensated for the increasing frustration of his work and the long and unanticipated separation from his family. Though not mentioned in his letters, there was also another factor. Bisson and other so-called "New Dealers" in the Occupation were being increasingly hounded by G-2 men.

The long-standing conflict within GHQ between G-2 and GS broke out into near civil war after General Willoughby circulated the results of his staff investigations on "leftist infiltration into SCAP." The secret G-2 reports, dated 15 January 1947, focused primarily on GS personnel, including Bisson. Drawing on the finding of the Dies Committee investigation of the Board of Economic Warfare, FBI information on *Amerasia,* and early China Lobby charges against the IPR, G-2 concluded that, prior to coming to Japan, Bisson "had pronounced leftist tendencies and some of his affiliations have had definite Communist implications." From the time that he was hired by GS, Bisson criticized the Yoshida cabinet as reactionary and had contact with the "left-wing cell" in the Tokyo Press Club which included Mark Gayn (*Chicago Sun-Times*) and Gordon Walker (*Christian Science Monitor*). Moreover, Bisson also had a very close relationship with Andrew Jonah Grazhdantsev [Grad], "well-known for his extremely leftist views." Bisson and Grad, the report claimed, were members of the leftist IPR and held their GS positions on the recommendation of Edward C. Carter, "a known communist sympathizer." Finally, G-2 charged Bisson with leaking secret information to his closest Japanese friend, Harvard-trained economist Tsuru Shigeto, who had been arrested before the war by the Japanese police "for his activities with the Japanese Communist Party." Ignoring the enraged protest of General Whitney, Willoughby defended the report on Bisson and others for presenting facts that were "irrefutable. I maintain that subversive elements are employed in this Headquarters. We are vulnerable, exposed to proven international espionage and local maneuvers [in Japan]."[35]

Critic of the Occupation

Bisson finally escaped from this poisoned atmospere of SCAP in April 1947. He had been in regular correspondence with William Holland at IPR, both about reorganizing a Japanese Council of IPR and about research and academic opportunities in the United States. Through Holland's good offices Bisson obtained a research grant from the Rockefeller Foundation during 1947 and a position as a visiting lecturer in the Department of Political Science of the University of California at Berkeley beginning in the fall of 1948.[36] For six years after his return from Japan, Bisson continued to write numerous articles and reviews and finished two books—outgrowths of his Occupation experience, and probably his most important writings.

Prospects for Democracy in Japan, published in 1949 under IPR auspicies, was a deft, hard-hitting critique of U.S. Occupation policy up until mid-1948. In the welter of self-congratulatory, success story literature by American students of the Occupation, Bisson's *Prospects* stood as one of the few significant works until the late 1960s to question seriously American policy and the meaning of Japanese democracy. Based on his firsthand observations in Japan, Bisson concluded that the United States

> failed to achieve the announced democratic aims of its initial post-surrender policy toward Japan, primarily because those aims could not be achieved through the instrumentality of Japan's old guard. Inasmuch as the economic machinery of Japan was left in the hands of Japanese . . . bent on sabotaging industrial recovery . . . [there was] a continued financial drain on the United States.
>
> This situation gave American Army and banking interests a plausible excuse to deplore the heavy financial burden placed on the United States. . . . However, instead of urging that SCAP cease to rely on the old regime and endeavor to develop a genuinely new and democratically-minded leadership in both government and industry, the [American] military-business interests represented by the [mission of General William Draper] took a very different stand. Their proposed solution of the problem was to restore Japan to what was, in essence, her pre-World War II industrial status, with one notable difference, Japan's economic life would continue to be ruled by the Zaibatsu . . . but henceforth American capital would be a partner of the Zaibatsu in prewar-style international cartels, or would simply take over certain key Japanese industries by means of large direct investments.[37]

Although American capital would never play the dominant role in Japan which Bisson predicted, clearly he did not think that prospects for real democracy in Japan after 1949 were very good. It was self-evident that the United States bore major responsibility for the fact.

The last and best known of Bisson's books, *Zaibatsu Dissolution in Japan,* was also the most scholarly and politically cautious. Published in 1954, it is a tour de force of economic and political analysis replete with tables and statistics carefully illustrating each argument. Following a historical survey of the growth and political influence of the Zaibatsu up to the surrender, Bisson emphasized the inherent social and political weaknesses of the Occupation sponsored dissolution program and hence the relative ease with which Zaibatsu executives and their allies evaded its most significant aspects. Though seeking to rid Japan of the despotic power of a small, privileged group over economic life, the dissolution program rested on concepts of free enterprise and individualism that had no popular roots in Japan. Not a single political party during the Occupation supported it. The conservative Liberal and Democratic parties that dominated postwar Japanese politics paid only lip service to free enterprise ideology and the principle of dissolution; they were historically the parties of the Zaibatsu combines and wedded by habit and self-interest to a monopolistic business order. The Communist and the Social Democrat parties also opposed the free-enterprise program. The Social Democrats (the "only real democrats in Japan, as the occupation defined the term"), who had the potential for gaining and holding control of the government, favored dealing with the Zaibatsu combines through a program of public ownership. In choosing to dissolve rather than nationalize the Zaibatsu combines, American policymakers destroyed the Social Democrats' raison d'être and played into the hands of the leaders of the Liberals and Democrats who believed that the combines stood the best chance of survival under a dissolution program.[38]

The core of *Zaibatsu Dissolution in Japan* is a detailed analysis of how conservative business and government leaders in Japan, aided after 1947 by their counterparts in the United States, effectively subverted the original dissolution program. The Occupation did score heavily in cutting away the monopolistic power of the ten leading Zaibatsu families and the holding companies at the apex of the Japanese corporate pyramid. But the net effect of even these most thoroughly carried out phases of the larger reform was far less drastic than appeared. By 1952, "the old networks had emerged in recognizable form [and] new concentrations of economic power have taken the place of the old." A look at the extensive redistribution of the shares of the holding companies and some of their subsidiaries, for example, showed that, early SCAP efforts at dispersal notwithstanding, there was an increasing trend toward concentration of stock ownership as the Occupation ended. In 1951, 8 percent of stockholders held 68 percent of all shares.[39]

Management control, Bisson also concluded, rested in the hands of these large stockholders. The Occupation effort to purge top business executives had been only partially successful. It never touched on the influence which purged business leaders, working behind the scenes, continued to exert on the policies of their successors. When the depurging began in 1949, these men "returned with greater rather than less prestige" to their old positions and began publicly attacking the whole dissolution program.[40] If ownership and management had not changed much by the end of the Occupation, neither had the most important part of the corporate structure, the large operating subsidiaries just below the holding companies. Prewar American investors in Japan, backed by an alarmed group of former Wall Street bankers in key policymaking positions in Washington, undercut the implementation of the 1947 law for the breakup of "excessive concentrations of economic power." The old

Zaibatsu banks managed to escape deconcentration entirely. Though the big commercial banks were divorced from the industrial and commercial units of their old combines and renamed, Bisson accurately predicted that a handful of them were "in a position to substitute for the old top holding companies as a nucleus around which former subsidiaries could gather in the effort to retain or recapture unity of operation."[41]

Deconcentration of industrial combines under the new law affected only a few firms and was not particularly severe. By 1951 three firms in the pig iron industry accounted for 96 percent of total output; three firms in the aluminum industry accounted for 100 percent of total output; two firms in the glass industry accounted for 90 percent of total output; and three firms in the beer industry accounted for 100 percent of total output. Only the liquidation of trading firms, including the two largest ones, Mitsui Bussan and Mitsubishi Shoji, was vigorously carried out by Occupation authorities. But despite the 1948 Anti-Monopoly Law, a classic process of competition, bankruptcies,absorptions, and mergers occurred so that by mid-1952 nine trading firms dominated the field and concentration was still continuing. In fact, the only question at the end of the Occupation concerning concentration in all sectors of the Japanese economy was how far the process of recombination would go.[42]

For Bisson, the Occupation dissolution program had clearly failed to create or maintain a competitive economy and new concentrations of wealth and power had emerged. Whatever changes the dissolution program had wrought in Japan's business life, he contended, were "incidental rather than primary." Without much elaboration, Bisson located the fundamental reasons for this failure in the unwillingness of American policymakers to conduct "an operation seriously designed to shift political power into new hands." The attempt to build a free enterprise economy through political parties linked to Zaibatsu interests was doomed from the start.[43]

Admitting to the many difficulties of nationalizing industry and agreeing that the Social Democrats were not an ideal party, Bisson nevertheless concluded that public ownership and control of Zaibatsu combines, mediated through the Social Democrats, "offered the best assurance available that the Occupation's democratic objectives in business and in other respects would be attained." The Occupation failed to gear its economic policy to the political reality that the Social Democrats, the largest popular party, favored nationalization not dissolution as the method for dealing with the Zaibatsu. In adopting a dissolution program the Occupation "weighted the odds against the one party through which liberal political as well as economic change might have been achieved."[44] Left unsaid, though clearly implied, was that Yankee

Zaibatsu, through their influence on the Truman administration, would never have consented to a program of nationalization or its political requisites in Japan.

The McCarren Committee Tragedy

Zaibatsu Dissolution in Japan was written during the most difficult years of Bisson's life. Despite his outstanding record of publications and distinguished reputation as a scholar of contemporary Asia, Bisson might have felt vulnerable at Berkeley without a doctoral degree or tenure even under ordinary circumstances. But beginning in 1949, circumstances at Berkeley and around the country for left-wing scholars, especially those in the Asia field, were far from ordinary. The collapse of Nationalist China, the Soviet explosion of an atomic bomb, the conviction of Alger Hiss for perjury, and the outbreak of the Korean War provided ammunition to those anxious for a purge of "subversive" influences from American life. When the Senate Internal Security Subcommittee, chaired by Senator Pat McCarren, set out in 1951 to prove that the IPR had been a captive organization of the Communist party with treacherous influence on American East Asian policy, Bisson inevitably was called to testify.[45]

For two days at the end of March 1952 a hostile McCarren Committee questioned Bisson about his role in *China Today,* his trip to Yanan, what he knew of Philip Jaffe's CP ties, why he had called Nationalist China "feudal" and Communist China "democratic" in a 1943 IPR publication, what his relationship was to Japanese Communists while serving in the Occupation, and much more. Senator James Eastland was not impressed by Bisson's answers, accusing him of always turning up "on the red side of things." Once during Eastland's questioning, Bisson lost his temper and said, "I have just been called a traitor." Eastland cut him off. "You have not been called a traitor, I said there was a question of whether you were a traitor."[46]

A badly shaken Bisson could not put the Washington experience and the attendant publicity behind him. State Senator Hugh M. Burns, chairman of the California Un-American Activities Committee, subpoenaed Bisson in the fall of 1952 for a one-day closed session at the state capitol. "After Sacramento," his wife recalled, "Arthur looked horrible. The nervous tension had built up so." Undoubtedly, Bisson's anxiety was related to the review by the Board of Regents of the University of California of his contract for the 1953–54 academic year. According to the only written account of Bisson's dismissal from Berkeley, in the spring of 1953 the chairman of the Department of Political Science was "ordered by the University Administration to release Bisson from the faculty.''[47] In all probability that order originated from the Board of Regents or a higher state official using undisclosed information supplied by California's "little HUAC" and the proceedings of the McCarren Committee.

At age fifty two, acceptance of his manuscript on the Zaibatsu by the University of California Press in hand, T. A. Bisson found himself without a job and unable to get one. Everywhere he turned the doors were closed. After a year of odd jobs and unemployment, Bisson was hired by the small religious Western Women's College of Ohio in Oxford, long known to his wife and her family. There Bisson became chairman of the international relations program and one of the most popular professors on campus. After a year on the academic blacklist, he found it attractive to teach at Western even though he earned a far lower salary than at Berkeley and never again had the time or facilities for further major research.[48]

Despite the trauma of the McCarren hearings and the loss of his job at Berkeley, Bisson did not swerve from his progressive political perspective. During the 1960s he regained the old punch of his younger years. The U.S. bombing raids on North Vietnam propelled Bisson into the antiwar movement sweeping college campuses. He sponsored the Inter-University Committee for Public Hearings on Vietnam, wrote a slashing critique of American policy in the widely distributed *Public Affairs Pamphlet* series, and contributed four pieces to the *Western Round-Up*, the student newspaper on his campus.[49] In his last published work, which appeared appropriately in the *Bulletin of Concerned Asian Scholars* in 1974, Bisson furiously assailed the "American-Japanese 'Co-Prosperity Sphere' " in Asia. The United States and Japan, he concluded:

pose as democracies, defenders of the "free world," but from end to end of the imperium they furnish arms and money to military dictators that betray local national interests, suppress the rights of free press and assembly, and shoot down students who seek to defend the true interests of country and people. [This] is not a matter only of Vietnam or Laos or Cambodia (it is just that in these cases imperialist force is directly applied), but also in Thailand, Indonesia, the Philippines, Taiwan, and South Korea where the ends desired can be achieved indirectly through the local military dictators. To the shame of all decent minded Americans, it is the United States that is the organizer and leader of this outrage, not only in its own right but also in carefully nursing Japan along so as to have a proper aide in handling the new co-prosperity sphere.[50]

Even as his health deteriorated, Bisson maintained a lively interest in current world affairs, particularly the struggles of all Third World peoples against the "modern imperial dispensation [of] the United States." But more and more Bisson turned in his final years to rereading literary classics from his vast home library, to enjoying the natural beauty of the Canadian homeland he adopted in 1969, and to gathering with his local friends who had little inkling of the reputation or controversies surrounding his life. On 7 July 1979, at age seventy-eight, Bisson died of heart failure in the Waterloo, Ontario area hospital.[51]

The demise of the scholarly career of T.A. Bisson and the oblivion to which his writings were cast highlights the determination of American policymakers after 1947 to develop Japan as a countermodel to revolutionary China for the unstable and developing countries of Asia. Inevitably, as John Dower has written, this task "required overtly or covertly enlisting America's Japan specialists in the task of cultural imperialism" and in providing a "selective portrayal" of Japanese history.[52] For the Occupation period that meant emphasizing such aspects of Japanese developments as the creation of parliamentary democracy, economic revival, and alliance with the U.S. Concomitantly, interpretations like those of Bisson that focused on the maintenance of traditional elites, unbalanced economic growth, inequality, exploitation, lack of freedom, and militarism were discredited.

It was hardly accidental that the conclusion of the peace and security treaties between the U.S. and Japan, locking Japan into the "free world" orbit, coincided with the effort in the McCarren hearings to paint as "Red" Bisson and many other of the best minds in the Asian field. The questions which Bisson asked, even the terms he used, were rendered taboo by the McCarren Committee assault. Subsequent Japan scholarship, heavily supported by the U.S. government, became preoccupied with the "successful" aspects of Japanese development and went about creating a counterideology to Marxism.[53] Only recently, in the wake of the Vietnam War and rising fear of the American and Japanese imperiums, have leftist critics of the "New Japan" like T. A. Bisson begun to emerge from the long neglected and sometimes buried history of the first generation of concerned Asian scholars.

Judged by his political affiliations and the point of view he took in his writings prior to working in Government Section, T. A. Bisson was undoubtedly one of the most radical of the "SCAP New Dealers." But more conservative members of that group experienced the same cycle of enthusiasm for and disillusionment with the reform project in Japan. The career of James Killen, chief of SCAP Labor Division in 1947 and 1948 and a staunchly anti-Communist "Cold War liberal," offers another instructive case study in the dynamics of the "reverse course" in Japan. Killen backed not only an anti-Communist but a strong trade union movement in Japan. For such politics he, like Bisson, would pay a price in MacArthur's Japan.

4   # JAMES S. KILLEN

American Labor's Cold War in Occupied Japan

The image of contented Japanese workers cooperating with company managers and enjoying guarantees of lifetime employment is deeply embedded in the American picture of contemporary Japan. This purportedly unique and constructive partnership is said to have developed not only from Japan's preindustrial social organization but MacArthur's liberation of Japanese workers and SCAP guidance of the union movement during the Occupation.[1] On closer inspection both the contemporary image and historical explanation prove deceptive.

While Japanese workers today enjoy a significantly higher standard of living than before the war, lifetime employment and relatively high wages are available only for that minority of "permanent" unionized workers employed in the largest, most modernized companies. The "temporary workers" in the large firms and workers in medium and small industries, who together comprise a majority of the labor force, are relegated to insecure nonunion positions at wages estimated between 70 and 80 percent of that of comparable workers in the large firms. Women, who are seldom in unions and comprise one-third of the labor force in Japan, receive an average wage of about half that of their male counterparts.[2]

It is true that American wartime planners hoped for a strong Japanese labor movement capable of offsetting the power of the industrial class and significantly improving wages of workers. SCAP established the legal framework for unionization in Japan at the outset of the Occupation and took other actions favorable to Japanese workers. But a series of explosive labor challenges to management prerogatives and conservative governments occurred in the first winter of the Occupation. Alarmed by the radicalism of the Japanese labor movement, SCAP gave crucial assistance after the spring of 1946 to the industrialists by which they were able to reconstruct much, though by no means all, of the pre-surrender system of exploitative employer-employee relationships.

There were two key elements in that system. The first was the "enterprise union" in which workers in the same firm organized together in a single union. By blocking efforts of labor leaders to develop ties amongst enterprise unions and create national unions which were more than merely federations of enterprise unions, refusing to negotiate industry-wide agreements, and hard-boiled policies of union busting, Japanese business and government, aided by SCAP, after 1947 recouped authority lost to labor in the immediate post-surrender period and produced unionists noteworthy for their stronger sense of allegiance to the firm than the working class.

The second element was the so-called seniority wage system. As before the war the monthly wage was primarily contingent on a man's seniority, rank, and evaluation in the firm and had little explicit relation to job content or skill level. The major portion of a worker's income, his base wage, rose regularly with each year on the job and was negotiated through collective bargaining. This seniority wage system obviously reinforced the lifetime employment tendency within large firms. While certainly regular and negotiated wages are a significant improvement for unionized workers over the arbitrary wage decisions of management before the war, the seniority wage system in practice divides permanent from temporary workers and effectively buttresses generally cheap, discriminatory, and inequitable wage rates.[3] In short, postwar Japanese business and government leaders overcame the upsurge of union militancy after surrender and successfully manipulated new levers of power provided by the Occupation to recreate in modified form key elements of the prewar labor system.

Though not generally appreciated, American labor officials played an active role in these Japanese labor developments during the Occupation. They participated in the planning of the Occupation's labor policies. They staffed the Labor Division of SCAP. They helped to write and monitor Japanese labor legislation. Finally they worked to establish an anti-Communist "free trade union" movement which after 1949 they hoped would be unified in one national federation affiliated with the International Confederation of Free Trade Unions (ICTFU).[4]

Perhaps the most important of the American unionists involved with Japan after the war was James Killen, a vice-president of the International Brother-hood of Pulp, Sulphite and Paper Mill Workers (IBPSPMW) affiliated with the AFL. As chief of Labor Division of SCAP in April 1947, Killen devoted

James S. Killen, Chief of Labor Division, with his daughter Linda and Japanese labor leaders in Tokyo, 1948. Courtesy of Linda Killen.

his energies to what he and other Americans saw as the complementary objectives of strengthening the Japanese union movement and combating communism within it. But in July 1948 he resigned with a sharp public denunciation of SCAP's anti-Communist labor policies for being, in fact, antiunion policies. Killen's brief career in Tokyo, set in the context of Japanese labor's struggle for autonomy and power, dramatically illustrates both the pro-Japanese labor ideal of American labor officials and planners in the early period of the Occupation, and its repudiation under the stress of anti-Communist hysteria and Cold War politics.

The Emergence of Militant Unionism

The dominant theme of American labor's involvement in Japan prior to Killen's appointment to SCAP was the creation of the legal and political framework for the emergence of a vigorous union movement similar to that in the United States. The principal Washington policy paper on Japanese labor organization, SWNCC 92/1 of 16 November 1945, was based practically verbatim on a Civil Affairs Guide prepared during the war by Theodore Cohen of the Foreign Economic Administration (FEA). Son of poor Russian-Jewish immigrants, the bright and affable Cohen imbibed the traditions of pro-unionism and anti-Stalinist radicalism of the 1930s. After graduation from City College of New York, Cohen learned Japanese and wrote a Master's thesis on the history of the Japanese labor movement at Columbia University. He worked closely at FEA with his boss Irving Brown, the staunchly anti-Communist former United Auto Workers union official who with Jay Lovestone, George Meany, and others founded in 1944 the AFL's foreign policy arm, the Free Trade Union Committee (FTUC). Brown, who became notorious after the war for directing the CIA funded campaigns of the FTUC to oust the Left from the European labor movement, liked the young Cohen. Cohen was one of the very few Americans knowledgeable about Japanese workers and clearly shared Brown's commitment to a strong and anti-Communist Japanese labor movement. Repressive trade union policies in prewar Japan, Cohen argued in the Civil Affairs Guide, restricted the Japanese home market and led to dumping and other unfair trade practices in world markets. Cohen viewed the emergence of a strong Japanese labor movement during the Occupation as a vital counterweight to the excessive economic power of the Zaibatsu which would then be forced to supply the domestic market rather than sell abroad in competition with American corporations. At the same time such a labor movement would also be a political bulwark against the Right and Left. "Brown and I were both terribly concerned about a possible upsurge of Stalinist influence in the new Japanese post-war unions," Cohen remembered, "just as much as we were with militarism and ultra-nationalism."[5]

In line with Washington policy, General MacArthur issued a series of sweeping political and civil liberties directives on 4 October 1945 that eliminated some of the greatest barriers to union organizing in Japan. Shortly thereafter he ordered the conservative government of Baron Shidehara Kijuro to draft legislation to protect the rights of Japanese wage earners in line with SWNCC 92/1. Though hedged with serious legal limitations which disturbed its American sponsors, the Trade Union Law (TUL), passed by the Diet in December 1945, guaranteed workers the right to organize, bargain collectively, and to strike. Taken together with the public encouragement of union organizing by SCAP officials in the first months of the Occupation, the new guarantees of civil liberties and the TUL sparked a phenomenal growth in the long repressed Japanese trade union movement. Within four months of surrender, the number of unionists in Japan had surpassed the prewar peak of 400,000 and in less than a year almost 13,000 enterprise unions with 3.8 million members had been organized. This upsurge continued until March 1949, when seven million workers, more than 50 percent of the labor force, belonged to unions.[6]

To direct the Japanese labor movement on the path of SWNCC 92/1, Cohen was appointed in January 1946 by MacArthur as chief of Labor Division, Economic and Scientific Section (ESS), SCAP. The articulate and energetic Cohen built up a staff carefully screened by him for anti-Communist labor union credentials: Assistant Chief of Labor Relations Branch John Harold from the AFL Restaurant Workers Union; Leon Becker, a troubleshooter in Labor Relations Branch from the International Ladies Garment Workers Union (ILGWU) and friend of its president, David Dubinsky; Chief of Labor Education Branch Richard Deverall from the anti-Communist wing of the UAW; and Samuel Thompson, an executive officer from the American Federation of Radio Artists. Candidates from the United Electrical Workers Union (UE) of the CIO and from the International Longshoremen's Union were rejected by Cohen because of "the pro-Communist slant of their union's leadership." Several American trade unionists already in Labor Division before Cohen's arrival were watched closely by the new chief, and those suspected of "close former connections with the Communists" in the American trade union movement were transferred out of Labor Division.[7]

As Cohen and other Labor Division officers immediately recognized, the principal spur to the rapid union growth in Japan was the increasingly desperate plight of the Japanese worker. The dislocations from the end of the war by themselves brought serious hardship. But the inept or deliberate inflationary economic policies of postwar conservative cabinets enormously aggravated the situation. Economist Tsuru Shigeto estimated that the annual rate of inflation in the first seven months after surrender was 947 percent, much higher than any time during the war.[8] The impact on workers' real income was dramatic. According to SCAP's official history, the average monthly earnings of a forty-year-old worker in January 1946 was 213 yen but the amount required to support him and three dependents approximated 509 yen.[9] John J. Murphy, New England regional director of the AFL, was acutely sensitive to the damage inflation and economic hardship caused to the objective of building an American-style labor movement in Japan. Sent by the War Department in January 1946, Murphy and other members of the Labor Advisory Committee reported after almost six months of study that few employers refused to recognize the newly formed unions although many covertly attempted to influence them. Nor did employers refuse to negotiate with the enterprise unions. The trouble was that the gains won by unions through picketing, demonstrations, and heated bargaining were so quickly wiped out by spiraling inflation that the process had to start over and over again.[10] In consequence, the number of labor disputes multiplied.

Some unions even resorted to a unique and controversial tactic known as production control. Unions temporarily operated establishments by locking out top management officials and, in Murphy's phrase, "proceeded to turn out much more production than [the companies] ever did before."[11] Production control, however, alarmed business and government leaders because it so openly flaunted traditional private property rights. It also stimulated demands by a hungry Japanese populous for control over production and distribution of food. Mass demonstrations in Tokyo and other cities in the spring of 1946 protested the persistence of the old order in the new Japan.

Alarmed by the drive for radical change, General MacArthur condemned "the growing tendency towards mass violence" and on 20 May 1946 threatened intervention against any further menace to orderly government. The speech threw the whole popular protest movement on the defensive, led to a crackdown on unions by business, and emboldened the Diet to pass the Labor Relations and Adjustment Law (LRAL) in September 1946.[12] Working with members of the Labor Advisory Committee and bypassing the Japanese labor movement, Cohen had drafted this legislation in April. He sought to contain the surge of labor-management disputes before production control, work stoppages, violence, or police suppression of unions occurred. The LRAL created the machinery for conciliation, mediation, and arbitration in cases of unresolvable labor-management differences, outlawed production control, and prohibited strikes among administrative employees of the government such as tax collectors. Yet to Cohen and the Labor Advisory Committee the success of the Occupation's labor policies rested less on LRAL or the expected passage of a Labor Standards law than the "prompt revival and stabilization of the Japanese economy" by the Japanese government.[13]

Most disturbing to SCAP and American labor leaders in the first sixteen months of the Occupation was the increasingly left-wing orientation of the Japanese union movement. Richard Deverall provided detailed reports on this ominous development to James Carey, Victor Reuther, and other friends in the CIO. Although he acknowledged inflation and the antilabor attitudes of employers, police, and the conservative cabinet of Yoshida Shigeru as causes of labor unrest and political involvement, Deverall's primary complaint was that "the labor leadership, being highly political has no interest in anything except a political solution of the problem: 'Overthrow the Yoshida Government.' ''[14]

Deverall and other American labor officials focused their worst fears on the Japanese Council of Industrial Unions, Sanbetsu, organized in August 1946 as a federation of twenty-one national industrial unions and claiming a membership of 1.5 million. Though Sanbetsu leaders did not state their political preferences it was an open secret that they were closely associated with the Japan Communist party (JCP). For Deverall, Sanbetsu's weaker archrival Sodomei, the Japanese Federation of Labor, was more compatible. The more conservative Sodomei claimed a membership of 900,000 members and was closely linked to the right-wing of the Socialist party. Many of the largest and most important unions, such as the Government Railway Workers Union, Kokutetsu, and the Japan Teachers Union, Nikkyoso, were not organizationally affiliated with any federation. But to Deverall's dismay, they were independent in name only. Like Sanbetsu, he thought, the major independent unions representing perhaps four million workers were by 1947 politically aligned with the JCP. Although the JCP before 1950 pursued a parliamentary strategy for attaining power and never officially had more than 110,000 members, American officials like Deverall always feared the potential of the party for revolutionary politics as the number of workers in Communist influenced or controlled unions increased.[15]

Free Trade Union News, the official organ of the Free Trade Union Committee (FTUC) that served as the AFL's foreign policy arm, first gave public notice in April 1946 that American labor leaders wanted a larger and more active role in Japan primarily to halt the leftward drift of the Japanese labor movement. Charles Kreindler, a vice-president of the militantly anti-Communist ILGWU, wrote that under prewar conditions the Japanese had failed to develop the leadership or experience for collective bargaining and would be susceptible to "anti-democratic forces." According to Kreindler, Matsuoka Komakichi, the "Gompers of Japan," and other leaders of Sodomei, were busily engaged in laying the foundations of a trade union movement patterned after the AFL. They needed "a helping and guiding hand" from FTUC before "other forces" took hold.[16]

A five week visit to Japan in the fall of 1946 by Mark Starr, educational director of the ILGWU, reinforced American labor's concern with left-wing political influences in Japan. Escorted on his trip through Japan by Deverall, Starr was struck by the naivete of the Japanese trade union leadership. Many of the unions he saw resembled revolutionary cells and evinced no interest in the sober business of wage agreements through collective bargaining. Starr recommended to General MacArthur a greater understanding of the problems of workers if they were not to turn to "black or red totalitarianism in despair." Starr believed that American labor experts were necessary to advise SCAP, Japanese labor, and Japanese management as well. As a result of Starr's visit and the persistent pressure by Matthew Woll, vice-president of the AFL and a member of the FTUC, MacArthur did authorize the hiring of an AFL representative on the staff of Labor Division in early January 1947.[17]

Faced with the second winter of cold, hunger, and privation since surrender, as well as the indifference of the Yoshida government, the entire union movement, led by Sanbetsu, joined in a call for a general strike on 1 February 1947. It was to be the culmination of a widespread program of demonstrations, food marches, strikes, and political agitation against the economic policies of the Yoshida government. But on 31 January, after the collapse of informal efforts by SCAP officials to pressure union leaders to call off the planned strike, General MacArthur intervened. "I will not permit the use of so deadly a social weapon in the present impoverished and emaciated condition of Japan. . . . The persons involved in the threatened general strike are but a small minority of the Japanese people. Yet this minority might well plunge the great masses into a disaster not unlike that produced in the immediate past by the minority which led Japan into the destruction of war."[18] MacArthur's action and his attack on the strike leadership sharply altered the context within which the Japanese labor movement had grown and provided American labor leaders with an opportunity long sought for a more important role in Japan.[19]

James Killen and the "Democratization League"

After the 1 February episode, both the Japanese government and SCAP underwent reorganization, a principal purpose of which was to combat the left-wing Sanbetsu labor federation more effectively. Fed up with the incompetent Yoshida cabinet, MacArthur called for new elections and provided support for a coalition government headed by Katayama Tetsu, leader of the anti-Communist right-wing of the Socialist party. Within SCAP, Cohen's supposed radicalism and leniency toward leaders of the general strike drew sharp criticism from Japanese and American conservatives and prompted MacArthur to transfer him to a new position in ESS in March 1947. At the time of his transfer, Cohen was in Washington, D.C. to attend a conference of labor administrators in the occupied areas and to hire an AFL representative to fill the labor advisor position MacArthur had authorized in January. Cohen was introduced to James Killen, the thirty-nine-year-old nominee of the AFL for the post. "As far as I was concerned, I was very happy to have him and I accepted him," Cohen recalled of Killen, and he was sent out to be my labor advisor, which was the original idea. Now, as it happened, while I was in America I was kicked upstairs. I didn't realize this. By the time I came back to Japan, Killen had already come, and he had gone to MacArthur. MacArthur wanted to speak to him because he represented the American unions, wanted to size him up. MacArthur liked him and he figured that this was a good opportunity now that he'd got somebody from the labor people. And he made Killen Chief of Labor Division and I was made Economic Advisor.[20]

Killen was the logical candidate to be selected by the AFL as a labor advisor in Japan. Born in 1908 in Port Townsend, Washington and raised in Olympia, Killen exhibited the tough-minded and hardworking traits of his Princeton trained, Presbyterian minister father. He excelled in high school and developed a lifelong habit of reading on his own, especially history, philosophy, and economics. With his family unable to afford to send him to college, Killen began work in the pulp and paper industry in Olympia in 1924 as a laborer. Exceedingly ambitious, Killen completed a Chicago correspondence school course in electrical engineering and advanced from electrician's helper to electrician. At the Olympia Forest Products mill in Port Angeles, the tall, handsome, and articulate young man helped organize a local of the Pulp Workers Brotherhood in 1933.[21] His abilities soon attracted the attention of the dominant personality of the union and its president for nearly fifty years, John P. Burke. A Debsian socialist before World War I, Burke had tempered his political views to become an adept power broker able to exploit the fears in the paper industry during the 1930s of the militant organizing tactics of the CIO and the Communists. In the summer of 1937, Burke appointed Killen as a full-time staff organizer for the union.[22]

Killen's very first assignment in his new post was to go to Ocean Falls, British Columbia to enlist Japanese workers into the Brotherhood. "Perhaps we did it at the time with the idea of protection of our occidental members, to prevent any further trespass, on jobs which we felt belonged to occidental labor, on the part of the Japanese," Killen confessed at the Brotherhood's national convention in St. Paul in March 1939. But after several months of organizing, Killen admitted that his "attitude toward the Japanese boys at Ocean Falls" had changed. Despite the language barrier and the very limited experience of the Japanese workers with trade unionism, Killen succeeded in getting all of the Japanese at Ocean Falls to join Local 76 of the union. "I hope the efforts of [our] organization can be directed in the future toward accomplishing more for them than we have been able to accomplish in the past," Killen implored the convention. "The management [at Ocean Falls] has been very, very hesitant—in fact they have almost been arbitrary—in the matter of making concessions to the Japanese workers and yet the Japanese have not criticized [the Brotherhood], they have not complained.''[23]

Killen developed a reputation as a shrewd organizer and orator. Suspicious of the CIO for its left-wing militancy, Killen saw himself as a practical trade unionist and New Deal liberal. He was first elected a delegate to the AFL convention in 1939 and served on important committees of the national organization through the war years. On the recommendation of Burke, in early 1944 Killen was appointed assistant director of the Pulp and Paper Division of the War Production Board, where his chief duty was working with the War Manpower Commission and other agencies in finding sufficient manpower for the nation's paper mills and combatting absenteeism and employee turnover. At the end of the war, Killen returned to the Brotherhood as eighth vice-president.[24]

Given his background in working with Japanese, contacts with the leadership of the AFL, and experience in Washington, Killen could not have been very surprised by Matthew Woll's request that he go out to Japan for six months as an AFL representative to SCAP. Killen spent several weeks weighing the decision, meeting with Burke and Theodore Cohen. Finally he agreed to go. ''Developments of the last two or three years tend to show, I believe, the extent to which totalitarian influences are still abroad in the world even after the defeat of Hitler and Mussolini,'' Killen explained to Burke in requesting a formal leave of absence. Woll was delighted by Killen's acceptance. He wrote MacArthur that Killen was devoted to the democratic cause and ''fully aware of the role of free trade unionism in preserving democracy and equally cognizant of the machinations and menace of totalitarians of all stripes.''[25]

Almost as soon as Killen arrived in Japan MacArthur asked him to take over as chief of Labor Division. Many in SCAP explained the general's action as an effort to win union support at home for his unannounced presidential bid. Whatever the reason behind his promotion, Killen found that the new position involved ''quite a change from the job for which I came out.'' The mushrooming growth of the Japanese union movement, he discovered, raised serious problems of finding experienced leadership, establishing collective bargaining relationships with employers, and securing rank and file participation in the unions. He worked strenuously to secure Diet passage of the Labor Standards Law of 1947, which established minimum wage standards and working conditions, workmen's compensation, and equal pay for equal work. But throughout his brief tenure, Killen was constantly amazed at the persistence of feudal patterns of labor-employer relations and the unwillingness or inability of the Japanese government, especially the Labor Ministry, to enforce laws protecting Japanese workers. He warned the State Department in November 1947 that if the United States did not retain direct control of Japan for another four or five years, ''trade unionism would be rapidly supplanted by traditional

Japanese labor practices [and] our efforts to bring about a democratic Japan would necessarily fail.''[26]

In practice, Killen's efforts to thwart a swing to the left in the Japanese labor movement soon took precedence over all his other work. The ''vigorous reaction to the rightist totalitarianism which has prevailed,'' Killen wrote Burke, ''inevitably creates a fertile field for the totalitarianism of the left under the guise of providing a complete break with and release from the tyranny of the past.'' When Killen arrived in Japan in April 1947, the Japanese union movement was still reeling from the impact of MacArthur's general strike ban and unable to judge the extent of freedom of action SCAP would tolerate. What was clear was that the so-called moderate, anti-Communist union elements that had initially opposed the general strike drive were attempting to displace Sanbetsu leadership from its dominant position in the labor movement. Within Sanbetsu itself, five newspaper locals withdrew from the organization in April amidst charges of Communist domination and too much emphasis on strike tactics. At the national Sanbetsu convention in early July, Killen learned from two Japanese informants, the main item of discussion at every session was a ''self-criticism program.'' Sodomei leaders attempted to capitalize on the swing to the right by organizing a liaison council, Zenroren, to attract all anti-Communist unions under one banner. (The plan, however, backfired and Zenroren became identified with Sanbetsu rather than Sodomei.) The large independent unions also participated in the purge of Communists from the labor movement. For example, only two of the sixty-two member executive committee of Nikkyoso, elected in June 1947, were Communists.[27]

Though aware of the resurgence of anticommunism in Japanese unions, Killen feared that the Communists had merely gone underground and were more dangerous there than when operating out in the open. More importantly, he believed, the ''growing severity of the economic situation facing Japanese workers generally tends to put the influence of the [moderate] Socialist party within the labor movement on the defensive. Without this economic crisis Communist influence would be substantially reduced because of the growing appreciation on the part of many people of the purposes and techniques of the Communist Party.''[28] Working in conjunction with the Katayama government and the FTUC, Labor Division sought to encourage such ''appreciation'' and intervened to strengthen the position of moderates over the radicals in the Japanese union movement. With the assistance of Richard Deverall, Killen drafted a document on ''Counteracting Communist Activities in the Labor Movement'' in May 1947 which was approved the next month by General William F. Marquat, chief of ESS, and General Paul J. Mueller, MacArthur's chief of staff.

Killen spelled out in his report the seriousness of Communist influence in the labor movement based on G-2 intelligence studies of the general strike. By the use of labor schools, cells, and publications from Russian sources, he claimed, small groups of Communists had penetrated Japanese unions with the ultimate objective of establishing a Communist police state. By lining up with the trade unionists and liberals, the Communists cleverly concealed this objective, for opposition to the Communists appeared to the workers as opposition to the trade union movement itself. The task for SCAP, therefore, was not to oppose the Communists "by sheer pressure of outside authority," but carefully to distinguish them from the "much broader group of active trade unionists. Among this group may be found some of the potential leadership which can take control away from the Communist minority. Every effort must be made to develop and encourage these people along constructive trade union lines." Concretely, Killen proposed that the TUL be revised to strengthen conciliation and mediation machinery, that SCAP employ more labor experts from the United States, and that Labor Division sponsor more conferences for democratic union leaders and distribute more labor education materials.[29]

The most notable immediate outgrowth of Labor Division's new policy was the formation of Democratic Leagues—Mindo—which were initially anti-Communist cells within the major unions. Mindo began during the fall of 1947 in the independent but Communist dominated Kokutetsu, an organization of about 400,000 members. Throughout the summer and fall, Labor Division staff met regularly with the leaders of Kokutetsu's right-wing faction in order to fan the flames, in the words of Deverall, "of rank and file revolt inside the railroad workers to overthrow the Red Fascists" who were running the union. This "anti-Communist, pro-trade union faction" so bitterly opposed the Executive Committee's leadership at the October 1947 convention that the convention was forced to adjourn. "Our office, I am happy to report," Deverall wrote to the FTUC, "has played a part in the development of the anti-Communist faction in the sense that as we continued to feed them educational material and ideas they became progressively conscious of the totalitarian rule of the Communists." By May of 1948 Deverall wrote AFL President William Green that, with the aid and advice of Labor Division, Kato Etsuo, leader of the Mindo of Kokutetsu, had "successfully driven out the Communists and done a good job in carrying on legitimate collective bargaining. They are the spearhead of the anti-Communists here in Japan."[30]

In fact, Deverall exaggerated. The Communist faction played a major role in Kokutetsu until the layoffs and strikes that accompanied the Dodge Plan in the summer of 1949. In other unions Mindo factions were organized but spread only slowly during 1948. When Mindo groups within Sanbetsu unions united in June to take control of the national organization, they were repulsed.

The Sanbetsu convention stigmatized Mindo as "an anti-labor movement" and ordered its expulsion, leading to the creation in 1949 of Shin (new) Sanbetsu.[31]

Throughout his tenure as chief of Labor Division, Killen carefully orchestrated support by the AFL and FTUC for the Mindo movement. He returned to the AFL's 1947 San Francisco convention as a delegate with a "cheering message of the organization of Japanese wage earners into free trade unions." He assisted Matthew Woll in writing a resolution, passed unanimously, pledging AFL's "full moral and material support" to a free trade union movement in Japan, "free from all control and domination by the government, the political parties, and employers." At a private meeting with FTUC leaders, Killen identified the problem more concretely as the "revolutionary communists" who were "appearing in increasing numbers." He contended that they had been encouraged by the visit in March 1947 of a delegation from the World Federation of Trade Unions (WFTU), the FTUC's principal nemesis in the foreign policy arena.[32]

One of the simplest and most effective forms of American labor support Killen organized was telegrams from AFL President William Green and other officials to the conventions of the anti-Communist unions. In addition, both Killen and Deverall obtained literature from the American unions which they passed on to Mindo for translation and distribution. These included the FTUC's map of slave labor camps in Russia, the Gulag Map; and ILGWU pamphlet, "Communists and Trade Unions"; the AFL's "Bill of Rights"; and copies of the *American Federationist.* Arranging with President Green for the AFL to invite a representative from the Japanese labor movement to attend the 1948 convention, Killen recommended as his first choice Kato Etsuo, leader of the Mindo in Kokutetsu. Neither SCAP nor American labor union records indicate the Mindo movement obtained American funds, although the AFL did send CARE packages to favored leaders.[33]

Despite the strenuous efforts of Killen and American labor unions to shift the balance of power within Japanese unions from the left to the right-wing factions and to channel working class discontent into the machinery of collective bargaining, worsening economic and political conditions continually hampered their progress. No one in SCAP was more sensitive to the problem than Killen himself. In reports and correspondence to AFL officers, Killen repeatedly emphasized the plight of Japanese workers in the face of unchecked inflation. Union leaders expressed their desire to avoid political activity and deal with "purely economic problems." But, concluded Killen, "if straight trade unionism is going to work it must have a stable economic foundation."[34]

Killen believed that Prime Minister Katayama and the Socialist party wanted to control inflation, increase production, and sincerely serve the interests of the Japanese people. Yet after a dinner with Katayama and several of his cabinet ministers, Killen was struck by their naivete in proclaiming themselves "the workers' best friend" and their assumption that workers would cooperate with rather than criticize the government's economic policies. While logical, Killen explained to William Green, "it completely overlooks the fact that when millions of people have empty stomachs they are inclined neither to cooperation nor logic." In fact, the Socialists under Katayama so compromised their principles and program to retain the support of their conservative partners in the coalition government that economic conditions deteriorated more rapidly than before. At the end of 1947, three-fourths of an average family's income went to essential food alone. "The Japanese worker is still confronted with problems of the greatest severity in obtaining the barest minimum in the way of food, clothing, and shelter," Killen wrote home in February 1948.[35]

The harsh economic conditions and the political fiasco of the Katayama cabinet led to an increase in labor disputes and a resurgence of Sanbetsu and the Left. Two million public employees, comprising almost 40 percent of the organized work force, were particularly militant by the winter of 1947. Of the 1.8 million workers involved in disputes in December, 1.7 million were government workers. Impatient with the government's budget policies, they demanded a revised wage standard on a par with private industry and triggered the collapse of the Katayama cabinet. Even with a substantial increase in wages early in 1948, by June the average monthly wage for a government employee was 2,290 yen, while for men in private industry it was 5,087 yen. Government workers quickly renewed dispute tactics and political agitation against the new, more conservative cabinet of Ashida Hitoshi, leader of the Democratic party.[36]

The upsurge of labor activism by government employees, however, coincided with the decision of Washington policymakers to restore Japan as the dominant economic and political power of Asia and a bulwark against communism. The new "reverse course" policy clearly entailed closer cooperation by SCAP with conservative management and political leaders and the suppression of working-class and leftist demands. "We should make it clear to the Japanese Government," the National Security Council insisted in NSC 13/2, "that the success of the recovery program will in large part depend on Japanese efforts to raise production and to maintain high exports through hard work, a minimum of work stoppages, and internal austerity measures." Under Secretary of the Army William Draper warned that unsettled labor conditions were one of the most serious obstacles to the coming of American foreign aid, without which recovery was impossible. The top State Department officer in Tokyo, William Sebald, forwarded to Washington the views of the Industrial

Club of Japan that labor unrest was the most serious impediment to economic recovery and supported the demands of Japanese businessmen for revision of the labor laws and measures to purge Communist influence from the trade unions. [37]

In conjunction with Washington's new economic program, Blaine Hoover, chief of the Civil Service Division of Government Section, offered SCAP a simple solution to labor unrest that ultimately placed Killen and the American labor movement at odds with Occupation policy. Without consulting Killen and Labor Division, Hoover recommended that all government workers in Japan be removed from coverage under the TUL. Instead, civil servants would be subject to a revised National Public Service Law (NPSL) which would sharply limit their union rights. They would be allowed to organize unions but neither to bargain collectively nor strike. Workers in government-owned enterprises like the Japan National Railroad would be subject to a new Public Corporation Law which would give them the right both to organize and bargain collectively but not to strike. [38]

Killen had grave reservations about the general change in American policy for the Occupation and offered sharp criticism of Hoover's recommendations in particular. "Talk about making Japan a bulwark against communism," he complained to Burke, "threatens to destroy . . . or at least effectively dilute many of the more liberal aspects of the Occupation." Certainly Killen shared in the increasing fears by American policymakers of communism. The Japanese Communist party, he wrote in April 1948, "was getting bolder in condemnation of everything American." He was dismayed by party documents circulating within the labor unions which applauded the new Communist regime in Czechoslovakia and prophesized a complete Communist victory in Italy. "In view of the severe economic situation which prevails here I sometimes marvel that the CP has not made even greater progress than it has." [39] But for Killen the proper method for dealing with the Communists was to extend democratic reforms, employ only limited and selective repression, and improve the economy.

In dealing with Hoover's recommendations, therefore, Killen accepted the need for the prohibition of strikes by civil servants, but questioned the practicality and desirability of a strike ban for workers in government-owned enterprises. Even more importantly, Killen insisted on the right of civil servants to bargain collectively under strengthened compulsory arbitration procedures. In Britain, Australia, and elsewhere, Killen pointed out, the concept of collective bargaining unsupported by the threat of strike was embodied in civil service legislation and had proven highly successful. To Killen, Hoover was a narrow technician attempting to implement an American type of civil service without recognizing the peculiar conditions within Japan, particularly the greater role of the national government as employer.[40]

Unfortunately for Killen, Hoover's recommendations had the strong support of General Whitney of Government Section who played on MacArthur's fears of a Communist uprising spearheaded by government workers unions. General Marquat and ESS Economic Advisor Theodore Cohen attempted to get Killen to accept a compromise plan that made concessions to Hoover's position. But Killen refused. A compromise would be better than a total defeat, he conceded. But Killen turned to Cohen tiredly and said, as Cohen recalled, "You are a career bureaucrat and for you it is right to compromise to save whatever you can. I'm a labor union man and I'm eventually going back to the labor movement. I can't agree to compromise my movement's principles."[41] In any event, Killen was confident that he could convince MacArthur of the peril of Hoover's course and intended to stake everything on his own considerable powers of persuasion.

Killen and Hoover had a six-hour showdown at headquarters in front of MacArthur and his top aides on 21 July. According to his own account, Killen argued successfully against Hoover in the opening few hours. But during a break General Whitney got to MacArthur privately and changed the supreme commander's mind. When the discussion resumed MacArthur repeatedly called attention to past and currently threatened government strikes and cited with strong approval the Hoover principle that the authority of the state must be supreme. Killen protested against the notion that collective bargaining necessarily implied strikes and warned of a "trail of labor resentment" if the Hoover plan were adopted. MacArthur made no move to explore a compromise and General Marquat did not volunteer the one he and Cohen had worked up. The next day, 22 July, MacArthur, in an open letter to Prime Minister Ashida, ordered changes in the NPSL in accord with Hoover's recommendations.[42]

The Ashida government used the MacArthur letter for a broad offensive against the Japanese labor movement. Pending Diet revisions of NPSL, all negotiations between government unions and national and local governments were suspended and strikes and delaying actions were made severely punishable offenses. Local officials introduced tighter restrictions on the holding of union meetings and demonstrations. Private employers openly suggested that their unions, like those in the public sector, must surrender the right to strike and bargain collectively. Naturally, all trade unionists reacted bitterly to these measures, and Communists led a determined legal and extralegal resistance to the newly imposed strike ban. Nevertheless, by the time of the Diet passage of the revised NPSL on 12 December 1948, the Japanese regime and large businesses, assisted by SCAP, had broken the public employees militant labor offensive and profoundly restricted the labor movement generally.[43]

Killen was thoroughly disgusted by this series of events. From the outset of his battle with Hoover, he had decided to return home at the earliest opportunity if MacArthur ruled against him. In his view, SCAP's 22 July letter effectively destroyed the substance of trade unionism for one-third of Japanese organized workers and was "another step—albeit a long one—in the rather sharp swing to the right gradually evidenced in the policies of this Headquarters." Moreover, the excitement of the job and the exhilarating sense of power he had felt were gone. Dealing closely with MacArthur during the NPSL fight convinced him that the general was a "somewhat self-inflated and pompous military bureaucrat."[44] Apparently not yet cognizant that "it was an unforgivable sin to publically disagree with theater commander when you are part of a military organization," Killen called a press conference in which he charged that the proposed revisions of the NPSL and other policies were "ill-conceived and will retard a healthy labor movement." Despite the wide publicity given his remarks, Killen naively believed that he would be allowed to stay on the job for several months to wind up his affairs in Japan and plan his return to the Brotherhood. He quickly realized that the press conference had been a blunder. His request to see MacArthur, with whom he had always been on friendly terms, was summarily rebuffed and headquarters assigned a first lieutenant to see that Killen left Japan within a few days.[45]

But Killen brilliantly recovered from the blow he received in Tokyo. First, he publicized his resignation from SCAP as a matter of loyalty to the trade union movement. He had warned MacArthur upon taking the job as Labor Division chief, Killen wrote in his union newspaper, that he felt himself to be primarily a representative of the AFL and would work for SCAP only so long as he could do so "with maintenance of some personal integrity." The revision of the NPSL had left him with "no other course" than to resign.[46]

Second, Killen led a vigorous campaign against the revised NPSL bill pending in the Diet. The new labor policies, he told officers of the FTUC on his return from Japan, were "not an anti-communist move . . . but entirely a proposal to restrain the field of collective bargaining and in that way lend aid to those opposed to trade unionism." He told the delegates to the 1948 AFL convention that MacArthur's actions served not to "weaken or cripple the Communist influence in those unions but give the Communists ammunition for their propaganda campaign against the occupation. It strengthens their hand in accusing the United States Government of being anti-labor and not desirous of advancing the interests of Japanese workers." No doubt it was Killen who was primarily responsible for the 1948 AFL convention resolution condemning the "restrictive and oppressive" labor laws in Japan and calling on the Army Department to get MacArthur to "discontinue repressive action that is being carried out under the guise of anti-Communism against legitimate trade union objectives."[47] Acting through the Labor Department's influential Trade Union Advisory Committee on International Affairs (TUAC), the CIO joined Killen and the AFL in condemning "the unwarranted denial by Occupation authorities of basic trade union rights of Japanese Government workers."[48]

Bowing to sharp criticism by not only the American labor movement and the Labor Department but from the State Department and foreign governments as well, Under Secretary of the Army Draper suggested to MacArthur some face-saving steps for modifying the proposed NPSL revisions. But MacArthur remained adamant. He was especially angered by Killen's statements, which Japanese unionists were using effectively in their campaign to prevent Diet passage of the revised NPSL bill. Killen was obsessed, MacArthur said, with the concept that society "should be organized on the basis of complete labor predominance." Changes in the draft NPSL bill, he insisted, would only encourage Japanese Communists and weaken the American position in Japan and the Far East. When the new law passed the Diet virtually intact in December, MacArthur hailed it as a major victory "over those who would leave the government prey to minority subjugation."[49]

Despite the ultimate futility of his campaign against the revised NPSL bill, Killen regained the full support of his own union and the AFL. He was promoted to seventh vice-president of the IBSPMW and placed in charge of all union operations on the Atlantic coast from Pennsylvania through South Carolina. On the recommendation of the AFL, he took a post in March 1949 as labor advisor to the Economic Cooperation Administration (ECA) in England. Late in 1951, Killen resigned from the Brotherhood to work as an administrator for the ECA. He then held a series of high-level positions in the foreign aid agencies of the Department of State in Yugoslavia, Pakistan, South Korea, South Vietnam, and Turkey until his death in 1972.[50] Ironically, the sixteen troubled months he spent in Occupied Japan as chief of Labor Division launched Killen on a second and successful career in the diplomatic service.

Sohyo and the ICTFU aftermath

The resignation of Killen and the fight over the passage of the revised NPSL severely strained the ties between the American labor movement and SCAP. Furthermore, they damaged the prestige of Labor Division through which American trade unionists had exercised their influence. Perhaps no longer interested in courting American labor unionists after his political defeats in 1948, General MacArthur blocked a proposed American Labor Mission to Japan in 1949 and rebuffed repeated efforts by the AFL to establish independent headquarters in Tokyo. The deputy chief of Labor Division and several other trade union officials resigned from SCAP along with Killen. With the exception of Valery Burati, a former organizer for the Textile Workers of America, SCAP Labor Division by 1949 had no American trade unionists on its staff and was unable to recruit any.[51]

Despite the tensions between American labor officials and SCAP after Killen's resignation, all parties involved with Japanese labor after 1949 agreed on the importance of a unified anti-Communist Japanese trade union movement which, it was hoped, would be affiliated with the AFL and CIO dominated International Confederation of Free Trade Unions (ICTFU). The concern for unity was a direct outgrowth of the fragmented and weakened condition of the Japanese trade union movement left in the wake of the economic stabilization plan designed by Detroit banker Joseph Dodge in 1949. The massive layoffs of government and industrial employees, increased taxes, wage freezes, higher prices for rice, transportation, and other necessities, and reduced public services which accompanied the Dodge Plan generated a renewed wave of strikes, demonstrations, and sabotage by the summer of 1949. The new Yoshida cabinet and Japanese employers mounted a campaign of repression aimed especially at the most militant and left-wing trade unionists. At the same time SCAP promoted the Mindo and other anti-Communists to take over union leadership. As a result, by the end of 1949, only about 1.5 million workers were estimated to be in unions under Communist influence or control, as contrasted with a high of over five million in 1947–48. Symptomatically, the number of unions fell by more than 5,000 and union membership declined by more than 800,000 in 1949.[52]

The significance of the ICTFU to the Japanese labor movement was outlined in October 1949 by Valery Burati, chief of Labor Relations Branch of Labor Division, to Jay Lovestone, principal architect of the AFL's foreign policies. Burati argued that the

> most important development in the Japanese labor movement as we see it at the present time is the struggle to unify it and its corollary, the struggle between the Communists and the anti-Communists representing various shades of moderate and leftist political opinion. The struggle of unification which now is quite intense revolves around affiliation with [IFTCU] in London in which I know you are especially interested.
>
> A group of the most important labor leaders in Japan have formed a Council to promote affiliation with the London conference. [Kato Etsuo, head of Kokutetsu] acts as Chairman inasmuch as his union is a strategic one. It is the hope of the Council members that around the issue of affiliation with the ICTFU they will be able to unify the Japanese labor movement which, as you know, at the present time is composed of shreds and patches. Unification means disintegration of Sodomei,

Shin Sanbetsu . . . and the virtual destruction of the federation Sanbetsu which stands outside the council.

With encouragement from the State Department, General MacArthur found funds to send Kato and four other delegates to the ICTFU's founding conference in London and hoped they would return as the core of a unified labor movement and a "bastion impervious to the scourge of totalitarian ideology."[53]

From the very start, the hopes of SCAP and American labor leaders for a Japanese labor movement affiliated en bloc with ICTFU were frustrated. Ironically, the first problem came from one of the AFL's closest allies in Japan, Matsuoka Komakichi, chairman of Sodomei. Matsuoka did not want Sodomei dissolved into the planned new national federation to be called the General Council of Trade Unions of Japan, or Sohyo. As a result, Robert T. Amis, new chief of SCAP's Labor Division and a professional arbitrator, forced Matsuoka to resign from the London delegation to which he had been elected. Following a bitter struggle at Sodomei's 1950 convention, Matsuoka organized the most right-wing unions of Sodomei and several conservative independent unions into the rump Shin Sodomei. Meanwhile, Labor Division and ICTFU cooperated with Takano Minoru and other Sodomei leaders willing to dissolve their federation and join Sohyo.[54]

An even more serious problem for SCAP and American labor leaders was the resurgence of union militancy in late 1949 and early 1950 by the very anti-Communist unions picked for participation in Sohyo and affiliation with ICTFU. Thirty-five of these unions, representing about two million workers and backed by the Socialist party, organized a Struggle Committee against the labor policies of the Yoshida cabinet and, implicity, against the antiunionism of the Dodge Plan. The committee's most important demand was that the government comply with the recommendation of its own National Personnel Authority (NPA) for a 25 percent wage increase for government workers. Fearing an imbalanced budget, Dodge and SCAP bolstered Yoshida's refusal to implement the NPA wage increase. Reluctantly the Struggle Committee posted notice of an illegal general strike and appealed to the American labor movement for support. "At present we find ourselves in fear of being deprived of the fundamental rights of laborers, . . . by the hands of avaricious monopolistic capitalists and the present Yoshida cabinet, their spokesman," the chairman of the Struggle Committee wrote to AFL President William Green. The general strike never occurred. The Japanese government and SCAP disrupted the March 1950 labor offensive by intervention in a coal miners' strike and a timid Struggle Committee called off the planned general strike.[55]

When the Japanese Communist party adopted a revolutionary posture early in 1950, after the Cominform attack on JCP leader Nosaka Sanzo, SCAP officials gave even greater importance to pushing Japanese labor into a unified labor center affiliated with ICTFU. MacArthur announced on 3 May 1950 a stepped-up drive to root out "destructive communist elements." Before the Korean War began, the leadership of the Communist party and of its newspaper, *Akahata,* were formally purged. The emerging Sohyo was to be the "focal point" in the Red Purge of the labor movement, according to a Labor Division document titled "To Reduce and Eliminate Communists in the Labor Movement." The creation of Sohyo would give an anti-Communist alternative to the auto, metal, and other unions still affiliated with the Sanbetsu dominated Zenroren. Sohyo would stand in direct opposition to Zenroren and "thus those who remain in Zenroren would be exposed and identified as Communists" and presumably purged. In August 1950, during the heightened anti-Communist frenzy of the Korean War, SCAP outlawed Zenroren as a Communist front organization. Sanbetsu, which in 1949 had 1.5 million members, dropped to only 47,000 just after the formation of Sohyo in July 1950. By 1953 there were only 13,000 members in Sanbetsu unions and, in 1958, the federation was dissolved.[56]

Encouraged by SCAP, American labor and ICTFU officials worked hard to bring about the formation of Sohyo. In March 1950 the big three of American labor—the AFL's William Green, the CIO's Philip Murray, and the United Mine Workers' President John L. Lewis—sent congratulatory telegrams to the Sohyo organizing committee, whose members represented about two-thirds of union workers in Japan. In one of its first decisions, ICTFU sent John Brophy and Jay Krane, top CIO officials, to Japan to attend the founding Sohyo convention in July. In meetings with Generals Marquat and MacArthur, Brophy and Krane appealed without success for concessions to Japanese labor as the best means for countering communism and supporting Sohyo.[57] Publicly, the ICTFU portrayed Japan as a model for free trade unionism throughout Asia. Its journal, *Free Labour World,* featured a front cover picture of Sohyo leader Kato Etsuo who was chosen as the Asian representative on the ICTFU's first executive board and was described as the "spearhead of the anti-communist movement in Japan."[58]

Ironically, the actions of Sohyo in the remaining months of the Occupation gravely disappointed its American sponsors. At its founding convention, the Dodge Plan was attacked, though not by name; the demands of the failed spring offensive were pressed anew; a call for the nationalization of the banks and large private industries was made; and "the overthrow of the reactionary [Yoshida] Cabinet" was considered paramount. Moreover, only individual unions in Sohyo, not Sohyo en bloc, affiliated with ICTFU.[59] The increasingly antilabor policies of the Yoshida cabinet aided Sohyo's left-wing and led the

ICTFU to back the legal overthrow of the government.

Meanwhile, such support as Sohyo did receive from the ICTFU, SCAP, and American labor officials quickly dissipated when Sohyo and the Socialist party with which it was linked attacked the American proposed peace and security treaties for terminating the Occupation. Sohyo favored an "overall peace" that did not exclude Russia or the People's Republic of China, insured Japanese neutrality, removed American military bases, and prevented any rearmament program. Fueling Sohyo opposition to the American proposals was the assessment, which proved correct, that they would accelerate the Yoshida cabinet's rightward thrust against the labor movement.[60]

By the summer of 1951, with the backing of the State Department, the ICTFU and American labor leaders were giving aid to the "practical trade unionists" in Sohyo who criticized Secretary General Takano Minoru and other antipeace treaty, left-wing socialist leaders of the union. As the Occupation ended, ICTFU and FTUC made plans to send Willard Townsend and Richard Deverall to Japan to attend Sohyo's July 1952 convention. Their goal, in Jay Lovestone's words, was to "fight side by side with those who are prepared to resist communism and every other form of totalitarian reactions."[61]

The hope of American labor leaders that Sohyo would serve as an anti-Communist labor center affiliated with ICTFU and representing the interests of the majority of Japanese workers, was never realized. By the spring of 1953, FTUC was convinced that Sohyo was "completely controlled by the Kremlin." Jay Lovestone ordered Deverall to abandon Sohyo and organize a new anti-Communist federation.[62] The CIO and ICTFU, though hopeful of a victory for Sohyo's right-wing faction, reluctantly joined in attacking Takano after 1953, especially for his opposition to the Korean War. Given such strains with American labor unions, Sohyo never joined ICTFU en bloc. In fact, at the end of 1954, only about one-third of the organized work force were in unions affiliated with ICTFU.[63] To the frustration of American unionists and the State Department, Sohyo remained the dominant labor federation in Japan until the mid-1960s, continuing to criticize and organize against the United States position on the revision of the Security Treaty and other foreign policy issues. Though Sohyo initiated numerous strikes and other militant dispute tactics which won its members increased wages during Japan's era of phenomenal economic growth, it never developed into a cohesive organization able to overcome the exploitative employer-employee relations reestablished during the Occupation. The Japanese working class remained divided by enterprise unions that excluded millions of "temporary" workers and by the prevailing seniority wage system.[64]

American labor leaders' primary goal during the Occupation was the creation of a unified anti-Communist trade union movement patterned after the bread-and-butter unionism of the American model. At the same time, they anticipated that this movement would endorse such fundamentals of American policy in Japan as the economic recovery program and the peace and security treaties. But even a majority of non-Communist Japanese union leaders correctly came to view these American policies as inimical to the interest of workers and, in some fashion, opposed them. American labor leaders were caught in the middle of this conflict. Generally they sided with American policymakers, condemning Japanese unions for their political activities and exhorting them to pursue strictly economic goals.

In the end, James Killen proved an important exception amongst the American unionists in Japan. Though sharing the anti-Communist animus of other SCAP officials, Killen gave higher priority to building an organizationally strong trade union movement. The SCAP-sponsored revision of the NPSL so obviously weakened the Japanese trade union movement that Killen and the AFL sought to embarrass SCAP and Washington policymakers into changing their position by publicly criticizing the policy. But ultimately United States government policy proved even more conservative than that of the bitterly anti-Communist AFL. Killen was bound to fail and American labor unionists' plans for a cold war in Occupied Japan soon turned into a skirmish. Efforts to use ICTFU to create a unified anti-Communist trade union movement faltered on the same shoals that had brought Killen home—namely, Japanese government officials and businessmen who despised organized labor and yet were supported by American businessmen and policymakers determined to integrate Japan into the American sphere of influence.

While Killen and the AFL complained that MacArthur's anti-Communist policies undermined legitimate trade unionism, Harry F. Kern, foreign editor of *Newsweek* magazine, organized a powerful lobby group called the American Council on Japan (ACJ) which contended that MacArthur failed to go far enough in crushing the Communists or disciplining the workers of Japan. In fact, no group of Americans more faithfully reflected the contempt which so many Japanese conservatives felt towards the working class than the ACJ. American policymakers paid heed to Kern and the ACJ and ignored Killen and the AFL. The reason they did offers a key to understanding the rightward thrust in American policy for Japan after 1947.

5   HARRY F. KERN

The Japan Lobby
in American Diplomacy

Curiously, the role of American pressure groups in the remaking of post-war Japan has been virtually ignored by all scholars of the Occupation. The most important such group concerned specifically with Japan was the American Council on Japan, the organizational umbrella for what may properly be termed the Japan Lobby. Unlike the China Lobby, with its sensationalistic record of activities, the Japan Lobby was a small, loosely-knit group of individuals who operated largely behind the scenes and often without acknowledgement of their affiliation with the ACJ.

Nevertheless, many contemporary observers agreed that the Japan Lobby provided a major impetus for the reorientation of America's Japan policy after 1947. The *New Republic,* for example, sharply condemned the reactionary assault on the "liberalism" of the early years of the Occupation and then explained that its "spearhead was the American Council for [*sic*] Japan, aided by *Newsweek* magazine, led by old Japanese hands of the State Department, and backed by major corporations with investments in Japan and friends among the Zaibatsu. Its program included the ending of reparations, the suppression of reform in the name of recovery, and the reinstatement of the Zaibatsu war criminals purged by MacArthur. These views found willing acceptance in Washington."[1] Even if this assessment of the ACJ is exaggerated, any analysis of the Occupation which fails to consider the tangled interplay between American policy in Japan and informal pressure groups like the ACJ is incomplete and, inevitably, distorted.

The Servant of Power

The principal organizer and leader of the Japan Lobby, Harry F. Kern, was a short, bespectacled, unimposing man who made a career as a journalist and public relations consultant out of his passion for intimacy with the wealthy and powerful. At one time or another since World War II, he counted amongst his closest friends Egyptian President Gamal Abdel Nasser, king of Saudi Arabia Ibn Saud, Shah Pahlavi of Iran, Prime Minister Kishi Nobusuke, Secretary of State John Foster Dulles, and Central Intelligence Agency Director Allen Dulles. His relationship with these men, like so much of Kern's life, is shrouded in secrecy. But Kern left a trail of letters to influential American friends whose papers or archives, upon their deaths, have been opened to researchers. In addition, Kern became the subject of intense scrutiny by the Japanese press in January 1979 for his suspected involvement in a politically charged aircraft bribery scandal. From these sources the outlines, and in some instances even the details, of Kern's postwar activities in Japan can now be known.

Born in 1911 and raised in Denver, Colorado, the bright and amiable Kern started at Harvard University in 1931. He studied history and literature through the worst years of the depression until his graduation in 1935. Neither he nor most Harvard students had any interest in Japan. Those few interested in the Far East, Kern recalled years later, specialized in Chinese studies, an outgrowth of Harvard's close connection with the Harvard-Yanjing Institute in Shanghai. Kern moved to New York City and in 1937 joined *Newsweek,* a new venture launched that year largely with the funds and encouragement of W. Averell Harriman, heir to the Union Pacific Railroad fortune and partner in the Wall Street investment house of Brown Brothers, Harriman. The ambitious young journalist thrived at *Newsweek* and rose from an assistant editorship to the prominent post of war editor after Pearl Harbor.[2]

"In my life, Japan is the country which has the most important meaning," Kern wrote his Harvard classmates in 1960. His interest in Japan he dated precisely: 7 December 1941. But it was not until immediately after the war when he became the prestigious foreign editor for *Newsweek* that Kern's intimate involvement in Japanese affairs began. By his own account, he became curious about the postwar fate of Japan after a business visit to Germany in July 1945. As he surveyed the wreckage of the Krupp works in Essen, he "heard the sound of iron striking iron and I was convinced that Germany would revive." Would Japan do likewise, he wondered? Dismayed by the hatred in the United States for the Japanese during the war, Kern also claimed that he wanted to glean a better understanding of the Japanese people and an insight into what really was happening in Japan beyond that available in the press. He may also have been influenced to pursue Japanese affairs by Eugene Dooman, Ambassador Joseph Grew's aide and the key figure in SWNCC in planning for the surrender and Occupation of Japan. But whatever the reason, Kern decided in the spring of 1946 to upgrade coverage of Japan in *Newsweek* by appointing Compton Pakenham as chief of *Newsweek*'s Tokyo bureau.[3]

Born in Kobe where his British father managed a shipyard, Pakenham had fluency in Japanese, an aristocratic pedigree, and an ultraconservative political outlook that led to numerous contacts before the war with high-level Japanese officials, especially those in the Imperial Palace. A professional journalist in the United States with the *New York Times* in the 1920s, Pakenham worked for Kern during the war as an "advisor" to *Newsweek,* especially on Japanese matters, and the two men became close friends and key figures in the Japan Lobby.

As soon as he arrived in Tokyo, Pakenham resumed contact with his prewar Japanese friends, many of them purged from political life for their prewar and wartime political activities. In dispatches to Kern, Pakenham told of his visits to such notables as Count Makino Nobuaki, Prime Minister Yoshida Shigeru's father-in-law and one of the emperor's most intimate confidants; Admiral Suzuki Kantaro, prime minister at the time of surrender; Admiral Nomura Kichisaburo, Japanese ambassador in Washington before the war and leading proponent of Japanese rearmament after the war; and Matsudaira Yasumasa, master of ceremonies for the Imperial Household. These men complained to a sympathetic Pakenham that while SCAP permitted Japanese Communists to return to public life, their own past records were being misjudged and misinterpreted. The initial enthusiasm for the Occupation by the Japanese people, they told Pakenham, was being dissipated by too far-reaching reform programs administered by leftist zealots. "Between ourselves," Pakenham wrote Kern on 24 July 1946, "there is no question but that the occupation here is failing, failing, failing."[4]

Kern's decision to follow up on Pakenham's reports was undoubtedly encouraged, perhaps even triggered, by Averell Harriman beginning in the fall of 1946. The new secretary of commerce, still a major stockholder in *Newsweek* and whose younger brother E. Roland Harriman was on *Newsweek*'s board of directors, met frequently with Kern to discuss Japanese affairs and convey his concern that Occupation reforms impeded the rehabilitation of a self-supporting Japan as the fulcrum of an anti-Communist American policy in Asia. In any event, using Pakenham's reports, Kern charged in a *Newsweek* story of 27 January 1947 that 30,000 Japanese businessmen, "the most active, efficient, cultured, and cosmopolitan" group in Japan and disposed to cooperate with the United States against the internal and external communist

Harry F. Kern, Foreign Affairs Editor, *Newsweek* (left), with
Compton Pakenham, *Newsweek*'s Tokyo Bureau Chief, visiting a
Japanese garden near Tokyo, ca. 1950. Courtesy of Harry F. Kern.

threat, faced removal from their jobs under a new purge order.[5]

In fact, the economic purge approved by MacArthur after much delay was a
very weak measure. A part of the initial post-surrender program for creating a
democratic Japan by policies which favored "a wide distribution of income
and ownership of the means of production and trade," the economic purge
related only to persons holding key positions in 245 large companies and

automatically required less than a thousand executives to give up their positions. Even after the closing of loopholes in the law, a mere 1,535 businessmen were removed or resigned in anticipation of removal under the law. That was less than 1 percent of the 210,000 Japanese who were purged in all categories.[6] But to Kern, the immature, untrained, and impractical officers in Government Section of SCAP were responsible for a purge program that undermined American capitalist principles in Japan.

A consummate egotist whose staff was vigorously promoting a favorable press for his 1948 presidential bid, MacArthur was infuriated by the *News-week* article. He told his closest political confidant that it was a smear and a "link in the campaign which is being so assiduously pressed in the east to discredit me." The general made it clear to his subordinates that Pakenham was persona non grata. General Charles Willoughby, the ultraconservative head of the Civil Intelligence Section who became an important contact for the emerging Japan Lobby, told Pakenham that if he had written the *Newsweek* article himself, not a word would be different; nevertheless, he told the journalist to stay away from his office for awhile. In the meantime, MacArthur prepared an immediate rebuttal for *Newsweek* in which he took full responsibility for the business purge and defended the actions of his close aide, General Courtney Whitney, chief of Government Section. MacArthur insisted the Zaibatsu had been in an unholy alliance with the militarists and only their breakup could lead to the realization of the American capitalist ideal.[7]

Under the direction of Kern and Pakenham, *Newsweek* continued to assail the economic policies of the Occupation and warn of the dangers of the Japanese Communist party. Ignoring the actions and inactions of Prime Minister Yoshida and the Zaibatsu leaders, *Newsweek* hammered away at the theme that the purge of the Zaibatsu, the radicals and incompetents on Mac-Arthur's staff, and the emergence of an aggressive and left-wing Japanese labor movement were to blame for the runaway inflation and economic distress which had reached crisis proportions.[8]

Early in June 1947 Kern decided to see developments in Japan for himself. Upon arrival, his first impression was that "Tokyo as a ruin was less impressive than Berlin." Instead of piles of stone rubble forty feet high along the streets, Tokyo was flat except for several districts, largely taken over by Occupation personnel, which had escaped the air raids. But the greatest contrast between Germany and Japan for Kern "lay in the fact that Japan had maintained a government [and] had kept its territorial integrity. . . . There were enough senior statesmen and men of integrity in the Japanese structure to guide Japan toward surrender." With Pakenham's help, Kern met with many of these men and began lifelong friendships with them. He regarded them as innocent victims of the purge, "the most destructive measure ordered by the

Occupation." He was particularly appalled by the entire Zaibatsu dissolution program and the general economic chaos he attributed to it. Kern also met with many officials in SCAP, personally observing the split between the reformers, housed mainly in Government Section, and their conservative adversaries led by General Charles Willoughby. Before his departure Kern was summoned to the office of General Whitney, chief of Government Section. Seated with two colonels on either side of him, Kern listened to Whitney deliver an angry tirade about what a dangerous man Compton Pakenham was and how harmful the *Newsweek* stories were to the Occupation. At one point, as Kern recalls, Whitney said, "'Everyday we look out here over the palace grounds, and I see Pakenham there praying in front of the Nijubashi to the Emperor.' At that point I said, 'I came here to listen to your point of view, not to hear fairy tales. Good morning gentlemen.' I walked out.'"[9]

Kern returned from his two-week trip to Japan more antagonistic to MacArthur and the reformist direction of the Occupation than ever before. He wrote a cover story featuring MacArthur that appeared in *Newsweek* on 23 June 1947. Kern offered the necessary pro forma praise for the popular general's handling of military affairs in Japan and tried to disassociate him from a bristling criticism of the purge of the Zaibatsu executives and other economic programs. But as General Frayne Baker told Pakenham confidentially, "I read that piece three times last night and twice this morning. If any one looks at it objectively it is aimed at one person [MacArthur]." With the publication of that *Newsweek* story on the Occupation, the Japan Lobby under Kern's direction became in great part a conservative anti-MacArthur lobby.[10]

Dismayed by what he had seen and heard in Japan and unable to publish all the important information he had gathered, Kern took the first tentative steps towards organizing a lobby by attempting "to see a number of people in positions of responsibility and tell them what I have found out." Retired Admiral William Veazie Pratt, a special editor on naval affairs for *Newsweek* during the war and a founding member of the ACJ, provided Kern with an introduction to his one-time commander in chief, Herbert Hoover. As head of the Famine Emergency Committee, the former president was taking an active role in advising Secretary of War Robert Patterson on economic policy for Japan. At his first meeting with Hoover, Kern obtained encouragement "to continue to do everything . . . to remedy the tragic mistakes made in regard to Japan." Hoover assured Kern that there were many in Washington who agreed on the necessity for a "radically new approach" to reparations, level of industry, food relief, the business purge, and other economic problems in Japan. He urged Kern to continue his campaign in *Newsweek* and even leaked to him confidential documents on reparations policy to be used as background for further articles.[11]

The FEC-230 Fight

One of the most important men Kern contacted that summer and fall was James Lee Kauffman, also a founding member of the ACJ and in whose New York law offices the organization made its headquarters. As senior partner in a Japanese law firm before the war, Kauffman had represented virtually every major American corporation there, including General Electric, Standard Oil, Libbey-Owens-Ford, and Dillon, Read & Company.[12] He went to Japan in August 1947 to provide his clients with a firsthand view of the business situation there and offer advice on "what course they should pursue in connection with their Japanese investments." Somehow Kauffman obtained a copy of the confidential document on the program for Zaibatsu dissolution, FEC-230, which he determined to make the focus of a sweeping and vitriolic attack on the whole reformist orientation of the Occupation.[13]

FEC-230, Kauffman claimed in his report, which quickly found its way to top Washington policymakers and the Japanese Finance Ministry, imposed an economic doctrine on Japan approaching the "socialistic ideal" and, if fully implemented, would lead to economic collapse in Japan. By going beyond simply the liquidation of the top Zaibatsu holding companies and directing a breakup of large operating combines, all business, Kauffman feared, would come "under the knife of the economic quack and split into as many small units as some gentleman sitting in Tokyo may deem appropriate." The provision in FEC-230 that SCAP assist labor unions in acquiring Zaibatsu properties, coupled with progressive labor laws already on the books, particularly galled Kauffman. Japanese labor had gone "hog wild" from the benefits handed them by the "economic theorists," "radical reformers," "mediocre people," and "crackpots" within the SCAP bureaucracy. "These workers are in many aspects like children and have to be treated as such." The critical conditions in Japan, Kauffman concluded, made the conduct of American business in Japan impossible, had discouraged the Japanese, and undermined Japan's potential as America's "Far Eastern bastion" against the Communist threat.[14]

The impact of the Kauffman report on top Washington policymakers and on SCAP was staggering. Under Secretary of the Army Draper, on leave from Wall Street's Dillon, Read and a key contact for the Japan Lobby, was immediately dispatched to Tokyo on the first of his critical missions to Japan. Upon his return in October 1947, Draper confirmed the accuracy of the Kauffman report to Secretary of Defense James F. Forrestal, also a former partner in Dillon, Read. Specifically, Draper reported that the National City Bank representative in Japan "had told him that [FEC-230] was disorganizing Japanese business" and that Civil Affairs Division lawyers believed the major deconcentration of industry bill then being pushed by Government Section through the Diet was "possibly in conflict with the Japanese Constitution." Moreover, after his own reading of the paper, he "disapproved of the preference granted trade unions and cooperatives as purchasers of divested Zaibatsu shares." The State and Army departments accepted Draper's revision of the deconcentration bill and "the need for carrying out the Zaibatsu program in such a way as to promote rather than hinder Japanese recovery."[15]

But General MacArthur, convinced of a conspiracy against his presidential bid, aroused the Army Department's worst fears by refusing to delay or revise the deconcentration of industry bill which had reached the final stages of passage in the Diet. Unquestionably, MacArthur's defiance was reinforced by Colonel Charles L. Kades, deputy chief of Government Section, leader of SCAP's trustbusters, and the Japan Lobby's most vocal critic. Kades prepared a point by point refutation of the Kauffman report and concluded that Kauffman's activities

stemmed from a desire to defend vested interest of his Japanese and American clientele against the application of [official Occupation policy]—possibly to lay the groundwork for a much larger Japanese clientele in the post-treaty period. Having no recourse to legal action, he apparently seeks to lobby his way to the end sought, and in so doing . . . has no slightest regard for the truth. He and others who . . . seek to preserve in Japan those very institutions, influences and practices which brought on the war [give] the American people a wholly distorted and false view of the occupation and . . . jeopardize primary American interests.[16]

MacArthur himself radioed Washington a lengthy defense of FEC-230, contending that opposition from the Zaibatsu (the advocates of "socialism in private hands") as well as the Communists proved the fundamental soundness of the program.[17] In so doing, MacArthur set the stage for a major showdown between top Washington policymakers and the emerging Japan Lobby, on the one hand, and SCAP, on the other hand.

Defense Secretary Forrestal took the lead in Washington in sounding the alarm that economic affairs in Japan must be given the highest priority. "The program, as outlined in that letter by [James Lee Kauffman]," Forrestal wrote Secretary of the Army Kenneth C. Royall, "indicates a degree of socialization in Japan which would make it totally impossible for the country's economy to function." Forrestal demanded and received the outlines for a new American policy that would put Japan on an economically self-sustaining basis within four to five years. Drawing upon a growing consensus in Washington that the economic rehabilitation of Japan was critical to American policy in Asia, especially in light of the collapse of the Nationalists in China, and that the reform program interfered with that objective, the Army Department concluded in mid-November that existing directives to SCAP, such as FEC-230, henceforth were to be "interpreted and implemented by the appropriate shift of emphasis so as to facilitate the early revival of the Japanese economy."[18] In short, key Washington policymakers, already inclined to regard the reforms of the Occupation as too far-reaching or a mistake, were prompted by the Japan Lobby to take the initiative in formally developing a new "reverse course" policy for Japan and getting MacArthur to carry out the new directives.

The emerging Japan Lobby played a crucial role in pressuring SCAP into line with the new policy. Throughout the fall Kern met with Washington officials. In addition he held "casual conversations" on the need for a formal lobby organization with Kauffman, Admiral Pratt, John L. Curtis (vice-president of First National City Bank and head of City Bank's Japan operation before the war), and Dooman, Ambassador Grew's counselor in the American embassy in Tokyo. The ideas discussed in these conversations were regularly communicated to Grew, the aristocratic leader of the State Department's "Japan Crowd," and former Under Secretary of State William R. Castle. Thus, when Kern decided to publish *Newsweek*'s controversial 1 December 1947 issue, he surely was not acting hastily or alone. The magazine featured portions of the still classified FEC-230 document, excerpts from the Kauffman report under the title, "A Lawyer's Report on Japan Attacks Plan to Run Occupation. . . . Far to the Left of Anything Now Tolerated in America," and a leak that the State Department had ordered the suspension of FEC-230.[19] The *Newsweek* stories were clearly meant to embarrass MacArthur into submission to Washington's views and to bolster Japanese opposition to the pending SCAP sponsored deconcentration bill.

MacArthur, however, remained adamant, pushing the Japanese Diet into passage of the legislation. Even after Senator William F. Knowland, who had been contacted by Kern, attacked FEC-230 on the floor of Congress and top-level administration figures had made public statements that the Zaibatsu dissolution program needed revision in light of changed world conditions, MacArthur stepped up a campaign to enforce the new law. In February 1948, he designated 325 companies representing 75 percent of Japanese industry as "excessive concentrations of economic power" and argued that their dissolution was central to displacing feudalism and militarism on the right and avoiding revolutionary violence on the left.[20]

Such stubborn and tenacious resistance in Tokyo to Washington's urgent pleas prompted the dispatch of two high-level missions to Japan in March 1948. The leaders of both missions were in regular contact with members of the Japan Lobby and were deeply influenced by them. Kennan was the first representative from the State Department to visit MacArthur. Throughout the fall and winter Kennan had devoted considerable time to Japan problems and frequently consulted with "leading outside experts," including Grew, Dooman, and Joseph Ballantine, former head of the Far Eastern Division of the State Department.[21] In language similar to the Kauffman report, which he no doubt had read, Kennan argued that FEC 230 would lead to "economic disaster, inflation, unbalanced budgets, resulting in near anarchy, which would be precisely what the Communists want." He told MacArthur not to feel bound by the Potsdam Declaration, which "made no provision for the security of the Japanese islands from aggression, overt or concealed, from outside." In short, Kennan impressed MacArthur with the broad views of the Japan Lobby and Washington policymakers that economic "recovery should be made the prime objective of United States policy in Japan" and that, therefore, SCAP "should be authorized not to press upon the Japanese Government any further reform legislation. As for reform measures already taken . . . SCAP should be authorized steadily but unobtrusively to relax pressure on the Japanese Government."[22]

To further underscore changed American policy and reorient MacArthur, Kennan was followed to Japan by Draper and a mission of five representatives from America's most powerful corporations led by Percy Johnston of Chemical Bank of New York. Though Draper knew very little about Japan, he was sympathetic to the Japan Lobby. He leaked confidential information for Kern to use in *Newsweek* and assisted Kern's efforts to establish contacts within the Army Department.[23]

Not surprisingly, Draper and the members of his mission made it known to SCAP that the reform phase of the Occupation had ended and that further dissolution of the Zaibatsu would hamper the realization of a self-supporting Japan as the foundation upon which the United States sought to build its policies in the Pacific. Even before the release of the Johnston report on 26 April 1948, it was clear that the condition for a multimillion dollar American aid program to achieve economic recovery in Japan and the integration of Japan into the world capitalist system was the abandonment of the dissolution of the Zaibatsu and the removal of all restraints imposed by the Occupation in the name of reform.[24] In short, the settlement of the FEC-230 controversy in which Kern, Kauffman, and Pakenham, the three leading figures of the Japan Lobby, had played crucial roles, resolved the ambiguities of early American Occupation policy in favor of an economic recovery program that entailed a sharp turn to the right in social and political policy.

Launching the American Council on Japan

By early 1948 Washington had altered its Occupation policies and pressured MacArthur into accepting them. Yet the implementation of programs in Japan to stem inflation, boost production, expand exports, reduce dependency on American aid, and achieve social and political stability faltered. Alarmed by these developments and buoyed by the successful outcome of the FEC-230 controversy, Harry F. Kern determined to build the lobby organization that he had been informally discussing for six months with Dooman, Pakenham, Curtis, Admiral Pratt, Grew, and Castle.

Kern drew up an outline for a formal organization and wrote twenty-one people outside of the core group to explore the extent of interest in the proposed lobby. Among the most important men on the list were leading figures from the business community: Philo Parker, chairman of the board of Socony-Vacuum Co.; Paulino Gerli, president of E. Gerli and Co., one of the largest importers of Japanese silk before the war; and Clifford Strike, president of McGraw Engineers and author of the controversial Strike report of February 1947 which revised American reparations policy for Japan. In addition, Kern contacted old State Department hand Joseph Ballantine, Admiral Ernest J. King, Harvard art curator Langdon Warner, and journalist Hanson Baldwin.[25]

Virtually every reply to Kern's circular letter expressed interest and some degree of approval for the proposed organization, though many would decline formal membership. Kern was particularly relieved that no one thought the organization might "lay itself open to the charge, however unjustified, of being pro-Japanese"—a charge constantly made at the close of the war against Grew and Dooman for their "soft peace" views. Some feared that the Japan Society and older groups would view a new organization as an unwelcome rival. But, in general, all the respondents applauded a new organization which would devote its primary attention "to fostering mutual trade" between Japan and the United States and which "stressed the necessity for a healthy, prosperous Japan simply as a matter of common sense strategy in the present situation existing between the United States and Russia."[26]

Kern, Kauffman, Pakenham, and Dooman constituted themselves as the Organizing Committee of the American Council on Japan. They drafted a constitution embodying the objectives of the group, created a committee structure with a strong executive, and established tentative policies on membership, dues, and meetings. At the Harvard Club in New York City on 28 June 1948, eighteen founding members of the American Council on Japan elected Grew and Castle as honorary cochairmen and Kern as chairman of the Organizing Committee.[27]

The interlocks between members of the ACJ and a host of American business groups, quasi-official policy-making bodies, and the highest circles within the national government gave credence to Kern's first public announcement that the purpose of the new organization was to inform the American public and assist the Truman administration in "solving those problems that must be solved if victory [in Japan] is to be assured."[28] Grew and Castle, as honorary cochairmen of the ACJ, symbolized the continuity of the Japan Lobby with the prewar advocates of American cooperation with Japan who favored moderating the Chinese revolution, containing the Bolsheviks in Russia, and keeping the Far East open to American goods, investments, and liberal democracy. The prominence in the ACJ of Kern, Pakenham, and Kauffman, who had so successfully deployed their corporate and political influence in the FEC-230 struggle, highlighted the conservative thrust the Japan Lobby would attempt to give to the Occupation. The organizational affiliations of other active ACJ members enhanced the prestige and authority of the whole group. Dooman served as a Japan expert on the Council of Foreign Relations. Clarence E. Meyer, a vice-president and director of Standard Oil and a close friend of Grew while stationed in Japan, linked the ACJ to the National Foreign Trade Council. Antonin Raymond, a pioneer modern architect in Japan, proved to be an important channel between the ACJ and the American Chamber of Commerce of Japan. Joseph Ballantine provided a tie between the ACJ and the Brookings Institution where he was an associate and regular consultant on Japan problems for the State and Army departments.[29]

The Japan Lobby's network of Japanese friends added to the strength of the ACJ among Washington policymakers. Proscribed from maintaining representatives in the United States, postwar Japanese government officials and their principal backers among the bankers and industrialists sought ways of circumventing the reform-oriented supreme commander in order to appeal to potential allies in the United States. One channel of communication was kept open by Lieutenant General Robert L. Eichelberger, a close associate of the Japan Lobby who became increasingly antagonistic towards MacArthur after 1947. As commander of the Eighth Army until the summer of 1948 and with headquarters in Yokohama, Eichelberger enjoyed a degree of autonomy from SCAP and was able to communicate directly with the War Department. Prime Minister Yoshida, a foe of most of the political and economic reforms of the Occupation, Foreign Minister Ashida Hitoshi, and Suzuki Tadakatsu, director of the powerful Central Liaison Agency, were on friendly terms with Eichelberger and eagerly availed themselves of his advice and assistance.[30]

Journalists like Harry Kern and Compton Pakenham, who frequently traveled between Japan and the United States, provided the Japanese with another means of overcoming the communication obstacle thrown up by MacArthur's tight rule in Japan. Even before the formation of the ACJ, Tokyo-based Pakenham linked his Japanese friends to Kern at *Newsweek* and through Kern to high corporate and governmental figures in the United States. Always careful to protect the identity of his Japanese sources in his dispatches and letters,

Pakenham was a regular visitor with high officials of the Imperial Palace, the Ministry of Finance, the Foreign Ministry, the National Rural Police, and, no doubt, many others.[31]

One of the Japan Lobby's most valued Japanese friends was Nomura Kichisaburo, a former admiral and foreign minister, and ambassador to the United States at the time of the attack upon Pearl Harbor. Nomura's goodwill was actively solicited by ACJ members throughout the Occupation. Following Nomura's purge in August 1946, Compton Pakenham arranged for regular (and illicit) gifts of food and cigarettes to the financially hard-pressed purgee. William R. Castle reopened a correspondence with Nomura by proclaiming that he would be "one of those who will help to rebuild Japan in the way which will make it, in the right way, an important nation once more." On each of his visits to Japan, Harry Kern entertained Nomura. And Admiral William V. Pratt, Nomura's closest American friend, kept his naval companion abreast of ACJ activities.[32]

Despite Nomura's temporary purge status, his continued importance to Japanese-American relations was well understood by the ACJ. On the Japanese side, Nomura provided a focus of activities for former officers of the Imperial Navy, including service as advisor or president of the major right-wing nationalist rearmament organizations; he was the "senior advisor and spiritual father" of the program for a new Japanese navy outside the mis-named Naval Demobilization Organization; he was a close friend of Ashida Hitoshi, a postwar foreign minister and prime minister well-known for his opposition to the no-war clause of the Japanese constitution; and, through Admiral Yamanashi Katsunoshin, Nomura had easy access to Prime Minister Yoshida Shigeru. On the American side, Nomura was in regular communication with such high-ranking officials as Admirals Arleigh Burke and Turner Joy and Special Ambassador John Foster Dulles.[33] These and many other contacts were begun or furthered with the assistance of the ACJ. To Nomura the ACJ was useful to his efforts to restore the Japanese naval establishment and for articulating to the American public and Washington the concerns of the so-called "moderates" within Japan's old ruling circles who felt the initial post-surrender plans threatened their position.

The ACJ got off to a slow start and never became the cohesive organization its founders had envisioned. Kern hoped to begin a profit-making monthly magazine to disseminate the lobby's views and finance its operations, but no such magazine appeared. Instead, Kern used the international pages of *Newsweek* as an unofficial organ of the ACJ and financed the organization from the small membership dues. Nor were the Japan Lobby approaches to high echelon policymakers as easy or rewarding as initially anticipated. Kern, Kauffman, and Dooman, the chief workhorses of the ACJ, consistently underestimated the risks involved for someone with official dealings with General MacArthur to be identified with the Japan Lobby. MacArthur had been terribly humiliated by the FEC-230 fight of 1947–48 and the resulting limitations on his discretionary authority as supreme commander. Characteristically, the general never forgave those who had been responsible or those whom he suspected of being in sympathy with them. Before his staff, MacArthur attacked Kern as an "unethical reporter and a reactionary," called Pakenham a "British Fascist," and denounced the ACJ as "unfair" to the Occupation.[34] He even had aides keep close watch on the activities of the ACJ.[35] By the fall of 1948 Kern became convinced that the ACJ should be a small organization which would be most effective by discreet approaches to those policymakers responsible for the Occupation.

In Lieutenant General Robert L. Eichelberger, Kern found an ideal person for carrying out his revised conception of the ACJ. A tough talking, ultraconservative geopolitician, Eichelberger retired from his Eighth Army command in the summer of 1948 and returned home to become the first and foremost public proponent of Japanese rearmament. At a luncheon meeting called by the ACJ in New York for executives from Westinghouse, Standard Oil, General Electric, and other firms with large investment interests in Japan, Eichelberger explained that a large army in Japan "would force the Russians to consider the possibility of a two-front war. . . . A rearmed Japan would doubtless act as a powerful deterrent to Soviet expansion in the West . . . and Far East." To his highly impressed audience, Eichelberger also criticized the early reform program for eliminating valuable Japanese in business and politics and fostering a strong internal Communist movement.[36]

Ecstatic over the success of Eichelberger's speech, Kern decided to use the general more often on behalf of the ACJ. Kern arranged a meeting between Eichelberger and the editors of *Newsweek* who offered the pages of the magazine for the dissemination of his views. Most importantly, Kern hosted a meeting at the Pentagon in February 1949 with Eichelberger and retiring Under Secretary of the Army Draper. Draper agreed to have Eichelberger hired as a consultant on Japan in the office of the new Assistant Secretary of the Army Tracy Voorhees. Though Occupied Japan was a direct responsibility of his office, Voorhees confessed to knowing almost nothing about the Far East and to having spent the bulk of his time on German matters. In the year Voorhees served first as assistant and then under secretary of the army he gained the highest respect for Eichelberger's broad knowledge of Japan and found his assistance "indispensable."[37] At the same time Eichelberger, who owed his job, in part, to the efforts of Kern, repaid the favor by serving as a principal liaison between the ACJ and top Washington officials.

While Kern was assisting Eichelberger at the Army Department, he also wrote an outline of the philosophy and policy recommendations of the ACJ. In a paper entitled, "American Policy toward Japan," Kern renewed charges that both the public and policymakers labored under the illusion that the Occupation was a magnificent success. In a vital area of economic recovery, Kern contended, the Occupation was failing miserably. Kern conceded that there were immense natural barriers to economic rehabilitation, but the major problem was that the Occupation had imposed on Japan "a set of social and economic reforms more embracing and immediate than those of the Russian Revolution." To be sure, since the FEC-230 crisis Japan policy had been moving in the right direction, but economic recovery was "still handicapped by American imposed controls and reforms" which were being vigorously carried out by an Occupation bureaucracy "not so very different from the discredited militarists in its self-righteousness, invincible ignorance, and occasional corruption."[38]

To solve these problems, the ACJ report made numerous recommendations, the prime target of which was the SCAP bureaucracy. Occupation personnel should be reduced; the reform-oriented Government Section should be abolished; and the State Department should make plans to take over Occupation authority from the Army Department (a proposal particularly galling to MacArthur, whose post as supreme commander would thereby be eliminated). Complementing these proposals were ones designed to give greater responsibility to court officials and Japanese business and political leaders who had fallen under the early purge orders. Thus the ACJ recommended the creation of a Purge Appeals Board under an agency independent of SCAP. It would "depurge" the prewar elites and allow the Japanese to "develop their own political institution and . . . deal with the Communists in their own way."[39]

The most detailed recommendations of the ACJ concerned the importance of American private investment in programs for the economic recovery of Japan. A uniform and fixed exchange rate for the yen was a prerequisite to the expansion of Japanese exports and foreign investments so necessary if Japan were to become self-supporting. To further encourage investment the ACJ called upon Washington to guarantee the principal and interest on loans to Japanese industry, to revise tax liability laws to allow American corporations to repossess their Japanese properties written off during the war, and to put pressure on the Japanese government to repeal or amend Japanese tax, patent, and antitrust legislation inimical to foreign investors. In the area of tax law the ACJ followed up its recommendations with a survey of business opinion and openly lobbied for a revision of American policy.[40]

Finally, the ACJ recommended changes in American military policy for Japan. The American army should be concentrated into combat units designed to repel invasion and to strike anywhere in Japan. The number of army dependents should be reduced as quickly as possible. Most importantly, the Japanese should be permitted a "well-armed and well-trained constabulary of at least 150,000 men . . . entrusted with guarding tunnels, bridges, and similar installations" against internal revolutionary sabotage. Only as a last resort should Japan "be permitted otherwise to revise its armed forces."[41]

Throughout the early months of 1949, Kern, Kauffman, and others propounded the Japan Lobby's view before powerful business forums, the national press, and within the government. Kern read portions of his report at a dinner meeting of the United States Chamber of Commerce. Kauffman spoke in New York on Japanese problems before the Bankers Club and the Export Managers Club. Kern prepared a full page report in *Newsweek* on "What's Wrong in Japan?" which contained renewed attacks on the business purge, reparations, and inexperienced Occupation personnel. The ACJ was also probably behind the publication of "A Two Billion Dollar Failure in Japan," an article in the prestigious *Fortune* magazine, or so the Japan Lobby antagonists believed.[42] Even before the approval of his report by the ACJ membership, Kern gave careful attention to reaching government officials. He arranged for Joseph Dodge, ultraconservative president of the Detroit Bank and newly appointed financial advisor to SCAP, to get a draft copy. Dodge, who held almost dictatorial power over the Japanese economy in 1949 and early 1950, gave Kern's report a close reading and required his five top aides to read it as well.[43]

Most important, Kern and the ACJ hosted a dinner party at the Willard Hotel on 16 February 1949 for twelve of the highest ranking State and Army department officials concerned with Japan. Kern and Kauffman made long comments on the inappropriateness of SCAP's organization and condemned its personnel and policies. They reiterated the recommendations in the ACJ report on Japan for the dissolution of SCAP and the substitution of a civilian advisory agency and the scrapping of the reform policies already carried into effect or about to be implemented. With great verve and pride Kern related his June 1947 confrontation with General Whitney and said he would brook no further criticism of Pakenham. Kauffman also made a plea for more loans to Japan guaranteed by the U.S. government. Army Department officials seemed offended at the ACJ's criticisms of the Occupation though, in fact, they agreed with most of them and had assisted Kern in organizing the dinner meeting. General Draper, for example, said that the major impediment to the restoration of Japan as a "bulwark of stability of great potential economic and political value to the United States was not Army Department or SCAP interference in Japanese affairs." Rather, the Japanese had been "permitted to try to rehabilitate their own economy but with the passage of time it has become evident that their own governments were not strong enough to achieve this end." Even General Eichelberger, who had helped Kern circulate the ACJ report at the Pentagon, complained that Kern and Kauffman had gone too far in describing the Occupation as a failure and said he "could point to many reasons for regarding it as a great success."[44]

State Department officials were sharply divided in response to the ACJ's position on Japan. Assistant Secretary Charles Saltzman admitted that "mistakes had been made" in Japan "which needed critical exploration by experts" but he took issue with the ACJ proposal to replace SCAP before the conclusion of a peace treaty. Saltzman's chief assistant, Philander Claxton, so vigorously assailed the American Council that, according to one account, both Dooman and Ballantine lost their tempers and shouted that Claxton "had always been against the Emperor and the 'better people' in Japan, the only ones who could be 'completely trusted.' "[45] But to the applause of the ACJ members, W. Walton Butterworth, director of the Office of Far Eastern Affairs, invited the ACJ "to continue badgering the State Department and other agencies of the U.S. Government insisting, if it desired, that SCAP be reduced, and that SCAP's intervention in the conduct of affairs by the Japanese be minimized so long as a self-denying program of that sort did not jeopardize our strategic interests." By the end of the meeting the sharp disagreements among the participants were buried in the recognition of the common objectives of the Japan Lobby and Washington policymakers. ACJ members were encouraged to continue studies of Japanese problems, "to develop a more widespread interest in Japan among the American people," to bring more Japanese to the United States, and to follow up on various other suggestions "which involved enlarging relationships between Japan and the U.S."[46]

The official basis for so amicable a conclusion to the ACJ dinner was the close parallel between the ACJ report and National Security Council (NSC) document 13/2 of October 1948 for which George F. Kennan was largely responsible: "Japan was to be strengthened economically and socially. . . . SCAP was to shift responsibilities to the Japanese, and SCAP personnel would be reduced; a 150,000 man national police force was to be organized."[47] In drafting NSC 13/2, Kennan appears to have been strongly influenced by Eichelberger, Grew, Ballantine, and other members of the Japan Lobby. In any case, so intertwined had the Japan Lobby become in official policymaking by 1949 that Kern should not have been surprised by the rather indifferent reaction of government leaders to the substance of the ACJ report. As Deputy Under Secretary of the Army Robert West assured Kern, his recommendations differed only in "some particulars" from NSC 13/2.[48]

The most unique aspect of the ACJ report, as the ACJ dinner made clear, was its attack on Washington's commitment to carry out the new policies for

Japan through the existing SCAP bureaucracy. The Truman administration believed it could implement NSC 13/2 without a political confrontation with MacArthur by appointments of advisors like Dodge and guidelines which would shift power within the SCAP bureaucracy away from Government Section towards the more conservative Economic and Scientific Section (ESS). Kern, on the other hand, believed as long as MacArthur remained supreme commander, he and his close aides would attempt to foil Washington policies. In Kern's view, SCAP remained wedded to the misguided notion that the Imperial Household and Zaibatsu leaders, as well as military officers, were war criminals and that early Occupation reforms should not be scrapped. By arousing public criticism against MacArthur's handling of economic affairs in Japan, the Japan Lobby hoped, at best, to hasten the restoration to power of the old ruling elites in Japan and displace the SCAP bureaucracy. At worst, the ACJ sought to undermine SCAP's ability to evade or defy Washington's policies which the Japan Lobby was helping to shape.

The Japanese Peace Treaty

The questions of timing, procedure, and the nature of a formal Japanese peace treaty and a final American position on post-treaty military security matters were explicitly left open in NSC 13/2. In the short run, primary emphasis was given to economic recovery policy. But prompted by the complete collapse of Nationalist China and pressured by wartime allies to clarify its policies, Washington reexamined the American role in Asia, particularly Japanese relations, during the fall of 1949. The obvious flux in American policy stimulated the directors of the ACJ to resolve to "advise and assist the State Department in the preparation of a peace treaty for Japan."[49] Virtually every member of the Japan Lobby participated during the next two years in the discussions and negotiations involved in the peace treaty.

Perhaps the informal debate between Joseph Ballantine and Owen Lattimore at the State Department's famous Roundtable Discussion of October 1949 best highlights the perspective of the Japan Lobby on the peace treaty and the dilemma of American policy in Asia. Ballantine, a founding member of the ACJ, argued that a treaty with Japan must not simply end the Occupation but must express America's ultimate objectives for Japan's role in the Far East. "We want a Japan that is going to be on our side," he told the large group of distinguished participants, even if the Russians and the Chinese Communists, at the very least, would not participate in a peace treaty conference that would ally Japan with the United States.[50]

Owen Lattimore, Oriental scholar, State Department consultant, and long an antagonist of the Japan Lobby, offered a trenchant critique of Ballantine's position. A post-treaty Japan "on our side" would not have normalized diplomatic and economic relations with Russia or China even though China was Japan's natural trading partner. Without the freedom to negotiate its own trading terms with Communist China, Japan would be forced to depend on continual "economic blood transfusions" from the United States and to rely upon Southeast Asian markets of doubtful stability. Instead of a unilateral treaty which would represent "a dangerous commitment of enormous American resources in a distant part of the world," Lattimore favored a multilateral peace conference that would allow Japan to negotiate its own terms with the Russians and Chinese and would lead to a closing of American bases in Japan.[51]

Under the guidance of George F. Kennan, the NSC attempted to reconcile these conflicting perspectives on post-treaty Japan in NSC 48/1 of December 1949. Seemingly rejecting the bipolar position of the Japan Lobby, the document proposed American support for a regime in Japan which would "maintain normal political and economic relations with the Communist bloc and, in the absence of open hostilities, resist complete identification either with the interest of the United States or the Soviet Union." But somewhat contradictorily, NSC 48/1 also stated that "a middle-of-the-road regime retaining the spirit of the reform program, even if not necessarily the letter, would in the long-run prove more reliable as an ally of the United States than would an extreme right-wing totalitarian government."[52] In any event, NSC 48/1 was vigorously opposed by Defense Department officials who distrusted both the Russians and the Japanese. They preferred an indefinite perpetuation of the Occupation to insure American preeminence in and control of Japan and succeeded in delaying any movement for a peace treaty conference with or without the participation of the Russians.[53]

The vacillation in Washington's handling of the Asian crisis, coupled with sharp criticism from large and articulate sectors of the Japanese populace and Far Eastern allies over any peace treaty designed to win Japan as an American ally in the Cold War, greatly alarmed the Japan Lobby. Compton Pakenham filed a report to Kern that his Japanese friends were very upset that Russia's offer to participate in a multilateral peace conference, while holding out the bait of a return of the Kurile Islands to Japan, was creating a very favorable response within Japan. Kern himself had concluded that it was both desirable and urgent to press for the early conclusion of a treaty of peace with Japan regardless of the objections of the Russians. Delay meant the Russians "would run away with the ball. I don't think there is any serious intention in the State Department in resisting communism in the Far East," Kern wrote Admiral Pratt in April 1950. "The peace treaty is being interminably redrafted. Meanwhile the situation in Japan is rapidly deteriorating."[54]

To help resolve the internal controversy which wracked Washington in the months prior to the Korean War, Kern produced a four-page position paper, approved by the ACJ, on the Japanese peace treaty and met with high State and Defense department officials about it. Although the containment of China was not explicit at this time, Kern's conception of a Japanese peace treaty rested on the assumption that Japan would have to find raw material resources and trade outlets to replace China in other Asiatic countries. Concomitantly, the United States would have to bolster the military defenses of Japan and Southeast Asian nations and encourage a Pacific pact similar to the North Atlantic Treaty Organization.

Given these critical assumptions, and fully recognizing that neither the Russians nor the Chinese Communists would find them acceptable, Kern proposed a Japanese peace treaty involving four major, interrelated areas. First, for purposes of external security, the peace treaty required "some provisions by which American Armed Forces will remain in Japan." Moreover, American policy should "consider measures for re-arming Japan and using Japanese fighting manpower" in a possible war with the Russians. Second, before calling a peace conference, the United States should "encourage the establishment of a unified, efficient, and well-armed constabulary, as well as coast guard" to deal with internal Communist subversion. Third, under any peace treaty, the Japanese should be given the right to repeal and revise legislation passed by the Occupation forces. Such terms would allow the repeal of SCAP sponsored reforms, particularly the purge. Finally, the peace treaty must insure that Japan be economically self-sufficient and the workshop of the Far East. The key to the success of this effort would be the stimulation provided by private American investments and loans. In negotiations of the peace treaty, the United States must encourage the Japanese to guarantee private property from expropriation, to allow repatriation of earnings, and generally to create a favorable climate for foreign investment.[55]

To what extent, if at all, Kern's ideas on a peace treaty with Japan influenced John Foster Dulles is uncertain. Appointed in May 1950 in a gesture of bipartisanship by President Truman as a special ambassador to conclude a peace and military settlement with Japan, Dulles did share Kern's conception of the treaty. Both men rejected the sanguine, middle-of-the-road approach of the National Security Council. The principal aim of any peace agreement with the Japanese, Dulles wrote Truman shortly after his appointment, would be to bring Japan into the Western bloc.[56]

Dulles soon developed close ties with the Japan Lobby in the difficult task of implementing American policy. To discuss his new assignment with General MacArthur and sound out the Japanese, he proceeded to Tokyo in mid-

June. Travelling on the same plane with the Dulles party was Kern. The journalist proposed that the ambassador break off his heavy schedule of meetings for an unofficial dinner meeting at Pakenham's residence with a few "well-informed" Japanese. Much to Kern's delight, Dulles later accepted the invitation. In so doing, Dulles highlighted what was to be the Japan Lobby's most important contribution to the peace treaty—bridging the wide gulf between American peace treaty objectives, particularly retention of American bases and Japanese rearmament, and what was politically acceptable to the Japanese governing class which was well aware of the nearly universal sentiment for an "overall peace" that would leave sovereign Japan a demilitarized and neutral power.[57]

Among the "well-informed" Japanese attending the 22 June 1950 private dinner Kern and Pakenham arranged for Dulles and John Allison, head of the Northeast Asia Bureau of the State Department, were Watanabe Takeshi of the Ministry of Finance; Matsudaira Yasumasa, member of the Imperial Household; Kaihara Osamu, chief of planning for the National Rural Police; and Sawada Renzo of the Foreign Ministry. Dulles emphasized the critical role of Japan in the global struggle with the Russians. At one time he had thought China essential to the economic viability of Japan. But he now thought that alternative markets for Japanese exports were available in the United States and Southeast Asia even if the future of Southeast Asia was a "big problem." Conversation then swung to the threat of communism in Japan and the successful prewar role of the emperor and a centralized police force as an anti-Communist bulwark. Dulles, however, expressed no sympathy with Kern's suggestion for a relaxation of the purge, perhaps holding that as bait to win the cooperation of the Japanese elites for his peace and military proposals. In any case, Dulles encouraged Kern and Pakenham to keep him in contact with Japanese opinion on his work.[58]

While Dulles and Kern were still in Japan, the Korean War opened. The war did not change American policy toward Japan so much as undercut Japanese opposition to it. Even before the outbreak of war, the Yoshida cabinet, with SCAP encouragement, had taken strong measures to silence the Left and other opponents of American peace plans for Japan. A Red Purge began in the public sector at the end of 1949 and was virtually completed before 25 June 1950; the Central Committee of the JCP was purged on 6 June 1950 and forced underground. After the war in Korea began, the Left and peace forces in Japan suffered crippling blows. The Red Purge was diverted to the private sector and by the end of 1950 approximately 22,000 public and private employees had been fired during the campaign. Student organizations were raided by police, leftist labor unions were stifled, and more newspapers were suspended.[59]

Dulles and Kern observed how the Korean War increased Japan's economic and strategic dependency on the United States. As SCAP gradually relinquished control to the conservative Japanese government and thousands were depurged, "special procurements" from the United States for the war effort in Korea resulted in an unequivocal militarization of the Japanese economy. In addition, under the guise of the National Police Reserve (NPR), the Japanese took the first steps toward creating a new Japanese army. By the end of the Occupation, 75,000 well-paid NPR recruits, led by former imperial captains, majors, and lieutenant colonels and directed by American officers, had received extensive training with tanks and other increasingly diverse and large caliber weapons.[60] As Dulles remarked, perhaps with exaggeration, the "problem of keeping Japan within the orbit of the free world [was] possible of solution only because of Korea. . . ."[61]

Throughout the year that Dulles torturously negotiated the Japanese peace treaty, he met and corresponded with Kern. In turn, Kern provided him with the views of the Japan Lobby and the Japanese elite and wrote helpful articles in *Newsweek* as well. No doubt Kern's greatest triumph was to link Dulles (and Averell Harriman) with Emperor Hirohito. "The Japanese do seem to consider us [the ACJ] a reliable and discreet channel," Kern explained to Dulles in forwarding what purportedly was the emperor's message, "and there is also, I am sure from the Japanese point of view, the consideration that by employing such an unofficial channel, they can, if they choose, deny everything at any time."[62] Not surprisingly, the emperor's principal themes, as filtered through one or more intermediaries, coincided with the policy views of Dulles and the Japan Lobby.

It has always been His Majesty's hope that Americans in authority visiting Japan for inspection and survey purposes should be allowed to discuss matters openly and frankly with prominent Japanese on their own comparative level. He is most gratified that a precedent in this regard has been set on the initiative of Mr. Dulles. So far as he knows this is a unique case.

He regrets that until this occasion irresponsible and unrepresentative advisers have generally been consulted. These usually give advice in accordance with what they consider Americans wish to hear. The reason for this is that these men feared they might be penalized for expressing opinions contrary to those held by Americans consulting them. . . .

It may be said that in the past Japan has suffered at the hands of ill-intentioned Japanese no less than has America and it is feared that occupation authorities, particular[ly] on middle and lower levels, have allowed themselves to accept the advice of such so that many misunderstandings have arisen.

In this regard he feels that the action which would have the most beneficial effect on the interests of both America and Japan and do most to foster goodwill would be the relaxation of the purge. . . . There are many people, now silent, whose opinions if openly expressed would have the profoundest effect on the public mind.

It may be said that had such men been in a position to express their thoughts publicly, the recent mistaken controversy over the matter of bases could have been avoided through a voluntary offer on the part of Japan.[63]

The most sensitive problem for Dulles in his negotiations with the Japanese was over the question of Japanese rearmament, and as earlier, the Japan Lobby attempted to be helpful. While Dulles privately and repeatedly urged Prime Minister Yoshida to create a force of 300,000 to 350,000 men, Kern sponsored numerous articles in *Newsweek* calling for the revision of the "no-war" Article 9 of the constitution and immediate rearmament. As Yoshida continued to resist pressures from Dulles for a rapid military buildup, Kern advised Dulles to let the Japanese have the "fun of doing a little bargaining. Heaven knows they have had small enough opportunity for bargaining during the last five years on anything from running their railroads to . . . cultivating sweet potatoes."[64] Even without deploying an army in Korea, Kern told Dulles, the Japanese were being very helpful in the war effort. He asked Dulles to assist Toshiba, "the GE of Japan," to win contracts for electrical equipment to be used in Korea. He also conveyed to Dulles a message from William Castle that Japanese intelligence agents, who formerly operated in China, could be recruited by the United States—a program which, in fact, was underway.[65]

The Japan Lobby also contributed to Dulles's careful effort to avoid any serious controversy in the public and Senate debates over the peace and security treaties. Openly joining hands with the China Lobby, Kern, Dooman, Ballantine, and Kauffman exploited the anti-Communist hysteria of the early 1950s to disarm any potential critics of the treaties and take out long sought revenge against old enemies as well. In a variety of forums they charged that the State Department's so-called "China Crowd" was not only responsible for the American defeat in China, but had almost succeeded in effecting a "quiet version of national revolution" in Japan. Before the McCarren Committee investigating the Institute of Pacific Relations in the fall of 1951, Dooman repeatedly contended that Dean Acheson, John Carter Vincent, and Owen Lattimore had laid the basis for programs in Japan similar to those in Russian occupied Eastern Europe: a capital tax levy of up to 90 percent, expropriation of land in excess of five acres, the purge of practically "the whole executive branch of Japanese business," and, once again, FEC-230, "in which all of the principles are laid out for atomizing Japanese industry."[66]

The peace treaty, signed by forty-nine nations at San Francisco in September 1951, formally ratified what Dulles had already achieved in bilateral negotiations. Though widely acclaimed as an example of American magnanimity, the peace treaty was tailored to America's needs and interest. It was essentially a peace without Asians. The three major continental countries of Asia—China, India, and Russia—did not sign the treaty. Australia, New Zealand, and the Philippines signed only under American pressure and after receiving assurances of separate security pacts with the United States directed against a resurgent Japan. Moreover, the peace treaty was contingent upon Japanese agreement to a military alliance with the United States which gave American forces virtual free rein in post-treaty Japan and which was premised on a rapid buildup of Japanese land and sea forces. Dulles also forced the Yoshida government to promise recognition to Jiang Jieshi's regime in Taiwan (a condition of obtaining Senate ratification of the peace treaty), even though this violated an agreement Dulles had just made with the British, who hoped that sovereign Japan would choose to normalize political relations with the People's Republic of China.[67]

Finally, before the formal end of the Occupation in March 1952, the Yoshida government summarized its future economic relationship with the United States: "Japan will contribute to the rearmament plan of the United States, supplying military goods and strategic materials by repairing and establishing defense industries with the technical and financial assistance from the United States, and thereby assure and increase a stable dollar receipt. . . . Japan will cooperate more actively with the development of Southeast Asia along the lines of the economic assistance programs of the United States."[68] In short, Japanese economic activity would be geared to United States needs in the Pacific thereby guaranteeing Japanese industrial growth and a supply of dollars to make Japan a market for American goods.

As the end of the Occupation approached, the organizational activities of the ACJ declined. Kern, Dooman, and Kauffman remained active but did not attempt to expand the membership of the ACJ. The signing of the peace treaty raised serious doubts in Kern's mind about the long-term viability of the ACJ. After a brief attempt to resuscitate the organization, the ACJ appears to have completely folded early in 1953.[69]

Epilogue

Though Kern abandoned the ACJ after the Occupation, he continued his own and *Newsweek*'s involvement in Japanese affairs. Upon assuming the directorship of the CIA in 1953, Allen Dulles sought to establish a recruiting and cover capability within America's most prestigious journalistic institutions and he quite naturally turned to *Newsweek,* among others. Agency sources told famed Watergate journalist Carl Bernstein in 1977 that the CIA engaged the services of several foreign correspondents and stringers for *Newsweek* under arrangements approved by senior editors at the magazine. Malcom Muir, *Newsweek*'s editor until 1961, admitted that Kern while foreign editor until 1956 "regularly checked in with various fellows in the CIA." The *New York Times* reported that during the 1950s *Newsweek*'s Tokyo bureau alone contained at least four CIA employees. "To the best of my knowledge," Kern told Bernstein, "nobody at *Newsweek* worked for the CIA. . . . The informal relationship was there. Why have anybody sign anything? What we knew we told them [the CIA] and the State Department. . . . When I went to Washington I would talk to Foster or Allen Dulles about what was going on. . . . We thought it was admirable at the time. We were all on the same side."[70]

Whatever his exact relationship to the CIA while at *Newsweek* and later, Kern moved in and out of Japan frequently, consulting with a succession of prime ministers and other of Japan's most prominent leaders. In 1952, if not before, Kern established a friendship with Japan's most infamous and powerful right-wing politician, Kishi Nobusuke. Despite three years in Sugamo prison as a suspected Class A War Criminal, Kishi made a remarkable political comeback within the ranks of the ruling Liberal-Democratic party, aided in some small way by Kern, Pakenham, and other Japan Lobby friends. In articles in *Newsweek* in 1955, Kern claimed Kishi "broke completely with Premier Hideki Tojo's war policy" in 1942, failing to mention that he later became vice-minister of munitions. Kern described Kishi as a democrat, "pro-American as Japanese politics permit," and the "chief hope for a more stable government" in Japan.[71] By 1956 Kishi was foreign minister, and the next year prime minister. Kern, who left *Newsweek* in 1956 to direct his own firm, Foreign Reports, advised and assisted Kishi in his relations with the United States and the Middle East. With the help of Kishi's press secretary, Kern also established in 1959 a Tokyo company with all the earmarks of an influence peddling operation called PR Japan.[72]

Using Foreign Reports and PR Japan as his base, Kern became a behind-the-scenes middleman and lobbyist for some of the most powerful interests in the United States, Japan, and the Middle East. A Kern letter to Foreign Minister Kishi in July 1956 is suggestive of Kern's business interests, particularly with four major international oil companies, after leaving *Newsweek:*

> As you know I am spending a great deal of time in the Middle East and I have set up a news and advisory organization of my own which deals primarily with that area. I enjoy especially close connections in Saudi Arabia and I count King Saud and Crown Prince Faisal as personal friends. It has long struck me that Saudi Arabia and the entire Persian Gulf area could be objects of great interest to Japan, especially as a market for Japanese goods. . . . What I would like to suggest to you is that King Saud be invited to visit Japan . . . Saudi Arabia, as is Japan, is regarded by the

United States as a firm friend. I should think it would be for the benefit of all concerned for contact to be established between Japan and Saudi Arabia. King Saud is strongly anti-Communist and I know he would appreciate meeting you and your colleagues and hearing your views.[73]

Kern's operations, by all accounts, were extraordinarily lucrative and successful. He was in regular contact with Secretary of State Dulles, CIA Director Dulles, Senator Knowland (who served as a conduit for Kern to the White House), and others on Japanese and Middle East matters.[74] As revealed in the Japanese press in 1979, Kern was suspected of having played an important part in several political scandals involving American military aircraft sales to Japan. His close relationship to Kishi in 1959 may have been a factor in the prime minister's decision to overrule the Defense agency recommendation for the purchase of the Grumman (F11F-1F) Super Tiger as the mainstay fighter for the Self Defense Force and select Lockheed (F-104) Starfighters instead.[75]

Ironically, Kern joined Grumman corporation as a consultant in Japan in 1969, an assignment no doubt awarded him because of his continuing relationship with Kishi and other top-level political and business leaders in Japan. According to a Grumman company report to the U.S. Securities and Exchange Commission, executives of Grumman learned in 1975 of the possibility that their Japanese sales company, Nissho-Iwai, had a secret contract with Kern. Under the contract Kern was to receive a portion of Nissho-Iwai's commission for selling Grumman's sophisticated E-2C Hawkeye early warning radar and reconnaissance planes to the Japanese Defense Agency and Kern "might in turn pay a portion of his commission to one or more Japanese officials."[76]

When news of Grumman's SEC report hit the Japanese press in early 1979, Nissho-Iwai officials admitted that Kern had held a contract with them under which he would receive 40 percent of their commissions on sales of the E-2Cs. But Kern, who resigned from Grumman in 1978 after the Japanese government's decision to purchase the E-2Cs, denied that any money was to be used to pay off Japanese politicians. Despite extensive media coverage of the tangled web of intrigue and alleged payoffs, a full and impartial judicial investigation of the Grumman affair and Kern's role in it never took place. Kern brought a thirty-million-dollar libel suit against Grumman which was quietly settled out of court at the end of July 1980.[77]

The activities of Harry Kern and the Japan Lobby highlight the fate of American Occupation policy. Although the ACJ was a small and loosely structured pressure group, its members were among the most strenuous participants in the debate over Japan policy, providing ideological, strategic, and economic rationales for the creation of a new capitalist structure in Japan. The peace and security treaties with Japan marked the culmination of efforts by the

Japan Lobby to reverse the reformist orientation of the early Occupation, to make Japan a bulwark against communism in Asia, and to rivet Japan onto an American dominated, world capitalist system. Those who pointed to the repression, militarism, class tension, and other reactionary consequences of the "reverse course" and who criticized the structure of military and economic dependence of Japan upon the United States faced the threat of being tarnished by the Japan Lobby's red brush.

The key to the success of the Japan Lobby lay in the conjunction of its interests with those of a few well-placed Washington officials. Under Secretary of the Army William Draper, a Wall Street investment banker before the war, proved to be among the most receptive to the goals of Kern and the Japan Lobby. From 1947 to 1949 the under secretary placed the Occupation in a context which emphasized global economic recovery under United States hegemony. Under such conditions the growth and profitability of large American corporations, he believed, would be assured. But Draper had no expertise on Japan. Members of the Japan Lobby did. Understandably Draper welcomed them as a valuable ally in his relentless struggle to overcome the political and bureaucratic obstacles in Washington and Tokyo to the implementation of a "reverse course" program for Japan. That the succession of conservative governments in Japan since 1952 have followed a path in their internal and external policies so distant from the reformist ideals espoused at the start of the Occupation is in great measure attributable to the successful collaboration of William Draper and the Japan Lobby in American diplomacy.[78]

6 WILLIAM H. DRAPER, JR.

The Eightieth Congress and the Origins of Japan's "Reverse Course"

Recently American scholars of the Occupation have given less attention to the ''political reorientation'' of Japan and focused on the policies designed to promote the rapid economic reconstruction of Japan. Why was a Japanese recovery program deemed necessary by Washington policymakers in 1947 and 1948? How did the program change during its implementation? To what extent, if at all, was the recovery program linked to a ''reverse course'' by Washington in its announced ''democratization'' program? Answers to these questions obviously provide important clues to the understanding of the roots of contemporary Japanese society and its relations with the United States.[1]

Though given only passing, if any, mention in most accounts of the Occupation, Under Secretary of the Army William H. Draper, Jr., was singled out by his contemporaries as the American policymaker most responsible for launching and setting the direction of the Japanese economic recovery program. The English-language *Nippon Times* bluntly stated in 1948 that Draper was the ''principal American official concerned with the United States drive to help Japan in its reconstruction plans.'' A liberal critic in the *New Republic* accused Draper of being the ''most important figure'' in establishing a Japan policy that ''takes the accent off reform and puts it on reconstruction.'' Conservative editors at *Newsweek* often hailed Draper for his ''vital role'' and ''realistic influence'' in promoting economic recovery measures that made Japan a bulwark against communism in Asia.[2] In fact, new evidence confirms the contemporary estimates of Draper's critical importance to the recovery program.

The Wall Street General

General William H. Draper, Jr., candidly admitted to a group of congress-men that, when he took office at the Pentagon with responsibility for all American occupied areas, he "knew nothing about Japan." What Draper did know about was the United States, and the basis for his influence on Japan was his intimate ties with America's largest corporations and his experience with the levers of American state power. Born in New York City in 1894, he graduated from New York University with a B.A. in economics in 1916 and an M.A. in 1917. He spent most of his year and a half of active military duty during World War I as an instructor at the Plattsburgh, New York officer training camp. Discharged as a major, he remained a reserve officer until recalled to the War Department General Staff as a colonel in 1940. By then he had established himself as a leader in the Wall Street banking community. Courteous and soft-spoken, the slender and always elegantly groomed Draper spent from 1919 through 1926 with National City Bank and the Bankers Trust Company. In 1927 he joined Dillon, Read, one of the largest investment banking houses in the world, and rose quickly to a vice-presidency. A lifelong Republican, Brigadier General Draper first served the administration of Harry S. Truman as the chief economic advisor to General Lucius Clay, deputy military governor for Germany.[3]

Draper's work in Germany foreshadowed his role in Japan. Even before VE day, he found himself fundamentally out of sympathy with the basic American policy directive for Germany, JCS 1067, a laboriously prepared but vague statement for reforming and reintegrating Germany into a liberal world trading system led by the United States. Among other things, JCS 1067 set out broad principles for the decartelization of German industry, reparations, denazifica-tion and other reforms which Draper felt would open the door to the Left and prevent Germany from sparking the revival of the entire European economy.[4] Unlike W. Averell Harriman and other "hard-liners" around President Tru-man, Draper's criticism of JCS 1067, as with his later criticism of initial Japanese Occupation policy, was not based on fears of Russian aggression. In Germany, Draper recalled, he discounted Harriman's views of the Russians because he was "hoping and thinking and wishing that we were going to reach a peaceful solution between our two countries." He pressed Washington to emphasize economic recovery, not decartelization, purge of Nazi manage-ment, or other reforms in Germany. For Draper, a former official in Germany asserted, "the investment banker's view was uppermost. He was fundamen-tally opposed to the idea that the cartels and combines required immediate reorganization and was convinced that the 'experienced German management' had to be retained."[5] In arguments he later used repeatedly in reference to

Japan, Draper insisted that key economic reforms were unnecessary or harmful to the German recovery program.

In the midst of the transition to the Defense Department organization of the military services and of a reshuffling of personnel, President Truman appointed Draper as under secretary of the army on 30 August 1947. Draper accepted the appointment primarily to effect the transfer of Germany from army supervision to the State Department. Having served in government for nearly eight years, he reportedly was anxious to resume his banking career. But delays in the change of regime in Germany and the pleas of the president and the new secretary of defense and fellow Dillon, Read executive, James Forrestal, persuaded him to remain at the job until 1 March 1949.[6] In the course of those critical sixteen months Draper coordinated all aspects of the Japanese Occupation around the core of an economic recovery program.

The First Visit to Japan

Two weeks after taking office, Draper and his aides headed off to Japan. They met General MacArthur, Prime Minister Katayama, and members of the cabinet and Diet. They assessed the military requirements in connection with a possible early peace treaty. Above all, they surveyed the economic problems there. The statistics and reports reaching Washington from Tokyo had already revealed the seriousness of the situation. After two years of Occupation, the industrial production index was only 45 percent of the 1930–34 average, exports about 10 percent, and imports about 30 percent. A spiraling inflation had pushed prices to ninety times their level at the end of the war. To prevent "disease and unrest" in Japan, Congress was providing under the Government and Relief in Occupied Areas (GARIOA) program about $350 million of food, fertilizer, medicine, and other relief items, with no end in sight. Discussion by Draper with Japanese and SCAP officials convinced him "that the economic and financial structure of Japan is tottering. Personal observations show clearly how present economic conditions threaten the accomplishment of U.S. objectives."[7]

On his trip to Japan, Draper carried a bulky draft of the still unapproved State-War-Navy Coordinating Committee document 381, "The Revival of the Japanese Economy," the principal U.S. statement on how to deal with the economic crisis in Japan. Crank-up, as SWNCC 381 was colloquially known, had been prepared under the direction of State Department economist Edwin Martin. It reflected the objective announced by Assistant Secretary of State Dean Acheson in May 1947 that the United States was prepared to take up the unilateral reconstruction of Germany and Japan as the "workshops" of their

Under Secretary of the Army William H. Draper, Jr., is greeted by General Douglas MacArthur on his arrival at Haneda Airport, Tokyo, 20 March 1948. Signal Corps Photo, National Archives.

respective continents. Highlighting both the greater importance Europe held in Washington's global concerns and the revolutionary turmoil throughout Asia, the crank-up of Japan was designed without a Marshall Plan for Asia. It was premised on an industrialized Japan exporting manufactured goods in exchange for the raw materials of its Asian neighbors. SWNCC 381 estimated that with $450 million of additional American aid appropriations and the expenditure of $150 million of convertible assets in Japan controlled by the U.S., Japan could be self-supporting by 1950. Specifically, this meant that Japanese exports and receipts from shipping and other invisibles would balance its import needs and that the standard of living, as measured primarily by food and cloth consumption, would be raised reasonably close to that in 1930–34.[8]

The "self-support" concept of SWNCC 381 did not mean economic or political independence of Japan from the United States—merely that U.S. appropriated funds to prevent "disease and unrest" in Japan would no longer be necessary. Coordinated with a similar, though much larger, program of grants and loans to Germany and other European nations, the Japanese program would enable the Truman administration to reach its elusive postwar goal of a self-supporting "open world" free from barriers to political democracy and economic opportunity. Dire consequences were predicted should Congress not fund these programs. With a vast surplus of goods estimated at $16 billion for 1947, but with foreign buyers holding only $8 billion in reserves, the war-enlarged flow of American exports would slow and lead to economic stagnation at home and abroad, political instability, and international conflict.[9]

More than anything else, the visit to Japan convinced Draper that crank-up required immediate and fundamental changes in U.S. economic reform policy, especially the Zaibatsu dissolution and reparations programs. A follow-up by Draper on a telegram from Secretary of the Army Kenneth Royall indicated the seriousness of the problem of reforming the Zaibatsu. Royall told of a meeting called by Defense Secretary Forrestal and Commerce Secretary Harriman at which John Biggers, president of Libbey-Owens-Ford Glass (LOF), had presented a summary of a blistering report on the economic situation in Japan by LOF attorney James Lee Kauffman. Among other things, the report accused MacArthur of staffing SCAP "with a superabundance of men" from the Office of Price Administration (OPA), blamed the former head of Labor Division for permitting half of the new unions in Japan to have closed shops, and above all attacked "imposition of laws which . . . are socialized in their nature, namely laws in implementation of FEC-230, [the Zaibatsu dissolution program]." Specifically Kauffman opposed the deconcentration of industry bill designed to break up the gigantic operating subsidiaries of the Zaibatsu holding companies, and which SCAP was pushing through the Diet. The Kauffman report, Royall ominously warned Draper, "might become the subject of discussion in the Senate. I believe you should look into the matter before your return, if necessary staying over two or three days longer."[10] After consulting with American businessmen and Civil Affairs Division lawyers, Draper reached nearly the same conclusions as Kauffman about FEC-230. He told MacArthur before leaving Japan that the FEC-230 directive was poorly written and if "carried out literally . . . would do real economic damage."[11]

Closely related to Draper's concerns over the Zaibatsu dissolution program was the U.S. reparations policy, SWNCC 236/43 of April 1947. After months of negotiations between the State and War departments, the new policy established final retention levels for major Japanese industries above which removals could be made. Reflecting the growing consensus in Washington that Japan was the fulcrum of Asian policy, SWNCC 236/43 was far more lenient towards Japanese industry than the proposals of Reparations Commissioner Edwin

Pauley during 1945 and 1946. Pauley had wanted to eliminate Japanese "war supporting industries," especially the top-heavy Zaibatsu controlled heavy industry structure, and to use removals from Japan to create a more balanced Asian economy.[12]

But even before Draper arrived in Washington, MacArthur had effectively stalled the implementation of the reparations program and War Department officials began plotting to lessen the potential burden of reparations removals from Japan under the comparatively lenient SWNCC 236/43 proposal. Purportedly, the Overseas Consultants Incorporation (OCI), a consortium of eleven engineering firms headed by Clifford Strike, was contracted by the War Department to provide technical advice to SCAP on inventorying, assessing, and selecting plants and equipment for possible removal. In fact, as economic officers in the State Department feared, the OCI mission was a War Department device to further delay any reparations removals and reopen the industry retention levels issue.[13]

"General Draper has again unsettled the basic question of levels of industry in Japan," complained OE officer R. Burr Smith after a briefing on the under secretary's September trip to Japan. "Apparently the General was sufficiently impressed by the Strike group to have doubts as to the levels contained in our present policy [i.e, SWNCC 236/43]." Smith was correct. From talks with OCI officers working under the direction of Rufus J. Wysor, former president of Republic Steel and a top aide to Draper in Germany, Draper learned that the OCI would recommend higher retention levels "on the basis that higher levels will be required to permit a self-supporting Japanese economy." Not surprisingly, he told the State Department "that we should not finalize the reparations levels in the FEC until we and the members of the FEC have the benefit of the present [OCI] report. . . . The American position should remain open." In a clear reference to the Eightieth Congress, Draper concluded that so "long as we are paying the Japanese deficit, any mistakes will be paid for in American appropriated funds."[14]

Convinced that Japanese businessmen were the key to a successful recovery program and would not rebuild enterprises which faced dissolution under FEC-230 or removal under SWNCC 236/43, Draper immediately launched a campaign on his return to Washington for a major reorientation of American Occupation policy. He asked his staff to draw up a brief directive to MacArthur for approval by SWNCC which would make "economic recovery the main objective and . . . give SCAP the authority to interpret other existing directives in the light of this primary objective." By 3 October SWNCC 384, a brief statement titled "The Economic Recovery of Japan," was ready for consideration by other departments. It amounted to the first explicit formulation linking economic recovery to a "reverse course" in other Occupation programs; henceforth the directives already approved by the U.S. and the Far Eastern Commission would be implemented with "the necessary shift of emphasis to accomplish economic recovery"[15] Behind the "shift of emphasis" phrase in SWNCC 384, Draper sought to reopen discussion with the State Department on the retention levels in SWNCC 236/43 and, most urgently, gain its cooperation in preventing SCAP from pushing through the Japanese Diet the deconcentration ordinance until the whole FEC-230 program could be reviewed.

Initially, Draper hoped that SWNCC 384 would be approved in advance of, not in place of, the detailed recovery plan in SWNCC 381. But he met strong and determined opposition from State Department economic officers who had designed crank-up with the idea that "the operation of the Economic Recovery Plan should not be allowed to prevent the successful implementation of programs looking towards democratization of the Japanese economy." These officials believed that, to avoid reparations and dissolution and maintain umhampered control over the nation's economic machinery, Japanese businessmen were deliberately abetting inflation and obstructing recovery, imposing thereby a continual financial drain on the United States. In their view, the rapid implementation, not the abandonment, of the reparations and dissolution programs was the appropriate means for ending the economic crisis and eventually winning the cooperation of Japanese businessmen with American recovery policy.[16]

That Draper wanted to issue a unilateral "interim" directive to MacArthur rather than seeking FEC approval highlighted the State Department's principal objection to SWNCC 384. The "shift of emphasis" phrase of SWNCC 384 would be bitterly resented by FEC nations. Their willingness to trade with Japan, the "absolutely essential" yet most doubtful part of the SWNCC 381 program, was gravely threatened by Draper's plan for unilateral changes in such internationally sensitive programs as reparations and dissolution. "The advent of Draper as Under Secretary of the Army and the results of his visit to Japan have stirred things up and I fear our troubles are only beginning," Roswell Whitman, head of the Division of Occupied Area Economic Affairs (OE), predicted. Though he recommended State Department rejection of SWNCC 384, he was not optimistic. For one thing, Draper would probably hold up approval of SWNCC 381 until SWNCC 384 was dealt with. Everyone knew that, in SWNCC, "only Draper's approval is required before [proposed papers] become final" policy. More important, what made Draper "so dangerous," in Whitman's view, "was the fact that he develops allies within the Department of State."[17]

Linking up with George F. Kennan

Draper's principal allies at Foggy Bottom were State Department political officers, particularly George F. Kennan, head of the newly created Policy Planning Staff (PPS). Since the early summer of 1947 Kennan and his staff had been studying U.S. policy toward Japan. They found a draft peace treaty which Hugh Borton of the Office of Far Eastern Affairs prepared after General MacArthur's surprise March 1947 call for an early end to the Occupation "highly dangerous" and wholly unacceptable. Rather than assuring the "central American objective [of a] stable Japan integrated into the Pacific economy, friendly to the U.S. and, in case of need, a ready and dependable ally of the U.S.," the Borton draft treaty appeared to PPS as "preoccupied with drastic disarmament, and democratization under continuing international supervision, including the U.S.S.R."[18] Guided by Kennan, the PPS developed the geopolitical rationale for a full-scale revision in policy for Japan that closely dovetailed with the work of Draper.

As one of the earliest postwar proponents of the view that Soviet behavior was inherently expansionist and hostile to the West, Kennan argued that the Truman administration should replace futile attempts at cooperation with Moscow with a program of Communist containment. The containment doctrine posited that the internal economic, political, and spiritual weakness of Western Europe, Japan, and the Middle East, not Russian military power, was the primary threat to postwar American security. After the damage and suffering from World War II, the Russians did not intend to risk another war. "Remember," Kennan told a National War College audience in October 1947 and would emphasize repeatedly in his writings, "it is not Russian military power which is threatening us, it is Russian political power."[19] The Russians advanced their objectives, especially within the demoralized, war-weary nations of Europe and Asia, by using reliable Communist parties abroad who through subversion, coups, or even victories in free elections sought to take power.

For Kennan, the key to thwarting the Soviets was to strengthen "the natural forces of resistance" against communism outside the Soviet empire. With economic aid from the United States, strong industrial capitalist economies under politically conservative governments in Europe and Asia would become bulwarks against communism. Kennan's first task at the PPS in May 1947 was work on what became the Marshall Plan for the economic recovery of Western Europe, especially the western occupied zones of Germany. The rehabilitation of Japan as a center of industrial-military power in Asia allied to the United States formed an equally important part of Kennan's strategic view of American security. Given limitations on American resources, some countries threatened by communism, most notably China, were not worth aiding in Kennan's view. Under the Nationalists, China was not only too chaotic and corrupt but lacked an industrial-military infrastructure so that its loss to the Soviets would not affect the world balance of power. The economic recovery of Japan, however, was a central feature of Kennan's global geopolitical containment strategy which ultimately contemplated the creation of such tension within the Soviet empire as to lead to a "mellowing" of Soviet power or its complete collapse.[20]

The Planning Staff's first preliminary study on Japan policy, PPS 10, submitted on 14 October 1947 by Kennan to Robert Lovett, under secretary of state and former Wall Street banker, attempted to define more precisely the requirements for making Japan a bulwark in the containment strategy. Kennan argued against any peace treaty plan until Japan could be economically and politically stabilized to prevent Communist penetration. The SWNCC 381 crank-up plan for the Japanese economy was a most important step in that effort. Without continuing U.S. control of Japan under an Occupation regime, the PPS feared difficulties in obtaining funds from Congress for crank-up and supervising the economic policies of the Japanese.[21]

On the issues of Zaibatsu dissolution, the purge, reparations, and other reforms raised by Draper's proposed SWNCC 384 "shift of emphasis" statement, the PPS study waffled. Kennan had indicated his personal preference for Draper's proposal by inviting old Japan Crowd stalwarts Joseph Grew, Eugene Dooman, and Joseph Ballantine to testify before the PPS. But given both the tactical and principled opposition of so many State Department officers to SWNCC 384, the PPS simply called for collecting more information and holding more discussion. Only then should "existing directives to SCAP be reexamined to determine whether they were such as to make the maximum contribution to Japan's eventual ability to meet the strain of renewed economic independence." In any case, post-treaty international control was politically and economically objectionable.[22]

The PPS study had an immediate impact on U.S.-Japan policy. The State Department scrapped the Borton draft treaty, and deliberately delayed discussion with FEC nations on holding a peace conference. Most importantly, Kennan was ordered to arrange a journey to Japan in preparation for a full National Security Council discussion on overall Occupation policy based on the PPS study. That the architect of global containment was assigned this mission signaled a clear victory by conservative political officers in the State Department for control of Japan policy.

Though the PPS paper was much closer than the Borton draft treaty to Draper's own thinking about Japan, he was not satisfied and sought to convince Kennan, Lovett, and others at the State Department to openly support the SWNCC 384 economic recovery statement. Draper's representative at the 23 October meeting of SANACC (State-Army-Navy-Air Force Coordinating Committee) rejected the State Department request to withdraw SWNCC 384 in favor of a compromise proposal for the addition of a new paragraph to SWNCC 381 on the primacy of economic recovery that avoided the explosive "shift of emphasis" phrase. "He went on to say," according to the minutes of the meeting, "that it would be extremely difficult to revive the Japanese economy and that it probably would be more difficult to continue to secure substantial funds from Congress for purposes of the occupation. Should SAN-ACC come up with a paper which indicated the economic recovery of Japan was a primary objective of this Government and if SCAP would be so notified, he felt it would be much easier to get funds from Congress."[23]

With SWNCC 381 as Draper's hostage, State and Army department officers resumed an intense bit of jockeying over the wording of SWNCC 384. The statement Draper wanted for gaining SCAP cooperation in undercutting the reform programs in Japan and for maximum effect in obtaining appropriations from Congress, the State Department leadership rightly feared would generate a storm of international protest and further hamper Japanese trade in Asia that was so vital to the crank-up program. As he maneuvered within the State Department and at the War Department to gain approval for the PPS study on Japan, Kennan played an important role in resolving what had become a tactical dispute and, in tandem with Draper, effecting a real "shift in emphasis" from reform to economic recovery.

The Green Book

While Draper sat on the SWNCC 381 crank-up program because it lacked a clear statement for a "shift of emphasis" from reform to recovery, economists from the Army, Treasury, and Commerce departments concluded by early November that it was also overly optimistic and based on unreliable data. Consequently, Draper sought approval for a new recovery program officially titled "Economic Rehabilitation for Japan, South Korea, and the Ryukyu Islands" prepared under the direction of Emmerson Ross of ESS, SCAP. Informally known as the Green Book because of the color of its binding, the ESS report became the basis for Draper's request for funding from Congress in early 1948.[24]

The Green Book followed the same "self-support" principles outlined in SWNCC 381 but was based not on a three-year but a four-and-one-quarter-year recovery program explicitly analogous to the Economic Recovery Program for Europe, better known as the Marshall Plan. With $1.2 billion in industrial raw materials as well as relief supplies from the United States, the Green Book predicted that, by 1953, Japan would be able to export $1.5 billion in goods and services (a figure nearly eight times that of 1947 and roughly twice that in the best years of prewar trade), pay for all of its own imports (thereby ending American aid appropriations), and reach a standard of living for the population reasonably close to that of 1930–34. The thorny issue of available markets for so rapid an increase in Japanese exports was simply avoided in the Green Book. Instead, focus was on the need to generate industrial momentum by breaking "the present log jam in raw material procurement." Iron ore, coking coal, raw cotton, pulp and other so-called recovery imports would be the "spark plug" for shifting the Japanese economy from its prewar emphasis on textile and other light industry exports to capital goods exports. Expanded textile exports were critical to launching the recovery program but, in light of the decline in the world demand for silk and the anticipated growth of the textile industry throughout the Far East, the Green Book emphasized that "Japan must look to expanded exports of machinery and metal products to bring its commodity trade into balance."[25]

There were many uncertainties in the Green Book plan, but for Draper the most immediate one was whether Congress would fund it. The Republican-controlled Eightieth Congress had made clear its determination to reduce taxes and cut government spending, especially foreign aid spending. Reflecting the public mood, key congressmen charged that foreign aid programs drained off scarce American goods, contributed to inflation at home, discouraged recipients from doing more for their own support, and threatened to increase competition for American business. These objections would have to be met and congressional support carefully cultivated, Draper knew, for the Green Book recovery plan for Japan, like the Marshall Plan for Europe, was premised on a large increase in foreign aid appropriations for 1948 and 1949 (though appropriations in subsequent years were projected to rapidly decline until the Japanese economy reached the self-support level in 1953).[26]

To launch the recovery program in Japan, the Army Department planned to request $376 million for GARIOA relief aid for FY 1949 and $180 million under a separate "Economic Rehabilitation Occupied Areas" (EROA) authorization for industrial raw material imports for fifteen months beginning 1 April 1948. That was a total aid request for Japan of $556 million, compared to the nearly $400 million in GARIOA aid that would be expended during FY 1948. Although beset by doubts that the $180 million EROA request was adequate to reach the Green Book goal of self-support, Draper and State Department officials agreed that "it would not be desirable to overemphasize this point to the Bureau of the Budget and to Congress."[27] Congress had to be convinced that funding EROA now would materially reduce and eventually eliminate GARIOA appropriations later.

The Eightieth Congress might wield the meat-ax on the army's request for funds to launch the Green Book recovery program. But that very threat, Draper certainly realized, provided a potential aid to his efforts for a "shift of emphasis" from reform to recovery in Occupied Japan. In earlier debate on Germany, Congress had already shown disgruntlement over reparations and decartelization programs which were presumably delaying economic recovery and, hence, costing the American taxpayer money for relief aid. When Draper testified before the House Foreign Affairs Committee in December 1947 to begin the legislative process for authorization of the EROA program, he was in the thick of a battle with SCAP over the Zaibatsu dissolution program, fending off State Department attempts to proceed on the basis of existing reparations policy, and awaiting SANACC approval of his version of SWNCC 384. If properly managed, Congress could be the key to a victory for Draper on all these fronts. Whether there would be a recovery program which supported or undermined key reform attempts, indeed whether there would be a viable recovery program at all, hinged more on the vagaries of Congress than Draper suspected.

The Zaibatsu Dissolution and Reparations Battles

On his return from Japan, Draper had met with Forrestal and Royall and all agreed that the most pressing issue was to block passage by the Japanese Diet of the deconcentration ordinance and then restrain future independent actions by MacArthur. But when Draper cabled SCAP to gain a delay in Diet consideration of the measure, MacArthur flatly refused. In a ten-page radiogram of 24 October the general contended that delay would only play into the hands of Japanese leftists or the Zaibatsu themselves, advocates of "socialism in private hands."[28] By implication MacArthur accused Draper of promoting both socialism and fascism.

Shocked by MacArthur's defiance, Forrestal took the lead in giving Japan policy top priority in the administration. Like Kennan, Forrestal regarded Japan as vital to an anti-Soviet containment policy in the Far East. Forrestal sent a memorandum to Secretary Royall on 1 November calling for the formulation of a new general policy for the reconstruction of the Japanese economy. "I think we should do everything possible to get the State Department to reexamine its economic policy on Japan. The program as outlined in that letter [by James Kauffman] and subsequently verified by you [through Draper] indicates a degree of socialization in Japan which would make it totally impossible for the country's economy to function if it were put on its own." Forrestal requested Royall to have a report prepared on the "extent the socialization program has been completed, and what steps we are taking to change course." Economic affairs in Japan, he concluded, were a matter of the highest priority. "In my opinion it has a very direct bearing on the future security of this country."[29]

Over the next three weeks Royall and Draper worked with Robert Lovett on strategies for getting MacArthur to understand the reorientation of American policy for Japan and then to revise his commitment to FEC-230. But when the lower house of the Diet passed the deconcentration bill in late November, Draper's hope of avoiding a direct clash with SCAP vanished. Writing for Royall's signature, Draper drafted one of the very few formal orders the army sent to MacArthur. If SCAP could not block final passage of the ordinance by the 8 December adjournment of the upper house, he was to delay implementation of the new law until all questions regarding FEC-230 were settled in Washington at the cabinet level.[30]

Draper now began a discreet collaboration with Harry F. Kern.[31] By orchestrating a public and congressional controversy over FEC-230 through Kern, Draper apparently hoped to impress MacArthur with the strong opposition of the Army Department to the FEC-230 program and to encourage Japanese Dietmen to stall consideration of the deconcentration measure. The "forthcoming [1 December] issue of *Newsweek* magazine would blast Army handling of the Zaibatsu holdings in Japan," Draper told General Robert Eichelberger on 24 November, and suggested that he condoned Kern's plan to publish a portion of the still classified FEC-230 document since it was, perhaps, "rightfully public information." Draper asked Eichelberger to reassure MacArthur "that any criticism of the Zaibatsu matter could be laid at the doorstep of the Army Department" rather than with SCAP.[32]

Draper badly misjudged the reaction in Tokyo. MacArthur read the controversial *Newsweek* article, with its watered-down version of the Kauffman report, as part of a "definite smear campaign" to undermine his bid for the Republican presidential nomination. Consequently, he continued to press for passage of the deconcentration ordinance. On 5 December Forrestal sent Draper a transcript of his telephone conversation with LOF President Biggers which indicated the seriousness with which the Pentagon had come to view MacArthur's actions and which outlined the strategy Draper would follow in handling the FEC-230 problem thereafter. Forrestal reassured an anxious Biggers that he had been hard at work trying to make MacArthur realize that FEC-230 was "cooked up of course by some crackpots here and I think that our best chance is to get some business people over there to administer that [deconcentration] law even if it is passed." The State and Army departments had just "got some modification of it now" but there were still problems.

"You can't unscramble what has been scrambled," Forrestal lamented to a surprised and grateful Biggers.[33] In a hectic all-night Diet session on 8 December with SCAP pressure evident, the deconcentration bill became Law 207 with a proviso that a Washington-appointed review board would administer the law in light of the primacy of economic recovery.

Draper found William F. Knowland an important ally in gutting FEC-230. A California Republican member of the Senate Appropriations Committee and one of the "cotton senators," Knowland had been quietly lobbying the Pentagon to develop the Japanese textile industry as a major foreign purchaser of surplus American raw cotton. After consulting with Kern and only eleven days after the passage of the deconcentration law, Knowland took to the floor of the Senate to excoriate FEC-230 as "contrary to our way of life." Shortly thereafter he requested the Army Department to provide the Senate Appropriations Committee and the Senate Foreign Relations Committee copies of documents on both the Zaibatsu dissolution and reparations programs in Japan.[34]

Knowland's threat to make not only Zaibatsu dissolution but reparations the subject of congressional scrutiny resulted from Draper's tactical differences with the State Department over the issue. Draper wanted the State Department representative to the FEC to delay any action on final retention levels based on the SWNCC 236/43 figures until the completion of the report by Clifford Strike's Overseas Consultants Incorporated. But Edwin Martin and other State Department economic officers argued that the reconsideration of the level of industry for Japan involved economic judgments outside the province of the OCI engineers. Martin angrily told Draper that the OCI "had been indoctrinated to reach certain conclusions and had gone out with preconceived ideas." But more importantly, Under Secretary Lovett based his refusal to accede to Draper's request for delay on his fear that any proposals more lenient to Japan than SWNCC 236/43 would jeopardize the willingness of American allies in the Far East to trade with Japan. For Lovett there was no need for OCI to revise SWNCC 236/43 since his staff had calculated that only 30 to 40 percent of the possible removals under SWNCC 236/43 would actually be taken. Moreover, if FEC nations claimed more than that SCAP could simply invoke paragraph ten of the FEC policy on "Reduction of Japan's War Potential" under which he was "authorized to except from reparations removals those facilities required to meet the needs of the occupation."[35] In essence, Lovett hoped to achieve the same higher retention levels for Japan as Draper but avoid the negative fallout from FEC nations that would certainly result from any formal change in reparations policy.

Draper was unimpressed. The Eightieth Congress was about to consider foreign aid requests. Knowland's actions carried the implied threat that, unless the closely interrelated Zaibatsu dissolution and reparations policies were revised, Congress would not authorize the Army Department request for funds to begin the critical economic recovery program outlined in the Green Book. Thus Draper insisted early in January 1948 on a public announcement of an official change in U.S. policy along the lines of the SWNCC 384 "shift of emphasis" proposal. Such a statement, Draper hoped, would satisfy Congress, provide him leverage in preventing MacArthur from implementing the deconcentration law before the so-called Deconcentration Review Board was in place, and facilitate negotiations with the State Department over delaying action on reparations until the completion of the OCI report. In proposing such an announcement, Draper, as one State Department official aptly put it, could afford to be "completely cynical about any international cooperation and . . . quite willing to disregard the FEC."[36] The time had come, Draper insisted, for an open shift from "punitive" reform policies to the implementation of the economic recovery program.

Announcing the "Reverse Course"

During the first quarter of 1948, Draper and Royall coordinated a series of official statements and releases that rang out the primacy of economic recovery in American Occupation policy and sounded what they hoped would be the deathknell for FEC-230, SWNCC 236/43, and the reform program generally. In a widely quoted speech on 6 January in San Francisco, Royall stressed the "increasing economic approach" Washington was taking towards Japan in order to relieve the burden of pouring millions of dollars into relief aid. That created "an inevitable area of conflict between the original concept of broad demilitarization and the new purpose of building a self-supporting nation." Royall gave examples of such conflict in the reparations, Zaibatsu dissolution, and purge areas. Anticipating the argument of the OCI report, Royall noted that the "destruction of synthetic rubber or shipbuilding or chemical or nonferrous metal plants will certainly destroy the war potential of Japan, but such destruction may also adversely affect the peace potential."[37]

The Zaibatsu dissolution and purge programs presented Royall with similar dilemmas. In an obvious reference to Washington's struggle with MacArthur, the army secretary argued that "at some stage extreme deconcentration of industry, while further impairing the ability to make war, may at the same time impair manufacturing efficiency of Japanese industry—may, therefore, postpone the day when Japan can become self-supporting." Royall also hinted at a reversal of the original purge program. "The men who were the most active in building up and running Japan's war machine—militarily and industrially—

were often the ablest and most successful business leaders of that country and their services would in many instances contribute to the economic recovery of Japan."[38]

Anxious to have a statement ready in time for the resumption of congressional hearings on the EROA authorization legislation, Draper agreed to the compromise worked out by State and Army department negotiators for the phrase "more emphasis" instead of "shift of emphasis" in the SWNCC 384 economic recovery document. General Frank McCoy, U.S. representative to the FEC, read the modified SWNCC 384 to dismayed foreign delegates on 21 January:

> Japanese industry and commerce are not yet sufficient to sustain the Japanese economy; there is not yet final Allied determination of the reparations which Japan will be required to pay; and Japan is not yet in a position to participate fully in world trade and to contribute its part to the rehabilitation of the world economy. Economic chaos in Japan has been prevented only at the expense of the American people. . . . It is the view of the United States Government that . . . a much greater effort must be made to bring about the attainment of a self-supporting Japan with a reasonable standard of living. To this end, my Government believes that the Japanese Government and people, [the FEC and SCAP], recognizing the conditions which now require more emphasis be placed on such a program, should take all necessary steps, consistent with the basic policies of the occupation to bring about the early revival of the Japanese economy on a peaceful, self-supporting basis.[39]

Though more ambiguously worded than Draper's original version of SWNCC 384, McCoy's statement indicated that Lovett and Kennan had led the State Department to support Draper's position on economic recovery despite anticipated objections from FEC nations. The announcement was correctly interpreted as a coupling of economic recovery with a "reverse course" that would strengthen the hands of Japanese businessmen and conservative politicians and spell the end to any chance that the United States would achieve the aims of its initial post-surrender policy for Japan.

To Draper the immediate public release of the final OCI report, completed at the end of February 1948, was another of the necessary steps to put Japan on a self-supporting basis. If somehow the OCI report leaked to the media, Draper threatened State Department officials, Congress, already "so stirred up about reparations questions in general," would be unnecessarily angered. Though only advisory, the OCI report confirmed SWNCC 384 and earlier indications that there probably would be little, if any, reparations removals from Japan. The critical Section B of the report did not tamper with the estimate of "primary war facilities" in SWNCC 236/43. However, it proposed only five instead of twenty-one categories of "war supporting industries'' from which removals would be taken—and with substantial reductions in each of those cases. All capacity in the pig iron, steel, machine tool, ball bearing, and twelve other theretofore ''war supporting industries'' would be retained. When the productive facilities to be designated for removals were added up in all categories exclusive of primary war facilities, the OCI report called for a mere 172 million (1939) yen compared with the SWNCC 236/43 proposal of 990 million (1939) yen. Anticipating adverse criticism by reparations claimants, the OCI report asserted that the balancing of the industrial needs of the Far Eastern region ''can be achieved most surely by leaving Japan free to reconstruct and use as quickly as possible the bulk of her industrial capacity.'' Japan needed more, not less, productive capacity if there was to be a self-supporting economy. Removal of ''productive facilities (except primary war facilities) which can be effectively used in Japan . . . would be expensive to the American taxpayer and, in our opinion, would not be in the best interests of the claimant nations.''[40] As Draper had hoped, the release of the OCI report provoked new debate over reparations policy in Washington and further delayed any removals of facilities from Japan to FEC claimants.

Much to Draper's dismay, the public declarations of a shift in American policy away from reform in early 1948 seemed to strengthen rather than weaken the resolve of General MacArthur to openly defend and carry out the Zaibatsu dissolution program. Perhaps in the belief his chances for the Republican party presidential nomination would be enhanced, SCAP responded to Draper's request for a statement to the appropriations committees of Congress considering the EROA program by emphasizing that the establishment of a ''more healthy economy'' in Japan depended on the destruction of an ''oligarchic system of economic feudalism'' under which the Japanese people had been ''exploited into virtual slavery.''[41]

That statement triggered another Congressional debate over Japan policy. Senator William Knowland took the floor on 19 January to again attack FEC-230 and former OPA officials in SCAP who had ''little experience in American business and industry.'' Avoiding a clash with a fellow Republican luminary, Knowland suggested MacArthur was simply uninformed about how his underlings were promoting socialism instead of building a ''beachhead of free enterprise.'' Senator Bourke Hickenlooper, a ranking Iowa Republican on the Foreign Relations Committee, applauded Knowland's speech and Senator Brien McMahon, Democrat of Connecticut, questioned why MacArthur did not return to Washington to support the recovery aid request and answer questions about FEC-230. MacArthur's response to the flurry of publicity that followed the FEC-230 debate in Congress compounded Draper's concern. In a letter dated 1 February to Senator McMahon and released to the press the general made his strongest statement ever in defense of FEC-230. If the

Japanese pyramid of economic power, MacArthur declared, were "not torn down and redistributed peacefully and in due order under the Occupation there is no slightest doubt that its cleansing will eventually occur through a bloodbath of revolutionary violence."[42]

It was SCAP's vigorous prosecution of the deconcentration program, not just MacArthur's rhetorical flourishes, that most alarmed Draper. During February the Holding Company Liquidation Commission (HCLC), under SCAP pressure, designated 325 firms, representing 75 percent of all Japanese industry and commerce, as possible excessive concentrations of economic power subject to reorganization. The HCLC also promised a later announcement on designation of banks and other financial institutions.[43] Clearly MacArthur had not grasped the critical importance which both the Army and State departments and their influential allies in the business community, the press, and Congress attached to the reversal of FEC-230. If passage by Congress of the EROA authorization legislation and appropriation requests for beginning the recovery program in Japan was to be assured and Japan was to become a bulwark of containment in Asia, strong and immediate action was needed to bring MacArthur into line with the shift in Washington's Occupation policy.

Kennan's Visit to Japan and PPS 28

Before Draper and the Army Department had fully developed a plan of their own for dealing with MacArthur's stubborn commitment to Zaibatsu dissolution, Secretary of State George Marshall dispatched Kennan on a delicate mission to orient SCAP to the new civilian-military consensus in Washington for a real "shift of emphasis" from reform to economic recovery in the context of the global containment strategy. Just prior to his departure Kennan called for the administration to dispense with concerns about human rights or living standards in its foreign policy and "deal in straight power concepts." In Asia that entailed recognizing the inability of the United States to prevent China from falling under the influence of Moscow, maintaining control of strong points in Japan and the Philippines as cornerstones of a Pacific security system, and aiding in the development of the economic potential of Japan as an "important force" once again in the affairs of Asia. For Kennan Japan's economic potential would never be realized if MacArthur carried out the deconcentration program. He insisted that the State Department notify the FEC that the deconcentration policy did not represent the "current views of the American goverment." The U.S. delegation to the FEC then began a deliberate policy of delaying consideration of FEC-230 and other issues while seeking to avoid "openly implying" that a revision of policy was underway.[44]

Draper hoped to use Kennan's visit to Japan to further undercut the ability of MacArthur to defy Army Department directives and reassure Congress that economic aid for Japan was warranted. His office leaked reports to the wire services that Kennan would order MacArthur to hasten economic recovery and perhaps rebuild Japan's military power. Newspaper stories on Kennan's trip soon appeared in the United States under headlines such as "Drastic Change in Policy of U.S. Envisaged—Kennan Visits seen as Move to Build Up Japan an Anti-Red Bulwark." The stories, which MacArthur ordered censored from the Japanese press, were essentially accurate.[45]

Following Marshall's advice on dealing with MacArthur, Kennan listened patiently for over two hours at his first meeting with the general on 1 March to a monologue on the success of the Occupation and the resulting lack of danger in Japan from Communist subversion or Soviet attack. A few days later Kennan met again with MacArthur to go over security and economic matters. They found themselves agreeing that permanent bases in Japan proper were not necessary for Pacific security as long as the Pentagon planned for an arc of military bases off the mainland of Asia running from the Aleutians to Midway, the former Japanese mandated islands, Clark Field in the Philippines, and above all Okinawa. But when Kennan turned discussion to the importance of an intensive economic recovery program to American security in the Pacific, MacArthur grew defensive. He blamed Japan's economic problems on Asian nations that discriminated against Japanese trade, denied that the purge of business leaders had a detrimental effect on recovery, and insisted that the deconcentration program was not as extreme as some claimed. Taking a page from the book of his critics, MacArthur blamed a few "academic theorizers of a left-wing variety" in SCAP and in the State Department for whatever problems there were with the program and hinted that he would not push it further. Finally, Kennan pleased MacArthur by attacking the FEC and denying it had any authority in the final phase of the Occupation over Zaibatsu dissolution or other SCAP policies. According to Kennan, MacArthur "slapped his thigh in approval" and told the disbelieving State Department envoy that they had achieved a "meeting of the minds."[46]

Delaying his return to Washington until he could meet with Draper and his hastily organized Economic Mission, Kennan began drafting a lengthy report for the Policy Planning Staff on Japan policy which he submitted to Secretary Marshall on March 25. PPS 28, as the report was designated, reflected Kennan's disgust with MacArthur and the SCAP bureaucracy and his fears for successful containment of communism in Asia. Because of the loss of Japan's sources of raw materials, decline in industrial production, repatriation of Communist indoctrinated Japanese from abroad, and the damage done by SCAP handling of the purge, decentralization of the police, Zaibatsu dissolution, and other reforms, Japan was extremely vulnerable to Soviet aided Communist subversion. Consequently, Kennan recommended temporarily delaying any peace treaty and using the additional period of Occupation to strengthen Japanese institutions. The first step, Kennan insisted, was for SCAP to "steadily but unobtrusively relax pressure" on the Japanese to carry out the purge, deconcentration, and other reforms which hindered the primary objective of economic recovery under a politically stable and conservative government. The Japanese government should assume more and more authority from SCAP and establish a centralized police force or even a small army to resist Communist subversion. Only when Japan was so strengthened, Kennan concluded, should peace treaty negotiations be considered. Whether American bases remained after the peace treaty and the Japanese fully rearmed would depend, Kennan concluded, on the "Russian situation" and the degree of American confidence in the internal stability of Japan.[47]

Though some within the State Department raised serious objections to key aspects of Kennan's report, PPS 28 quickly gained the endorsement of Under Secretary Lovett and Director of the Far Eastern Division W. Walton Butterworth.[48] In mid-April it was forwarded to the Army Department for comments. As Kennan knew, the final form his PPS 28 report would take before its consideration by the National Security Council and approval as official policy depended above all on the reaction of General William Draper who had just returned from leading the Economic Mission to Japan.

The Origins of the Draper Mission

Initially, Draper did not anticipate the necessity of a high-level army mission to Japan in order to effect a change in MacArthur's handling of deconcentration and other reforms. He pinned his hopes instead on the rapid organization of the Deconcentration Review Board (DRB). If its members were properly chosen, Draper believed that the DRB could prevent most of the firms designated by the HCLC as possible excessive concentrations of economic power from ever being broken up. "Congress and the public," one Pentagon economist reported to Draper, "particularly those associations interested in the status of their remaining vested interests in Japan, were exhibiting keen interest in the constitution of the Deconcentration Board."[49]

Brushing aside a State Department request to participate in the selection of DRB personnel, Draper consulted early in February with Clifford Strike, then putting the finishing touches on the OCI report. Previously Strike had told Draper that Japanese management was timid and frightened and had recommended that OCI mission head Rufus Wysor replace Edward Welsh, a staunch proponent of the dissolution program, as chief of the Antitrust and Cartels Division of ESS. Wysor, Strike indicated, was a "man more familiar with industry." Following the same principle, Strike recommended for the DRB Roy Campbell, a former president of the New York Shipbuilding Company and in charge of the Japanese shipping section of the OCI reparations survey.[50] With Strike's assistance Draper persuaded Campbell to accept membership on the DRB. In the person of Roy Campbell the assault on the reparations program was symbolically linked with that on FEC-230.

Draper's proposal to appoint officials from International General Electric, Carrier Corporation, and Caltex oil to the DRB was aborted by MacArthur's opposition. SCAP warned that such officials would be exposed to "allegations of personal interest" since their companies were attempting to restore extensive prewar links with Zaibatsu combine partners. International General Electric, he pointed out, had a 20 percent share interest in Toshiba, a firm designated for possible deconcentration. Beating a tactical retreat, Draper wound up appointing to the DRB (in addition to Campbell) an Ohio banker, a New York manufacturer of railroad train couplers, an Ohio utilities executive, an antitrust lawyer friend of Attorney General Tom Clark, and a member of the Securities Exchange Commission.[51] By 4 May, when the DRB arrived in Japan to begin its work, Draper was rightly confident that the board would subvert the deconcentration program.

While working on finding suitable personnel for the DRB, Draper and Royall planned a solo mission for "a man of real stature . . . and armed with authority" to review the whole Zaibatsu dissolution problem. As late as the end of February, Royall hoped to recruit George L. Harrison, president of the New York Life Insurance Company or Thomas McCabe, president of Scott Paper, "to come to some conclusion as to whether [there was a] necessity for a change in direction of course . . . in view of profound changes in the world situation and the attitude of the American people toward the economic circumstances of the Occupied areas." But both Harrison and McCabe declined to go to Japan.[52]

Unexpected developments in Congress during the first two weeks in March triggered a new approach by Draper and Royall to the Zaibatsu dissolution controversy and other economic issues in Japan as well. Representative Charles Eaton, Republican chairman of the House Foreign Affairs Committee, decided that the army's EROA request for Japan of $180 million should be considered as part of a new omnibus foreign aid bill. The core of the bill was the $6.8 billion request for the Marshall Plan but it also included an aid proposal for China and other items. Fearing that lengthy debate on the various parts of the omnibus bill would delay passage of the top priority Marshall Plan, the Truman administration applied intense pressure on the Foreign

Affairs Committee to remove the Marshall Plan request from the omnibus bill for separate consideration. In a vote by the committee on 11 March, the administration effort failed.[53]

Senator Arthur Vandenberg, chairman of the Senate Foreign Relations Committee and the principal Republican proponent of the Marshall Plan, conferred with Draper about the EROA request. In the interests of the passage of the Marshall Plan, the Army Department should withdraw the EROA request from the omnibus foreign aid bill. Vandenberg said he was not familiar with the Japanese program and discussion of it might further delay passage of the Marshall Plan request beyond the scheduled 1 April start-up date. He also implied that the EROA request might jeopardize a few votes on the omnibus bill as well. In any case, he assured Royall and Draper of his support for the EROA program once the Marshall Plan was safely through Congress. The Army Department did withdraw the EROA request from the omnibus bill and asked that it be handled separately.[54] In the midst of a war scare around a Communist coup in Czechoslovakia, the omnibus foreign aid bill without EROA was reported out of the House Foreign Affairs Committee on 19 March. Less than two weeks later, while EROA languished in committee, Congress authorized funding for the Marshall Plan.

The uncertain fate of the recovery aid request for Japan and congressional insistence during debates that the Marshall Plan be run on a business basis convinced Draper and other Army Department officials to expand the scope of the Zaibatsu dissolution mission. Accompanied by Royall and a few other Pentagon officials, five or six top-flight businessmen would survey the entire spectrum of economic problems in Japan and return to assure Congress that the Japanese, SCAP, the State Department, and the FEC all understood the new emphasis in American policy on recovery in Japan. Initially Draper's only connection to the Economic Mission was the recruitment of the business-men members of the mission. But on 12 March, less than two weeks before the departure of the mission, Royall assigned Draper to take his place so he could testify before Congress in support of the Universal Military Training bill.[55] Thereafter, the Economic Mission, though officially headed by Percy Johnston, chairman of the Chemical Bank, was usually referred to in the press as the Draper Mission.

The Textile Crisis

Of Draper's appointees to the Economic Mission, Sidney H. Scheuer was the least known but, in many ways, the most important. Head of Scheuer and

Company, a New York business consulting firm with an international textile trading subsidiary, Intertex, Scheuer had been advising Draper for several months on what was for the army under secretary the most time consuming and most complex of all the Japanese problems he handled—the restoration of the Japanese textile industry and the marketing of Japanese textiles abroad.

For more than a year before Draper took over responsibility for Occupied Japan, Washington policymakers encouraged the rapid rehabilitation of the once mighty Japanese cotton textile industry. The failure of plans for restoring the Japanese silk industry, the relative technical and financial ease of raising cotton textile output, the pressure of raw cotton producers in the United States for foreign markets, and above all the expectation of a large foreign exchange surplus from Japanese textile exports figured heavily in the decision of economic planners to make cotton textiles the key to launching a successful recovery program. As the Green Book projected, foreign exchange from cotton textile exports would finance the purchase not only of raw cotton but of other raw materials necessary for the recovery of those heavy industries engaged in the export sector. By the end of the recovery program, capital goods rather than cotton textiles would account for the bulk of Japanese exports and provide the basis for a self-supporting economy.[56]

But for Draper this whole recovery plan was in danger even before it started. He noted the "alarming rate" at which output and export sales of Japanese cotton textiles had fallen off during the summer and fall of 1947. The heart of the problem was the shortage of dollars in world markets. The Japanese needed dollars to pay for necessary imports of surplus raw cotton stocks held by the U.S. Commodity Credit Corporation (CCC).[57]

Draper's first attempt at solving this crisis was to modify the terms of the CCC raw cotton contract to allow the sale of Japanese cotton textiles for dollars in the American market. But he was immediately lobbied by Dr. William Jacobs, president of the American Cotton Manufacturers Association (ACMA), who warned that his organization would use its influence in Congress against Japanese aid requests if the doors were opened to cheap Japanese textiles. To appease the ACMA, Draper arranged for Jacobs to head a Textile Mission to Japan and promised to postpone action on Japanese textile imports until after his return. All interested departments, SCAP, and Sidney Scheuer informed Draper that the Jacobs report of 30 January 1948 made recommendations that were already being carried out, impractical, or dangerously protectionist. Scheuer charged that it evidenced "a desire to fortify the domestic raw cotton and textile industry rather than the imperative necessity to reestablish the Japanese economy."[58] Obviously impressed by Scheuer, Draper called him to Washington to develop a strategy for circumventing Jacobs and the

ACMA until after congressional action on the recovery and relief aid requests and appointed him to the Economic Mission to come up with marketing plans for Japanese textiles.[59]

While working to close the dollar gap and fending off the ACMA, Draper and the staff of the Civil Affairs Division also sought a more secure flow of raw cotton to Japan than provided by the CCC contract. Though there was some raw cotton included in the EROA request to Congress, they counted on private financing for the bulk of raw cotton supplies to Japan. In September, Draper had hoped that four large New York banks and the U.S. Export-Import Bank would quickly agree to arrange a $60 million credit for raw cotton sales to Japan. But the bankers were skeptical of Pentagon terms that called for the loan to be paid off by the sale of Japanese textiles in uncertain world markets and was backed only by the Gold Pot. Officially known as the Occupied Japan Export-Import Revolving Fund (OJEIRF), the Gold Pot could not be shipped from Japan and distributed to the banks in case of default or war except by permission of the FEC.[60] After nearly six months of haggling with the bankers and others, Draper had no accord on an OJEIRF-backed raw cotton loan as he left for Japan with the Economic Mission. With the Japanese lacking the dollars to purchase CCC cotton and continuing uncertainty over the passage of the EROA aid request with its provision for raw cotton, Draper and the Army Department feared further delay in reaching a settlement on an OJEIRF-backed raw cotton loan would damage the Japanese cotton textile industry and "seriously endanger Japan's economic survival and the political situation in the Far East."[61]

Just as the Economic Mission began its work in Japan, a bill was introduced in Congress, perhaps at Draper's request and certainly with his approval, proposing a $150 million revolving fund to finance shipments of raw materials to occupied areas, such as cotton to Japan. Authored by Senator James Eastland, a Mississippi Democrat and large cotton producer, and strongly backed by Knowland and three other "cotton Senators," the bill aimed to insure Japan as a major market for American raw cotton.[62] "We have a big cotton crop coming in 1948," Eastland told reporters, "and we have to find an outlet for it." Forty-one senators sponsored the "Eastland bill," which offered better terms for raw cotton shippers than contemplated by the New York bankers under the stalled OJEIRF proposal.[63] Unlike that proposal, Draper knew, the Eastland bill had to be debated and passed upon by Congress. Thus as Draper and his party started work in Japan, virtually the entire financial underpinning of the Occupation—GARIOA relief aid, EROA recovery aid, and the Eastland cotton financing bill—rested in the none-too-reliable hands of the Eightieth Congress. The personnel, the press releases, and the final report of the Draper Mission were shaped by this consideration more than any other.

The Draper Mission

The selection of the businessmen personnel for the Economic Mission was for Draper the key to its success. For chairman of the mission, Draper recruited Percy Johnston, chairman of the Chemical Bank and Trust Company of New York. His name was apparently suggested by Defense Secretary Forrestal. In an undated, penciled memo bearing no signature in Draper's files, Johnston was described as a ''close friend Mac[Arthur] & handles investments for him.'' The appointment of Paul G. Hoffman, Republican, president of Studebaker Corporation, and chairman of the board of the influential Committee for Economic Development, was a particularly savvy one by Draper. Nominated director of the Economic Cooperation Administration (ECA) to administer the Marshall Plan program on his return trip from Japan, Hoffman was highly regarded by Senator Vandenberg and other Republicans in Congress. With Draper at his side, Hoffman summed up his outlook to the press in a single sentence: ''Our greatest responsibility today is to fortify capitalism against all attacks.'' Robert F. Loree, formerly vice-president of the Morgan Guaranty Trust Company and chairman of the powerful National Foreign Trade Council (NFTC), also joined the Economic Mission. NFTC represented all of the major U.S. investors in Japan and Loree had been strenuously lobbying on their behalf against FEC-230 and other reforms that ''adversely affect foreign business.''[64] Completing the business membership of the Economic Mission was Sidney H. Scheuer.

Ostensibly the purpose of the Draper Mission was to study and make recommendations to the Army Department concerning the economic problems of Japan. In fact, the primary objective of the mission, as Draper recalled in an interview nearly twenty-five years later, was political. ''I took this group of businessmen over, because I had become convinced from what I'd known in Germany and what I had learned in Japan in two or three visits, that the orders concerning the economy of Japan had to be changed. I took [them] there to buttress my own recommendations to the President and the Secretary of State and the Congress to change the instructions to MacArthur in Japan.'' Those instructions, in Draper's view, amounted to a Morgenthau Plan for Japan which had left the country ''so far as industry was concerned, a morgue.''[65]

General MacArthur was more blunt about the real purposes of the Economic Mission. He told the British Minister in Tokyo that, for ''all intents and purposes,'' the mission's report had been written before Draper ever left Washington. The Economic Mission had ''only come to Japan to furnish Congress ocular evidence in support of its plans for large appropriations.'' The general ''spoke most bitterly'' against American ''Tycoons'' like Draper,

Forrestal, Royall, and Harriman who were against the purge and Zaibatsu dissolution measures "because they thought they would conflict with their own business interests."[66]

The very first meeting Draper had with MacArthur upon arriving in Japan bore out a State Department prediction that he and his businessmen friends would "become involved in a number of rather explosive political considerations. . . . [The] outcome of the Army's effort to reorient SCAP's policies is unpredictable." Joined by Kennan, Draper opened by asking MacArthur his opinion on the controversial question of rearming Japan. "[There] is a general trend in recent War Department thinking," Draper noted, "toward the early establishment of a small defensive force for Japan, to be ready at such time as U.S. Occupation forces leave the country." MacArthur retorted that such a plan was contrary to the international commitments of the United States, violated the no-war clause of the Japanese constitution, and would delay economic recovery. In short, he was "unalterably opposed" to Japanese rearmament. Rather than build up Japan's military forces and rely on U.S. naval and army bases on the Japanese home islands, the general outlined his strategic view that U.S. air power based in Okinawa was adequate to defend Japan in the post-Occupation era.[67] Draper did not challenge MacArthur's views directly but later made it clear to others in Tokyo and Washington that he emphatically disagreed with him.

Draper's initial meeting with Prime Minister Ashida Hitoshi, head of the Democratic party, set the tone for the next two weeks of high-level conferences between American and Japanese officials. Taking over from the fallen Katayama government, Ashida counted on American aid to hold together his shaky right-of-center coalition government. He presented Draper a memorandum containing a list of requests prepared by his aides and business groups for exemptions from possible reparations removals, a higher level of shipping tonnage, the reconstruction of oil refineries, and more U.S. foodstuffs and raw material imports. The prime minister blamed the continuing inflationary spiral and lack of progress in industrial recovery primarily on very strong labor agitation, particularly from Communist infiltrated government employees unions. Ashida joined Japanese business circles and the press in "telling the Draper Mission almost with a single voice" that industrial recovery was dependent on "better control over labor" through "revision of the occupation's liberal labor laws" and appeals "to labor asking greater moderation in its demands." If that were done and U.S. aid were forthcoming, Ashida argued, inflation would be eased and real recovery begun. Draper responded by pointing out "that getting money for Japan depends upon the U.S. Congress and . . . Congress will be more generous if convinced that Japan is helping itself to the maximum extent in meeting the problems of inflation, foreign trade, etc. Japan can become self supporting only if it works hard and intelligently, establishes . . . stabilized exchange conditions, and increases food, coal, and other production. This requires a calm political situation."[68]

Draper took personal charge of impressing on MacArthur and SCAP personnel that the business purge and Zaibatsu dissolution program were to be effectively halted. In addition, members of the Economic Mission openly conferred with purged business leaders such as Asano Ryogyo and staunch opponents of the dissolution program such as Ishikawa Ichiro, president of the Japan Federation of Economic Organizations (FEO). The final report of the Economic Mission, known as the Johnston Report of 26 April 1948, confirmed the fears of SCAP's leading trustbuster, Edward Welsh, that Draper wanted "such drastic curtailment of the deconcentration program as to amount to virtual abandonment of the principles of FEC-230."[69] The period of uncertainty caused by the dissolution program, the report concluded, "should be made short and the area of uncertainty lessened as rapidly as possible. The possible disturbing effects should be allayed by care not to hurt production, and by limiting reorganization to the minimum necessary to insure reasonable competition."[70] Of course, what constituted reasonable competition would be determined primarily by Draper's handpicked DRB.

In finalizing U.S. reparations policy Draper found General MacArthur an unexpected ally and brushed aside the arguments of some SCAP liberals who were critical of the leniency of the OCI report. Paul Hoffman advised that the Economic Mission would "play safe, take the most liberal estimate for retention in every case, and protect American taxpayers."[71] The Johnston Report findings on reparations were far worse than Draper's most severe critics anticipated and opened yet another phase in the rapid subversion of the original program. The report bluntly stated that plants "which are needed in bringing about the recovery of Japan should be retained [and the] excess capacity that can be spared without affecting Japan's useful peacetime productivity is not great." The Economic Mission recommended a 40 percent decrease in reparations availabilities from the five remaining "war supporting industries" in the OCI Report. Most shocking, the mission called for more than a 60 percent reduction in available reparations from arsenals, airplane factories, and other theretofore "primary war facilities."[72]

For Draper and his colleagues, halting the spiraling inflation, attracting foreign investment, and stimulating textile and other exports in the face of the world dollar shortage were key interrelated parts of a successful recovery program for Japan. From the start of the Occupation until 1949, the Japanese economy was beset by severe and chronic inflation, accompanied by low levels of industrial output and even lower levels of exports. As already noted, Draper had at first tended to blame these problems on the Zaibatsu dissolution, reparations, purge, and other reform programs which, he felt, undermined the confidence of the Japanese business community. But despite his largely successful efforts to halt and begin the reversal of the reform program, Draper saw no abatement of the inflationary spiral on his second trip to Japan. He told Prime Minister Ashida that the enforcement of a balanced government budget was the key to stemming inflation.[73] By reducing the number of government employees, eliminating subsidies to industry, raising railroad fares and prices of other governmental services, strengthening efforts at tax collection, and other steps the national budget could be balanced and the main source of inflation choked off. Such measures, Draper knew, were politically unpopular. In fact he did not think the weak Ashida cabinet would be any more successful than its predecessors in stabilizing the economy unless the American aid program was directly linked to the government's enforcement of an austere balanced budget. Draper told MacArthur that, as soon as he returned to the United States, he would ask Joseph Dodge, president of the Detroit Bank and architect of occupied Germany's currency stabilization plan, to map out a balanced budget solution to Japan's economic woes.[74]

Not surprisingly, members of the Economic Mission regarded the introduction of foreign capital into Japan as extremely important to the recovery program. American investment could be profitable, a source of scarce dollars for the Japanese, a means of boosting the export competitiveness of Japanese industry, and a help in gaining congressional support for the recovery aid requests. But the Draper Mission publicly warned that American investors were "not satisfied with Japan's current economic picture and generally feel that the Japanese have not done everything possible to encourage private investments from the outside." The unstable multiple foreign exchange system, Draper told Ashida, made it difficult for Japan to resume its old trade channels and, hence, was one of the most important obstacles to greater foreign investment in Japan. Until there was a single, fixed exchange rate for the yen, which could not be established until inflation was controlled, "there could not be much [foreign] investment. Everything seems to revolve around stable exchange conditions, and this around the need for a balanced budget." In addition, the Draper Mission considered many other obstacles to foreign investment in Japan—Japanese tax laws, lack of legal protection for property acquired, no provision for repatriation of profits, and lastly the lack of a Washington policy on restitution and compensation for damage of the assets of prewar American investors in Japanese companies.[75]

Finally, Draper and his aides discussed with SCAP and Japanese officials the manifold problems encountered in boosting Japan's export trade, the most important index to the success of the recovery program. Congress, Draper told Ashida, would not indefinitely pay for the food and other imports to Japan.

The none-too-high standard of living in Japan itself would have to be restricted, Draper warned Ashida, in order to channel production from the Japanese home market to the export market and thereby earn foreign exchange to pay for necessary imports.[76] The Draper Mission reaffirmed the need for trade to be taken out of the hands of both SCAP and the Japanese government and returned to private companies even before a peace treaty; for diplomatic pressure to be exerted on countries which discriminated against Japanese trade; and for the Japanese shipping industry to be revived to cut down on the foreign exchange drain.

Sharing in the consensus developing in Washington, Draper and members of the Economic Mission considered the reorientation of Japanese trade from the United States to within Asia critical to the success of economic recovery planning. Some analysts argued in 1947 and 1948 that only Northeast Asia, especially China, offered the raw materials and markets needed for Japanese economic recovery, adding that increased Sino-Japanese trade would soften the radicalism of the Chinese Communists and prevent China from falling under Soviet domination.[77] Like most planners, however, the Draper Mission looked primarily to the economic integration of Japan with its southern neighbors without ever fully appreciating the obstacles which existed to such plans. Leaders of Southeast Asian nations, for example, resisted any plan that smacked of a renewal of Japanese economic domination and therefore might add to the political turmoil throughout the region. When they sought an infusion of American aid dollars in a Marshall Plan for Asia as the price for ending their discrimination against Japanese trade and investment, the State Department consistently responded that these countries were at such a low level of industrial development that the program could not succeed.[78] In rejecting some form of a Marshall Plan for Asia, American officials heightened the fears in Southeast Asia of the Japanese. New weapons for achieving the economic integration of Japan with Southeast Asia had to be found in order to insure the economic recovery of Japan and to contain communism in Asia.

The one concrete suggestion of the Draper Mission for reorienting Japanese trade to Southeast Asia eschewed these delicate foreign policy problems and was clearly designed to win the political support of both Southern raw cotton and textile interests for the package of aid and loans still awaiting passage in Congress. The Johnston Report used the idea of Dr. Jacobs and Sidney Scheuer for the development of a triangular trade arrangement by which American cotton would be sold to Japan for production of textiles to be exported to the Dutch East Indies. The Dutch would pay for the textiles with tin and other raw materials that were needed for the U.S. strategic stockpile program. Such an arrangement was of "great interest to American cotton growers,'' the Draper Mission candidly admitted. They wanted a solution to Japan's trading problems "so that the large potential Japanese market would not be lost.''[79]

At his final news conference in Tokyo, Draper, according to Burton Crane of the *New York Times*, "strongly emphasized that the United States was not attempting to build Japan into a base against the Reds and that his mission was 'purely economic.' '' Apparently Draper had not yet changed his view that the Soviet military threat was exaggerated. He certainly wanted to contain labor and the Left in Japan. But talk of Japan as an anti-Communist military bastion might jeopardize Japanese trade in Asia, including trade with Communist governments there. No doubt referring to China, Draper stated that trade between democratic and Communist controlled areas "was possible regardless of their beliefs.''[80]

Securing the Recovery Aid Package

The Economic Mission, as Draper intended, thwarted any SCAP plans for implementing FEC-230, further delayed State Department efforts to finalize the reparations program, boosted the political fortunes of the conservative Ashida cabinet, and gave the Japanese business community and political conservatives encouragement that they would survive the Occupation relatively unscathed. That the Economic Mission helped spark anti-American mass demonstrations in China and extraordinarily sharp outcries, official and unofficial, from virtually all FEC nations fearful of the revival of Japanese economic domination and militarism, did not appear to trouble Draper.[81] His primary concern remained to effect a "shift of emphasis" in Occupation policy in time to win congressional support for the Army Department's EROA and GARIOA requests and for the passage of the Eastland bill.

Soon after his return from Japan and Korea in early April, Draper contacted Senator Styles Bridges, chairman of the Senate Appropriations Committee. He went over the changes in the Zaibatsu and reparations policies and asked for his support of the EROA request for Japan, Korea, and the Ryukyus. It had been revised from the original fifteen-month basis to the twelve months of FY 1949 for a total of $200 million of which $144 million was for Japan.[82] At the end of the month he wrote to Senators Bridges, Knowland, and Vandenberg and Congressmen John Vorys, John Taber, and Charles Eaton that he had been assured by MacArthur that the deconcentration law would be administered in light of the proposed recovery program and enclosed a copy of a conciliatory statement by MacArthur in Tokyo welcoming the Deconcentration Review Board. "Discussion of recovery program with House and Senate Committee

chairmen have had generally favorable reaction,'' Draper reported optimisti-
cally at the end of April to MacArthur: "We are continuing to push this
program vigorously."[83]

In an appearance before the House Appropriations Committee on 11 May,
Draper's optimism about the prospects for the EROA program must have been
shaken. Following a recital by Draper of the standard litany that only recovery
aid for Japan could lead to self-support and eventually reduce costs to the
American taxpayer, Draper was closely questioned by Representative Francis
Case, Republican from South Dakota, who had taken charge of the Japanese
bill for the committee. If American raw materials were going to be converted
by the Japanese into manufactured goods for exports, he asked, where would
they be sold? "Largely through the east and also the United States," Draper
responded. Pressed by Case, Draper conceded that most Asian countries
"still have very much in their minds the Japanese domination before the war
of the trade areas, and it is a slow business getting them to accept the Japanese
to come to their countries." Case persisted in questioning Draper about Japanese exports to the United States. "We have some cases, such as textile
manufacturers who are not eager" for increased Japanese trade with the
United States, Draper testified. But even they were reassured by Dr. Jacobs of
the ACMA that the Army Department was "not going to flood the market
here with Japanese textiles." The congressmen complained not only of the
potential dangers of Japanese trade competition but of the "run around"
Draper gave them on whether aid to Japan was a loan to be paid back or a
grant. And why had the Army Department failed to get MacArthur to come
home and testify for the Japanese appropriation as General Clay had done for
the German appropriation? A statement from MacArthur, Case lectured
Draper, would have created grassroots support for the aid program which did
not then exist.[84]

With time growing short before Congress adjourned for the summer Draper
was forced to revise the administration's tactics for securing aid for the EROA
program. "Have been continually pressing Japanese Korean recovery
program," Draper telegramed MacArthur on 12 May, "but legislative jam has
developed and Representative Vorys of Foreign Affairs Committee and Chairman Taber of Appropriations Committee advised me . . . that House calendar
such that legislative authorization [for EROA] and subsequent appropriation
was out of question for this session. . . . Suggestion was made by them that we
broaden language in GARIOA request to permit recovery items to be paid
from appropriations as well and food and fertilizers." Draper immediately
contacted Frank Pace, acting director of the Bureau of the Budget, who
agreed to such an approach. For reasons which are not clear, Pace recommended to Congress that only $150 million, instead of the $220 million

amount requested for a separately authorized EROA program, be tacked on to the $1.25 billion GARIOA item; nor did he specify how much of that $150 million was directed specifically for Japan, Korea, or the Ryukyus. But if the chairmen of both congressional appropriations committees agreed to support a GARIOA deficiency appropriation early in 1949, Pace told Draper, he would permit "over expenditure" for the recovery program during the remainder of 1948. After a talk with Senator Styles Bridges, Draper was hopeful that the new approach to funding the recovery program in Japan would succeed and "generally accomplish the same result [as a separate EROA appropriation] for the balance of this year and permit the whole issue to be resolved early in the new [fall congressional] session."[85]

In the hope of salvaging the long delayed and already reduced Japanese aid package, Draper arranged for the public release of the Johnston Report and gave a major address in San Francisco on "Japan's Key Position in the Far East" in mid-May. For the first time since becoming army under secretary, Draper emphasized that the recovery program in Japan was part of the political and military effort of the United States against world communism. "In Europe and in Asia economic health and well-being," he said, "must be regained so that democracy will find good soil in which to grow and in which those philosophies and ideologies which thrive upon hunger and confusion will lose their appeal." The recovery of the Japanese economy and foreign trade, Draper added, required increased American military strength to "maintain the peace. . . . We must deny to any potential enemy any foothold or any base on or near the American continent, and if war should come we must be ready to seize and hold airbases perhaps far from our shores but so located that our bombers could carry the war decisively to the enemy."[86] These statements may have reflected an actual change in Draper's strategic thinking. That such military arguments had wrenched foreign aid dollars from the niggardly Eightieth Congress before, Draper was certainly well aware.

Despite Draper's efforts, Congress proceeded to mangle the administration's foreign aid request, including that for Japan. No longer under the war crisis atmosphere of mid-March, when the Marshall Plan authorization was railroaded through Congress, the House Appropriations Committee rebelled and on 3 June reported out a bill that cut European Recovery Program requests by $1.7 billion and the total foreign aid requests by 25 percent. Committee chairman John Taber challenged the administration to state the real aims of its foreign aid programs which, he claimed, had been "grossly misrepresented to the American public." While the committee approved the principle of the EROA request, it proposed that the funding for and administration of EROA come from the Marshall Plan program. At the Senate Appropriation Committee meeting a week later, Paul Hoffman, chief administrator of the Marshall Plan, decried the House committee's action and argued that EROA be funded as proposed by adding $150 million to the GARIOA appropriation rather than subtracting money from the Marshall Plan.[87]

After troublesome negotiations between House and Senate conferees and considerable pressure from the administration, Congress finally approved on 20 June the FY 1949 foreign aid program. The multi-billion dollar Marshall Plan was funded as had been planned. The $1.3 billion GARIOA appropriation, however, was $100 million less than the administration had requested and included $125 million instead of $150 million for an EROA program for Japan, Korea, and the Ryukyus subject to the same guidelines as the Marshall Plan.[88] The new language of P.L. 793 governing the GARIOA appropriation was so vague, however, that Tracy Voorhees, Draper's successor as army under secretary, suggested that, in fact, there were "no directions or recommendations as to the amounts to be spent on either [the GARIOA or EROA] program" in Japan during FY 1949.[89] With deficiency appropriations added in, total U.S. appropriated aid to Japan in FY 1949 was $530 million. This figure was $108 million under EROA and $422 million under GARIOA guidelines, or some 50 percent more than the previous year's GARIOA expenditures for Japan.[90]

With the highly confused and uncertain standing of the EROA and GARIOA appropriations in Congress, the passage of the Eastland bill and the finalization of the OJEIRF cotton credit took on heightened importance for Draper after his return from Japan. Inadequate financing for raw cotton had reached the point where drastic cuts in textile production in Japan were contemplated. Unless the depleted stocks of raw cotton were replenished from American sources, Japanese textile exports would cease and jeopardize the whole recovery program even before its official start. Thus Draper was pleased to learn that the Senate Committee on Agriculture and Forestry had reported out favorably the Eastland bill. Anticipating opposition to the bill from domestic textile manufacturers, Draper shrewdly brought Dr. William Jacobs to Washington. No doubt unaware of how critical Draper was of the Textile Mission report or his scheme to drop the prohibition against Japanese textile imports to the United States after Congress adjourned, the naive Jacobs spent a great deal of time in Washington promoting the passage of the Eastland bill. By mid-April Jacobs reported to Draper that Senate passage of the bill was certain. The next month Jacobs returned to Washington to push the bill through the House.[91]

The hearings and brief debates in Congress on the bill made clear that the program was viewed primarily as a good business proposition. Surplus raw cotton would be sold and the cheaper quality textiles manufactured from it would be unsuitable for the American market. Representative Joseph Bryson, Democrat from South Carolina, told his colleagues that his support for the Eastland bill was not out of love for the Japanese. "What is proposed is to restore the Japanese textile industry to relieve us of the burden of paying the way of our former enemy. . . . Japan should be provided with access to the natural Japanese markets [of Asia] but should not be permitted to compete with and undersell the American producers in the American markets." With such support, the final bill passed Congress on 29 June 1948. The first procurement of cotton under P.L. 820 for Japan did not begin until April 1949, but by the end of 1950, 220,000 bales had been shipped.[92]

Given the critical cotton supply problem for Japan in the early spring of 1948 and unavoidable delays in passing and implementing the Eastland bill, Draper wanted the quick completion of arrangements for the OJEIRF credit. He personally attempted to negotiate a lower interest rate from the New York bankers. Despite his failure, the Truman administration finally approved the terms for the $60 million OJEIRF credit for raw cotton on 20 May 1948. Ironically, with the certain passage of the Eastland bill, Draper and other officials saw the significance of the new cotton loan as establishing a pattern for the use of the OJEIRF for imports from all over the world of raw materials to Japan other than cotton.[93] In any case, by the end of 1950, 603,000 bales of U.S. raw cotton had been financed to Japan under the OJEIRF credit, making it more important, in fact, than either P.L. 820 or EROA appropriations as the financial source of U.S. raw cotton to Japan during the Occupation.[94]

By the end of June, the whole aid and loan package for the critical first year of the Japanese recovery program was finally clear to Draper. When they compared it to the treatment given by the Eightieth Congress to the German occupation and the Marshall Plan, the army under secretary and his aides often expressed resentment at the delays and reductions suffered by the Japanese recovery program. Yet Draper betrayed a sense of satisfaction with the final outcome. "We are now in position for the first time," he told a top aide, "of having a Congressionally approved recovery program." Coupled with P.L. 820 and OJEIRF credits, SCAP and the Japanese government could "coordinate an actually operating program for the next six months." It should begin as quickly as possible, Draper warned, for the Army Department would have to run the gauntlet of congressional committees again in the fall for both FY 1949 deficiency appropriations and the FY 1950 aid requests.[95] The next Congress would want to see results from the new aid program and be reassured that by 1953 no further relief or recovery aid would be necessary to make Japan self-supporting.

Conclusion

As under secretary of the army until 1 March 1949 Draper remained deeply involved in the key aspects of Japan policy. Not surprisingly he fully supported the central feature of Kennan's PPS 28 document which made the achievement of the primary objective of economic recovery dependent on a continued shift away from pressing the Japanese for further reform legislation and temporizing what was already on the books. "Strengthen economic recovery objective" and "get in thought of new instructions" to MacArthur which would not require FEC approval, he wrote in the margins of PPS 28 on a first reading.[96]

Concretely, Draper's support of PPS 28 meant the demise of key economic reforms. By the end of 1948, Draper's handpicked Deconcentration Review Board had eliminated all but nine companies from the list of those designated for possible reorganization and the State Department had withdrawn FEC-230 with the statement that the objectives of the program had already been accomplished. In collaboration with Kennan, Draper engineered the complete cessation of any reparations removals from Japan, although the public announcement of that policy did not come until May 1949 after Draper had left office.[97] He persistently pressed MacArthur to depurge those Japanese who had been designated as militarists and ultranationalists while giving full backing to SCAP's assault in the summer of 1948 on public employee unions and labor generally. Clearly the well-known NSC 13/2 statement on U.S. Japan policy of October 1948, while based primarily on George Kennan's PPS 28 paper, represented the consensus in Washington on the relationship of recovery to reform that Draper, more than any other policymaker, articulated and implemented throughout his tenure as army under secretary.[98]

In reviewing Kennan's document before it was forwarded to the National Security Council, Draper was forced to give attention to security issues for Japan. He had already discovered on his visit to Japan that Kennan and MacArthur did not include permanent American bases on the Japanese home islands in their concept of an Asian defense perimeter and that MacArthur objected to Pentagon plans initiated in February 1948 for "limited remilitarization" by the Japanese. Reflecting the views of the Joint Chiefs of Staff, Draper sought to include in the final NSC document a paragraph which made the termination of the Occupation conditional on abandonment by the Soviet Union of its policy of Communist expansion or the inclusion in the peace treaty of the American right to undefined numbers of forces and bases and some degree of Japanese rearmament. What the military planners wanted was to deny Japan to the Soviet Union and utilize Japanese territory for offensive air attacks that could rapidly destroy the effectiveness of all enemy forces in

East Asia. But Kennan viewed these proposals as resting on the unwarranted premise that war with the Soviet Union was inevitable. He also feared an army ploy for an indefinitely prolonged Occupation of Japan.[99]

In the end the NSC in 1948 adopted Kennan's view on the timing and terms of a peace treaty. The whole question of bases and Japanese rearmament in the post-treaty period which loomed as a major issue dividing the State and Defense departments would be postponed until the economic recovery program was far enough along to start actual peace treaty negotiations. At that point both Russian policy and Japan's internal stability would be reevaluated and the question of post-treaty bases and rearmament settled accordingly. It would be Draper's successors who were left to consider the Army Department's security requirements and other terms for ending the Occupation.[100]

To Draper's consternation,the enlarged flow of aid to Japan and rapid demise of the reform program did not win the cooperation of Japanese business and government leaders, to say nothing of Japanese workers, in the American designed recovery program. Throughout the summer and fall of 1948 exports lagged behind imports and were appreciably below the levels indicated in the Green Book as necessary and possible. Only part of the difficulty was attributable to excessive optimism about market conditions throughout the politically unstable Far East or inadequate recovery funds from Congress, argued the SCAP economists who prepared the Blue Book recovery plan of November 1948. The root of the problem was that the "Japanese Government and people . . . give undue priority to internal rehabilitation and expansion projects." Unlike the Green Book, the Blue Book recovery plan made no assumption that a domestic standard of living reasonably close to that of 1930–34 should be achieved by 1953 in Japan. In fact, emphasis in the Blue Book Plan (which Draper used as justification for the congressional appropriations needed for FY 1949 deficiency requests and the second year of the recovery program) was "upon the necessity for Japan to expand exports first, and to restrict its consumption to . . . minimum levels. The rise in domestic consumption will be contingent upon demonstrated performance in the export program."[101]

The continued inflation and inadequate export performance during 1948, Draper admitted to the much alarmed NSC, required more direct intervention by Washington in the economic policies of the Japanese government. Largely at Draper's insistence, Joseph Dodge, president of the Detroit Bank and a former colleague of Draper's in the Economics Division in occupied Germany, agreed in December 1948 to supervise an economic stabilization plan for Japan. As explained in the following chapter, the Dodge Line had a profound impact on every segment of Japanese society in 1949 and 1950.

Working from his New York offices of Dillon, Read after March 1949,

Draper continued to shape Occupation policy and became the principal spokesman promoting American investments in Japan. Through contacts he had developed with Prime Minister Yoshida and Finance Minister Ikeda Hayato, Draper and Dillon, Read became the "informal and unofficial" representatives of the Japanese government on matters of aid, trade, and investments in the United States. From 1949 to 1952, Draper lobbied the World Bank, the International Monetary Fund, the State Department, the Council of Foreign Relations, and other agencies on a variety of projects designed to promote recovery in Japan and its integration into the global capitalist system.[102] With considerable pride in his own role, Draper told a group of American businessmen in 1950, a year before the signing of the peace treaty ending the Occupation, that the "Rising Sun of Japan, long in eclipse, was indeed rising and is again taking its honorable place in the world today."[103]

William Draper, as the American official most directly responsible for Japan policy from 1947 to 1949, was the first to directly link the Japanese economic recovery program to a "reverse course." In his view, a successful recovery program required the restoration of the Japanese capitalist class and a secure conservative government while, conversely, the trade unions and the political Left in Japan had to be contained. Draper constantly and successfully battled those in the State Department, SCAP, or the FEC who fought to implement or preserve key aspects of the original reform program. The hold of the conservative Eightieth Congress on the foreign aid funds needed for carrying out the recovery program strongly reinforced Draper's determination that a "reverse course" accompany the recovery program.

Draper was supremely confident in 1948 that the United States had the power to overcome the obstacles thrown up by Japan's neighbors or by the Japanese themselves to his conception of economic recovery. Draper was not motivated in his Japan policies by ideological or strategic fears of the Soviet Union. Rather, global economic issues had the most profound influence on his policies for Occupied Japan, and those policies significantly contributed to—and did not just reflect—the Cold War atmosphere of international distrust. Above all, the creation of those conditions in Japan and elsewhere for the security, growth, and profitability of large American corporations was William H. Draper's raison d'etre and that of the capitalist class he so ably represented.

7   JOSEPH M. DODGE

The Integration of Japan into the World Economy

A short, solemn American with thin graying hair and rimless glasses arrived in Tokyo on 1 February 1949, with the innocuous title of financial advisor to SCAP. Within two months the *Economist* in England commented that this financial "expert has finally taken over from the soldier in Japan." General Douglas MacArthur might still be the supreme commander but Joseph Dodge, president of the Detroit Bank, was "the new power behind the throne."[1] Japanese newspapers and magazines soon were filled with articles analyzing, criticizing, and occasionally praising the Dodge Mission and Dodge Line. Though virtually unknown in the United States today, Dodge is remembered in Japan along with General Douglas MacArthur and John Foster Dulles as one of the triumvirate of Americans who shaped the course of Occupation history.

The Man

Joseph Dodge was a shy and introverted man who never sought attention from the public. But his recognized competency in the banking field thrust him to the heights of power in the world of national and international affairs. Dodge did not have the credentials of most of his colleagues in business and government. He was born in Detroit in 1891, the son of a poor Quaker artist. He never attended college. After graduation from high school he worked as a bank messenger and in clerical and bookkeeping positions. Then in 1911 he began employment with the state of Michigan in the securities and banking regulatory fields. The founder of the Bank of Detroit was so impressed with Dodge's abilities that in the early 1920s he invited him to become an operating officer of the bank. During the depression Dodge assisted several Detroit banks in mergers and reorganizations and, in 1933, became president and director of the Detroit Savings Bank, the oldest bank in Michigan. He developed a reputation as a granite-like, no-nonsense banker who got the job done. Under Dodge's leadership the Detroit Bank, as it became known, grew from assets of $60 million in 1936 to $550 million in 1948, at the time of his assignment to Japan as SCAP financial advisor.[2]

From his headquarters at the Detroit Bank, Dodge extended his influence widely. He served as a member of the board of directors of Chrysler Corporation, the Standard Accident Insurance Company, and other firms. For years Dodge was active on committees of the Michigan Bankers Association and the the American Bankers Association. (He was the president of the former during 1944–45 and of the latter during 1947–48.) Like many Republicans of his generation, he did most of his government service for Democratic administrations. In 1937 he joined the advisory committee from Detroit to the Reconstruction Finance Corporation and the next year he began a six-year term as director of the Federal Reserve Bank of Chicago. During the war, Dodge held several economic posts at the request of Secretary of War Henry Stimson, including chairman of the War Contracts Board and of the Price Adjustment Board.

Dodge played his part in building the American Century as soon as the war in Europe ended. When the German monetary system collapsed, General Dwight Eisenhower wired Washington, "Get Dodge to Germany fast." He served as a deputy finance advisor to Military Governor General Lucius Clay and designed a deflationary currency reduction which precipitated the Berlin blockade of 1948. In May 1947, Dodge went to Vienna for the State Department as U.S. Representative on the Austrian Treaty Commission and returned to advise Secretary of State George Marshall on Austrian affairs. From 1947 to 1951 Dodge also was a member of the advisory committee on fiscal and monetary problems to the Economic Cooperation Administration which handled Marshall Plan funds. But none of these varied assignments proved as significant or as challenging as that of financial advisor to General MacArthur. By 1948, the highest officials in Washington regarded Dodge as one of the most vital troubleshooters around on the vast problems of the international economy.[3]

Throughout his career Dodge adhered to an orthodox banker's view of the world. For him, wealth was created by private accumulation of capital through incentives for profit. An available supply of relatively cheap and mobile labor was an important incentive to capitalists. Full employment, he argued, was a "road to disaster. [S]ome competition for job opportunities . . . results in an increase in worker productivity."[4] Rejecting Keynesian theories, Dodge criticized government expenditures on social welfare and public works as expensive and dangerous luxuries. Dodge was also a vigorous nationalist, promoting investment by American corporations overseas and denouncing foreign critics of American policies. He was convinced after the war that "with an aggressive revolutionary communism loose in the world, there can be no such thing as neutrality—as appealing as it is."[5]

In applying his conservative principles to Japan, Dodge often found himself at odds with Japanese businessmen and their representatives in government. Unlike early U.S. planners who called for the creation of a competitive market for small- and medium-sized businesses, Dodge envisioned a capitalism of Zaibatsu combines operating in an environment of limited government control or regulation. But in his view the pursuit of short-run advantage by these companies lay behind the biggest problem facing postwar Japan, inflation. While inflation enabled Zaibatsu companies to repay debts in devalued yen and more easily acquire smaller competitors, it also priced them out of export markets. High priced exports limited Japan's foreign exchange earnings, and thus left the American taxpayers with the expense of supplying relief imports.[6]

Japanese companies, Dodge often remarked, were "facing a war of economic survival" in international markets and would have to become price competitive through adherence to a program of "dis-inflation" that served American needs and objectives in Asia. "The better class of Japanese is a highly educated and sophisticated world trader," Dodge recorded in his diary. Viscount Kano Hisaakira, probably Dodge's most regular Japanese contact, epitomized just such an individual. Vice-Director of the Central Liaison Office into which the Foreign Office had been transformed during the Occupation, Kano was a short, self-assured international banker with vast prewar experience, owner of a large shipbuilding company, and someone who shared Dodge's political and economic outlook on the world.[7]

In seeking the restoration of Japanese capitalism within an American defined global order, Dodge found common cause with all Zaibatsu executives in weakening the union movement and creating a cheaper source of labor. When one SCAP labor official pointed out that Dodge's anti-inflationary program would depress wages of the Japanese workers and might lead to political unrest, Dodge replied that the standard of living had been permitted to go too high. "We cannot give them everything they want," he insisted. To make Japanese companies more competitive in world markets, Dodge favored an "increase in unemployment" because that would "in turn lead to universal efficiency of labor and greater production." Invariably Dodge recommended that SCAP use repression against those Japanese workers who engaged in strikes and left-wing political agitation to protest his policies.[8]

As a conservative nationalist Dodge anticipated resistance to his policies from Japanese business, labor, and government officials. What angered him most were the many "smartees," "do-gooders," and "hobby-riders," he encountered in SCAP who favored more unemployment insurance, health services, and other social welfare programs for Japan and otherwise remained committed to the original goals of the Occupation. These Americans wanted to make the Japanese "democrats by edict," he charged while in Tokyo, and "transplant here anything that worked in the United States" at the expense of the American taxpayer. Little wonder that *Fortune* paid a glowing tribute to Dodge's leadership in the American banking community in 1948 by calling him that "rare phenomenon—the complete rationalist . . . who does not permit sentimental considerations to affect his decisions."[9]

The Stabilization/Aid Crisis and the Origins of the Dodge Mission

The Dodge Mission arose out of the failure of American efforts by 1949 to establish Japan as the "workshop of Asia." Japanese production and trade revival had been disappointingly slow. Production at the end of 1948 was only about 65 percent of the levels of 1930–34, when population was fifteen million less. The international trade picture had hardly improved. The total level of trade was less than 20 percent of 1937 levels. The outstanding feature of the trade picture in 1948, however, remained the extent to which Japan depended on American aid to correct its unfavorable trade balance. The trade deficit totaled $203 million in 1946, $352 million in 1947, and $426 million in 1948.[10] In 1948 Japan took 65 percent of its imports from the U.S. but sent only 25 percent of its exports there. By contrast, Japan sent 43 percent of its total exports to Southeast Asia but took only 10 percent of its imports from that region.[11]

To American economic planners, Japan had to break its dependence on U.S. aid imports, which were threatened by congressional budget cuts, and do so by increasing its production and selling more products in Asia in exchange for more foodstuffs and raw materials. Given the chaos on the Chinese mainland, Southeast Asia was considered the most critical region for Japanese trade expansion. Solving these Japanese economic problems meant far more than just ending the drain on American resources. Like Kennan, Dodge was convinced that Japan was "an important border area in the worldwide clash between Communism and Democracy and that only a self-supporting and democratic Japan can stand fast against Communism." A rebuilt Japan would be able to protect itself and deter "totalitarian pressures" in the entire region emanating from a "Pan-Asiatic movement" under Soviet or Communist leadership. Through an economically healthy Japan, Dodge contended, the United States could "exert tremendous influence over our relations with all the Orient."[12]

In the eyes of American policymakers, the most serious obstacle to making Japan a self-supporting, anti-Communist workshop in Asia was the rampant postwar inflation which made Japanese exports uncompetitive in world markets. Even with SCAP directives ordering strict controls over the economy, prices from September 1945 to August 1948 rose more than 700 percent. Dodge believed that the spiral of inflation in Japan resulted primarily from the deliberate policies of postwar Japanese governments. Those policies reflected the influence of Ishibashi Tanzan, former editor of the *Oriental Economist* and finance minister in the first Yoshida cabinet until his purge in 1947 under charges of obstructing SCAP policies. Ishibashi emphasized business recovery through deliberate government budget deficits to finance capital accumulation. Taxes were kept low while easy credit was made available from the Reconstruction Finance Bank.[13] Prior to the Dodge Line, loans from the RFB accounted for roughly three-fourths of investment in all industries. A program of "priority production" directed 84 percent of these loans mostly to large firms in the coal, iron and steel, fertilizer, electric, shipbuilding, and textile industries. Since the funds for RFB loans came from debentures subscribed to by the Bank of Japan, they were highly inflationary. But far from opposing price increases, the Ishibashi Line welcomed their effect on production, denied their long-run inflationary character, and ignored the resulting cost to consumers and labor.[14]

Army Under Secretary Draper returned from his trip to Japan in April 1948 extremely alarmed at the threat Japanese inflation represented to the U.S. sponsored recovery program and overall U.S. objectives in Asia. The Ashida cabinet's failure to balance the national budget as a way of controlling inflation did not result from lack of understanding SCAP policy. Rather, any stabilization program involving increased taxes and budget cuts would be politically unpopular and threaten Ashida's fragile coalition in the Diet. Draper was convinced that only more direct American intervention would succeed in solving the Japanese problem and he immediately set out to obtain the services of his former colleague in Germany, Joseph Dodge.[15] The matter was urgent. The powerful National Advisory Council (NAC) warned the Army Department on 6 April that approval of economic recovery aid for Japan was contingent upon enforcement of a stabilization program. Without stabilization, recovery-imports from the U.S. would neither boost production nor increase Japanese exports. To Draper's grave disappointment, Dodge would not consider government service until the end of his term as president of the American Bankers Association in October.

Even before Draper had time to sound out other candidates for the stabilization job in Japan, the seriousness of the inflationary threat to the recovery program was brought home by an interdepartmental mission (without army representation) that had been dispatched to Japan to make recommendations on yen foreign exchange policy. Headed by Federal Reserve Board member Ralph Young, the mission members were appalled to find Japanese government officials not being "fiscal policy or monetary policy minded" and SCAP enforcement efforts wholly inadequate. "The inflationary situation was becoming worse and the tax problem was acute," Young told the NAC on his return.[16]

The Young Mission Report offered a ten-point stabilization plan in the traditional pattern of the International Monetary Fund for attacking the inflationary problem. The plan laid particular emphasis on a balanced budget, including stepped-up tax collections and rigid wage controls with no explicit allowance for cost of living adjustments. With the ten-point stabilization plan in effect, the Young Mission argued, a single fixed exchange rate in the range of 270 to 330 yen to the dollar could be effected before 1 October 1948. The early introduction of a single exchange rate, replacing the chaotic, multiple exchange rate system, would contribute to the overall stabilization of the economy. The immediate implementation of the whole program, Draper told MacArthur in summing up the Young Mission's work, was necessary to "1) avoid threatened and perhaps imminent economic breakdown through continued inflation; 2) to move toward the stage at which economic controls can be relaxed; and 3) to meet self-help obligations implicitly imposed on Japan by U.S. grants of economic aid."[17]

SCAP's denunciation of the Young Mission Report failed to shake Washington's determination to gain greater control over the Japanese economy. MacArthur claimed that the ten-point stabilization plan of the Young Mission was redundant, that "impressive results" were already being achieved in bringing inflation under control, and that the introduction of the single exchange rate before achievement of full economic stability would accelerate inflation and delay relaxation of economic controls. "I am apprehensive of complete disaster," he warned, accurately noting that the essence of the recommendations amounted to a sharp cut in the nation's current consumption, and specifically to a reduction in workers' real wages.[18] But at a tense meeting held on 28 June the NAC adopted the Young Mission recommendations, with a single change. Pressed by Army Secretary Royall, the NAC agreed to lift the 1 October deadline for establishing a single exchange rate and substitute the language "as soon as administratively possible" instead. The change, NAC members warned Royall, did not imply a one- or two-year extension of the time for a single exchange rate but merely a few additional months.[19]

The NAC adoption of the Young Mission stabilization program heightened the pressure on the Army Department to find a means of getting MacArthur and the Japanese to cooperate in imposing what were certain to be unpopular measures. After meetings with Robert Loree and other bankers on the Young Plan, Draper was more than ever convinced that the sending of a top-flight financial advisor to MacArthur with adequate authority to implement stabilization was the only prospect of meeting NAC conditions for further aid to Japan. When several candidates Draper approached over the summer proved unwilling or unable to go to Japan, Draper renewed contact with Dodge. If Dodge would not go to Japan, Draper hoped he might at least help draw up a detailed and workable stabilization plan and lobby Congress for foreign aid for Japan.[20]

Most reluctantly, Dodge agreed to consult for Draper. He first reviewed the data on unemployment, money supply, the budget, manufacturing output, and so on prepared by SCAP economists for the "Blue Book" recovery program, the basis for the Army Department's FY 1950 request of $165 million in recovery aid (up from the $108 million in FY 1949) and $370 million in GARIOA funds. At a meeting called by Draper at his Pentagon office shortly after Truman's election, Dodge told Young and other officials that "every report [from Japan] seems to indicate an adverse or continuing undesirable trend of economic events." Until there was more complete and accurate statistical data on all phases of the Japanese economy, Dodge warned, the Army Department was in the awkward position of only being able to urge SCAP to intensify existing, though obviously ineffective, stabilization efforts. Since stabilization of the economy was the sine qua non for a successful recovery program, Dodge concluded, the Army Department would not be able to defend its aid request for Japan before the NAC or Congress. Dodge suggested the immediate dispatch of a technical mission for data collection to be followed up late in January 1949 by a "key group," possibly including himself, which would remain in Tokyo to force an overall solution to the stabilization problem.[21]

The stabilization/aid crisis reached its climax at the NAC meeting of 3 December. With Draper and Royall present as guests, the NAC reviewed a report by its staff committee which sharply criticized the Army Department and SCAP for failing to halt the deterioration of the Japanese economy and presented the NAC the choice of rejecting the army request outright or accepting it on condition that "appropriate steps will be taken promptly looking toward the desired economic stabilization of Japan." Royall and Draper vigorously pressed the NAC to choose the latter course of action. Royall spoke of the importance of Japanese recovery in view of the debacle in China. Draper argued that the primary problem was the "lack of strength" in the Japanese government in enforcing the Young Plan program. The real question, therefore, involved a decision by the U.S. government to direct Japanese officials in the stabilization field even if "it would be contrary to the desire to have a democratic Japanese Government that makes its own decisions." He recommended that the National Security Council be asked to issue a separate stabilization directive "so that there could be no doubt in General MacArthur's mind that the proposal was national policy."[22]

Draper's recommendation was accepted. The NAC gave its conditional acceptance to the FY 1950 rehabilitation aid request. The next week, on 10 December, the NSC approved a nine-point stabilization directive to MacArthur (which was virtually identical with the Young Report plan) and called for establishment of a single general exchange rate within three months of the initiation of the stabilization plan.[23] As the editors of *Fortune* magazine perceptively noted, the NSC stabilization directive was a confession of failure. It established "as new goals the very thing SCAP has supposedly been doing."[24]

More so than before, the Truman administration desperately sought the services of Joseph Dodge to implement the new NSC directive. At Draper's urging President Truman on 11 December requested Dodge fly down to Washington for a meeting at the White House. With Royall and Draper present, Truman pointed out that the collapse of the Nationalists in China had increased the importance of economic recovery in Japan, that the NSC regarded the economic situation in Japan as critical, and that all Washington agencies were unanimous that Dodge was the one person who could take charge of the problem.[25] Much to the relief of everyone, Dodge succeeded in getting a three-month leave of absence from the directors of the Detroit Bank to launch the stabilization plan.

Dodge negotiated his status as financial advisor with ministerial rank and won assurance that once the stabilization program was in place he would not have to stay in Japan to handle its implementation. The appointment of Ralph Reid, Draper's assistant, to the Dodge Mission provided Dodge with an experienced liason person to the Army Department. Dodge also selected as members of his team William A. Diehl of the Treasury Department, Orville J. McDiarmid of the State Department, Paul O'Leary of Cornell University, and Audley Stephens of Rutgers. Dodge warned Draper that there were no "quick or easy answers" for the "fix we are in," and many mistakes would be made in the attempt to change the prevailing trends.[26] But the Army Department felt confident that Dodge had the authority, know-how, and resoluteness to finally carry out a successful stabilization program. Secretary of the Army Royall accompanied the Dodge Mission to Japan to underscore the importance of its work.

The Dodge Line

Though often lost in the complex technical debate over the many facets of the stabilization program of 1949, the major objective of the Dodge Mission was to link Japan on a competitive basis to the world capitalist economy dominated by the United States. To do that required controlling inflation and gearing Japanese industry for increased exports. In practice, Dodge emphasized three major policies with enormous economic and political implications: 1.) achieving a balanced national budget by curtailing expenditures and expanding revenues; 2.) creating "tight money" through the U.S. Aid Counterpart Fund and the phasing out of the Reconstruction Finance Bank; and 3.) establishing a single yen-dollar exchange rate to replace the then existing multiplicity of commodity export and import rates.

The bulk of the Dodge Mission's attention and energy during its three-month stay in Japan focused on the balancing of the consolidated national budget. That was the key to the control of inflation, and it had to be done quickly. The National Security Council had ordered the establishment of a stable single exchange rate within three months which meant, in effect, stopping inflation immediately. Dodge and his staff held major conferences with General William Marquat, other officers of ESS, and Finance Minister Ikeda Hayato on the Japanese budget in the first week after their arrival. Dodge was aghast at the chaos in the procedures by which the Japanese government drew up a budget and SCAP approved it. The data used by the ministries in compiling the budget was "not reliable or accurate, the real meaning of the figures is often obscured, and information supporting the figures sketchy."[27]

While the Japanese national budget was required to be balanced to gain SCAP approval, Dodge emphasized that past practice indicated only a paper balance. When Ikeda claimed that the balanced budget did not seem much of a problem since the 1948 budget had actually generated a surplus, Dodge was incredulous. Ikeda simply referred to the general account but ignored the large government expenditures in the special accounts, such as those for national schools and hospitals, government loan funds, and government owned companies such as the Japan National Railway. Invariably the government covered the deficits in these accounts by inflationary bond issues and increased loans from the Bank of Japan. Thus, the consolidated government budget deficit in 1946 was 62 billion yen, in 1947 it was 149 billion yen, and in 1948 it reached 348 billion yen. In these years the deficit constituted roughly between 10 and 15 percent of the national income and hence played a major role in the inflationary process. Though the Japanese had made some progress in 1948 toward a balanced budget, it was still inflationary, reflecting in Dodge's words, a "crossfire between the political parties, unions, and industry."[28]

Joseph M. Dodge, president of the Detroit Bank and Finance Advisor to General MacArthur, is welcomed upon his arrival in Japan by Ikeda Hayato, Finance Minister, and Masuda Kameshiachi, Chief Cabinet Secretary, 31 October 1949. U.S. Army Photo, National Archives.

After numerous conferences, Dodge and his mission presented to ESS on 8 March a draft of the Japanese national budget which, according to Japanese press accounts, was "handed to Japanese Government by SCAP officials" on 23 March for passage by the Diet. For the first time in Japanese financial history, the government had to balance a consolidated budget that included the general and special accounts and the activities of government affiliated railroad, communication, banking, and other companies. Although the new budget was 24 percent larger in real terms than the 1948 budget and was superficially larger than the budget compiled by the Yoshida cabinet, it represented, as the State Department reported, "appreciable cuts" from totals which would have been derived from the former method of budgeting.[29] The cuts were primarily in public works projects, subsidies to industry, and layoffs of government workers. For example, the proposed Japanese budget contained appropriations for building 21,000 classrooms of the 40,000 which educational authorities said were needed to implement SCAP requirements for students to attend school through the twelfth grade. These were cut out of the Dodge budget. Subsidies on raw materials such as zinc, aluminum, iron, and steel were cut or eliminated. As the consumer prices of these commodities were not to be raised, industry would be forced to cut production costs through "rationalization," primarily layoffs and improved technologies. In Dodge's view, prices had been so long controlled and their structure so distorted by subsidies that they did not reflect anywhere near the actual cost of production. The hidden subsidies of the earlier exchange rate system on imported goods for domestic consumption, including foodstuffs, were also slashed, compelling consumers to pay higher prices. The cost of rice, the staple of the Japanese diet, was raised 13 percent, for example.[30]

Large-scale reduction of the government workforce was a key part of the Dodge budget plan. Dodge accepted in principle the Yoshida cabinet goal of a 20 to 30 percent retrenchment, affecting some 600,000 government employees. He was especially determined to put the traditionally deficit-financed Japan National Railways on an independent footing by curtailing operating costs as well as raising passenger fares by 60 percent. Unquestionably there were "surplus employees" on the railroad, mostly demobilized soldiers unable to find work. But railroad workers were also organized in a Communist-led union sharply critical of Japanese conservative rule. The firing of some 126,000 railway employees, representing 20 percent of the workforce, in the spring of 1949 precipitated a wave of violent strike actions culminating in the still mysterious death of the president of Japan National Railways on 6 July. Government repression was swift, with many Communists arrested and charged in connection with the violence.[31] By the end of 1949 the weakened union was in the hands of its right-wing members. Official estimates hold that total government employment for 1949 fell only by a net total of 140,000, or about 5 percent. But that figure underestimates the total number actually affected by retrenchment, which was at least 260,000.[32]

At the same time there was a relative decrease in total expenditures in the 1949 budget, tax revenues were sharply increased to balance the budget and prevent further inflationary borrowing by the government. SCAP estimated tax revenues would increase almost one-third over 1948 figures. Dodge assumed that the additional revenues were obtainable by strengthening the programs of tax collection under the existing tax structure and insuring prompt and vigorous prosecution of tax evaders. The new tax strategy, however, was contrary to the ruling Liberal party campaign promise in the previous election of a reduction in income taxes and the elimination of the sales tax on grounds that inflation combined with the progressive tax structure had generated unfair "bracket creep." The average tax rate on income rose from prewar levels of about 4 percent to a high of 21.2 percent in 1947 and, as inflation slowed, declined to 16.6 percent in 1949.[33]

The *Nippon Times* noted the impact of the new enforcement of tax collections early in the visit of the Dodge Mission. There was a hike in the number of public auctions of goods taken from delinquent taxpayers. The explanation was simple: "a considerable proportion of the people of Japan have reached the point where they are no longer able to pay taxes out of current income." An American economist confirmed the point by estimating that approximately 65 percent of Japanese consumption in 1949 was for food while taxes comprised 60 percent of the remainder, "a figure difficult to duplicate elsewhere." In any case, when Ikeda sought a modest reduction in the income tax burden by increasing the number of exemptions, Dodge sternly lectured him on the heavy tax burden in the United States. The time had come for the Japanese to stop "ducking the issues. . . . The history here showed a continued series of concessions made on promises that have not been performed; what we needed was a record of performance."[34]

The key to the success of the balanced budget as an instrument of stabilization was the U.S. Aid Counterpart Fund. In the enforcement of our "basic policy," Dodge told General Marquat, "the biggest single stroke was the creation of the Counterpart Fund through which there is tremendous and effective leverage."[35] Similar to the mechanisms used by recipients of Marshall Plan aid, the Counterpart Fund was one of "two pockets" in the Japanese government's budget. The first pocket held funds raised from Japanese tax revenues. The Counterpart Fund pocket was filled through the transfer by the government of the yen equivalent of the dollar value of wheat, raw cotton, and other imports provided by the U.S. under GARIOA and EROA aid programs. Expenditures from the Counterpart Fund, unlike those from the general revenue accounts, required the approval of SCAP which, in practice, meant Dodge.

As Dodge saw it, the Counterpart Fund, representing about 20 percent of the total budget for 1949–50, had two primary purposes. First, the return flow of these funds to the Japanese economy, either directly or through commercial banks, was a major factor in the nation's money supply. By making the largest single item from the fund retirement of RFB debentures and other government debts—63 billion of the estimated 140 billion yen—Dodge expected there would be a restriction on credit and a marked "disinflationary" effect.[36] If "disinflation" became "deflation," as Dodge's critics predicted, the size and flow of counterpart funds could be increased.

Secondly, the Counterpart Fund would replace the RFB as the source for long-term, low interest loans to priority industries. To the Dodge Mission the RFB, controlled by the minister of finance and the director of the Economic Stabilization Board, had been the principal engine of inflation since 1947. Its activities revealed unsound banking practices, corruption, and the use of political rather than economic criteria in making loans. Dodge was appalled to learn, for example, that many RFB loans went to industries with unused capacity whose purchase of new equipment added to the demand for scarce materials. Since only 12 percent of RFB loans had been repaid by the end of 1948, the evidence indicated that many industries treated the loans as subsidies which might never have to be repaid. Dodge obtained Washington approval to quickly phase out the RFB and by September 1949 the bank's loan making authority was completely terminated.[37]

By curtailing the RFB, Dodge anticipated that industries would have to rely more heavily on the commercial banking system. But major capital construction loans to private industries vital to economic recovery and expanding exports would come from the Counterpart Fund. When the Japanese government submitted its request for private industry loans from the Counterpart Fund, Dodge and SCAP officials cut them back roughly 40 percent. General William Marquat explained that the Japanese proposal was "based upon desire to afford maximum stimulus to economic activity to counteract alleged deflationary movement [while] SCAP policy is to make counterpart funds available for particular 'bottleneck' situations where . . . private financing is not available." Major loans from the Counterpart Fund were scheduled for the coal, iron and steel, electric power, and shipping industries.[38]

The ultimate objective of the Dodge program was the integration of the Japanese economy into the global capitalist system through the establishment of a stable single yen-dollar exchange rate. The existing multiple exchange rate system in which every traded commodity had a government determined exchange rate had been ingeniously devised, in Dodge's view, to insulate Japanese producers from the pressures of competitive world prices. The single foreign exchange rate was the key to the return of Japan's foreign trade from government control to private contracts, to the rationalization of Japanese industry, and to a substantial increase of Japanese exports which would eliminate U.S. aid imports. As early as May 1947 SCAP had considered such a rate. But with inflation rates five and six times world rates, a stable exchange rate could not have been maintained. The stabilization program, by putting the brakes on inflation, made it possible for Japan to perform as the workshop of Asia, Dodge hoped.

From the outset of the Dodge Mission, studies were made by SCAP and Japanese officials of the impact of different levels of exchange rates ranging from 270 to 400 yen to the dollar on import prices and government import subsidies and export prices. Dodge's greatest fear was that setting too low a rate "would lead to a diversion of export goods into the domestic market when the objective is a diversion of domestic market goods to export."[39] In the calculations of Counterpart Fund revenues from U.S. aid imports, import subsidies in the General Account of the budget, and export revenues in meeting Blue Book recovery goals, Dodge and ESS officials settled on an exchange rate of 330 yen to the dollar. With that rate Japan could import the maximum with its foreign exchange resources and export the maximum for those imports.

Much to Dodge's surprise, on 30 March the National Advisory Council urged SCAP to adopt a rate of 360 yen per dollar to provide additional incentives for increasing exports. Dodge was reluctant to make the change, particularly since the 1949 budget which was then before the Diet had been based on the lower rate. As the most knowledgeable person on the Japanese economy, he was also annoyed that Washington had gone over his head. In a secret cable to SCAP, the Pentagon explained that England was planning to shortly devalue the pound sterling. Since Japan had extensive trade with the sterling bloc countries, the Japanese would be forced to devalue a 330 exchange rate too soon after it had been set. Dodge accepted Washington's recommendation for the 360 rate, but deferred announcement of it until after Diet passage of the budget. On 25 April the exchange rate of 360 yen to the dollar became effective and was kept fixed there for the next twenty-two years.[40]

In the Maelstrom of Japanese Politics

The Dodge program became the centerpiece of Japanese political controversy from its inception until the Korean War. While agreeing on the priority of economic rehabilitation, the Yoshida cabinet opposed the Dodge Line on such basic issues as taxation, funding of public works, unemployment and wage policy, and governmental support for small industry. In general, the conservatives were convinced that Dodge's tight credit and balanced budget policies threatened to plunge the country into a severe recession or depression. Certainly they welcomed the "disinflation," "rationalization," and export-oriented production which favored the larger enterprises. They particularly applauded the Dodge Line's restraints imposed on the labor movement and the political Left. But the Liberal party endorsed a more gradual approach to stabilization and recovery which allowed for easier credit and deficit spending.

No less important, the ruling party was acutely sensitive to the domestic political liabilities of the Dodge program and sought to avoid them. A program that openly required extensive layoffs of workers in the public and private sector, increased railroad passenger fares, postage fees, and staple food prices, increased the real level of taxes as much as 50 percent, curtailed school construction and other public works projects, kept a ceiling on wage increases, and forced numerous small- and medium-sized firms into bankruptcy was one that no political party could publicly endorse.[41] The strategy of the Liberal party leaders for dealing with the politically untenable austerity policies was perceptively outlined by W. Walton Butterworth of the State Department. In the first five months since the formation of the Yoshida cabinet in January 1949, the government had "adopted a policy of refusing to carry out orders not to its liking without a formal written instruction from GHQ. This relieves Yoshida's party of the responsiblity for unpopular measures [and requires GHQ to] assume an openly greater degree of direct control of Japan's internal affairs—particularly in connection with the [stabilization plan]. It also places the blame for resulting hardship and difficulties more directly upon the occupation."[42] In fact Dodge personally became a lightning rod for all the bolts of criticism striking the Japanese economy.

The principal responsibility for representing the ruling party position to the Dodge Mission fell to the new Minister of Finance Ikeda Hayato, formerly head of the Tax Bureau. Prime Minister Yoshida reportedly was sick and resting in his home at Oiso outside Tokyo during most of the budget negotiation but clearly felt Japan had no choice except to cooperate with Dodge. Ikeda did not appreciate being handed the draft budget from the Dodge Mission on 23 March in the expectation it would be rammed through the Diet before the start of the new fiscal year on 1 April. He met with Dodge on 23, 25, and 28 March to appeal for changes in the budget. He was especially anxious to secure tax concessions in line with the Liberals' campaign promises. Other points Ikeda raised were the lack of funds for unemployment relief and school construction, and steep passenger fares on the national railroad. Dodge listened but in the end refused to make any concessions. He defended the tax program as necessary to reduce domestic consumption so that more goods were available for export, avoid the appearance of submitting to political pressure, and prevent demands for revision on other budget items. When Ikeda told Dodge he might refuse to handle the budget in the Diet, Dodge retorted gruffly that "strike and resignation proposals seemed to be the usual answer when the Japanese did not get what they wanted."[43]

In fact, when the Liberal party recoiled in shock upon being presented the budget and then opposed it, Ikeda seriously considered resigning. Only Yoshida's determination to see the Dodge program implemented kept Ikeda from doing so. In the end, Yoshida recalled in his memoirs, "I decided to accept the general framework of the [1949] budget drafted by SCAP. But I instructed cabinet members to spend about one week for a resurrection of negotiation involving particularly a tax cut."[44]

Liberal party leaders had no more success than Ikeda with Dodge. They told him on 26 March that stabilization was a "surgical operation" in which it was important to keep "the bleeding to a minimum." Without a reduction in taxes there would be a renewal of social and political unrest from which only the Communists would benefit. But to Dodge, the ruling party was playing a dangerous game of narrow partisan politics instead of trying to establish stabilization as a national policy. "Oriental politics," he concluded early in his stay in Japan, was a "devious business" and intrigue was "carried on as an art and is prevalent everywhere."[45] Why had the party leaders not considered the positive features of the new budget, he wondered. "Japan had been travelling on soft-rubber tires supplied by the U.S.," he told them in rejecting their request, "and the ride was more comfortable than the means of the nation warranted." When Liberal party members of the House of Representatives Budget Committee made a last ditch effort on 14 April to win concessions, Dodge expressed his sympathy for their political problems but said he could not "overlook the fact that these arose from promises which should never have been made."[46]

The opposition parties tried with little success to take advantage of the popular disaffection with the Dodge Line. The Socialist party, weakened and divided by its participation in the coalition Ashida cabinet in 1948, grudgingly accepted the stabilization program in pincipie but criticized the "one-sided" sacrifices being forced on the mass of workers and small businessmen. Several Socialist dietmen used parliamentary and legal maneuvers to try to block the passage of the 1949 budget. But in general the Socialist party and its large allied unions recognized they had little power to prevent enforcement of the Dodge Plan and tried to mitigate the required sacrifices. The left-wing faction of the party encouraged the trade union opposition to use militant tactics to fight layoffs, wage ceilings, and inadequate relief assistance. The right-wing favored moderate labor union offensives and rejected any attempt to use the general strike weapon.[47]

On the surface, the Japanese Communist party appeared in a much stronger position than the Socialists to challenge the Dodge program. The Communists scored spectacular gains in the January 1949 House of Representatives elections, winning 10 percent of the total vote (compared to 4 percent in 1947) and thirty-five seats in the Diet (compared to four earlier). But while extremely gratifying to party leaders, the election results largely reflected disillusionment with the Socialist party and not an increase in strength in their major constituency—the labor movement. In fact, since the abortive strike of 1 February 1947, the SCAP supported Democratization Leagues had weakened the Communist controlled labor unions. The retrenchments of government employees under the Dodge stabilization plan brought conflict between the Communist and right-wing factions of the trade union movement to a violent pitch. Opportunistically, the leadership of the Democratization Leagues cooperated with the Japanese government and SCAP to gain control of the unions. Aided by the ouster of key Communist leaders during personnel reductions, they gained firm control of the government railway union and the government communications union. Secessions by anti-Communist union leaders from the Communist dominated Sanbetsu and Zenroren were numerous. In effect, the Dodge program dovetailed with a Red Purge which centered on the union movement. By the end of 1949, only 1.5 million workers were estimated to be in Communist-influenced or controlled unions compared to over five million in 1948.[48]

Not surprisingly, Dodge was even more unsympathetic to the demands and actions of the labor unions and the Left than those of the ruling party. He lashed out at the Communist party for attempting to exploit problems unavoidably created by the balanced budget. He was "not disposed to be blackmailed by the Communists under any conditions," Dodge told conservative dietmen. "They capitalized on what you did do and what you did not do. Changing the budget would not change their objectives or their activities." Dodge, the *Economist* noted, shared Prime Minister Yoshida's method for handling the Communists: "crush them."[49] To Socialist party complaints of large-scale layoffs under the Dodge Line, the financial advisor retorted that much propaganda was "used to encourage a demand for large government appropriations for unemployment which does not now exist." Dodge encouraged the right-wing trade unionists' efforts to take over the labor movement and ignored the demands of the left-wing unions. No doubt, he was delighted to hear from Marquat that the anti-Communist factions were "gaining ground in spite of the use of the 'austerity' bugaboo used by Communist propagandists."[50] When the Dodge Mission was deluged with petitions, telegrams, and visiting delegations from the left-wing Japanese Teachers Union pleading for school construction funds to relieve a severe shortage of classroom space, Dodge stood behind the drop in the educational share of the national budget from 8.1 percent in 1948 to 6.3 percent in 1949. School construction, he said, was "directly inflationary. What the country needs is productive projects. [P]ublic works should be eliminated entirely until productive capacity has been replenished."[51]

Frustrated by more than two weeks of delays in the passage of the budget by the Diet, Dodge decided to warn the Japanese people of the dangers ahead. On the day the Lower House was to act, he delivered what an American journalist described as probably the toughest speech ever issued by a high-ranking Occupation official. The Japanese were living beyond their means and failed to comprehend the real situation in the economy. Instead of planning on the assumption of long-term hardship and self-denial, previous Japanese governments spent more and more by relying on a cushion of American aid. The Japanese people should demand a balanced budget and help eliminate "excessive expenditures, wastefulness, subsidies, overemployment, and the general dependence on government instead of individual or group accomplishment." Only then, Dodge stressed, could later tax reductions be made.[52]

Apparently Dodge's speech helped ward off amendments to the budget by the Liberal party. Using their large majority, the ruling party switched to a policy of voting for its budget without revision. Cabinet members gave flip answers to critical questions coming from the opposition and cut off debate. The normally cautious *Nippon Times* editorialized that the Liberals showed an "utter lack of understanding of democratic parliamentary procedure."[53] Predictably, the vote was along party lines, with the opposition voting en bloc against the Dodge budget measure. The final tally in the key Lower House vote was 231 to 113; in the House of Peers, the vote was 102 to 40. Two days after the Dodge Mission left Japan, the government announced on 25 April the new 360 yen to one dollar exchange rate.

Enforcement of the Dodge Line

Upon his return to Detroit, Dodge carefully monitored the impact of the stabilization plan on the Japanese economy, provided Tokyo officials advice on adhering to the Dodge Line, and aided the Army Department in securing aid funds from Congress. Both before and after the Korean War, Dodge privately accused the Yoshida government of attempting to sabotage his program. Suspicious of Japanese politicians, he feared there were "almost unlimited possibilities of completely unbuttoning the budget by one means or another." The government might attempt to prove the program unworkable by deliberately creating large and unnecessary employment and then appeal for larger U.S. appropriations or by using counterpart funds for "non-productive and primarily political" public-works projects. Dodge was appalled to learn that the government had targeted the statistical units in various ministries for large layoffs or even their complete elimination as part of a governmental reorganization carried out in the name of compliance with the Dodge Line. The effect, General Marquat pointed out, would be to hamper the ability of those agencies responsible for allocation of raw materials and other economic controls to enforce the stabilization directive.[54]

Ironically, Dodge viewed the government's Economic Stabilization Board as one of the greatest obstacles and biggest liabilities to the success of his program. "I have always believed the ESB," he told one ESS officer, "did not either fulfill its function or live up to its name. [It] has been a propagandizer of panic. It rushes to the press on any pretext with ill-considered or inaccurate statements." While in Japan, the ESB had issued a report that argued that severe and immediate stabilization under the Dodge Plan would cause a decline in capital accumulation, delay progress toward a self-supporting economy, increase unemployment from 1.4 million to four million, and create serious social unrest. Inflation could not be terminated within so short a time without causing a deflationary crisis.[55] Achievement of Dodge's goal of "disinflation" required at least two years or a highly planned economy. The ESB continued its criticisms of the Dodge Plan and by the fall of 1949 issued a lengthy white paper which charged that the Dodge program contributed to an unfavorable business climate at home, prevented industry from obtaining funds, created hardships upon small business, and fostered the slump in exports. But to Dodge the ESB reports were disguised formulas for inflation. He forwarded a letter for use by General MacArthur on the "tendency of certain ostensible financial and economic authorities in Japan to overestimate the adverse effects of the Stablization program and underestimate or ignore its benefits." Dodge explained to one SCAP official "that was as close as I wanted to come from here in putting a finger on the ESB."[56]

Outside the government, the influential *Oriental Economist* was considered by Dodge and SCAP officials as the principal source of "pro-inflationist" propaganda directed at reversing the stablization program. In an analysis of the Dodge budget before its passage in the Diet the *OE* predicted that full implementation would lead to a steadily "aggravating condition of depression." The journal displayed an uncharacteristic sympathy for the misery and suffering of the Japanese people caused by the increased tax collection. While admitting that the export slump which began after the departure of the Dodge Mission was primarily caused by the recession in the United States, the *OE* proposed modifications in the Dodge program to shift emphasis from export to domestic market production. By the end of July the editors saw unmistakable signs of the economic depression they had predicted and recommended steps contrary to the Dodge Line such as suspending redemption of government bonds to make for easier credit, more money for public works, and unemployment relief. SCAP handling of the Counterpart Fund came in for particularly strong criticism. While industry hungered for capital, counterpart money went to retire the national debt. "Conditions could not be worse," the *OE* claimed in August. "We must rid ourselves of the morbid fear of inflation and start out on measures to counter depression without delay and indecision."[57] Dodge was scornful and contemptuous of the *Oriental Economist* though he recognized that it reflected the views of a large segment of business and government leaders.

Whatever its impact on the Japanese economy, the adherence of the Japanese to the Dodge Line was the principal weapon in the Army Department's struggle in May and June 1949 for $654 million in combined GARIOA and EROA aid funds for Japan for the 1950 fiscal year. Dodge lobbied in Washington for the funds but ironically refused to testify before Congress. According to Ralph Reid, Dodge did not want to review Japanese misuse of earlier appropriated funds. Nor did he feel sure that the additional funds would lead to the self-support goal of $1.5 billion in balanced trade for the Japanese economy set for 1953. Dodge considered that there was in Japan, despite the stabilization program, an indefensibly "high production for the domestic market which has reduced goods available for export." In addition, Japanese trade with non-dollar countries in the Far East would remain below estimated targets because of political unrest.[58] Nevertheless, Dodge believed the stabilization program the "most constructive factor" in the testimony of Army and State department officials for the total GARIOA program including recovery funds.

As Dodge reviewed reports from Japan over the summer of 1949 on the impact of the stabilization program, he was satisfied in all areas except the crucial one of exports. The rate of inflation, the principal target of the new policy, dropped dramatically to an annual rate of only 24 percent in 1949, compared to 80 percent for the previous year. "It's a textbook example of how a [balanced] budget can stop an inflation cold," Dodge proudly told ESS economists. Even the rate of increase in industrial production did not trouble Dodge. (After increasing by 50 percent in the year previous to the implementation of the Dodge Line, industrial activity remained constant during the first six months of the stabilization program. It rose somewhat during the fourth quarter of 1949, but then stagnated in 1950, until the outbreak of the Korean War.) To Dodge, previous increases in the index of industrial production were misleading because of the Japanese economy's dependence on U.S. aid. If Japanese inflation was to be halted and an export recovery made, an initial slowdown in industrial growth and increase in unemployment were unavoidable.[59]

Initially, Dodge supported a State Department public relations campaign targeted at the unemployed, small- and medium-sized business groups, and the labor movement to reduce the inevitable opposition to the stabilization program to "managable proportions." The campaign would emphasize that real long-term economic recovery and reduction of unemployment were only possible if based on the stabilization program. When public relations failed, Dodge accepted repression. Following two months of bitter and violent clashes between labor and police, Dodge was pleased to hear from Tokyo that the labor situation had never been quieter. "The truth of the matter is that it seems the people are getting along fairly well and the [stabilization plan] with its austerity threat, actually has caused far less suffering than anyone expected."[60]

Despite Dodge's general satisfaction with the success of stabilization, by the fall it was evident that powerful business interests and the Japanese government sought to undermine the program and exerted pressure for its modification. The initial battle ground was the Counterpart Fund. The government's proposals for larger loans to industry and funds for public works projects were essentially political and inconsistent with the stabilization program in Dodge's view. Failure to agree on the use of the Counterpart Fund delayed the expenditure of the monies and contributed to what the Japanese increasingly referred to as a "deflationary crisis." In a long letter to Ikeda drafted in August 1949, but which was never sent on the recommendation of SCAP, Dodge indicated he accepted the theory that the Yoshida cabinet sought to create a false stringent credit condition in order to bolster its program for the use of the Counterpart Fund. He complained of the "tendency of certain ostensible financial and economic authorities of Japan to over estimate the adverse effects of the stabilization program and underestimate or ignore its benefits." All this suggested to Dodge a "possibility of a deliberate attempt to reverse the Stabilization Program and return to outright inflation."[61] Only SCAP vigilance and control over the Counterpart Fund, Dodge believed, sustained the program.

U.S. Containment Policy in Asia and the Japanese Trade Problem

American planners of Japanese economic recovery saw the necessity for Japan to play the major role in U.S. containment policy in Asia. When the triumph of communism in China appeared inevitable by early 1949, the State Department sought to focus congressional and public attention toward the "great crescent" of nations that formed an arc from Japan to India. A secure Japan would be part of an offshore "defensive perimeter" and would help support Southeast Asian nations wracked by nationalism and threatened by Chinese communism. Following numerous discussions in Washington, Dodge commented in June 1949, that "everyone seems to be convinced of the importance of the situation in the Far East and the relationship Japan bears to the problem and the interest of the United States." By the end of 1949, the National Security Council in NSC 48/2 formally adopted a much debated containment policy for Asia that was anchored in the link between Japan and Southeast Asia. Above all else, U.S. containment in Asia required that Japan have access to the markets and raw materials of Southeast Asia while minimizing trade with China.[62]

The first step in making Japan the economic hub of the region, in the view of Dodge, was to end government control over trade. The scope of private export trade activities was broadened in January and February 1949. (Imports remained largely governmental, due to the need to limit and allocate them to priority industries.) The single-exchange rate established in April was central to expanding the scope of private commercial trade. By August only government approval of export contracts was needed. With Dodge's encouragement, new agencies of the Japanese government were organized to boost private trading efforts, the most important being the Ministry of International Trade and Industry (MITI), founded in April 1949.[63]

Dodge anticipated that the stabilization plan and new exchange rate would temporarily reduce Japanese trade levels. But by the summer he saw Japan "facing a war of economic survival" in an extremely hostile international environment. The Dodge Plan in Japan coincided with a fall in world commodity prices, especially in the United States, the continued shortage of dollars in the non-dollar areas, difficulties in the convertability between the dollar and pound sterling, and a 30 percent devaluation of the pound in September 1949. While trade had improved sharply in the first half of 1949, the last half of the year saw decreasing exports and a trade deficit of 104 million yen.

The extrication of Japan from its export slump through more direct U.S. intervention became the focus of discussion in Tokyo and Washington. Pressure was stepped up to speed negotiation on the Anglo-Japanese Trade agreement, which was finally signed in November at double the level of 1948 trade. Ormond Freile of the Army Department convinced Dodge that a devaluation of the yen to offset the British devaluation would hurt the long-run trade position of Japan. Dodge concurred in Freile's alternative recommendations that there be a complete return to private trade, and trade financing be done by commercial banks, not SCAP, that a trade promotion campaign, including development of a Japanese consular system be launched, and most importantly that SCAP remove the 70,000 price floors on exports which had been established to prevent the "dumping" practices of the prewar era. That measure heightened international tension and increased British demands that the Japanese be given access to the China market to lessen the anticipated Japanese trade interest in Southeast Asia.[64]

During his second visit to Japan at the end of October, Dodge found that the foreign trade problem threatened to unravel the whole stabilization program. Many Japanese business and government officials who had formerly acquiesced in the Dodge program considered the slump in trade a last straw. The Japan Management Association, for example, argued for sweeping revision in tax policy, easier credit, release of export stockpiles for the domestic market, and devaluation of the yen because "trade is stagnating, stockpiles are mounting, employers are failing to meet payrolls, and panic is just around the corner. In an open letter to Dodge before his arrival, the *Oriental Economist* called for wholesale revisions in the Dodge Line and a 20 percent devaluation of the yen to enhance exports in order to deal with an economy "forced into a severe disinflationary depression."[65] But Dodge remained convinced that more, not less, adherence to stabilization was necessary. Ultimately, higher quality production at lower prices was the only answer to intensified international competition.

After close to three weeks of difficult negotiations, Dodge obtained commitment from the Yoshida cabinet for approval of the supplemental 1949 and 1950 budgets substantially as he wanted, and returned home to join the army's battle of the budget with Congress for aid funds to Japan. While Dodge reportedly was "genuinely optimistic" about the economic developments in Japan, particularly the decline in inflation and black market activity, the decontrol of prices, import subsidy reductions, and less-than-expected unemployment, the Army Department's initial request for $394 million exceeded Blue Book projections for attaining self-support.[66] Faced with a budget stringency and convinced that it had to reduce aid to Japan considerably below that appropriated for 1950, the Budget Bureau slashed the army request by more than half, to around $150 million. The Army Department rushed Dodge to testify before the Budget Bureau and the NAC for a restoration of aid. He told the NAC on 12 January 1950, that Japan was the key to Far Eastern economic recovery and the "sole Asiatic nation in which we have a major influence and complete control over all the factors to achieve our objectives." He described those objectives as the integration of Japanese trade and investment in the region. "It is probable that the development of our future Far Eastern policy will require the use of Japan as a springboard and source of supply for the extension of further aid to the Far Eastern areas." As far as Army Department and SCAP officials were concerned, Dodge's testimony was the key to gaining final approval to go to Congress with a $271 million GARIOA request with which to carry on the work of the Occupation successfully.[67]

The formal embrace of an anti-Communist Asian containment strategy in NSC 48/2 coupled with the slow recovery of Japanese industry and trade prompted a host of reports and recommendations for linking Japan and Southeast Asia in the six months prior to the Korean War. Aided by Dodge and Ralph Reid, Army Under Secretary Tracy Voorhees played a key role in developing the theme of "regional integration." He sent his assistant, Robert West, and Agriculture Department expert Stanley Andrews on an eleven-nation, eight-week trip to Southeast Asia in January 1950. With unemcumbered funds of $75 million appropriated for the "General Area of China" for the Military Assistance Program (MAP), Economic Cooperation Administration funds, and other aid funds available, Voorhees pushed the National Security Council to coordinate all Far Eastern aid programs toward using Japanese industry to promote economic development in Southeast Asia. Voorhees, Dodge, and others contemplated such schemes as dollar grants to Thailand tied to the purchase of irrigation equipment in Japan. A portion of the increased Thai rice production would be sold to Japan to pay for more Japanese capital imports. In Voorhees's view, maintaining Japanese economic recovery and ultimately reducing the need for U.S. appropriated funds to Japan depended on keeping communism out of Southeast Asia and developing it as the principal trading area for Japan. Japan had adequate plant capacity, know-how, and labor but insufficient markets. U.S. economic and security objectives in Asia were best achieved through finding those markets in Southeast Asia for a revived Japanese economy.[68] These schemes took on a distinctly military cast as work finished in June on a major review of American defense policy that contemplated a tripling of defense spending. Voorhees envisioned Japanese industry earning dollars by helping to produce low-cost military equipment for Southeast Asia. At one and the same time, Japan would be defending the region from communism, promoting trade integration, and saving the U.S. taxpayers money.[69]

Dodge heartily endorsed Voorhees's efforts, seeing in them a reflection of his own ideas. Almost as soon as he had arrived in Tokyo on his first visit in 1949, Dodge advised ECA administrator Paul Hoffman that one of the principal areas of U.S. policy in the Far East "must be the greatest possible integration of U.S. aid programs to the end that U.S. appropriated dollars may be used several times over in the achievement of our goals of recovery and reconstruction throughout the Far East." As Japan's trade picture clearly worsened by 1950, Dodge pointed to the use of U.S. aid funds to help solve problems in Southeast Asia. He told the ECA administrator, in April 1950, that to protect Japan as the natural workshop of Asia and get Japan off "our shoulders" required relating "the effect of aid from one area to another" so as to promote Japanese trade with Southeast Asia.[70]

The plans of Voorhees, Dodge, and other policy makers to accomplish greater integration of Japan and Southeast Asian trade prior to the Korean War were slow in developing. There was opposition from ECA officials who regarded Southeast Asia as Europe's backyard rather than Japan's. There was competition between the State and Defense departments for control over funds. More importantly, there was continued political unrest and economic chaos in Southeast Asia. The Bank of Japan report on the performance of the Japanese economy in the first quarter of 1950 noted that exports had failed to expand as expected especially in metal products, machinery, and minerals. In view of tariff discrimination, Asian nationalism, inconvertability of currency, and the global dollar gap, the ESB in early 1950 considered it virtually impossible for Japan to increase exports to meet U.S. balance of trade objectives. The *Asahi* newspaper summed up the outlook of most observers in February 1950 with the comment that "Japan's foreign trade is now faced with a grave situation by causes that are beyond control."[71]

The Dodge Plan Crisis of 1950 and Japanese Banks

As Diet consideration of the budget worked out by Dodge and the Finance Ministry in the fall approached, renewed debate in Japan erupted on the economic impact of the stabilization program. In general, the consensus amongst Japanese was that Dodge's policies were responsible for a severe deflationary crisis evidenced in all economic indicators—industrial production, trade values, stock market, housing starts, employment, wages, and prices. Dodge and most SCAP officials, however, dismissed Japanese complaints as alarmist and self-interested, pointed to stable prices, and predicted increased production and export figures as the recession in the United States lifted.

While economists are still debating whether Dodge's medicine helped cure the patient, there is no argument that, as a secret State Department report of May 1950 put it, "every major power element in the Japanese body politic considers itself injured and its interests jeopardized" by the Dodge Line.[72] Representatives of the forty thousand large enterprises that had initially acquiesced in the Dodge Line complained bitterly of stagnation, depression, excess inventories and panic throughout the spring of 1950. When Ikeda told Diet critics of the Dodge Plan in March that suicides and bankruptcies amongst the nearly four million smaller businessmen were inevitable, he was sharply rebuked for his callousness. By some accounts, the tight credit of 1949 forced 30 percent of small businesses into bankruptcy and those that survived laid off employees and skipped wage payments.[73] Organized labor, despite the purges and splits of 1949, launched a new offensive against the second Dodge budget which once again proposed to keep wages of government workers frozen. The newly dominant anti Communist leadership rebuffed SCAP's effort at maintaining industrial peace; any truce between labor and management first required a "recharting of the Dodge line."[74] Even farmers suffered economic setbacks in the Dodge Plan period and feared a loss of their status as independent landowners.

Under pressure from so many sectors, the political parties continued to make opposition to the Dodge Plan the prime issue of the day. The ruling Liberal party sought concessions from SCAP and Dodge as the Diet began consideration of the budget in March 1950. The Political Research Committee recommended using Counterpart Fund money for investment purposes instead of debt retirement. Most importantly, Prime Minister Yoshida announced that Ikeda would visit Washington. Early in May Ikeda met with Dodge, Carl Shoup, whose recommendations were the basis of a new tax policy, and others to present proposals for modification in the Dodge Line. Dodge had been forewarned of Ikeda's visit and was not sympathetic. Of course there were business complaints about the stabilization program, Dodge lectured Ikeda again. "The minute inflation stops business is thrown on its mettle and the weak sisters go into bankruptcy." Inflation hurt the majority, Dodge continued, while disinflation hurt only "a small segment of the population."[75]

Dodge got his way again. Over a clamor of opposition, the ruling party by the end of May had pushed through the Diet the Dodge-backed budget and tax legislation. When one of Dodge's aides suggested that the rigid enforcement of the stabilization program threatened the power of the Liberals, Dodge made clear that he considered the Yoshida cabinet "our best asset. I fully explored the possibility of concessions suitable for some political advantage."[76] Dodge and SCAP officials simply did not comprehend demands for wholesale revisions in a policy which, to them, had produced a more efficient economy able to take advantage of the end of the American recession and consequent easing of the world dollar crisis.

To many Japanese, however, the satisfactory economic developments to which Dodge pointed occurred in spite of, rather than because of, the stabilization plan. In a lengthy assessment of the impact of the Dodge Plan after one year, the *Oriental Economist* concluded that it "must be regarded as an excess" for precipitating a sudden drop in prices, increasing unemployment, slowing production, and generally upsetting the stability of the economy. If the Japanese financial world had not been "busy stopping up the holes made by the deflation policy," a major economic collapse would have occurred. By easing its lending policies the Bank of Japan encouraged large commercial banks to help financially hard-pressed companies. In fact, the *OE* pointed out, commercial bank loans were substantially larger than deposits over the year of the Dodge Plan, creating a dangerous "overloan" problem. Whereas the normal prewar ratio of lending to deposit volume was 60 percent, by 1 March 1949, the ratio had become 91 percent. The cause of such an abnormal situation, argued the *OE* in a swipe at the Dodge Plan, was first, the suspension of RFB lending and the delays in the release of the Counterpart Fund loans to industry and second, the demands for financing of large inventories resulting from the slack in domestic sales and the export slump. "It may therefore be said," concluded the *OE*, "that bank loans have been the principal means of fending off the crisis engendered by the depression."[77]

A later analysis of the Bank of Japan policies during the Dodge Plan period by a former member of the U.S. Federal Reserve Board and advisor to SCAP, Frank Tamagna, supports the *OE* position. Initially, the Bank of Japan cooperated in the Dodge retrenchment program, sharply tightening credit. But to counteract the adverse effects of the balanced budget and tax program in mid-1949 the central bank began "easing its own rates, lowering maximum rates on loans by other banks, and arranging to have part of the government deposits transferred from its own books to the accounts of certain large banks." In addition, the Bank of Japan permitted two or more banks to pool their resources to provide big companies with large loans unobtainable from a single bank. Tamagna concluded that these policies succeeded in maintaining the volume of credit and currency unchanged in the period before the Korean War, "thus softening the impact of a 'super-balanced' budget."[78]

Certainly Dodge was aware that the policies of the Bank of Japan and expansion of commercial bank credit could subvert the Dodge Line. On his first trip to Japan Dodge met with Ichimada Hisato, governor of the Bank of Japan, who SCAP officials regarded as a member of the pro-inflationist camp of Ishibashi Tanzan. Dodge sought to wrest one-man control of the bank from Ichimada by restructuring the policy-making function of the Bank of Japan to include five to seven representatives from other government agencies. Although Dodge succeeded in pushing through his Policy Board proposal, Ichimada managed to maintain his previous grip on real power over the bank.[79]

To SCAP officials the new Policy Board seemed wholly ineffective in dovetailing financial policy with the stabilization program. "In actual fact the evidence indicates that the Governor of the Bank of Japan has considered his function to be one of primarily correcting the real or financial imbalance or error in government fiscal policy," General Marquat wrote Dodge in June 1950. Marquat requested Dodge's assistance in getting statutory regulations requiring commercial banks to hold some measure of reserves with the Bank of Japan and limit the loans of their banks to single borrowers to amounts that would not endanger the solvency of the bank. Dodge agreed. In his opinion, the lending policies of the private banks were the clearest indication of "why [the] inflationary situation is not yet under control."[80] Years later, a member of the Dodge Mission recalled that Dodge often lectured Japanese bankers "at great length about the policies of overlending and of lending on a revolving line of credit."[81]

Nevertheless, the failure of the Occupation to impose controls on the commercial banking system proved to be the principal safety-valve by which Japanese ruling circles escaped from the worst effects of the Dodge Plan. Perhaps Dodge failed to impose such controls because he himself was a commercial banker and had a misplaced confidence in their willingness to cooperate voluntarily with his program. More likely, Dodge and his superiors, while maintaining an atmosphere of austerity, tolerated banking violations of stabilization principles because of a fear of economic collapse.

Whatever the utility of the Dodge Plan as an economic program, the State Department considered that it had caused a deterioration in the U.S. position in Japan. The stabilization program had evoked "intense criticism from the press, rebellious behavior from organized labor and the opposition parties, and covert objection from the cabinet and government party." Moreover, SCAP had to intervene repeatedly in Japanese affairs when, theoretically, its role had been reduced to prepare Japan for democracy and independence. A State Department report concluded that "for the first time since the surrender there is in Japan an appearance of wide political resistance to American control—a resistance more impressive because it comes from responsible organizations acting through channels and institutions sponsored by the occupation."[82] In the context of the State Department's Asian containment policy and the just launched effort under John Foster Dulles to negotiate a peace treaty ending the Occupation—one that would allow U.S. bases to remain in Japan, promote industrial remilitarization, and begin full-scale Japanese rearmament—the Dodge Plan had become a serious liability. Only the unexpected outbreak of the Korean War rescued the American position in Japan from the political and economic morass left in the wake of the Dodge Plan.

Economic Cooperation and the "New Japan"

The Korean War radically changed the economic and political context in which Dodge continued his work on Japanese problems for the next two years. First, his personal influence and power in Japan was drastically reduced from the towering heights of 1949. Though he remained a key player, Dodge's importance inevitably declined as the U.S. relinquished control to the Japanese government in preparation for the peace treaty ending the Occupation. Second, the Korean War touched off an economic boom in Japan as a result of an upturn in world price levels and demand for military supplies by the United States. The index of industrial production, which stood at 86.6 percent of the 1936 level in May 1950, surpassed the prewar level by October and reached 131.5 percent by May 1951—an increase of more than 50 percent in one year compared to only 10 percent during the year of the Dodge Line.[83] When the boom began to fizzle out in the spring of 1951 in anticipation of a settlement in Korea, U.S. planners, including Dodge, developed a program of "U.S.-Japanese economic cooperation" which rested on "new special procurements" of Japanese military goods and services as a part of a global rearmament effort well beyond the requirements of the Korean War. These new procurements helped sustain the rapid economic growth of the first months after the start of the war. Third, Japan's central strategic importance to the United States, implicit in NSC 48/2 of December 1949, now became manifest, and Dodge's economic policies had to dovetail closely with the U.S. containment strategy in Asia.

Dodge followed the fighting in Korea closely. He fully supported the Truman administration's "firm stand" there. "We are no longer running away while being milked to death," he wrote Marquat. Dodge often wondered about the "place and time of the next communist move." MacArthur, Dodge thought, was probably glad "to have his hand back in the war games." Occasionally, he even put his own hands into the war game, lobbying for the creation of an American Foreign Legion.[84]

But the Detroit banker's main concern remained the economic health of Japan. Initially he was cautious about drawing any conclusions as to the long-term effect of the Korean War boom on the Japanese economy. He was pleased that John Logan, his aide in late 1949 on exports, was "covering the waterfront in D.C. through all agencies" to get U.S. dollars to be used to purchase Japanese exports. Dodge favored the principle of a Japanese Export Bank, which both the State Department and the Japanese Finance Ministry were pushing as a means of stimulating Japanese exports. But, in July 1950, Dodge wrote Marquat that, "in an attempt to make Japan the source of financing the reconstruction of the Far East, this specific project for Japan should be part of a coordinated program of the whole area."[85]

By late summer the Army Department grew increasingly alarmed at the inflationary impact of the Korean War expenditures on the stabilization program and once again requested Dodge to go to Japan to help work on the Japanese budget and other matters. SCAP officials were pleased that Dodge agreed to come. In their view, Ikeda and especially Ichimada were "getting out of line and no one could straighten them out as effectively as [Dodge]." Dodge himself agreed that the Bank of Japan's policies were greatly complicating such inflationary pressures from the Korean War as the costs of the 75,000-man National Police Reserve established in July under U.S. auspices as the start of a full-scale rearmament program. "Ichimada's policies apparently have been designed to offset the fiscal restraints imposed by our program," Dodge complained. "[He] is likely to be the goat for most of the trouble we have from now on."[86]

Dodge arrived in Japan on 7 October. Production in Japan was booming, and consecutive export records were recorded for August, September, and on into October. All indications were that those trends would continue. But Dodge wanted to impress on the Japanese that fundamental problems remained. The recovery was only a result of Korean War procurements, and Japan had yet to prove its "ability to earn its own living with normal exports in increasingly competitive world markets. To do this the export effort has to be accelerated and strengthened and not weakened by the unexpected windfall of foreign exchange."[87] Dodge warned that Korean War procurements were probably temporary and that the expansion of normal exports was the only way to assure a higher standard of living in Japan.

Dodge held his usual round of meetings with SCAP and Japanese government officials. His greatest concern was the proper use of the foreign exchange windfall produced by Korean War procurements. The windfall, he warned Ikeda, should be invested to help modernize basic industries and increase financial incentives for exports.[88] Dodge hoped to encourage that approach by approving eighty-two billion yen in counterpart funds to railroad, telecommunication, electric power, and shipping industries. He also deposited 7.6 billion yen of counterpart funds for the Equipment Trust Fund, which financed long-term credit offered by commercial banks to export industries in need of advanced foreign technology. When Ikeda expressed interest in an export-import bank, Dodge overcame his earlier skepticism. The Export Finance Bank would aid capital goods exporters by covering the time lag between purchase orders and payment on delivery. The bank opened in February 1951, with partial financing from counterpart funds and the next year expanded its operation under the restructured designation of the Export-Import Bank of Japan.[89]

Dodge and ESS officials also pushed the Japanese for a balanced budget at a lower level of expenditures than earlier. The major plan for reduction was in subsidies that had been in place to soften the impact of the new exchange rate in 1949. When Ikeda raised the politically sensitive issue of tax reduction, Dodge countered that first subsidies had to be reduced even further.[90]

For the first time on his trips to Japan, Dodge took a careful look at the financial side of the Japanese economy and was appalled by what he saw. In a memorandum for General Marquat, he claimed that the Bank of Japan was encouraging banks to make the maximum amount of credit available as part of an expressed policy of cancelling out the disinflationary fiscal policies of the government. It did no good, he stated, to close the "spigot of inflation arising from government deficits while leaving another spigot open in terms of an excessive expansion of bank credit." Dodge expressed these same ideas directly to the governor of the Bank of Japan. Unless the bank fell into line with the objectives of the stabilization program, he and interested Washington agencies would push for a revision of Japanese banking laws.[91]

By late 1950, the Korean War boom had reversed Japan's recovery problems and prompted calls in the U.S. for cuts in congressionally approved economic aid packages for Japan. Instead of inadequate foreign demand, unused plant capacity, inventory stockpiles, and increasing unemployment, there were now serious problems of high prices for imported raw materials, import shortages, production bottlenecks, and the reappearance of an inflationary spiral. Since military related U.S. procurements were counted as exports in Japan's balance of trade, it was also evident that Japan would reach its $1.5 billion level of self-support in 1951. That was more than a year ahead of the original target set in 1948 when the recovery program was launched. In fact the deficit in Japan's commodity trade balance in 1951, which amounted to $540 million, was more than covered by U.S. special procurements and consumption expenditures of military personnel to the tune of $800 million.[92] Hence plans for GARIOA aid in the Army Department's 1952 budget request were dropped.

But neither Dodge, the Army Department, nor Japanese officials were wholly sanguine about these developments. All continued to see fundamental weaknesses in Japan's ability to compete in normal commodity export markets. If the fighting in Korea stabilized and U.S. special procurement orders fell, they feared, the Japanese economy would be thrown into a tailspin. Inevitably, General Marquat predicted, pressures would then develop in Japan for a resumption of large-scale trade with Communist China, "attended by a strong movement of local dissident elements to achieve a political reorientation with the communist orbit."[93] When the uncertainties of the Korean War situation triggered an end to the industrial boom in Japan in the spring of 1951, American planners, including Dodge, developed and implemented what became known as "U.S.-Japan economic cooperation" as the major program for maintaining Japan as the focal point in the U.S. containment strategy for Asia.

The first element in the program was "new special procurements." Japan would produce military hardware and provide services for the U.S., its own new military, and eventually counterrevolutionary regimes in Asia on a scale that would more than compensate for any loss of Korean War orders. SCAP economists prepared three enormous studies of *Japan's Industrial Potential* (in February and October 1951, and February 1952) which provided an industry-by-industry analysis of military products which could be purchased by U.S. defense agencies. All the studies boasted that, if provided adequate raw materials and specialized tools, Japanese industry could manufacture virtually anything desired. Industrial rearmament through the "new special procurements" would sustain economic growth in Japan without requiring economic aid appropriations from a politically sensitive Congress. Furthermore, "economic cooperation" through the new special procurements entailed Japanese adherence to the political and economic policies of the U.S. in Asia, particularly developing an anti-Communist capitalistic bloc. The U.S. would accelerate implementation of plans made before the Korean War for Japan to obtain raw materials and foodstuffs from Southeast Asia and develop export markets especially in military supplies there as well. Not until the end of 1951, however, did the Yoshida government reluctantly acknowledge that the triangular U.S.-Japan-Southeast Asia relationship of economic cooperation meant a sharp and indefinite restriction of future economic relations with the People's Republic of China.[94]

Once the shift from "self-support" to "economic cooperation" objectives occurred in early 1951, Dodge helped translate this high-priority policy into a practical program. In April 1951, General Marquat went to Washington for three weeks with SCAP officials as head of an Economic Cooperation Mission. He lobbied for military procurement orders for Japanese industry and the coordination of U.S. aid between Japan and Southeast Asia. He also met with a cross section of the national security bureaucracy, including Dodge, in developing what became the thirteen-point Marquat Plan for economic cooperation of 16 May 1951. The main point in the plan, confirmed in the secret NSC 48/5 document the following day, was that the U.S. would assist Japan in producing large quantities of low-cost military supplies for use in Japan and anti-Communist countries in Southeast Asia.[95]

Dodge heartily approved the Marquat Plan. He, Ralph Reid, and others met with Charles Wilson, director of the Office of Defense Mobilization, and found him to be in agreement on the importance of letting contracts to Japanese industries even after an armistice agreement in Korea. Dodge wrote Marquat in July that he could soon expect "the expansion of Japanese production of aluminum and products made of aluminum for U.S. defense procurement. This will be a notable example of U.S.-Japanese economic cooperation." In addition Dodge closely followed the numerous studies by

SCAP and Japanese officials on developing extractive enterprises in Southeast Asia for supplying the needs of Japanese industry under the economic cooperation program. Though still not formalized into an agreement, "economic cooperation" was reflected in U.S. military procurements from Japan during 1951. Despite the peace talks that began at Kaesong, Korea in July, procurement orders rose from $141 million in the first half of the year to $241 million in the second half.[96]

One of the most serious threats to the future success of the U.S.-Japan economic cooperation scheme, from the American planners' point of view, was the renewal of a sharp rise in prices in Japan. Since U.S. procurement agencies would show no special favoritism towards the Japanese, the quality and price of export goods had to be internationally competitive. Yet in the first half of 1951, prices in Japan rose about 70 percent compared to only 40 percent in the U.S. Given the threat of the Japanese pricing themselves out of world markets, both the Army and State departments requested that Dodge meet with Japanese finance officials at the September peace conference in San Francisco. Then he was to go to Japan to work on the Japanese budget so as to prevent the complete unraveling of the economic stabilization plan. The situation was "rather critical," Army Secretary Frank Pace told Dodge. "The inflationary pressure must be dealt with."[97]

In San Francisco, Dodge first met with John Foster Dulles, architect of the peace and security treaties with Japan, and then held meetings with Ikeda, Ichimada, and Prime Minister Yoshida. Dodge emphasized to them that the ratification of the treaty meant substantial financial obligations for Japan which had to be built into a balanced national budget to prevent inflation. Dodge feared the Japanese were greatly underestimating their post-treaty obligations for increased security forces, reparations, property restoration to the Allies, repayment of the GARIOA debt to the U.S., and payment and servicing of the Japanese external debt. When the Japanese talked blithely of the increased tax revenues generated by the Korean War boom, Dodge insisted the surplus revenue be used first for post-treaty obligations rather than inflationary tax reductions. Moreover, minimum Japanese government controls on foreign exchange, credit, and the like were needed to prevent the inflationary danger of forcing Japan out of foreign markets. The U.S. would help Japan with procurements under economic cooperation agreements, international lending agencies, and otherwise but if concrete steps were not taken to meet obligations and control inflation, Dodge warned Ikeda, "there may be little case for additional United States aid."[98] Ikeda and Ichimada found out just how serious Dodge was when he blocked their publicly announced plan for negotiations with the Treasury Department for a major loan. The Japanese had no choice but to fit in with the economic cooperation program as designed by the Americans. As Dodge later bluntly informed representatives of the Ministry of International Trade and Industry, "Japan can be independent politically but dependent economically."[99]

In the interim between the signing of the peace treaty in September 1951 and its coming into effect in April 1952, Dodge remained more active than ever with respect to Japanese economic problems. He returned to Japan in November, his fourth trip in two years, to try to compel Japanese adherence to stabilization as a prerequisite for successful U.S.-Japan economic cooperation. Once again, publicly and privately, Dodge criticized Japanese complacency about controlling inflation and lack of attention to developing normal export markets. He thwarted an inflationary Japanese government proposal to decontrol prices and sought recognition of more strict governmental controls on imports and credit to protect and improve Japan's balance of trade and payments position. The dissipation of foreign exchange for domestic construction projects was particularly galling to Dodge. Efforts by SCAP to involve the Japanese in using their reserves in some forty potential ventures for developing raw material sources in the Pacific region had, with one exception, been unsuccessful. Again and again, Dodge reminded the Japanese that the U.S. would not "blueprint a recovery for Japan and revamp the U.S. economy to meet Japan's needs."[100]

As on his previous visits, Dodge spent the bulk of his time and effort in meetings with Finance Ministry officials on the national budget. The major difference between the 1952 budget and earlier ones was the large new obligations Japan faced as a result of the peace and security treaties. The Yoshida cabinet strenuously resisted implementation of many of these U.S.-imposed plans through budgetary legerdemain. The largest item in the projected budget, nearly one-fourth of total expenditures, was "reserves." Ikeda insisted that the 200 billion-yen line included not only domestic security costs but all the other post-treaty obligations which Dodge had discussed in San Francisco. The U.S. position, Dodge told Ikeda, was that this item was solely for security costs, including the expansion of the National Police Reserve from 75,000 to about 180,000 in 1952 and about 350,000 by 1953. Dodge estimated that, by including nonsecurity related expenditures such as reparations and settlement of the foreign debt in the item, the Japanese were attempting to shave 55 to 60 billion yen off security requirements. In the end, Dodge was forced to use General Matthew Ridgway, the new supreme commander, to obtain Yoshida's agreement in principle to the American position before he could proceed with planning the budget.[101]

Dodge was incredulous at Japanese reparations estimates as well. The proposed budget included only 35 billion yen for reparations in 1952 to nations overrun by the Japanese, while providing 30 billion yen in claims to war injured Japanese and families of Japanese war dead. "That is ridiculous," Dodge told Ikeda, and would infuriate Indonesians, Filipinos, and others. It would also "undoubtedly result in much larger claims and requirements for payment than expected."[102]

Finally, Dodge criticized Japanese budget forecasts for being based on the assumption of a continuation of Korean War procurement orders. When Ikeda reiterated Yoshida's view that expenditures in Japan for the rehabilitation of Korea after an armistice would offset the drop in military procurements, Dodge's legal aide Ralph Reid explained that was unlikely. If "Japan could hence trade with China, its position would be eased," Ikeda responded. That too was a "false assumption," Dodge insisted.[103] Without ever acknowledging the charade, Dodge and Ikeda both avoided discussing the principal solution to the cutoff of Korean War orders, namely post-treaty U.S.-Japan economic cooperation.

Upon his departure from Japan Dodge delivered an unusually harsh speech. He charged that the Japanese were "suffering from a plague of false legends" and dangerous delusions, including the idea that the "Korean windfall will be followed by another equally good or fair wind. Clearly Dodge did not want the Japanese to assume the flow of new special procurements for fear that they would then ignore his familiar case for controlling inflation and increasing normal exports. Privately Dodge was even more caustic. Noting that there were several new large office buildings in Tokyo, "of which every pound of steel could have been exported," Dodge charged that the psychology of the Japanese he met was "inflationary, opportunistic, overoptimistic, and unrealistic."[104] The Japanese assumed that no matter what they did, the U.S. would foot the bill. Dodge felt he had to tell them they were wrong.

Ironically, it was Dodge who finalized a much debated memorandum setting forth the official understanding of Japan's post-treaty economic relationship with the United States, one that was premised on a large flow of U.S. military procurements from Japan. Two months before the end of the Occupation, Dodge wrote that "economic cooperation" entailed substantial American reliance on Japan in the post-treaty period for:

a) Production of goods and services important to the United States and the economic stability of non-Communist Asia.

b) Cooperation with the United States in the development of the raw material resources of Asia.

c) Production of low cost military material in volume for use in Japan and non-Communist Asia.

d) Development of Japan's appropriate military forces as a defensive shield and to permit the redeployment of United States forces.

In the same memorandum Dodge criticized the Japanese government's expectation that the U.S. "will plan and blueprint the needs of Japan and then fit the economy of the United States into those needs—instead of the reverse."[105] In short, the Japanese economy had to be reintegrated into the American economic orbit.

The Yoshida government had little choice but to accept the terms laid out in the Dodge memorandum. Suto Hideo, head of the ESB and one of the six members of the Supreme Council on Economic Cooperation, summarized Japan's responsibilities under economic cooperation in a memorandum of 12 February. It privately assured the U.S. that "Japan will contribute to the rearmament plan of the United States, supplying military goods and strategic materials by repairing and establishing defense industries with the technical and financial assistance from the United States, and thereby assure and increase a stable dollar receipt. . . . Japan will cooperate more actively with the economic development of South East Asia along the lines of the economic assistance programs of the United States." The memorandum went on to specify the concrete measures for developing all key sectors of Japanese industry in conjunction with military "special procurements" program—manufacture of vehicles and aircraft, ship repair and shipbuilding, textiles for U.S. military uniforms, and so on.[106]

The final SCAP report on Japanese industrial potential, dated February 1952, indicated that Japan had already laid the groundwork for this Dodge-formulated "economic cooperation." More than 2,700 Japanese firms were working on contracts for military supplies. Japan was already playing a "major role" in Southeast Asia, which was absorbing some 42 percent of Japanese exports as opposed to 20 percent in 1935. Under the impetus of procurements, Japanese production for 1951–52 had already outstripped that of 1934–35. The pattern of Japanese export trade had also shifted under American direction, from its reliance on textiles to heavy industrial goods in 1951.[107] In essence, Japan agreed to accelerate an ongoing program of industrial rearmament as economic policy rather than as a short-term response to war in Korea in the post-treaty period and, under U.S. auspicies, develop an updated version of a co-prosperity sphere in Southeast Asia.

For several years after the Occupation, Dodge was called upon by American policymakers to deal with the conflicts that plagued the "economic cooperation program." When Dodge was appointed by Secretary of State Dean Acheson as a consultant on Japanese economic affairs in August 1952, the Japanese press conjectured accurately that U.S. "attitudes" on procurement, rearmament, foreign debt, reparations, and foreign investment would reflect Dodge's ideas. Dodge gave particular attention to the Japanese dependence on U.S. procurement orders and failure to adopt politically unpopular austerity measures he regarded as essential to more "normal" trade with the U.S. The $800 million of procurements in 1952 represented 38 percent of Japan's total foreign earnings; calculated as exports, they were a staggering 65 percent of the total, up from 44 percent in 1951. Yet even with special procurements, the Japanese trade deficit continued to grow, so that by the end of 1953 it was over a billion dollars, nearly eight times the figure for 1950. Dodge feared that the end of the Korean War and new "Buy American" policies would make that problem worse and even wreck Japan's "shallow economy."[108]

Though chosen in 1952 by President-elect Eisenhower as director of the Bureau of the Budget, a position he held until March 1954, Dodge maintained an active concern with Japan policy. He vigorously promoted Japanese trade with Southeast Asia, working with Secretary of State John Foster Dulles to use reparations as an instrument for opening up markets and U.S. aid funds to develop sources of supply for Japan. Just as important, Dodge insisted that the Yoshida government halt its dissipation of U.S. procurement dollars through increases in domestic consumption and an improved standard of living. Thus when Ikeda journeyed in late 1953 to Washington for a mission on Japan's military buildup, Dodge urged him, as he had done since 1949, to adopt strict credit and consumption controls and programs to reduce manufacturing costs so as to boost exports. Once again, Dodge suggested that perhaps only reducing procurement orders from the U.S. would force industry to modernize and cure the economy of its ills. Ikeda responded simply to Dodge, "Patient will die instead of 'cure.' "[109]

In 1954 Dodge returned to the Detroit Bank where he remained until his death in 1964, at age seventy-four. Throughout that decade, Japanese officials visited Dodge to seek his advice, and the emperor decorated Dodge in 1962 for his service to Japan.[110] The tradition of the balanced budget set by Dodge in 1949 continued to be Japan's basic fiscal policy into the late 1960s. But in 1949 and 1950, Dodge had imposed a balanced budget at less than full employment with the intention that it would be contractionary and halt inflation. Later Japanese government budgets, however, were intended to be expansionary. In fact, as the *Economist* of England wrote in 1962, in the decade following the Dodge Line, Japan had experienced rapid economic growth by continuing and following almost precisely the domestic policies which Dodge opposed.[111]

On the other hand, the "economic cooperation" programs which Dodge helped to design in 1951 and 1952 lay behind the Japanese economic "miracle" of the 1950s and 1960s and the transformation of Japan into the chief bulwark of the American containment strategy against communism in Asia. U.S. military procurements, amounting to $10 billion from 1950 to 1970, were crucial to the growth of major industries in Japan and resolved crippling problems in Japan's trade balance and balance-of-payments situation. This was especially true in the 1950s, as the link between Japan and Southeast Asia upon which Dodge and other planners of ''economic cooperation'' placed so much emphasis did not develop as rapidly or extensively as hoped.[112] By the 1960s, however, the importance of this triangular U.S.-Japan-Southeast Asia policy which Dodge had pushed became tragically evident with official Japanese support for American intervention in Indochina.

Joseph Dodge gained a towering reputation for success in the world of national and international economics. His personal selflessness was coupled with a banker's conservative economic and political philosophy that emphasized the interests of American business first and foremost. Dodge was impatient with any rhetoric that suggested otherwise. In his work in Japan, the most significant of his career, Dodge continually preached the necessity of subordinating Japanese objectives to those of the United States in Asia. More than any other single American during the Occupation, Joseph Dodge defined the economic contours of the U.S.-Japan alliance.

If American scholars are prone to separate economic from political and strategic affairs, Joseph Dodge was not. He kept careful tabs on plans developed in the State and Army departments for peace and security treaties with Japan. The ''economic cooperation'' program, Dodge recognized, had to dovetail with the terms of those treaties. Not surprisingly, Dodge kept in close contact with John Foster Dulles, the Truman administration's special ambassador on the Japanese peace treaty. Dodge knew that more than any other single American, Dulles defined the political and strategic aspects of the U.S.-Japan alliance.

8 JOHN FOSTER DULLES

American Bases, Rearmament, and the China Questions in the Making of the Japanese Peace Treaty

The reintegration of Japan into the American-dominated postwar global order found its formal expression in the peace and security treaties signed by delegates to the San Francisco Conference on 8 September 1951. John Foster Dulles was the principal figure in negotiating these accords. Brought into the State Department on 6 April 1950, Dulles hurdled many hazardous obstacles along the road to San Francisco. The most formidable of these were the security issues of American base rights and Japanese rearmament as well as the question of the future of Sino-Japanese relations. The Pentagon resisted any movement towards a peace settlement that compromised the unilateral control it exercised over bases under the Occupation; the Japanese government tenaciously fought against pressures by Dulles for extensive base rights and immediate, rapid, and large-scale rearmament; and the British government, aided by the Japanese, opposed Dulles's plans to link Japan in the post-treaty era to the rump Nationalist Chinese regime on Taiwan and thereby restrict Japanese trade with the Chinese mainland. In each instance, Dulles used his diplomatic acumen or American might to prevail over his opponents.

Publicly, Dulles and other American officials proclaimed that the U.S.-Japan Security Treaty deepened and broadened cooperation between Washington and Tokyo. They also maintained that the Japanese decision to establish diplomatic relations with the Nationalist Chinese on 28 April 1952 was in the best interests of the entire "free world" and was voluntarily entered into by the Japanese. Yet, contrary to Dulles's public expectations, the security treaty became the most consistent and serious source of friction in U.S.-Japanese relations during the 1950s, culminating in the bitter Diet debates and riots of

1960 over revision of the original agreement. In the 1960 congressional hearings on the revised treaty, Secretary of State Christian Herter acknowledged that Dulles had extracted a high price from the Japanese. There were, he said, "a number of provisions in the 1951–1952 Security Treaty that were pretty extreme from the point of view of an agreement between two sovereign nations."[1] Like the security treaty, Japan's relations with the Communist and Nationalist Chinese were imposed by the United States. For more than two decades, Sino-Japanese relations proved a major source of additional tension between the United States and Japan and a festering sore in the Japanese body politic.[2]

In most accounts by American historians of the Japanese peace and security treaties, Dulles is acclaimed for successfully negotiating arrangements that

Special Ambassador John Foster Dulles congratulates Premier Yoshida Shigeru after the signing of the U.S.-Japanese Security Treaty as Japanese and American delegates look on. The signing took place at the Presidio of San Francisco, 8 September 1951. Signal Corps Photo, National Archives.

took into account the ultimate interests of victors and vanquished alike. Particular emphasis is placed on the brief and nonpunitive peace treaty which contrasted sharply with earlier draft treaties prepared by the State Department and the more restrictive treaty terms favored by other countries. Even the related security treaty is usually presented as a generous arrangement. The frictions with Japan over base rights, rearmament, and China policy are often explained as Communist inspired, temporary, or the unavoidable cost to the Japanese for American protection against hostile neighbors and support for Japanese economic growth and world trade.[3]

Recently, a number of younger scholars have questioned this traditional interpretation of Dulles and the Japanese treaties. They have underlined the strong American self-interest behind support for the alliance, the many negative features of the U.S.-Japan security relationship, and the legitimacy of Japanese resentment and fear of American power in the Pacific.[4] Research into new archival materials in the United States, Britain, and Japan for the period 1950 to 1952 has not and can not settle these problems of interpretation. But certainly the presently available documentation allows for a more sophisticated understanding of how Dulles succeeded in negotiating the treaties and the price paid by all parties for his success.

The Missionary Diplomat

The Senate ratification of a set of peace and security treaties in the Far East in the spring of 1952 placed John Foster Dulles on the threshold of appointment as secretary of state in the administration of Dwight D. Eisenhower. For almost as long as he could remember, Dulles wanted to be secretary of state. Born in 1888, the son of a Presbyterian minister, Dulles considered becoming a clergyman himself. But his grandfather, John Watson Foster, secretary of state for Benjamin Harrison in 1892–93, and his uncle, Robert Lansing, Woodrow Wilson's secretary of state, had a more telling influence on him. While still an undergraduate at Princeton, Dulles accompanied his grandfather to the Second International Peace Conference at the Hague in 1907. There Dulles acted as secretary to the Chinese delegation. After his graduation from George Washington Law School, Dulles secured, with the help of his grandfather, a position in the prestigious Wall Street legal firm of Sullivan and Cromwell which specialized in international trade and finance. By 1917, Dulles's experience with foreign legal, financial, and political matters convinced "Uncle Bob" to give him a clandestine assignment to Central America. His reputation enhanced, Dulles was appointed by Bernard Baruch as chief counsel to the American Reparations Mission to the Versailles Conference. During the interwar years, Dulles aided American corporations, international cartels, and even European governments with sundry legal problems and became a senior partner in his law firm. But he grew bored and restless in his law practice. Anxious about the war clouds gathering in Europe and Asia, Dulles decided to return to public life at the end of the 1930s.[5]

Though fear and distrust of the Soviet Union became the hallmark of his outlook on the world after the war, during the war the staunchly Republican Dulles worked with the Federal Council of Churches promoting the idea of a world governmental organization that would guarantee future peace by fostering intellectual, political, and economic freedoms. He assumed that cooperation would continue between the United States and its wartime Communist ally, envisioning Soviet participation in an international order without spheres of influence and controlled by the United States.

But in several important postwar advisory roles in the Truman administration, earned by his espousal of bipartisanship in foreign affairs, Dulles discovered the Soviets wanted cooperation on the basis of agreed upon spheres of influence in the world. At the San Francisco United Nations Conference in the spring of 1945, Dulles's suspicion of the Soviets was aroused and, by the time of the first Foreign Ministers conference in London in September, his attitude had hardened. He rejected Secretary of State James Byrnes's suggestion of a compromise with the Russians on the troublesome Balkan question. Determined to establish his own American brand of morality in the world, Dulles felt compromise with the Soviets was a step down the road of appeasement.[6] For the remainder of his career, the fiercely self-righteous Dulles considered the Soviet Union to be set upon a program of planned expansion and the chief obstacle to world peace. All Soviet initiatives for a reduction of tensions with the West were merely Communist traps. For Dulles the world was bipolar. He feared that national aspirations within the Western world would only assist Soviet expansion and considered neutrality in the Cold War as unworkable and immoral.

As one of the most prominent voices on foreign affairs within the Republican party after the war, Dulles expected to take over as secretary of state after the triumph of presidential candidate Thomas Dewey in 1948. But when Dewey lost, Dulles sought means for remaining publicly visible in the foreign affairs field until the 1952 presidential election and a better showing by his party. He agreed to fill the unexpired term of New York Senator Robert Wagner and run in the special election of 1949. His losing campaign against Governor Herbert Lehman, however, left Dulles fearful that his dream of becoming secretary of state might never be realized. Ponderous and pious in manner, careful and slow in speech, Dulles tenaciously set out to salvage his reputation as the leading Republican spokesman on foreign affairs by seeking a position within the Truman administration.[7]

His timing was fortunate. Truman desperately needed to deflect Republican criticisms of his foreign policy in the Far East. Senators Robert Taft, William

Knowland, and other prominent Republicans offered particularly sharp denunciations of the handling of China policy by Secretary of State Dean Acheson. In their view, the Nationalist government of Generalissimo Jiang Jieshi had lost the civil war to the Communists not, as Acheson claimed in the White Paper of August 1949, because of its own flaws but through the failure of the Truman administration to support Jiang adequately. When news leaked out early in 1950 that Acheson, over the opposition of the Pentagon, had convinced the president not to intervene to prevent the Chinese Communists from taking Taiwan, longtime Nationalist sympathizers charged that a final betrayal and sellout of an American ally had occurred. Some even suggested that China policy was being shaped by the treasonous activities of left-wing Far Eastern experts and State Department officials. Acheson recalled that the Republicans were preparing a "veritable witches brew" for public consumption and readying for "partisan infighting as bloody as any in our country."[8]

Bringing a prominent Republican like John Foster Dulles into the State Department might provide public reassurance of maintaining a bipartisan foreign policy, key Truman advisors argued. Certainly Dulles had indicated strong interest in that objective. In numerous public speeches and in his book *War or Peace,* written in early 1950, Dulles offered, by Republican standards, mild criticism of the administration's Far Eastern policy that was coupled with homilies on the importance of bipartisanship. Though Acheson did not like Dulles, the pressure to appoint him mounted. Republican Senator Arthur Vandenberg, the central figure of bipartisanship after the war, wrote Acheson on 31 March that bringing Dulles back into "active and important cooperation" with the State Department was "indispensible" to restoring a bipartisan foreign policy.[9] Within a week Acheson, with the president's approval, appointed Dulles as one of his top advisors.

The Bureaucratic Knot

To no one's surprise, Dulles was assigned to work on Far Eastern policy where he might mute some of the noisy criticisms coming from angry Republicans. For five weeks Dulles participated in policy deliberations on general problems in the Far East, especially Korea, Taiwan, and Japan. On 18 May Acheson decided to give Dulles responsibility for arranging a peace settlement with Japan. Unlike China, Japan had been insulated from partisan wrangling after the war by the esteem in which the public, especially Republicans, held General MacArthur. But the Defense and State departments had become entangled in a bureaucratic knot over Japan's place in the emerging containment strategy for Asia. Dulles's first task was to untie it.

For more than a year, Dulles learned, the State Department had struggled without success to reach a consensus with the Pentagon on post-treaty security arrangements. The dispute became intense beginning in June 1949 when dour and irascible Secretary of Defense Louis Johnson submitted a controversial program, "Strategic Evaluation of United States Security Needs in Japan" prepared by the Joint Chiefs of Staff, to the NSC. Reacting to the impending victory of the Red Army in China, NSC 49 argued for American strategic control of an "offshore island chain" running from the Aleutians to the Philippines in which American bases on Okinawa and the Japanese main islands would be key "staging areas from which to project our military power to the Asiatic mainland," including atomic air attacks against the Soviet Union. The JCS opposed a neutral Japan, unequivocally asserting that bases in the area near Japan did not meet "essential needs without bases on the Japanese mainland." If U.S. bases within Japan were to be dismantled as part of the peace settlement, however, "prevention of friendly control of Formosa" was of even greater strategic importance to the entire Pacific security system.[10]

The plan of the Joint Chiefs of Staff had several other key components. It called for the creation of a Japanese military establishment which could be used to tie down Russian forces on the eastern front and thereby prevent them from mobilizing against the United States and Europe in the west in the event of war. It postulated an active Japanese alliance with the United States in a war with Russia. The "developing chaos on the Asiatic mainland" and the growing unrest in Japan in the wake of the Dodge austerity program convinced the JCS to support a continued American military presence in Japan under the Occupation regime of control and oppose any peace settlement limiting the deployment of American forces in Japan. Not until after the creation of Japanese armed forces for self-defense and an agreement with the Japanese which would grant unlimited American rights to bases indefinitely did the joint chiefs want peace treaty negotiations to begin.[11]

NSC 49 clashed with many of the ideas on the peace and security questions held by the State Department. Ironically the Policy Planning Staff under George Kennan, so instrumental in promoting the "reverse course" in 1947–48, took strongest exception to Pentagon assumptions about Soviet intentions towards Japan and the dangers of war in the Pacific. Kennan called for a rapid conclusion of a peace treaty which entailed neither the stationing of American bases in Japan proper nor Japanese rearmament. To do otherwise, he feared, would unnecessarily arouse Soviet suspicions and narrow opportunities for negotiations leading to a modification of aggressive Soviet behavior in the international arena.[12] But Kennan's influence in the State Department had already declined.

After a delay of more than two months, Dean Acheson outlined the department's official position on NSC 49 which revealed that the differences with the Pentagon were more tactical than substantive. Acheson favored a reduction of the American presence in Japan leading to the rapid conclusion of a peace treaty ending the Occupation. There was a "growing weariness and restiveness among Japs" with the Occupation, according to Acheson, who questioned whether the Japanese were committed to "sound friendly relations with non-commie countries." An indefinite Occupation threatened to alienate the Japanese from the West and make it more likely that Japan would slip into the Soviet orbit. He argued that the principal problem for Japan was not overt attack and invasion from the Soviet Union but "a conspiracy inspired by the Kremlin . . . conducted by Japanese. It is essentially a conspiracy from within—and whether it succeeds depends primarily on the political, economic and social health of Japan." The main thrust of American policy, therefore, was fostering conditions in Japan "conducive to a pro-western orientation." The State Department favored increasing the military strength of the police forces but feared limited rearmament for self-defense would create political problems in negotiating a peace treaty.[13]

Acheson did not differ with the joint chiefs over securing the Yokosuka naval base near Yokohama or maintaining a large American military presence in Okinawa. More importantly by September 1949 the State Department accepted the key principle of NSC 49 that U.S. troops should not be withdrawn from the country following the restoration of sovereignty to Japan. It was clearly understood that this would be unacceptable to the Soviet Union and other Communist countries and therefore lead to a "separate peace" involving Japanese alignment with American Cold War policy. Acheson did oppose any Pentagon plan for the "continued dispersal of American forces in many Japanese cities and towns" because they "would constitute an irritating and not a stablizing influence on the Japanese population." Proceeding promptly with a peace treaty that assured essential U.S. military needs in Japan was necessary for the "development within that country of indigenous resistance to Communism and of spontaneous orientation toward the west."[14]

Pressed by U.S. allies, Acheson announced in September 1949 that the State Department would soon begin negotiations on a peace treaty settlement with Japan. Even though the crucial security question remained unresolved with the Pentagon, the department circulated to other agencies of the government a draft treaty of 13 October 1949 which laid out the fundamental approach which Dulles would later follow and which presaged the September 1951 San Francisco settlement. There would be a brief, unrestrictive, nonpunitive multilateral peace settlement covering territorial, political, and economic matters. The State Department requested that the Defense Department submit specific security terms. But the draft treaty provided for a supplementary agreement for the stationing of U.S. forces in Japan for ten years after the peace settlement in "defined base areas on a self-supporting basis." In short, an informal consensus had emerged in the department by this time that the security terms would be separated from the rest of the peace treaty and negotiated as a bilateral pact between the United States and Japan. To Acheson, the implementation of the draft treaty would reintegrate Japan into an American security sphere without provoking the fears of most U.S. allies. If the Soviets balked, Acheson would not hesitate to conclude the peace and security agreement without them.[15]

But Acheson did need the cooperation of the Pentagon to proceed with work on the draft treaty. When the joint chiefs on 22 December insisted on maintaining American forces throughout Japan "generally as at present," Acheson was outraged. In a meeting two days later with General Omar Bradley, chairman of the JCS, he accused the military leaders of ignoring Japan's needs for a treaty and complicating U.S. relations with the British. At that point Bradley opened the door to a possible compromise. In essence, Bradley intimated that if the State Department changed its position against further military assistance to Jiang Jieshi on Taiwan, the Pentagon would consider proceeding with the security terms for Japan.[16] Acheson was not interested. Backed by the president, he succeeded in deflecting the Pentagon's program for an aggressive rollback of communism in China and seizing control of Taiwan in the final NSC 48/2 paper of 30 December 1949. The paper, "The Position of the United States With Respect to Asia," reaffirmed earlier State Department policy on China and emphasized American economic and military assistance to strengthen the ability of Japan and Southeast Asia to maintain internal security and prevent further encroachment of communism in the region. The troublesome question of a Japanese peace treaty was left open for separate consideration at a later date.[17]

Despite NSC 48/2 the State Department and Pentagon continued to wrangle over Asia policy in early 1950. The Pentagon remained committed to rollback in China and, still desirous of using Japan as a forward base in the event of war and distrustful of an independent Japan, held out against a peace settlement for Japan as well. The State Department clearly opposed any rollback approach to China. But secret proposals, as well as public statements, indicated as much concern for a permanent, if more limited, American military presence in Japan, Japanese rearmament, and the strengthening of Japan as a Cold War ally as found in the Pentagon.[18] The disagreement amongst the principals in the Japan security policy debate by 1950 came down largely to whether or not the Japanese could be trusted after a peace treaty and independence to carry out those commonly held objectives.

The State Department was aware that neither the Yoshida cabinet nor the

Japanese public wanted the infringement on sovereignty represented by American forces remaining in Japan. Initially Prime Minister Yoshida hoped that a peace settlement could be arranged in which U.S. forces would be stationed only in areas adjacent to Japan proper, such as Okinawa, while Japan maintained bases within the country for use by American forces in an emergency. But he also believed that granting base rights to the Americans in Japan, even if that meant the Soviets and the Chinese Communists would not be party to the peace treaty, was preferable to an indefinite continuation of the Occupation. The prime minister recognized he would face popular opposition to such a settlement. By the spring of 1950, the Left and independent intellectuals had gained wide support for an "overall peace" in which Japan remained neutral in the Cold War, free of any foreign bases, and without armed forces of its own. Yoshida scorned such thinking as unrealistic. In April he decided that some U.S. military presence within Japan was an unavoidable price to pay for regaining sovereignty.[19]

Well aware that the dispute in Washington over the bases question was causing a delay in the peace treaty process, Yoshida launched a bold initiative of his own. He instructed Finance Minister Ikeda Hayato, who was heading to Washington on an economic mission, to discuss the possibility of American bases in Japan. In a secret meeting on 3 May 1950 with Finance Advisor Dodge, Ikeda noted the strength of the opposition to U.S. bases, the restlessness with the continuation of the Occupation, and the uneasiness, in the wake of the China debacle, over the American commitment to defending Asia. He conveyed the message from Yoshida that the Japanese government "desires the earliest possible treaty. As such a treaty probably would require maintenance of U.S. forces to secure the treaty terms and for other purposes, if the U.S. Government hesitates to make these conditions, the Japanese government will try to find a way to offer them." Besides the initiative on possible security arrangements, directed toward resolving the American intragovernmental dispute, Yoshida's message included an attempt to pressure the United States into a peace treaty by veiled references to the possibility that the Soviets might offer a peace treaty in advance of the United States and include in that offer the return of Sakhalin and the Kuriles.[20]

In summary, when Dulles took over the Japanese peace treaty assignment on 18 May, the State Department had worked out the basic principles of the peace treaty but was deadlocked with the Pentagon over security terms. The Japanese attempt to break the deadlock with a tentative offer to accept American forces on the home islands was still being considered. More significantly, the Pentagon had intimated that the disagreement over Japan policy could be resolved if the administration adopted a more activist containment policy elsewhere in Asia, particularly Taiwan.

Opening Gambits

Predictably Dulles's first memorandum on a peace treaty of 6 June endorsed the principal ideas within the State Department for transforming the former enemy into an ally in the Cold War. As the role of SCAP steadily declined, the Japanese would be assisted in economic development. The peace treaty would insure the Japanese against any reparations or restrictions on industries or raw material supplies demanded by the Allies. Dulles feared that Japan might develop a "dangerous dependence" on continued American aid or on trade with the Chinese mainland, "which would expose Japan to successful communist blackmail at a subsequent date." But he hoped that American pressure on Pacific and Southeast Asian countries to avoid discrimination against Japanese trade would offset that danger.[21]

On controversial security matters, Dulles's memorandum was deliberately vague. Dulles reiterated a long-standing consensus in Washington on the need for a buildup of Japan's paramilitary forces. But he eschewed any specifics on the U.S. bases question beyond proposing a phased withdrawal of Occupation forces except for "certain agreed points . . . held by combined forces" of Japan and the United States. The entire matter was a "technical military problem" requiring the immediate attention of the Pentagon so as not to delay a peace treaty. In truth he was uncertain about the strategic concepts that were undergirding the Pentagon's reluctance to proceed with the peace treaty. Did the JCS want to use Japan "generally as a major advanced offensive air base" or as part of a defensive containment line off the Asian mainland? He clearly doubted that the "dynamic and aggressive tendencies" of Communist powers near Japan could be stopped "merely" by passive defense and hinted at "some counter-offensives of a propaganda and covert character designed to prevent the easy and quick consolidation by Soviet inspired Communists" of areas near Japan. The fundamental assumption for Dulles in the development of the peace treaty was that Japan become a center for the American effort to "resist and throw back communism" in Asia.[22]

The conception of the Japanese peace treaty which Dulles had was perhaps more militant than that of Acheson and other State Department planners. But his singular advantage over them in dealing with the Pentagon was his opposition to the State Department policy on Taiwan. Like the military brass, he did not accept Acheson's prediction that intervention by the United States to defend Taiwan against an anticipated invasion from the mainland would arouse the anger of the Chinese people, thwart hopes of detaching Beijing from Moscow, and undercut American efforts to ally with non-Communist forces elsewhere in Asia.

In a top secret memorandum dated the same day he received the Japan treaty assignment, Dulles spelled out the peril to U.S. global interests, especially economic, created by the Chinese becoming "junior partners" of Soviet communism. If the U.S. continued to show a disposition, as in China, to "fall back" in the face of Soviet aggression, there would be "an accelerated deterioration of our influence" in all areas outside Europe and Latin America. "The situation in Japan may become untenable and possibly that in the Philippines. Indonesia, with its vast natural resources, may be lost and the oil in the Middle East will be in jeopardy." Such a series of disasters, Dulles argued, could probably be prevented only by a "dramatic and strong stand" by the U.S. at some "doubtful point." Of these, "Formosa has advantages superior to any other," for it was not subject to immediate influence from Soviet land power, was close to U.S. naval and air power, and was occupied by non-Communist friends and allies to whom this was a moral responsibility. If the U.S. was not prepared to risk war to prevent the fall of Taiwan to a "joint Chinese-Russian expedition," then in the eyes of the world, Dulles concluded, "we are making another retreat" which would lead to disaster everywhere. Dulles favored an effort in the United Nations to create an international trusteeship over Taiwan with American naval forces preventing an invasion of the island from the mainland.[23]

While devoting the bulk of his time to Japan problems, Dulles worked closely with Assistant Secretary of State Dean Rusk and Pentagon officials throughout May and June for a change in the administration's Formosan policy. He perceived that the pressure on Acheson was having an impact, telling a meeting of seven leading pro-Jiang Republican senators that they should not start any "fireworks" over Taiwan policy until he had more time with the secretary of state. At a press conference in Tokyo on 22 June, Dulles also predicted "positive action" by the United States to preserve peace in the Far East, and he specifically mentioned that American policy towards Taiwan was subject to revision.[24] Picking up on statements from the JCS, Dulles apparently believed that if Taiwan, and South Korea as well, were maintained within the American security perimeter, he could convince the Pentagon to compromise on security terms for Japan.

Recognizing the need to get a firsthand grasp of the complexities of security policy in the Pacific in order to proceed with the peace treaty, Dulles and his chief aide, John Allison, director of the Bureau of Northeast Asian Affairs, arrived in Tokyo on 17 June and immediately departed for South Korea. The envoy toured the defenses along the thirty-eighth parallel, met with the increasingly despotic South Korean president, Syngman Rhee, and implied to the South Korean Assembly that the United States would provide aid in the struggle to loosen the Communist grip on North Korea.[25]

Back in Tokyo on 21 June, Dulles received an unusually cordial reception from General MacArthur, whose views on Taiwan and key aspects of the Japanese peace treaty were remarkably similar to his own. In a memorandum prepared on 14 June which he gave to Dulles, MacArthur made clear that he opposed any further delay in peacemaking and expressed fear that extensive U.S. bases in Japan would arouse a "wave of intense nationalistic opposition within Japanese political circles" and give credence to Communist propaganda that the U.S. wanted to colonize Japan. He also warned that, contrary to Dulles's thinking, any rearmament scheme was certain to cause "convulsions" throughout Asia and within Japan as well. He contended that the most desirable and realistic military security arrangement for Japan was one he misleadingly called "neutrality." It would deny Japan to the Soviets rather than making Japan an "active military ally of the United States." Such neutrality, however, entailed American access to some military and naval bases to assure Japanese political alignment with the West.[26]

Coinciding with the Dulles visit to Japan was a mission headed by Defense Secretary Johnson and the Joint Chiefs of Staff to study the military aspects of the Japanese peace treaty. Johnson publicly denounced the "State Department crowd" while Dulles was in Korea. Privately, he considered Dulles an "impractical man who approaches the world's problems with a religious, moral, and pacifistic attitude."[27] Given such hostility, Johnson and the chairman of the JCS, General Bradley, were happy to use MacArthur as as intermediary with the Dulles mission, even though they objected to MacArthur's 14 June memorandum on the Japanese peace treaty. The Pentagon war plans called for Japan to be a forward offensive base against the Soviets in the Far East and MacArthur's conception of a neutral Japan without its own arms was contrary to basic strategy. Only on the issue of defending Taiwan did MacArthur make any sense to them.

Hoping to end the conflict between the two visiting missions, MacArthur drafted a second memorandum on Japanese security problems on 23 June which ultimately became the basis of American policy. In flagrant contradiction to his position only two weeks earlier, he now argued that the "entire area of Japan must be regarded as a potential base for defensive maneuver with unrestricted freedom reserved to the United States as the protecting power through her local commander. . . ." To reduce the "adverse psychological effect upon the national sentiment of the Japanese people" of such a policy, MacArthur proposed several reservations. Any changes in the disposition of American forces in Japan would have to be done in consultation with the prime minister of Japan. The security forces should not have authority to intervene in the internal affairs of Japan. To sweeten the bitter medicine of extensive U.S. base rights to the Japanese, MacArthur also proposed that U.S. forces operate on a "pay-as-you-go" basis, which would contribute under existing conditions about $300 million to the Japanese economy and make Japan completely self-sufficient. He also suggested a softening of his position on rearmament arguing that the no-war clause of the constitution did not deny Japan the right to self-defense.[28]

While considering MacArthur's proposal on security matters, Dulles met with a host of American, Japanese, and allied diplomats, businessmen, politicians, journalists, intellectuals, and labor leaders to sound them out on what kind of treaty would be acceptable. He focused much of these discussions on the controversial issue of Japanese rearmament. Since the approval of a new 150,000 paramilitary force in NSC 13/2 in November 1948, American policymakers had moved rapidly away from the initial demilitarization programs. While rejecting full-scale rearmament in March 1949, the joint chiefs favored further increases in civilian and coastal police forces for handling internal security problems and as a "vehicle for the possible organization of Japanese armed forces at a later date."[29] State Department officials like Max Bishop opposed any reference to a prohibition or ceiling on Japanese armed forces in the peace treaty and, prior to the signing, wanted "a strong constabulary [to] be created and an end put to the communistic menace through the outlawing of the party and the jailing of the leaders." When Dulles told the Tokyo chapter of the American Chamber of Commerce on 22 June that if Japan aligned itself with the West it would have the "primary responsibility of protecting itself by its own efforts against the ever present menace of indirect aggression," he was publicly expressing the consensus in Washington that the Japanese had to launch a more serious rearmament effort as well as accept some U.S. bases.[30]

But Dulles found Japanese leaders remarkably vague about questions of post-treaty security. On 23 June, two days before the Korean War broke out, Prime Minister Yoshida met with Dulles and refused to commit himself on the bases question. Though Yoshida implied that a satisfactory arrangement could be concluded, he was not willing to be tied down to any specific terms. On the rearmament issue, Yoshida was even more noncommital. Neither Dulles nor the joint chiefs had set a specific level for a Japanese troop buildup, but John Allison recalled that, in prodding Yoshida for some contribution to Japan's own defense, Dulles had in mind about 100,000 troops. Yoshida, Dulles later recorded, "seemed to be hoping that Japan's renunciation of war and armed force in her new Constitution would make it possible for Japan to remain apart from the struggles and dangers of the rest of the world." With Dulles visibly disturbed, Yoshida suggested that General MacArthur, with whom he had a "secret understanding," be consulted. MacArthur told Dulles what Yoshida had wanted to hear on rearmament and then proposed as an alternative that the Japanese rehabilitate idle weapons factories to assist in the reconstruction of

American armaments. For the time being, Dulles and Yoshida accepted this compromise.[31]

With the single exception of a representative of the Japanese labor movement, all the Japanese with whom Dulles spoke vigorously opposed rearmament. Former Foreign Minister Shidehara, a respected conservative in the House of Councillors, told Dulles he expected American forces to remain in Japan after a treaty, but he emphatically opposed a "revival of militarism" or the expense of rearmament. The leader of the large Socialist party, Asanuma Inejiro, and several trade union officials voiced support for an "over-all peace" settlement, without U.S. bases or rearmament. One of the more radical spokesmen charged that the United States was designing a treaty to serve its own, not Japanese, interests but the Japanese "wanted independence for themselves; they wanted to be left alone and they did not like the occupation, particularly the effect of the Dodge policy on the laboring man." With dismay, Dulles summed up the "general opinion" of the Japanese on security matters before the Korean War this way: "Japan should not rearm but should nevertheless continue to be protected by the United States, preferably from long range."[32]

The Impact of the Korean War

Within five days of the onset of the Korean War on 25 June, the Truman administration created the conditions under which Dulles was able to finally gain Pentagon support for an early peace treaty and reluctant Japanese acceptance of a "separate peace" that required both American bases in Japan and Japanese rearmament. With Dulles's support, U.S. air, sea, and ground forces were sent from Japan to defend South Korea against what was assumed to be Soviet inspired Communist aggression whose real target was Japan. On 27 June, Truman ordered the Seventh Fleet to sail from Sasebo, Japan to prevent any attack on Taiwan from the mainland and called on the Nationalists to cease operations against the People's Republic of China from Taiwan. With the neutralization of Taiwan accomplished by unilateral American intervention, the president announced that the future status of the island would await the restoration of security in the Pacific, a peace settlement with Japan, or consideration by the United Nations. At the same time, U.S. aid to the French forces in Indochina and the Philippine government, both of which were facing well-organized Communist led insurgencies, was dramatically increased. Dulles was elated with these fundamental changes in American policy taking place throughout Asia. According to Allison, before leaving Japan Dulles "completely forgot that he was a Republican" and hailed Truman as the "greatest president in history."[33]

The first step for Dulles on his return to Washington was winning Pentagon approval for a post-treaty security arrangement with Japan. During July, Dulles and State Department officials prepared a draft of prospective articles on "International Peace and Security." The draft was intended to follow General MacArthur's 23 June compromise proposal and, as Dulles explained to Acheson, "give, in a form as inoffensive as possible to the Japanese, the broad power to the United States to place military forces wherever in Japan the United States may determine to be desirable." In the context of the changes in American policy throughout Asia wrought by the Korean War, especially the maintenance of American control over Formosa, Dulles expected that Pentagon officials would not object to this proposal, since it met their previously reiterated demands on base rights and rearmament. Thus Dulles was incredulous when Defense Secretary Johnson refused to meet with him to discuss the draft security proposal. But when he explained that the proposal "gave the United States the right to maintain in Japan as much force as we wanted, anywhere we wanted for as long as we wanted," Johnson relented and told the envoy he thought the Pentagon and State Department on that basis could "get together and go places."[34]

Johnson was right. Though objecting to some vagueness in the language of the State Department's "unlimited bases" proposal, the JCS informed Johnson that the "portentious events" in Asia since the Korean War made a separate peace settlement with Japan advisable. At the end of August, John Allison began negotiations with high-level Pentagon officials to find a mutually acceptable revision of the State Department's draft proposal. The resulting top secret Joint Memorandum on Japanese security terms, signed by Acheson and Johnson on 7 September, was approved the next day by the National Security Council and the president as NSC 60/1.[35]

Dulles finally had won a truce with the Pentagon so that he could proceed to negotiate the peace treaty. But the cost was somewhat higher than State Department officials had expected to pay when the peace treaty was formally placed on the agenda a year earlier. The Joint Memorandum, U. Alexis Johnson of the Office of Northeast Asian Affairs pointed out, was put in "brutally frank terms, a concession to the military's desire to avoid any possibility of future misunderstanding with the U.S. Government as to the terms of the agreement reached. Public disclosure of a document so phrased could be disastrous for the whole treaty project."[36]

Several provisions of the Joint Memorandum Johnson found particularly explosive. First was the right of the United States to maintain "armed forces in Japan, wherever, for so long, and to such extent as it deems necessary," the details of these arrangements to be spelled out in a supplementary bilateral security agreement with Japan which would come into effect at the same time as the multilateral peace treaty. Secondly, American forces would not be obligated to stay in Japan even in the event of war or threat of war, but could not be removed from Japan except with the consent of the United States government. Thirdly, nothing in the security treaty would prohibit American forces from acting, at the request of the Japanese government, in putting down large-scale riots and disturbances. Finally, NSC 60/1 stipulated that there should be no prohibition, direct or implicit, in the peace treaty on Japan's "right to self-defense," a signal, in fact, of the American intention to push the Japanese into a large-scale rearmament program.[37]

In the first weeks after the outbreak of the Korean War, Dulles was buoyed by the changes he observed in the attitude of the Japanese towards the prospect of American bases in post-treaty Japan. Before his return to Washington at the end of June he reported that the Japanese finally showed an appreciation of the "increasing Communist menace" and hence gave "more open admission than had previously been obtained of the continuing need of United States military forces remaining in Japan." The stepped-up campaign of the Yoshida government and the business community against left-wing labor unions and the Communist party after the Korean War further undercut much of the popular resistance to a "separate peace" with American forces in Japan.[38]

But Dulles also recognized that the importance of Japan as a forward base for American operations in Korea afforded the Japanese more bargaining power in reaching a settlement on the bases question. The first sign of that was a statement on 29 July 1950 by Yoshida that he opposed the leasing of military bases to any foreign country. It was the most forceful public comment he had made on the vital security question and, in effect, withdrew the secret offer on base rights he had made through Ikeda on 3 May.[39] In sum, while Dulles believed the Korean attack had shocked the Japanese people into accepting United States forces in Japan, he also was aware that the longer the war continued the more opportunity the Japanese gained for bargaining on the bases issue.

To the initial satisfaction of Dulles and other American planners, the Korean War undercut some of the Japanese opposition to rearmament and accelerated the transformation of Japanese paramilitary forces into a small armed force. The first American troops sent to Korea were from Japan and it was soon clear that, by early September, only one of the four divisions comprising the Occupation force before the war would remain. To protect American bases and approximately one-quarter million American dependents, General MacArthur dispatched a letter to Prime Minister Yoshida on 8 July authorizing the formation of a 75,000-man National Police Reserve. Formerly the staunchest advocate of a completely demilitarized Japan, he now envisioned the NPR as a paramilitary force, distinct from other Japanese police forces, which could become a small army of four infantry divisions. As long as the NPR could be publicly presented as a police unit, Yoshida was receptive to the proposal. It promised a solution to the problem of maintaining civil order without American troops and perhaps would satisfy Dulles's requests, made before the outbreak of war, for Japanese rearmament.[40]

But Dulles had more ambitious notions than Yoshida anticipated. In July he finished a memorandum urging immediate attention to the rearmament of Germany and Japan and abruptly dismissed Kennan's search for a diplomatic approach to the Soviets by avoiding military settlements with the former Axis powers.[41] Since the no-war article of the Japanese constitution and basic Far Eastern Commission-approved directives for the Occupation explicitly prohibited rearmament, Dulles and other top ranking American and Japanese officials adopted a surreptitious approach to operating the NPR. American military officers responsible for creating a viable Japanese fighting force were placed under the cover of the Civil Affairs Section Annex, so as to suggest a civilian mission. The instructions given by Colonel Frank Kowalski, chief of staff for Major General William Shepard, the commander of CASA, to the first American officer assigned to a camp of new NPR recruits ludicrously illustrate the secrecy and duplicity by which the NPR became a de facto Japanese army:

> You will be the only one in the camp who will know that you are organizing an infantry battalion. Others, of course, will suspect it. But only you will know. As far as the Japanese are concerned, and that applies to all Japanese, the governor, the police and the NPR [recruits themselves]—you are organizing a police reserve. The Constitution of Japan prohibits an army. You will not call the men soldiers, and you will not call the officers by any military ranks. The men are policemen and the officers will be superintendents. If you ever see a tank it isn't a tank, it's a special vehicle. You can call a truck a truck.[42]

Initially, American military officers performed planning and operational tasks so as to make the NPR a "little American Army." After several months, control was turned over to about a thousand Japanese civilians recruited from business, the professions, and government service and an elite of 320 American-trained Japanese commanders. Then began, in Kowalski's words, "calculated creeping rearmament tuned to the will of the Japanese public and Allied reaction." When no serious protests erupted in Japan or elsewhere, CASA grew bold, first issuing to the "police" American carbines, M-1 rifles, and .30-caliber machine guns and gradually escalating to .50-caliber machine guns, 60- and 81-millimeter mortars, bazookas, flame throwers, artillery, and tanks. Dulles and Pentagon officials, however, considered the slow strengthening of the NPR an inadequate contribution to Japanese self-defense and, as will be indicated, privately pressured Yoshida to create an army of ten divisions of between 300,000 and 325,000 troops. Throughout 1950 and 1951, Yoshida stubbornly resisted such massive and rapid rearmament while publicly maintaining that the NPR was simply a police force. But, in fact, by the end of 1951, the NPR force of 75,000 was based in thirty-seven camps throughout Japan under highly trained officers, and was provided with a variety of heavy American armament. In Kowalski's view in the closing months of 1951, NPR, as battalions, could "have put up a whale of a fight. Beyond that the capacity of the force for war was very limited, although in the opinion of many, the organization possessed a great potential for future development."[43]

The Korean War also greatly accelerated the pace of naval rearmament in Japan though, as with the NPR, not fast enough to satisfy Dulles and military planners. The Maritime Safety Agency, founded in April 1948 with twenty-eight small patrol type vessels, was modeled after the U.S. Coast Guard, its duties legally limited to non-military tasks. But as James Auer has carefully documented, the head of the new agency, Okubo Takeo, former Japanese naval officers, and high-ranking U.S. Navy officers began planning for the MSA from the outset as the nucleus of a new navy. With the outbreak of the Korean War, MacArthur authorized an increase of eight thousand in the number of MSA personnel and plans were made to increase the number and tonnage of ships and remove restrictions on speed and armament. Even before the buildup could be completed, a dramatic, but secret, demonstration of the MSA's transformation into a naval unit occurred. In accordance with the desires of the U.S. Navy, Prime Minister Yoshida reluctantly decided in early October 1950 to authorize forty-six Japanese minesweeping units for duty off Korean waters.[44] Despite these developments, Dulles expected a more substantial naval role for Japan. During his crucial negotiations with the Japanese on security terms early in 1951, he met with Admiral Nomura who presented a proposal for a complete defense organization with a 200,000-man army and 50,000-man navy-airforce with 200,000 tons of shipping and 700 aircraft. According to Nomura, Dulles was very impressed by the plan and the two men continued discussions of it.[45]

The Security Issue in Negotiating the Peace Treaty

With the Pentagon no longer blocking his way and a mandate from the NSC and the president to proceed, Dulles began a series of informal meetings with members of the Far Eastern Commission on a memorandum spelling out the seven "principles" for a Japanese peace treaty. The fourth principle called for the retention of American forces in Japan and no restrictions on Japanese rearmament but did not reveal the "brutally frank terms" of NSC 60/1. It appears from the record to have drawn the heaviest fire from the delegates with whom Dulles met in New York and Washington from mid-September until his second trip to Japan at the end of January 1951.

Representatives from Australia, Burma, New Zealand, and the Philippines expressed strong reservations about the absence of military restrictions on the Japanese. As Australian Foreign Minister Percy Spender read the seven principles, John Allison recalled, his

> face drew more and more suffused with color, and at one point I thought he would burst a blood vessel. Japanese troops had come close to Australia and the bitterness caused by the war was still intense among his people. And here was their ally, the United States, proposing a peace treaty with no restrictions on the remilitarization of Japan and no provision for reparations of any kind. Sir Percy did not hesitate to express his opinion in colorful and uninhibited language.[46]

Indeed, Spender wanted "firm guarantees" from the United States in the form of some kind of Pacific Pact "against Japanese aggression" if there were no restrictions on rearmament. New Zealand's foreign minister voiced a similar opinion. The security issue seemed "uppermost" in the mind of Philippine Foreign Minister Carlos Romulo, Dulles reported. Romulo reminded Dulles that the security of the Philippines from another Japanese invasion rested on the "willingness of the United States to stand by a long-time friend."

The Indians and Russians complained not only about potential Japanese rearmament but about American base rights as well. Madame Pandit, Indian ambassador to the United States, told Dulles that India's most serious concerns were "with the problem of security, and in general it feels Japan should be demilitarized and its security guaranteed by the U.N." As for post-treaty U.S. bases, she said, "they will in practice constitute a military occupation and thus limit the free exercise of Japanese sovereignty." Though Dulles had little expectation that the Soviets would ever accept the peace and security terms he was negotiating, he met three times with Jacob Malik, Soviet representative to the U.N. Security Council. Malik had many objections to the seven principles, starting with the exclusion from the negotiations of the People's Republic of China, the most publicly critical of American security plans for Japan. While Malik questioned Dulles about Japanese rearmament, he spoke out firmly against U.S. bases in Japan, noting that the Soviet Union was surrounded by American military bases. Retention of bases in Japan in the post-treaty era would be "in effect the same as United States troops remaining in Occupation."[47]

Despite all the criticisms of the security principle, Dulles's talks with the Allies had, on the whole, been encouraging. By mid-November Dulles was convinced that if he could get "as a fixed and solid point" Japanese agreement to American peace terms, particularly on security, that other countries, except for Russia and Communist China, would "come into line [by a] combination of firmness with some placating modifications which will be of form rather than substance." Though the rapid success of over 300,000 Chinese Communist troops in pushing American forces out of North Korea during late November and December stunned Dulles and temporarily delayed his work on the Japanese peace treaty, he was soon persuaded that rapid conclusion of the treaty was necessary to prevent Japan from falling to the Soviet Union's "aggressive policies." Time was of the essence, he wrote Acheson on 8 December, for the United States "still possesses prestige in Japan and the full political and military implications of the Korean defeat are not yet apparent." The longer treaty negotiations were delayed, the more likely the Japanese would be to resist American terms.[48]

Standing in the way of Dulles's proposal once again was the Pentagon. The Joint Chiefs of Staff argued that the defeats in Korea had so shaken the American position throughout Asia that peace treaty negotiations would be conducted "under circumstances of extreme weakness [and] the United States would be expected to offer many military and other concessions to the Japanese which under other circumstances, probably would not be necessary." Expressing their continuing doubts about Japanese commitment to American policies in Asia, the JCS saw a "strong possibility" that if peace negotiations were concluded quickly the Japanese could "deprive the United States forces of the use of Japan as the major base of operations in the Korean War." Nor were Japan's own security forces yet ready to deal with either a possible Soviet attack or an escalation of internal Communist activity in the chiefs' view.[49]

The beginning of a successful counteroffensive by General Matthew Ridgway in pushing North Korean and Chinese forces out of Seoul and back to the thirty-eighth parallel, the more accommodating posture of General George Marshall who succeeded Louis Johnson as secretary of defense in September 1950, and the upper hand which the State Department gained over the Pentagon on Japan policy after the Korean War began led Truman to elevate Dulles from consultant to ambassadorial rank on 10 January 1951 in order to begin formal negotiations on the Japanese peace treaty. Contrary to a Pentagon proposed stipulation in NSC 60/1, Dulles was instructed to conclude a treaty, if necessary, without waiting for a favorable resolution of the Korean crisis. In addition, Dulles had authority to negotiate a mutual security arrangement with Japan, the Philippines, Australia, New Zealand, and perhaps Indonesia. The principal purpose of the peace and security treaties, Dulles was told, was to "secure the adherence of the Japanese nation to the free nations of the world and to assure that it will play its full part in resisting the further expansion of communist imperialism."[50] Ironically, as Dulles knew, not one other country in the world wanted the kind of peace treaty with Japan that he was now finally entrusted to negotiate.

The Showdown with Japan

The most critical work of the whole peacemaking process for Dulles occurred in meetings with the Japanese on the bases and rearmament questions during his visit to Japan from 25 January to 11 February 1951. Dulles recognized that, because of the heightened importance of Japan to American security in the wake of the Chinese intervention in Korea, concessions which once he could have obtained from the Japanese "merely by suggesting them [had now] to be negotiated for and obtained as fully as possible."[51] He learned in his first meeting with Prime Minister Yoshida on 29 January the price the Japanese demanded for acceptance of American bases. Yoshida expressed the hope that numerous Occupation sponsored reform ordinances still on the books, such as those affecting the family system, should be rescinded with American permission before the end of the Occupation. He also mentioned pressing Japanese economic needs for expansion of fishing areas, increases in shipbuilding capacity, and investments from the U.S. He spoke of the "long-term necessity" for Japanese trade with the Chinese mainland, even if China was governed by the Communists. Dulles politely countered Yoshida's position on China trade and warned that many of the Allies would want to impose restrictions on Japanese fishing, shipbuilding, and other matters in the peace treaty.

The tone of the discussion abruptly changed, however, when Dulles turned to the rearmament question. He chided the prime minister for advocating the restoration of Japanese sovereignty without specifying what contribution Japan would make to the "free world." Dulles did not mention the size of the force he expected the Japanese to develop, but SCAP headquarters at the time was using the target figure of ten divisions of between 300,000 and 325,000 troops. Yoshida's vague response upset Dulles, who complained to his staff the next day that he had been treated to a "puffball performance." Yoshida said it was necessary "to go very slowly" in rearming Japan. He argued, as he had the previous June, that rapid rearmament would bring back the militarists and expose the government to the danger of being dominated by them. Secondly, the Japanese economy would be severely strained by massive rearmament. There would be a decline in the standard of living that would create social unrest which the Communists would exploit.[52] Though not stated to

Dulles, Yoshida also feared that rapid and large-scale rearmament would lead to overt Japanese involvement in the Korean War, reviving the antagonism of Asian neighbors whose trade was vital to economic recovery. In any event, Dulles was openly disappointed with Yoshida's position and insisted that the Japanese had to make some sacrifices by "at least a token contribution" to the collective security of the region. Yoshida conceded the point without committing himself to a figure.

Yoshida strenuously labored to ease the pressure by Dulles for rearmament. Once again he and Dulles paid General MacArthur a visit wherein MacArthur, official policy notwithstanding, supported Yoshida's position against large-scale, rapid rearmament. MacArthur and Yoshida considered Dulles's Cold War fears of a direct external threat to Japan exaggerated; as MacArthur observed in the congressional hearings that followed his dismissal in April 1951, the Soviet Union and China simply lacked the amphibious capacity to invade Japan. The two also agreed that Dulles's concern over a Kremlin sponsored Communist conspiracy in Japan was also unwarranted. Through his relatives, the crusty prime minister secretly encouraged left-wing socialists to step up their antirearmament campaign so as to impress Dulles with the political difficulties of accepting American policy.[53] Finally, on 31 January, he threw down on the negotiating table his best card. The Japanese would cooperate as "equal partners" with the United States in the stationing of American forces for defense of Japan against outside attack in return for a slow, gradual, and limited rearmament.[54]

After two days of negotiations over Yoshida's quid pro quo at the staff level, American officials grew angry at Japanese reluctance to promise more and faster rearmament. They threatened to enumerate the rights and privileges of U.S. forces in the body of the security treaty instead of in a supplementary agreement. Such an approach would stimulate domestic opposition, Yoshida feared, and endanger the overriding objective of regaining independence as soon as possible. Consequently, on 3 February Yoshida instructed his negotiators to submit to the Americans a document on "Initial Steps for Rearmament Planning." The Japanese proposed the establishment of a 50,000-man national defense force which would exist separately from the National Police Reserve and the Maritime Safety Agency. It would include a navy and an army, as well as a Peace Preservation Agency and a Headquarters for Defense Planning. The prime minister's top military advisor, Tatsumi Eiichi, was not even aware of the existence of this document at the time, and, in a recent interview, said he would never have recommended a force of only 50,000 since that had no meaning in military terms.[55] That, no doubt, was the point for Yoshida. To accept the American proposed target of 300,000 or more troops aroused Yoshida's long-standing fears of the revival of militarism, direct Japanese involvement in Korea, opposition from other nations, the strain on the economy, and domestic unrest.

After reviewing the various documents and negotiations on bases and rearmament, Dulles was not satisfied with Yoshida's concession, as important as it was. The proposed Japanese version of the security treaty bound the United States to come to Japan's defense in case of an attack. Until Japan was in a position to make more definite commitments to contribute a certain number of divisions by a certain date, "the US would want rights rather than obligations [in the security treaty]," Dulles told a morning staff meeting on 5 February. Moreover, he continued, "the US cannot press the Japanese to assume military obligations until they have dealt with their Constitutional problems [namely, revision of the no-war article 9], and are in a position formally and publicly to assume such obligations." Bluntly Dulles reiterated his understanding of his instructions from the president. The United States was prepared to station troops in Japan and desired the right to do so, "but it was not stated that the US was prepared to guarantee Japan's security. By not assuming such an obligation we remain free to pull our troops out at any time."[56] In short, even after Yoshida's concession to the principle of rearmament and a promise of 50,000 troops, Dulles refused to make any significant revision in the terms for unrestricted post-treaty American base rights. Dulles knew that his position was precarious, though he concealed his uncertainty.[57]

By the last meeting between Dulles and Yoshida and their staffs on 7 February, agreement was reached substantially on American terms. There would be a package of three interconnected accords dealing with the security and rearmament issues. The peace treaty would have only a brief section on security, which simply stated Japan's inherent right to collective self-defense in phrasing taken from the United Nations Charter. The rest of the American drafted peace treaty offered the Japanese sovereignty without any of the major restrictions which most of Japan's former enemies wished to impose. Japan would not be obligated to pay any reparations. There would be no restrictions in the peace treaty on Japanese commercial activity, including shipbuilding and fishing. The signators to the treaty would retain Japanese assets in their countries but they would have no continuing right to reclaim property looted by the Japanese during the war. There would be no treaty requirement that the reforms of the Occupation period be maintained.[58] Such extraordinarily lenient peace terms, designed to consolidate the power of Japan's ruling elite and integrate Japan into the American dominated world economy, convinced Dulles that the Japanese would be willing to swallow the two remaining accords in the package.

The first, the U.S.-Japan Security Treaty to which Dulles and Yoshida agreed, was to be signed immediately after the peace treaty and, unlike the peace treaty, required only the ratification of the Japanese Diet and the U.S. Congress. The core of this brief treaty was a Japanese request to the United States for the stationing of "land, air, and sea forces in and about Japan." The primary purpose of the forces was for the defense of Japan against external attack, but there was no specific commitment. The United States was permitted to use its bases in Japan without consulting the Japanese for actions in the Far East that might involve Japan in a war. If requested by the Japanese government, American forces could be used to put down large-scale internal riots and disturbances. The United States exercised a veto over any arrangement for the entry of forces of a third power into Japan. The United States would only consent to the Japanese request for American forces "in the expectation, however, that Japan will itself increasingly assume responsibility for the defense of its own homeland against direct and indirect aggression." No rearmament targets were specified but Dulles had obtained Yoshida's commitment to an initial 50,000-man force in addition to the 75,000-man NPR. Finally, there were no provisions for a termination of the treaty except by mutual consent.[59]

The second of the remaining two accords in the package would be a deceptively innocuous sounding "administrative agreement" in which the "conditions which shall govern the stationing of armed forces" by the United States would be arranged by a joint committee of American and Japanese representatives after Diet ratification of the peace and security treaties. The key to the acceptance of the American security proposals, practically without change, Assistant Secretary of the Army Earl Johnson told Dulles, was "the concept that while the Diet would approve the [security treaty] the administrative agreement would be a Cabinet action only" and would not be negotiated or made public until after the peace and security treaties were approved.[60] The Japanese had made clear their fear that enumerating the details of facilities and areas for U.S. security forces and their rights would create the impression that the Occupation was continuing in the post-treaty period and thus cause severe political complications within and without Japan. Dulles appreciated that concern. He attached great importance from the outset of his negotiations with the Japanese to winning broad based political support for the final treaty arrangements.

Upon leaving Toyko for visits to Manila, Canberra, and Wellington, Dulles told a press conference that he was quite pleased with how smoothly the negotiations had gone. He ascribed his success to the readiness of the "Japanese people" to have their nation become "a sustaining member of the free world."[61] But if that was the case, then why did Dulles and Yoshida agree to keep the terms of U.S. base rights hidden in an administrative agreement until after the peace and security treaties were ratified? And why did these two diplomats agree not to make public the promise of 50,000 troops and to continue the charade of calling the National Police Reserve a police force? Perhaps a better explanation for the success of Dulles in his negotiations of security terms with Yoshida was the leniency of the peace treaty and the desperate desire of the Japanese for independence. Once independent, Yoshida believed, the Japanese would gradually be able to gain leverage against the more onerous requirements of both the security treaty and the still to be negotiated administrative agreement.

Patchwork Security and the San Francisco Settlement

With little success, many American planners had attempted from 1948 onward to adopt a regional rather than a "country by country" approach to the economic and military reintegration of Asia into the postwar world order. A formal military alliance known as a "Pacific Pact," analogous to the Atlantic Pact or NATO, originated with Philippine President Elpidio Quirino in the summer of 1949. The National Security Council endorsed the principle of such collective security arrangements in Asia in NSC 48/2 at the end of 1949. But Washington officials were suspicious of Quirino's motives and skeptical that a general agreement of Asian nations to such a pact could be reached. In an attempt to break the deadlock with the Pentagon over the Japanese treaty, lower ranking State Department officials considered in March 1950 an "offshore" Pacific pact. But in his very first briefing on the Japanese peace settlement on 7 April 1950, Dulles joined top State Department planners in underscoring the drawbacks to the Pacific pact concept. The Senate would not want to offer Japan, an ex-enemy country participating in a Pacific pact, the "one for all and all for one commitment of the Atlantic Pact" when so many former allies of the United States were not given similar guarantees, he said.[62]

The outbreak of the Korean War rekindled interest in Asian capitals and Washington in a Pacific pact. Dulles, John Allison, and others argued that the North Korean attack showed Asian nations the "true nature of the Communist threat" and, hence, the necessity for some kind of regional security pact with the United States. Moreover the Japanese would be more amenable to rearmament, Dulles believed, if their armed forces attained international status. At the same time, a multilateral pact would give Pacific allies "a right to have a voice in what Japan does so that they may be assured that Japanese rearmament does not get out of hand and become a threat."[63] Dulles was officially authorized by his instructions of 10 January 1951 to negotiate a regional pact, if necessary, with Japan, Australia, New Zealand, the Philippines, and possibly Indonesia.

During his second visit to Japan, Dulles found the Japanese extremely interested in a Pacific pact. But, at the same time, he received from the British Foreign Office the first indication that the latest version of the pact was in as much trouble as earlier ones. Without the participation of the United Kingdom, British prestige in the Far East would suffer a serious blow. Moreover, the proposed island pact only increased the jeopardy from the mainland to British possessions in Hong Kong and Malaya. Dulles, however, did not want the British in the pact. "If you bring in the British," he told General Ridgway, "you must bring in the French, then the Dutch—which would make it a Colonial Pact." Yet Dulles was not distressed. The main point was that as long as the U.S. and Japan—"the only significant sources of power in the Pacific, we actual, they potential"—were in accord on peace and security terms, "the lesser Pacific powers will get security and will, sooner or later, formally or informally endorse that accord. If the United States and Japan fall apart, the situation in the West Pacific is grave for a long time."[64]

On his visits to Manila, Canberra, and Wellington to win assent to the Japanese peace treaty terms he had negotiated, Dulles encountered further resistance to his concept of a Pacific pact. The Australians and New Zealanders emphasized the popular revulsion which would attach to any pact which included the Japanese. "Russia seemed a long way off," Dulles concluded in Canberra after witnessing intense popular "resentment, fear, and hatred of the Japanese." It was not possible "to change public feeling, or to persuade the Government it could go along with us without committing political suicide." Colonel C. Stanton Babcock reported for the Dulles mission that there was a "surprising lack of enthusiasm for the Pacific Pact" in the Philippines, which he attributed to the fact that Nationalist China was not included and because the Filipinos "realize that we are already committed to their defense—actually although not by treaty."[65] The newly independent Indonesian government opposed the whole plan. Dulles quickly recognized he would have to make major changes in the Pacific pact proposal.

Instead of incorporating the Japanese security terms into a Pacific pact, Dulles negotiated two separate additional security agreements primarily to assuage fears of a resurgent Japan—a trilateral security treaty amongst the United States, Australia, and New Zealand and a bilateral U.S.-Philippine security treaty. Canberra and Wellington were not wholly satisfied with the new agreement, mainly because the only clear obligation of the parties in case of a threat to territorial integrity or political independence was to "consult together." If there was an armed attack, the treaty promised action but without a requirement, as in the NATO agreements, for an immediate military response. In effect the ANZUS Pact, as the agreement was called, meant that

American forces could be used to defend Australia and New Zealand from an armed attack only after congressional approval. Based on his own participation in the Senate debates in 1949 over the Atlantic Pact formula, Dulles anticipated that the Senate would not likely ratify a similiar formula in the Pacific which further increased the power of the executive branch. Despite its limitations, the ANZUS Pact had great value to political leaders in Australia and New Zealand in mollifying public criticism of the Japanese peace treaty.[66]

The Philippine security agreement was designed to appease Philippine public opinion more than alter the American military relationship with the island nation. By the terms of the Military Bases Agreement of 1947, the U.S. exercised extraordinarily favorable rights to naval, air, and army bases in its former colony. President Quirino and other Filipino government officials assumed that the United States would defend the islands against any outside threat from those bases. Their interest in a Pacific pact rested primarily on the hope of greater American economic assistance. When Dulles arrived in Manila from Tokyo in February to discuss the Japanese peace treaty, the Filipinos stressed not security but the necessity for reparations. A presidential advisory commission had estimated that Japan owed the Philippines eight billion dollars for the damage done during the war. But Dulles told the Filipinos their reparations demands were impossible, for they would impose on Japan an intolerable burden.[67] Nor could he offer any specific guarantee against Japanese military aggression.

Initially Dulles was convinced that any Filipino objections to the reparations and security provisions of the Japanese peace treaty could be overcome by the "reasonable prospect of future aid from the United States."[68] But by the end of his visit he recognized that American aid by itself would not be adequate compensation to gain Manila's acquiesence to the Japanese peace treaty. Consequently, after leaving Manila, he negotiated a revised reparations article in the treaty that he felt went far enough to meet Filipino objections. Rather than being absolved of all reparations, Tokyo would compensate for war damages by providing services to the victims of Japanese aggression. That concession failed to satisfy the Filipinos, who submitted a proposal that left open the possibility for cash reparations. Dulles got President Truman himself to approve a stinging rejection of that plan.[69]

To soften the blow on reparations, Ambassador Myron Cowen recommended conclusion of a Philippine-American security treaty pact. Washington liked the idea and by the end of August the two nations signed a bilateral security pact. The new treaty merely recognized existing obligations and put them on a mutual basis even less specific than the ANZUS treaty. As critics of the U.S.-Philippines security pact (and the ANZUS Pact as well) pointed out, it was questionable whether this kind of treaty guaranteed anything more than the United States would likely do in its own interest anyway. Its real significance, as Dulles understood, was in reconciling the governments of Australia, New Zealand, and the Philippines to a peace treaty which did not provide any restrictions on Japanese industrial or military rearmament or offer reparations in the form or amount expected.

With the important exception of a dispute with the British over the handling of China's representation at the Japanese peace treaty conference, Dulles felt ready early in June to proceed with a conference designed to gain formal approval of U.S. allies for the draft peace treaty and related security treaties already negotiated bilaterally. Underscoring Dulles's care in keeping the Senate informed about his negotiations, American political leaders and the press, with little dissent, welcomed the treaty draft and plans for the San Francisco Conference. But no such reception was given the draft treaty abroad. The Russians and Chinese Communists, as expected, vigorously denounced the proposed settlement, particularly its security provisions. In a bitter note that reflected the fear of an emerging aggressive threat on their Far Eastern flank, the Soviets charged that the treaty was being imposed on the people of Japan by American imperialists in cooperation with Japanese reactionaries. The Chinese Communists, who were never consulted by Dulles and, unlike the Russians, were not invited to the peace conference, were even more critical of the draft peace treaty. As the chief victim of Japanese imperialism, the Chinese especially feared the threat of a rearmed Japan.

The reaction of most U.S. allies in Asia to the draft treaty was one of apprehension or outright opposition. As already indicated, Australia, New Zealand, and the Philippines were induced to approve the treaty only by the ANZUS and U.S.-Philippine security pacts, as well as timely and cosmetic concessions on reparations terms. India, whose approval of the Japanese peace treaty was considered by the State Department to be especially important because of its influence as a leading non-Communist power in the region, raised four major objections, including the stationing of U.S. troops in Japan. Failing to win any compromises, India declined at the end of the summer to participate in the San Francisco Conference. The Burmese, who had suffered under brutal Japanese occupation during the war, were distressed that the draft treaty failed to provide for sufficient reparations payments and also rejected the invitation to attend the San Francisco Conference.[70]

Carefully stage-managed by Acheson and Dulles, the San Francisco Conference ended after four days when forty-nine nations, beneath the glare of television lights, signed the Japanese peace treaty on 8 September 1951. Surprisingly, delegates from Russia, Poland, and Czechoslovakia attended to register their objections, but were quickly ruled out of order by Acheson, the chairman of the conference. Most of the delegates, primarily European and

Latin American allies of the United States, followed the prepared script. With his usual hauteur, Acheson described in his memoirs the feelings of those who attended the conference. "Never was so good a peace treaty so little loved by so many of its participants." The ink had barely dried on the peace treaty before Prime Minister Yoshida and Acheson drove across town to the Presidio. With only Dulles and two other Americans looking on, they quietly signed the U.S.-Japan Security Treaty worked out in Tokyo in February. The signing of the two treaties on the same day symbolized, as John Dower has written, that the peace treaty had "no separate existence of its own but rather was contingent upon Japan's agreeing to a military alliance with America: magnanimity under lock and key."[71]

Japanese opposition to Dulles's handiwork developed only gradually, as the unpleasant details of the security treaty were revealed in stages over several months' time. The treaty's final text was kept secret until it was signed and then rode the wave of satisfaction that greeted the peace treaty and the coming of independence. In a *Mainichi Shimbun* poll of 13–14 September 1951, 80 percent of respondents supported the security treaty. But William Sebald reported on 30 September a "sizable body of opinion which is strongly opposed to [rearmament]," as well as to the general purpose of the security treaty. Communists, socialists, trade unionists, liberal intelligentsia, and students "appear convinced that any rearmament, even for self-defense, or any military understanding with the United States will only draw Japan into the vortex of a struggle which could otherwise be miraculously avoided." Even more serious, Sebald argued, the ruling Liberal party and other Japanese conservatives offered only shallow support for rearmament and the security treaty. A "semi-colonial attitude on the part of the United States and a failing standard of living" could lead Japanese leaders to take their "chances in the role of a third or neutral force, possibly oriented toward Nehru's India."[72]

When the peace and security treaties came before the Diet at the end of October, the security treaty was the major focus of debate. The opposition pressed Yoshida to spell out the details of the security treaty, at that point no more than a vague agreement that Japan would both allow American troops to stay on after the Occupation and would assume responsibility for its own defense. The prime minister was deliberately evasive and aroused his critics. The Communists and left-wing Socialists led the opposition to both treaties; right-wing Socialists supported the peace treaty but opposed the security treaty; and the majority Liberal party and the Democratic party favored both treaties. The final tally in the House of Representatives for the peace treaty was 307 to 47 and for the security treaty 289 to 71. In the House of Councillors the vote was 174 to 45 in favor of the peace treaty and 147 to 76 for the security treaty.[73]

With the Japanese ratification of the peace and security treaties accomplished, Dulles did not fear to sharply increase the price demanded for the return of Japanese sovereignty. Two major issues remained outstanding. The first was the negotiation of the "administrative agreement" which implemented the security treaty. The second was assurance of Japanese cooperation with the United States in the containment of the People's Republic of China. Not to gain Japanese acceptance of American terms on these issues, Dulles believed, would jeopardize ratification of the treaties in the U.S. Senate.

Administrative Agreement

Dulles played a small but important role in the design of the "administrative agreement," the final critical link in the U.S.-Japan security chain. As agreed to by Dulles on 6 February 1951 at the insistence of Japanese negotiators, the detailed terms for the stationing of American forces in Japan were to be placed in a separate executive agreement which would not require Diet approval. Under the direction of Earl Johnson and General Carter Magruder a rough draft of the administrative agreement was prepared on 9 February and approved by the Japanese government. The Joint Chiefs of Staff, however, found the draft wanting and after more than six months of study submitted a revised version to the State Department for comment on 22 August 1951.[74]

Once again Dulles and other State Department officials were stunned by what they regarded as the Pentagon's political obtuseness and apparent tactics of delaying the return of Japanese sovereignty. John Allison prepared an immediate critique of the memorandum for Assistant Secretary of State for Far Eastern Affairs Dean Rusk, and sent a copy to Dulles. For Allison the JCS position against allowing the Japanese criminal jurisdiction over off-base American personnel, for example, amounted to a return to the despised unequal treaty system from which the Japanese had freed themselves in 1899. Allison recommended to Rusk, who was assigned to negotiate the administrative agreement, that the highest officials of the State Department meet with their counterparts in the Defense Department "to make clear the unacceptability of the general philosophy exhibited" in the JCS memorandum. Dulles shared Allison's frustrations with the Pentagon. In San Francisco he met William Sebald, Earl Johnson, Carter Magruder and others to discuss launching an educational campaign for the JCS so that they would not continue treating the Japanese as "defeated enemies and as orientals having qualities inferior to those of occidentals." Upon returning from San Francisco, Dulles insisted that the task of reconciling State and Defense department views on the administrative agreement had to begin at once.[75]

At the request of the president and Dean Acheson, Dulles assumed formal responsibility for handling the ratification of the peace and security treaties in the Senate on the condition that he push for action as soon as Congress reconvened in January. Dulles agreed that early consideration by the Senate of the treaties was important to avoid having them become political footballs in the 1952 presidential election and endangering ratification. The only potential obstacle to that plan, Dulles told Acheson on 22 October, was that the Defense Department probably wanted to postpone ratification in order to "bargain for position" on the terms of the administrative agreement. He appealed to Acheson for presidential support behind the State Department's contention that the Defense Department had ample time to make arrangements for the administrative agreement without delaying Senate consideration of the treaties. A few hours later Acheson returned from a meeting with the president and told Dulles Truman was "in full agreement" with the department and would brook no delays by the Pentagon.[76]

Dulles immediately prepared a two-page memorandum for Dean Rusk outlining the general principles he felt should be followed in resolving the conflict with the Pentagon and negotiating the administrative agreement with the Japanese. He admitted that the achievement of American security objectives in Japan involved "some burdensome and irksome conditions" which the Japanese would have to accept in good spirit. But when the peace treaty came into effect the Japanese would properly expect to be treated as sovereign in their homeland. To seek an administrative agreement that met "all possible contingencies and conceded to the United States elaborate extra-territorial privileges, command relationships, and prestige position" would be self-defeating. The Japanese would deeply resent such an agreement and seek to terminate it. Moreover, the Pentagon conception of the agreement would encourage many American soldiers who had fought against the Japanese or served in the Occupation to continue in the "habit of treating the Japanese as inferiors" and thereby weaken the chance of Japanese-American cooperation. Finally, Dulles emphasized that,

> if it is demonstrated to all Asia, which is intently watching, that Westerners as represented by the United States find it congenitally impossible to deal with Orientals on a basis of respect and equality, that will have grave repercussions throughout all of Asia. It will make it likely that all of the Asiatics will unite, under communist leadership, against the West. Then the situation would be more dangerous to us than when Japan attempted this same result under the same slogan.

In brief, Dulles wanted Rusk to accommodate Japanese sensitivities about national sovereignty and, in *New York Times* columnist James Reston's phrase, "avoid suspicion that the United States is clamping a phony independence on

Japan while at the same time preserving the facilities essential to the United States military command.''[77] That those might be contradictory objectives from the Japanese perspective seemed not to trouble either Reston or Dulles.

Generally adhering to the principles laid out by Dulles, Rusk negotiated a complex compromise with the Defense Department on all articles of the draft administrative agreement except the one on criminal jurisdiction over U.S. forces (which required the intervention of Acheson and the president to settle).[78] The approved draft in hand, Rusk began four weeks of strenuous negotiations in Tokyo on 30 January 1952 with Foreign Minister Okazaki Katsuo and Treaty Bureau Chief Nishimura.

After raising initial procedural objections, the Japanese accepted a slightly revised article 2, the heart of the administrative agreement. A joint committee of high-level Americans and Japanese would immediately begin consultations on selecting specific facilities and areas for use by American forces after the peace and security treaties came into force. The U.S. would have the right and authority to garrison and control such places, including the right to remove buildings, deepen harbors, install radar apparatus, and acquire rights of way for pipelines.[79]

The Japanese vehemently objected to two of the American drafted articles. Article 15 on criminal jurisdiction not only stipulated that the U.S. military had the power to arrest Japanese outside of base areas but it gave American authorities exclusive jurisdiction over U.S. personnel for all crimes committed in Japan. Thus American courts would have primary jurisdiction even when Americans committed crimes against Japanese outside base areas during off-duty hours. Okazaki complained that these terms were inferior to the U.S.-Philippine base accord and warned of domestic protest against such humiliating legal immunities for Americans in Japan. Rusk remained adamant, however, and ultimately the Japanese accepted a face-saving provision which stated that the U.S. would give sympathetic consideration to a request by Japan for waiver of the American right to exercise jurisdiction in particular cases.[80]

Finally, the Japanese objected to article 22 which stated that, in the event of actual or threatened war, Japanese military forces would be placed together with U.S. forces under the ''combined command'' of an American designated officer. Moreover, in such an emergency, U.S. forces would not be limited to the facilities and areas worked out by the joint committee under the terms of the administrative agreement. Okazaki presented a host of reasons, most of them rooted in the fear of a political backlash against the Yoshida cabinet, for not including ''combined command'' in the administrative agreement. With the crucial assistance of Supreme Commander Ridgway, Rusk and the State Department convinced the JCS to drop the requirement for specific reference to ''combined command.'' Undoubtedly most persuasive to the chiefs were assurances that the Japanese government accepted the principle of combined command and would act accordingly. In the end, the Japanese and Americans settled on a quite general statement which simply called upon the two governments to "consult together" on defense issues in the event of an emergency.[81]

The entire negotiations on the administrative agreement were conducted in secret. But press leaks stirred uneasiness amongst the Japanese. A coalition of representatives from all parties in the Diet demanded assurances that Japan would not be turned into an atomic base either for storage or attacks against other nations. They pressed Yoshida for an outright declaration against extra-territoriality. The most intense controversy focused on the defense share of the Japanese budget. In a budget primarily designed once again by Joseph Dodge, in consultation with General Ridgway, the Yoshida cabinet railroaded approval in the Diet for sixty-five million yen for support of American forces remaining in Japan by the terms of the still secret administrative agreement and fifty-six million yen for the NPR and MSA. That was about 30 percent of the total budget and more than the costs to Japan of the Occupation in the previous year.[82]

On 28 February 1952, the day the agreement was signed, it was made public. Criticism of the pact was strong and widespread throughout Japan. The conservative business paper *Nihon Keizai* bluntly said the agreement was "not satisfactory to the Japanese. Frankly speaking, we get the impression that the will of the United States has been forcibly imposed upon Japan." The largest newspaper in Japan, *Asahi,* offered some of the frankest criticism of the agreement, contending that there was not a clause that gave even the appearance of an independent Japan. "Friendship between Japan and the United States will become everlasting only when the two peoples stand in equal autonomy," the editors warned.[83] The Japanese press, one U.S. Foreign Service officer reported, "generally took the view that the agreement was not concluded on an equal basis and that it failed to answer important questions regarding criminal jurisdiction and emergency defense measures." The opposition parties called for a protest rally and issued a statement condemning the Yoshida government's conduct of the negotiations, the restrictions on sovereignty and basic human rights, and the use of "dictatorial politics" in pushing through legislation required by the agreement.[84]

Much of the criticism centered on the secrecy of the Yoshida cabinet's handling of negotiations. The administrative agreement highlighted the ignorance of the Japanese people of the critical details necessary for informed judgement during the public debates and Diet vote only a few months earlier on the security treaty. Certainly the Japanese people did not expect to have to play host, in 1954, to 210,000 American troops stationed in about three hundred installations across the country. Nor did they anticipate that an implicit condition for the reduction of these American forces was the buildup of the Japanese Self-Defense Forces (which emerged from the NPR and MSA) to an actual strength of over 200,000 by 1957, complete with an inventory of the latest U.S. model tanks, heavy artillery, jet fighters, and destroyers. Nor did they imagine that within a few years the United States would attempt, unsuccessfully, to introduce Honest John missiles capable of carrying nuclear warheads on the Japanese main islands. The latitude of criminal jurisdiction given to the Americans, as the Japanese negotiators had warned Rusk, became a particular sore point.[85]

The administrative agreement, the *New York Times* accurately editorialized, "appears to have aroused greater opposition in Japan than the preceding pacts." The "mood of concern tinged with bitterness," concluded one American official after surveying reaction to the agreement, "would appear to presage a period of difficulty in United States-Japan relations." A Dutch observer with friendly ties to the Americans in Japan reported that "the United States delegation was surprised at the strong anti-American feeling revealed in the Diet and the press."[86] But, as Dulles recognized, the crucial audience was at home. The Pentagon's conditions were met and one major obstacle on the path to Senate ratification of the peace and security treaties was cleared with the signing of the administrative agreement. One more obstacle remained.

The China Question

Despite geographical proximity, mutual trade needs, and cultural affinity, Japan did not give diplomatic recognition to the People's Republic of China until 1978. Formally, the major obstacle to normalized relations between the two Asian nations was the peace pact Japan signed with the rump Nationalist Chinese government on Taiwan on 28 April 1952 a few hours before the termination of the Allied Occupation of Japan. This Japanese decision was preceded by more than a year of heated controversy in the United States, Britain, Japan, and both Nationalist and Communist China. To Dulles, the central figure in the controversy, the outcome of the Anglo-American conflict over Sino-Japanese relations was crucial to the ultimate adherence of Japan to the "free world" and Senate ratification of the Japanese peace treaty.

As the United States recognized only the Nationalists and Great Britain only the Communists as the legitimate government of China, Dulles decided after the outbreak of the Korean War to conduct bilateral talks with FEC members recognized by the U.S. on the Japanese peace treaty. The negotiating strategy worked well until the formulation of a final draft of the peace treaty was prepared by the end of March 1951. To Dulles's dismay the British Labor government responded with its own draft treaty which took a tougher position on reparations, limits on shipbuilding capacity, rearmament, and especially a divergent approach on handling Japan's relations with China.[87] The British, who scoffed at continued American support for the hapless Jiang Jieshi regime on Taiwan, proposed that Beijing "be invited to participate in any negotiations for the conclusion of a treaty." If Nationalist China signed the Japanese peace treaty for China, British diplomats feared, Japan would be foreclosed from resuming its important trade relations with the mainland. Not only would Japan's economic viability in the long term be thrown into question but Japan, with American assistance, would attempt to compensate for the lost trade with the mainland by invading traditional British markets in Southeast Asia. The British, Dulles correctly gauged, were principally worried about "the impact of Japanese commercial competition during the post-Treaty period."[88]

Coming only a few months after the Chinese Communist entrance into the Korean War and amidst the continuing furor in Congress over the bloody combat, the British proposal for PRC participation in the Japanese peace settlement was wholly unacceptable to the State Department. Dulles complained to Sir Oliver Franks, British ambassador to Washington, that Anglo-American relations were "drifting seriously apart" over the issue and warned that he was prepared to take unilateral action to effect a rapid conclusion to the treaty. Secretary of State Dean Acheson was even more blunt with Franks. Only "American and Japanese power—the latter potential—existed in the Far East. Japan was now a primary end in itself. We could not be paralyzed by looking only at the difficulties."[89] The China issue in Anglo-American relations had become a major stumbling block on the road to the Japanese peace treaty.

To break the deadlock with the British, Dulles planned a trip to London for early June. He wanted the input of the Japanese before he left, while making clear to them that participation of the PRC in the treaty settlement was "absolutely out."[90] Dulles received assurances from the Japanese Foreign Ministry that, basically, the Japanese government wished to make peace with the Nationalists at some time separate from and after the other Allies. The Japanese and Americans recognized that to insist that the Nationalists be cosigners of the treaty with the other Allies would mean the British, Australians, and many other Allies would not sign the treaty. On the other hand, failure to give Nationalist China an opportunity to become party to the treaty would delay ratification by the Senate with its powerful bloc of Jiang Jieshi supporters.

Arriving in London on 2 June, Dulles plunged into meetings with Foreign Office officials to reach an acceptable Anglo-American draft treaty and settle the Chinese participation issue. The British diplomats were eager to compromise, Dulles discovered, backing off their demand for PRC participation in the treaty settlement. They never had any illusions that the Americans would accept that proposal, but it was a good bargaining chip. After further discussion, British Foreign Secretary Herbert Morrison agreed on 6 June to a proposal by Dulles that no Chinese government would be invited to sign the multilateral Japanese peace treaty at the peace conference anticipated for early September in San Francisco. But Japan would be permitted to conclude a separate bilateral peace treaty with the Nationalists or the PRC on terms substantially the same as the multilateral treaty *after* the coming into force of that treaty. "This w[ou]ld permit Japan to determine which Chi[na] it wished to do business with," Dulles cabled Acheson, confident that Japan would make peace only with the Nationalists.[91]

However, to Dulles's shock, on 7 June the disintegrating government of Prime Minister Clement Attlee rejected the formula negotiated with Morrison. The majority of the cabinet felt that to leave Japan, while under American tutelage, free to make her own arrangement with China merely "facilitated Japan's recognition of the Nationalist Government of China and in effect yielded to the U.S. demand that that Government participate in the Treaty."[92] Dulles flew off to Paris for three days, threatening to end negotiations if the cabinet did not accept the Dulles-Morrison formula.

Dulles's tactics worked. At a cabinet meeting on 11 June Morrison strenuously argued that Dulles had taken a "major step to meet us" in not having the Nationalist Chinese cosign the multilateral treaty. He would be subjected to vehement criticism by the right-wing of his own party. Moreover, Morrison felt Dulles appreciated that the British did not want Japan to align with the Nationalists and that he would not pressure Japan in that direction. In fact, Dulles had suggested to him that the British use their influence to dissuade Japan from a pact with the Nationalists. Dulles, Morrison naively asserted, was "known to be opposed to Chiang Kai-shek."[93]

Persuaded by Dulles's tough negotiating stance and Morrison's appeal, the cabinet voted to approve the formula it had rejected only four days earlier. As spelled out in a joint British-American memorandum of 19 June, no Chinese government would participate in the multilateral peace treaty. Japan's "future attitude toward China" was to be determined by "Japan itself in the exercise of the sovereign and independent status contemplated by the treaty." To Dulles the agreement meant that the British "acquiesced in the United States thinking that Japan should conclude a peace treaty with the Nationalist Government."[94]

Though he knew the Nationalists would not be happy with anything less than full participation in the Japanese peace settlement, Dulles was confident he could obtain their acquiescence to the London formula if he consolidated support of some key senators sympathetic to Jiang Jieshi. On his return from

London, Dulles saw senators William Knowland, Robert Taft, and others. Apparently with little objection, they indicated their approval of Dulles's approach.[95]

Then Dulles met with Ambassador V. K. Wellington Koo to persuade him to recommend acceptance of the Dulles-Morrison agreement to Taipei (Taibei). But the Nationalists were deeply disappointed, not only at the prospect of being excluded from the Japanese peace conference, but of signing a bilateral peace treaty which seemed to place the Japanese, the defeated enemy, in a position to decide with whom they wished to deal and China, an ally, in the position of a supplicant. Dulles did promise, in violation of the spirit of the London accord, that the Sino-Japanese pact might be negotiated and signed by Japan *between* the signing and entering into force of the multilateral treaty. That way, Dulles told Koo, "the two treaties come into effect about the same time so that in fact [Nationalist] China would be on an equal footing with the other Powers vis-à-vis Japan."[96] After futile efforts to rally American supporters against the Anglo-American agreement, the Nationalists resigned themselves to watching the peace conference from the sidelines and hoped bilateral negotiations with the Japanese would start as soon thereafter as possible.

Though delegates from neither the PRC nor Nationalist China were seated at the San Francisco Conference, their presence hovered over the entire proceedings. Acheson told Prime Minister Yoshida that, when the issue of Sino-Japanese relations came up, he should be evasive and say no decision would be reached until after the treaty was signed. But Herbert Morrison, for one, was suspicious of American pressure on Japan to enter into relations with the Nationalists, and issued an oblique warning in his conference speech that Japan would have to make her own relations with the PRC. "We cannot and must not presume to set the pattern for the future relationship of these two great nations of Asia. That momentous decision they must make for themselves."[97]

The signing of the Japanese peace treaty by forty-nine nations on 8 September and the conclusion of the mutual security pact by the U.S. and Japan later the same day brought the unresolved issue of Sino-Japanese relations to the forefront of State Department concern. Morrison insisted to Dulles that the June agreement meant nothing should be "done to crystallize the Japanese position toward China until after the Treaty of Peace came into force."[98] But a large group of senators feared that, left up to the Japanese themselves, there was a serious danger of Japanese recognition of the PRC. Senator Knowland organized fifty-six senators to sign a letter to President Truman on 12 September declaring that, prior to the admission of the Japanese peace treaty to the Senate, "we desire to make it clear that we would consider the recognition of Communist China by Japan or the negotiating of a bilateral treaty with the Communist regime to be adverse to the best interests of the people of both Japan and the United States."[99]

To the distress of Dulles, Prime Minister Yoshida made statements in October and November that appeared to flaunt the Knowland letter and brought down the wrath of the Nationalist Chinese and Congress upon the State Department. Several times Yoshida announced a "wait and see" policy on recognition of the PRC in answer to criticism of the Japanese peace treaty by Socialists in the Diet.[100] Yoshida and powerful sectors of the Japanese business community clearly considered Japanese trade with the mainland a necessity. Wellington Koo told Dulles Yoshida's statements indicated the Japanese were not interested in a bilateral treaty with the Nationalists and British influence had been active in tilting Japan toward the PRC. Dulles reassured Koo that he was prepared to use Japan's economic and military dependency on the U.S. to force her into line with U.S. policy on China. Yoshida's statements, he explained, were greatly disturbing Congress and threatened ratification of the peace treaty.[101] Consequently, Dulles decided in early November to take Senators John Sparkman and H. Alexander Smith, the ranking Democratic and Republican members of the Far Eastern subcommittee of the Senate Foreign Relations Committee, with him to Tokyo to get a reliable indication of Japanese intentions on the China matter.

In preparation for his trip, Dulles hoped to gain the approval of the new Conservative party government of Winston Churchill for the Japanese to begin as soon as possible negotiations on a bilateral treaty with the Nationalists limited to the de facto authority of Jiang Jieshi. But Foreign Minister Anthony Eden refused to initial any accord that was not fully consistent with the Dulles-Morrison agreement, and would therefore jeopardize passage of the Japanese treaty in Parliament. At an impasse, Acheson agreed to Eden's suggestion that Dulles meet in Tokyo with Sir Esler Dening, the new head of the British Mission in Japan, to further discuss the matter. Once the House of Commons ratified the peace treaty, State Department officials believed Eden might not be so "hypersensitive" about the Dulles-Morrison agreement.[102]

Ten days after Parliament ratified the Japanese peace treaty, Dulles left for Japan on what he claimed was merely an information gathering visit prior to the Senate consideration of the peace treaty. In fact, his primary purpose was to obtain written assurances from the Japanese that they would sign a bilateral pact with the Nationalists. He laid the blame for Japanese equivocation on the issue squarely on the British. The continued British recognition of the PRC and rejection of U.S. efforts to induce Japan to begin negotiations with the Nationalists, he believed, was part of a plan by Churchill to come to Washington early in January "with the maximum number of bargaining points in order to increase . . . chances of getting aid economically Britain so badly needed." But that strategy endangered Senate ratification, and Dulles decided to brook no further opposition. The British had to realize "their former empire, particularly in the Near and Middle East, was a pathetic shell and that our help was essential to their survival."[103]

With the aid of SCAP officials, Dulles prepared a memorandum on 13 December on Sino-Japanese relations for approval by Yoshida and Sir Esler Dening. Since Senate ratification of the peace and security treaties depended on Japan following a policy on China "generally compatible" with that of the United States, Japan should begin negotiations as soon as possible on a pact with the Nationalists on the basis of their de facto control of Taiwan to come into force immediately after Japan regained sovereignty. Yoshida did not openly object to the Dulles memo though, according to Dulles, he "showed obvious reluctance to take this course if UK strongly opposed." The prime minister pleaded for a reconciliation of American and British policy on China for Japan was "in an almost impossible position when confronted by major differences between two leading nations of the free world." He also told an incredulous Dulles that, by increasing Japanese trade with the mainland, the PRC might be weaned from the Soviet bloc.[104] Sir Esler Dening was visibly shocked by the Dulles memorandum, which he considered an open violation of the Dulles-Morrison agreement. He would have to refer the whole matter back to the Foreign Office, which instructed him to have no further discussions with Dulles. Churchill and Eden would handle it on their trip to Washington.[105]

In consultation with Senators Smith and Sparkman, Dulles prepared a letter for Yoshida's signature which embodied the 13 December memorandum. The letter indicated Yoshida's presumed desire for normal relations with the Nationalists through a bilateral treaty, the terms of which would be "applicable as regards the territories now or hereafter under the actual control of the Japanese and Nationalist governments." In addition, the letter sharply indicted the PRC and gave assurance that "the Japanese Government has no intention to conclude a bilateral treaty with the Communist regime." Yoshida said he had no objections to signing the ghosted letter. He would send it to Dulles who would hold it until a suitable opportunity for publication during or just prior to Senate debate on the Japanese peace treaty. In any case, Dulles promised not to release the letter until he had met with Churchill and Eden early in January in the hopes of "changing the British attitude on China."[106]

Despite the efforts of Japanese Foreign Ministry officials to hold off making a decision on the recognition of Nationalist China, the prime minister signed the infamous "Yoshida letter" on 24 December. He did not want to risk difficulties over ratification in the Senate, about which Dulles, Sparkman, and

Smith repeatedly warned. Furthermore, Yoshida no longer had to fear that a treaty with the Nationalists would adversely affect the British Parliament's ratification of the treaty. Finally, as Yoshida insisted later, the proposed bilateral treaty with the Nationalists was a limited one which would not foreclose trade and other ties with the mainland.

The visit of Churchill and Eden to Washington provided the State Department with one last opportunity to line up British support for the American position on Sino-Japanese relations. Acheson, Dulles, Eden, and their aides met on 10 January to hammer out a final settlement. Without specifically discussing the text of the Yoshida letter, Dulles referred to a "direct communication" from Yoshida "stating the intentions" of the Japanese government towards Taiwan which would be made public during Senate consideration of the peace treaty. Though Eden reiterated his often stated view that he did not want the Japanese to commit themselves to the Nationalists before the coming into force of the San Francisco treaty, he left Dulles with the impression that "he would not press the U.K. position strongly on Japan or expect it to prevail or feel aggrieved at the Japanese government if it did not follow the U.K. line." On that basis Dulles arranged for the public release of the Yoshida letter on 16 January. "Senate has reassembled and there is urgent need of clarification [of the China issue]," Acheson explained to one diplomat.[107]

The publication of the Yoshida letter shocked Eden. In his memoirs Eden emphasized that he had not been shown the Yoshida letter to read nor did he understand its significance from Dulles's reference to it. Moreover, he assumed that Dulles appreciated that the British did not want to be "regarded as having acquiesced" in U.S. policy on Sino-Japanese relations. But the release of the Yoshida letter the day after Eden arrived back in London had done just that. "Neither date nor announcement had been agreed with me," he insisted. "Its publication so soon after my visit to Washington was embarrassing and could give the impression that I had agreed to its contents."[108]

The Foreign Office made a formal complaint to Secretary of State Acheson about the Yoshida letter. Acheson conveyed his regret and assured Eden the incident was unintentional. Few, if any, in the Foreign Office accepted that explanation, believing instead that Dulles had masterminded both the timing and substance of the release of the Yoshida letter. It was "obviously American dictated," wrote Dening from Tokyo. "The extent to which it commits Japan and provokes China could hardly have been drafted by any Japanese."[109]

The release of the Yoshida letter stirred up a political furor in Britain and Japan. "The British press at home and abroad is in full cry against me," Dulles wrote. Back as a member of Parliament, Herbert Morrison charged Dulles with blatantly violating the Dulles-Morrison agreement of June. The Japanese public attitude was more restrained but, according to Dening, that was no clue to the strong feelings of resentment towards the U.S. for forcing Yoshida's hand on China policy. Most criticism focused on Yoshida's failure to consult the Diet and "giving the impression that important matters are handled behind the people's back." The Japanese, however, had little choice but to acquiesce in American wishes if they were to secure the earliest end of the Occupation. Yoshida attempted to minimize the political damage to himself by stressing that the proposed treaty with the Nationalists gave them only limited recognition and did not foreclose diplomatic relations with the PRC if conditions changed. Moreover, the British, Yoshida incorrectly claimed, had raised no objection to a Japanese treaty with the Nationalists.[110]

Neither the criticisms of the British and Japanese nor the more open hostility of the PRC towards the Yoshida letter appeared to disturb Dulles. "I know that what we did put an undesirable strain upon our U.K. relations," Dulles later admitted to Acheson, "but it was not nearly as bad as what seems to me was clearly the alternative," namely passage in the Senate of a crippling reservation to the Japanese peace treaty on the China issue.[111] Dulles, in fact, made the Yoshida letter an important part of his testimony during the Senate hearings on the ratification of the treaty at the end of January. If Yoshida made good on his pledge to open negotiations with the Nationalists on a bilateral pact, Dulles and Senators Smith and Sparkman were confident that the China bloc would not succeed in breaking up bipartisan support for the Japanese treaty.[112]

The exceedingly slow pace of the negotiations in Taibei for a Sino-Japanese pact that began on February 20 greatly alarmed Dulles and his Senate allies. The problem developed when the Nationalists presented a draft treaty in which the Republic of China was to be recognized as the legal government of all China and the Japanese delegation insisted on the limited recognition language of the Yoshida letter. The State Department instructed Chargé Karl Rankin to mediate the dispute, and just prior to the opening of Senate debate on the Japanese peace treaty, Senator Smith flew out to Taibei and Tokyo. His intervention was apparently instrumental in the resumption of serious talks between the Japanese and the Nationalists.[113]

The Yoshida letter and the renewed negotiations in Taibei effectively undermined the efforts of Senator William Jenner to obtain support for a reservation to the Japanese peace treaty which reaffirmed the U.S. open door policy against any partition of China and recognized the Nationalist government as the sovereign government of China. Senators Smith, Sparkman, and Knowland all warned that adoption of any reservation to the treaty would require the State Department to reopen negotiations with U.S. allies and probably topple the whole treaty structure. More importantly, they suggested that nothing in the treaty permitted Japan to act contrary to U.S. policies towards the PRC.

Though the Sino-Japanese pact had not been formally signed yet, the Japanese, Sparkman noted, indicated an attitude of "sympathy with us and an attitude of opposition to Communist China."[114] The Jenner reservation on China was defeated 48 to 29 with 19 abstentions, and the Japanese peace treaty was ratified on 20 March by an overwhelming margin of sixty-six to ten.

As the Nationalists had feared, the Senate ratification of the Japanese peace treaty stiffened the Japanese negotiating position in Taibei. Intense pressure by the State Department failed to budge the Japanese who appeared to be deliberately stalling until after the coming into force of the San Francisco treaty on 28 April. But the Japanese ended ten weeks of negotiations and signed the bilateral pact with the Nationalists only seven hours before regaining sovereignty. "It seems almost as if, having demonstrated their power, [the Japanese] contemptuously made this last minute concession to Chinese 'face,' " observed one British diplomat in Taiwan.[115]

Whatever the reason for the change in Japanese negotiating tactics, the text of the treaty and an accompanying exchange of notes were designed to allow both the Japanese and Nationalists to claim that their position on the scope of application of the treaty had been upheld. The treaty itself contained no reference at all to the territorial limits of Japanese recognition of the Nationalists. That was dealt with in an exchange of letters that followed the Yoshida letter formula. With confusing and self-serving rhetoric and limited domestic opposition, the governments in Japan and Taiwan easily won legislative approval for the Tokyo-Taibei pact, which came into force on 5 August 1952.[116]

Though Dulles alienated a considerable body of British and Japanese sentiment, the State Department regarded his handling of the China question in the making of the Japanese peace treaty a success. By not inviting the Nationalists to the peace conference, Dulles had insured the participation of all major U.S. allies except India. Above all, the subsequent Sino-Japanese pact, which Dulles carefully supervised, greatly mollified the angry Nationalist Chinese and their supporters in Congress. Throughout the negotiations of the Japanese peace treaty and the Sino-Japanese treaty, Dulles disregarded the strenuous protests of the PRC that those treaties were part of a plan to restore the Nationalists to power on the mainland. But the prevailing wisdom in the State Department was that the Chinese Communists were puppets of the Russian enemy, without an independent foreign policy. The opposition of the British to his handling of China in the Japanese peace treaty was regarded by Dulles as politically misguided and based on narrow economic self-interest. After all, the cabinet had recognized that the Dulles-Morrison agreement would "almost inevitably lead Japan to align herself with United States," he told Acheson.[117] Dulles was essentially correct. But, by ignoring both British sensibilities and arguments in favor of a Japanese modus vivendi with the PRC that the Tokyo-Taibei pact appeared to make impossible, Dulles greatly strained Anglo-American relations. British global weakness and reliance on U.S. economic aid allowed the U.S. the luxury of treating its principal ally with scarcely veiled contempt in an area it regarded as having preeminent jurisdiction.

Finally, Dulles was well aware of the strong opposition within Japan to a pact with the Nationalists that helped isolate Japan economically and politically from the mainland. But he was convinced that, with adequate markets for Japan in Southeast Asia and U.S. military procurements, Japan could prosper until the PRC collapsed and a friendly regime was installed. Subsequently, when Southeast Asia markets for Japan failed to grow rapidly and the Chinese Communist regime survived, Dulles faced as secretary of state the full brunt of Japan's economic and military dependency on the United States.

The ratification of the Tokyo-Taibei pact which followed the coming into force of the Japanese peace and security treaties marked the successful completion by John Foster Dulles of his project for reintegrating Japan into the American dominated postwar global order. Dulles characterized these arrangements as in the best interests of the United States, Japan, and the "free world." They prevented the manpower and industrial resources of Japan, he often said, from being joined with Communist China and exploited by the Soviet Union. But the presence of American bases, the American insistence on Japanese rearmament in violation of the Japanese constitution, and the economic straightjacket imposed by the Tokyo-Taibei pact severely compromised Japanese sovereignty and contributed to Cold War tensions. Resentment and fear of American power in Japan and the Pacific quickly developed. For most Asian peoples, Dulles's handiwork placed the United States and Japan on a new and more dangerous path of imperialism and war.

CONCLUSION

When the Occupation ended in 1952 the United States had superficially accomplished its goals in Japan. The government of Japan was conservative and staunchly anti-Communist. The working class, for the time, was effectively stilled. With the conspicuous exception of the left-wing parties and a good portion of the intelligentsia, the Japanese people as a whole appeared to look favorably upon the United States. Above all, the peace and security treaties and the "U.S.-Japan economic cooperation" agreements had transformed Japan into America's key military and economic ally in Asia which no other power in the region was strong enough to challenge. Certainly when compared to the revolutions, civil wars, and foreign interventions that wracked the rest of Asia, U.S. policymakers could reasonably claim a success in Japan.

American planners nevertheless remained nervous about the future of Japan in its new and crucial role in the global balance of power. First, the Japanese economy had become dangerously dependent on massive military procurements for the Korean War. Secondly, rearmament and strategic plans more generally were jeopardized by the continued embrace of the Japanese people of the "no-war" clause of the new constitution. Finally, fears remained about Japan's political inclinations. Extremists of either the left or the right might assume power.

The six major themes threaded through the chapters of this book offer clues to how American policymakers devised the policies for perpetuating Japan's economic, strategic, and political subordination to the United States into the post-Occupation era. First, American policies for Japan rested primarily on enlightened self-interest, not goodwill. Behind the progressive democratization program of the early Occupation lay a determination to crush forever Japanese militarism that might again threaten the American stake in Asia. By 1947 the definition of the primary threat to American interests in Asia had shifted from Japan to Russia and the Communist movement in China. American policy moved towards making Japan an ally of the U.S. in the Cold War.

The key to that process for American policymakers was the recovery of the Japanese economy under the strong leadership of industrialists and financiers. Such issues as levels of production, exchange rates, reparations, economic concentration of industry, trade, and dollar aid received more careful and more sustained attention in both Washington and Tokyo than any others. Supremely confident in the strength of the entire American economy, planners did not worry (and could hardly have been expected to worry) that the rebuilding of Japan as the economic workshop of Asia might lead thirty or forty years later to an autonomous Japanese challenge to American industry. Rather U.S. economic policies for Japan were part of a global program for insuring continuing American economic supremacy and were closely intertwined with United States strategic objectives. A strengthened capitalist class and increased industrial production in Japan reduced the threat of a resurgent left-wing movement in Japan or the possibility of Japanese accommodation to communism abroad. Moreover, the power and responsibilities of Japan in the struggle against communism in the region would grow as its economy expanded.

The outbreak of the Korean War in 1950 further underscored the self-interestedness behind the economic role American planners assigned Japan in its global Cold War policies. The large-scale U.S. military operation in Korea, as well as the global rearmament program, required logistical support from Japan. Between June 1950 and 1954 the Pentagon spent close to three billion dollars in Japan for everything from blankets, canvas, chemicals, truck parts, and small arms to the use of Japanese shipyards for repair of naval vessels. These procurements triggered an economic boom in Japan and assisted American efforts at Communist containment in Asia. Far more important in explaining the Japanese "economic miracle" and competitiveness of Japanese exports today than American mercy and generosity has been the Pentagon's continuing demand for war materials from Japan, estimated at nearly ten billion dollars from 1950 to 1970.

A second theme emerging from this study challenges the suggestion that the Japanese committed themselves during the Occupation to American objectives in the world only to later, ungratefully and unfairly, turn against their benefactors. American policies were frequently not to the liking of the Japanese oligarchy that held power after the war. Throughout the eighty months of the

Occupation, Japanese officials, by exploiting differences within the American policy-making community, quiet subterfuge, and noncooperation, managed remarkably well to achieve key objectives of their own. The first post-surrender cabinets of Prince Higashikuni, Baron Shidehara, and Yoshida Shigeru generally opposed Occupation policies except—as in the instance of the dissolution of Japan's armed forces—where the traditional civilian leadership, especially its industrial and financial core, was strengthened. Contrary to American policy, these cabinets attempted to strengthen popular loyalty to the emperor system that sanctified the old regime, continued to pay accounts due on war production contracts with the large Zaibatsu, took measures that set off an inflationary spiral, and had to be pressured to release political prisoners and accept the ending of restraints on freedom of speech, press, assembly, and religion. The implementation of the Occupation's purge orders, proposed labor union legislation, plans for reparations and breakup of large combines, provisions for the emperor in the new constitution and other reforms were, as T. A. Bisson recorded, constantly delayed or openly resisted by the Japanese leadership.

The shift in American policy after 1947 from emphasis on reform to economic recovery was an anticipated and welcome relief to the Japanese conservative oligarchy. Yet it would be a mistake to suggest that this shift resulted in a congruence of interest and full collaboration between American and Japanese officials. The Ashida and Yoshida cabinets from 1948 until the Korean War regarded the American proposed economic stabilization programs as politically unacceptable and economically misguided. Only by tieing vital American aid to compliance with a balanced budget and other stabilization measures did Joseph Dodge compel Japanese officials to implement the unpopular program. Even at that the Yoshida government succeeded in deflecting most of the criticism against the Dodge Plan unto Dodge and Washington while working through the Bank of Japan and other financial institutions to moderate the impact of the stabilization program.

Prime Minister Yoshida had his own definition of Japanese peace and security needs as well. At his very first meetings with John Foster Dulles, Yoshida made clear his own and popular disagreement over fullscale rearmament for Japan and planned U.S. restrictions on Japanese trade with the People's Republic of China. Despite tough and unrelenting pressure by Dulles, Yoshida in the end managed to fend off the American demands on the rearmament issue, agreeing to it in principle but failing to find the level of funds expected by the United States. On Japanese trade with China he was not so successful and the issue remained a festering sore in U.S.-Japanese relations until 1971.

In short, Japanese political and business leadership during the Occupation often found American policies anaethema to their own interests. Within the limitations of the relative weakness of their position vis-à-vis the United States they managed remarkably well to achieve their own goals. For more than two decades after the Occupation ended the Japanese gave every indication that when the balance of power within the alliance inevitably shifted more favorably to them, they would challenge perceived restrictions, economic or otherwise, imposed by the United States.

A third theme which emerges from this study is the importance of the "reverse course" decisions of 1947 and 1948 for the entire postwar U.S.-Japan relationship. In order to avoid international criticism and diplomatic complications in a nominally Allied enterprise American policymakers deliberately downplayed and disguised a unilateral "shift in emphasis" from reform to economic restoration. But the signals of closer American collaboration with Japanese conservatives and the business class were unmistakable. Purge orders were soon halted and depurging of former ultranationalists begun, many of the gains of the trade union movement were slowly rolled back, and deconcentration of big combines and reparations removals were effectively halted. And though the Imperial Court's formal authority under the new constitution was sharply reduced, the emperor system continued to serve its old function as the ideological center of conservative class rule. The retreat from reform did not occur at once. It began slowly and sharply accelerated after the Korean War. Nor did American and Japanese leaders always agree on how far these early reforms should be modified. The Japanese people tenaciously defended many of the freedoms and rights they already enjoyed. Through strikes, petitions, mass marches, and the like Japanese labor unions, for example, managed to survive repeated assaults to emerge from the Occupation weakened but still with far more organizational strength than at any time before the war.

Fourthly, the "reverse course" had an external dynamic as well. The economic reconstruction of Japan under the aegis of conservatives and business leaders required, in George Kennan's famous phrase, that Japan seek an "empire to the south." Fearful of both Japanese accommodation with the Chinese Communists and permanent dependency on U.S. aid imports, American policymakers prior to the Korean War pushed the Japanese to develop trade with Southeast Asia. After the start of the Korean War Americans accelerated efforts to integrate Japanese trade with Southeast Asia. Such integration would permit continued Japanese economic recovery once procurement orders for the war fell off and prevent the "fall" of Southeast Asia to communism.

American diplomats emphasized the opposition of the Soviet Union and the People's Republic of China to these plans. But Great Britain and most of the nations of Asia also feared a Japanese-American Co-Prosperity Sphere. A central justification for American aid to the French war effort in Indochina from 1950 to 1954 and later American military intervention there was to prevent the collapse of Japan. Ironically, the development of a Japanese economy requiring much wider markets than Southeast Asia and able to challenge American industry was spurred by additional Pentagon procurements for the Indochina war.

A fifth theme of this book, one that even New Left historians of the Occupation have largely overlooked, is the significant role that American businessmen and their representatives played in shaping the Occupation program. Just as enterprising Northerners swept into the South behind Union troops after the Civil War, American businessmen sought opportunities and special advantages in Occupied Japan. With a few exceptions General MacArthur blocked their entry until 1947. Frightened by the chaotic economic and political conditions they discovered in Japan, representatives of the major U.S. companies with prewar investments in Japan took the leadership in clamoring for new policies in Washington and Tokyo that would insure restitution of their properties and profitable trade relations. Though not formally a business organization, the American Council on Japan headed by *Newsweek* editor Harry F. Kern became the principal and most effective lobby in Washington for powerful American companies interested in Japan. Weaker American industries like textiles and Pacific Coast fishing, which were already faced with Japanese competition by the end of the Occupation, received a sympathetic hearing from policymakers in Washington, too (and, to the annoyance of the Japanese, a measure of protection).

Despite its successes in Washington and Tokyo in pushing for and implementing "reverse course" policies favorable to foreign investment and trade during the Occupation, Japan never became a large investment area for American companies. American policymakers like Dodge, who saw Japan most useful to the United States as a junior partner in the American dominated Pacific region, did not want to alienate the Japanese by the presence of American companies exploiting Japan's weakened industrial system. Certainly the Japanese carried the protection of their own industries further than American policymakers envisioned. But Japanese restrictions do not appear to have been the principal deterrent to direct investment in the 1940s and 1950s. American firms had many opportunities for investment around the globe and were leery of directly entering a new and uncertain market in Japan. After the outbreak of the Korean War, they made indirect investment through technological assistance agreements with their Japanese counterparts. Confident they were not nurturing dangerous future competition, American corporations exchanged trade secrets, fabrication rights, and engineering know-how with Japanese companies in primarily military-related Japanese industries such as chemicals, oil, electrical supplies, and engine construction and reaped windfall profits in the form of royalties. In so doing, they maintained a large stake in the growth of higher quality Japanese production and the expansion of Japanese trade.

Finally, these chapters, by testifying to the impact of the global Cold War, ideologically, politically, and militarily, challenge the long tradition in studies of the Occupation of treating Japan as an isolated experiment in social engineering. From the outset American policymakers struggled with the question of Japan's relation to the Soviet Union and world communism. In Tokyo and Washington in 1946 some Americans called for making Japan a place d'armes against the threat of Russia. By 1947 American and Japanese conservatives alike openly attacked the reform program and its proponents as communistic. Whether such attacks were propaganda masking other concerns or firmly held beliefs is historically unimportant. With the start of the "reverse course" in Japan the raison d'être of virtually every program of the Occupation was its contribution to the struggle against communism in and outside of Japan. Well before the Korean War Japanese leftists were put on the defensive as they struggled to preserve as much of the legacy of the early reforms as possible. Of course liberals and leftists in SCAP such as James Killen and T. A. Bisson and their friends in the State Department were similarly victims of the swelling anti-Communist hysteria after 1947.

The Korean War strengthened the political right in the U.S. and Japan. U.S. offshore procurements geared the major industries of Japan for military production and institutionalized militarism in the U.S.-Japan economic relationship. By the terms of the U.S.-Japan Mutual Security Treaty the United States gained an indefinite use of numerous military installations in Japan and a reluctant Japanese commitment to rearmament. The Japanese government crushed the campaign by Japanese intellectuals and leftists for neutrality in the Cold War. At the same time it rapidly depurged former high officers of the Japanese army and navy and constantly used subterfuge to get around the popularly supported no-war clause of the new Japanese Constitution.

Americans attempted to remake Japan from a "feudal" and militaristic society to a peaceful democracy during the Occupation. Yet they were never agreed on what it was in prewar Japanese society that accounted for aggression in Asia and war with the United States, and hence what needed changing in Japan to achieve the objective of a peaceful democracy. Under the strains of economic chaos in Japan and Cold War confrontations around the globe, conservative American policymakers, backed by representatives of large American corporations, offered a benign diagnosis of Japan's past ills and pushed aside those who considered major surgery necessary to bring about a peaceful democracy in Japan. By the end of the Occupation in 1952 these conservative American officials, with good reason, prided themselves on their success. Defying popular protests in Japan and revolutionary nationalism in most of Asia, the dominant class in Japan maintained power under a constitutional monarchy and accepted a privileged position in the American dominated system of global capitalism.

NOTES

INTRODUCTION

1. Jon Halliday and Gavan McCormack, *Japanese Imperialism Today* (New York: Monthly Review Press, 1973); Herbert Bix, "Japan's New Vulnerability," *Monthly Review* 34, 7 (December 1983): 10–17; Ezra Vogel, *Japan as Number One* (Cambridge: Harvard University Press, 1979).

2. Theodore White, "Danger of Japan," *New York Times Magazine,* 28 July 1985, 22, 59.

3. Ibid., 37.

4. See particularly Edwin O. Reischauer, *The United States and Japan,* 3d rev. ed. (Cambridge: Harvard University Press, 1965); Robert E. Ward, *Political Development in Modern Japan* (Princeton: Princeton University Press, 1968); and Herbert Passin, "Occupation Reforms as Experiments in Guided Social Change," *The Legacy of the Occupation-Japan* (New York: Occasional Papers of the East Asian Institute, Columbia University, 1968). These scholars might, with justification, just as easily be considered "liberal." I have preferred the "conservative" label to emphasize their generally uncritical perspective on American Occupation policies and to distinguish them more sharply from the members of the other two schools.

5. Two outstanding historiographic essays on the Occupation from which this section draws heavily are John W. Dower, "Occupied Japan as History and Occupation History as Politics," *Journal of Asian Studies* 34, 2 (February 1975): 485–504, and Carol Gluck, "Entangling Illusions: Japanese and American Views of the Occupation," in Warren I. Cohen, ed., *New Frontiers in American-East Asian Relations: Essays Presented to Dorothy Borg* (New York: Columbia University Press, 1983), 169–236. See also Howard Schonberger, "The Occupation of Japan Through American Eyes," *American Studies Newsletter* 41 (May 1976): 1–4.

6. Owen Lattimore, *Solution in Asia* (Boston: Little, Brown, 1945); Owen Lattimore, *The Situation in Asia* (Boston: Little, Brown, 1949); T. A. Bisson, *Prospects for Democracy in Japan* (New York: Macmillan, 1949); T. A. Bisson, *Zaibatsu Dissolution in Japan* (Berkeley: University of California Press, 1954); and Miriam Farley, *Aspects of Japan's Labor Problem* (New York: John Day, 1950).

7. John W. Dower, "E. H. Norman, Japan and the Uses of History," in John W. Dower, ed., *Origins of the Modern Japanese State: Selected Writings of E. H. Norman* (New York: Pantheon Books, 1975), 44.

8. See particularly John W. Dower, "Occupied Japan and the American Lake, 1945–1950," in Edward Friedman and Mark Selden, eds., *America's Asia: Dissenting Essays on Asian-American Relations* (New York: Pantheon Books, 1971), 146–206; John W. Dower, *Empire and Aftermath: Yoshida Shigeru and the Japanese Experience, 1878–1954* (Cambridge: Harvard University Press, 1979), 273–470; William Borden, *The Pacific Alliance: United States Foreign Economic Policy and Japanese Trade Recovery, 1947–1955* (Madison: University of Wisconsin Press, 1984); Joe Moore, *Japanese Workers and the Struggle for Power, 1945–47* (Madison: University of Wisconsin Press, 1983); Michael Schaller, *The American Occupation of Japan: The Origins of the Cold War in Asia* (New York: Oxford University Press, 1985); and Howard Schonberger, "Zaibatsu Dissolution and the American Restoration of Japan," *Bulletin of Concerned Asian Scholars* 5, 2 (September 1973): 15–31.

1 JOSEPH C. GREW

1. George H. Gallup, *The Gallup Poll: Public Opinion 1935–1971* (New York: Random House, 1972), 1:512.

2. Waldo Heinrichs, Jr., *American Ambassador: Joseph C. Grew and the Development of the United States Diplomatic Tradition* (Boston: Little, Brown, 1966), 3–162.

3. E. Herbert Norman, *Japan's Emergence as a Modern State* (New York: Institute of Pacific Relations, 1940), 3–10, 206–9; David Titus, *Palace and Politics in Prewar Japan* (New York: Columbia University Press, 1974), 318–29; and Reischauer, *The United States and Japan,* 171–72.

4. James Crowley, *Japan's Quest for Autonomy, National Security and Foreign Policy, 1930–1938* (Princeton: Princeton University Press, 1966), 3–121; and Akira Iriye, *After Imperialism: The Search for a New Order in the Far East, 1921–1931* (Cambridge: Harvard University Press, 1965), 227–303.

5. Jon Livingston, Joe Moore, and Felicia Oldfather, eds., *Imperial Japan, 1800–1945* (New York: Pantheon Books, 1973), 199–201; Stephen S. Large, *Organized Workers and Socialist Politics in Interwar Japan* (Cambridge: Cambridge University Press, 1981), 51–162; and Gail Lee Bernstein, *Japanese Marxist: A Portrait of Kawakame Hajime, 1879–1946* (Cambridge: Harvard University Press, 1976), 117–73.

6. Heinrichs, *American Ambassador,* 193–95; and Dower, *Empire and Aftermath,* 108–12.

7. Heinrichs, *American Ambassador,* 202, 210–11; and Akira Iriye, "The Role of the United States Embassy in Tokyo," in Dorothy Borg and Shumpei Okamoto, eds., *Pearl Harbor as History: Japanese-American Relations, 1931–1941* (New York: Columbia University Press, 1973), 116–17.

8. For the MacMurray memorandum and Grew's reaction see Joseph C. Grew, *Turbulent Era, A Diplomatic Record of Forty Years, 1904–1945* (Boston: Houghton Mifflin, 1952), 2:929–30, and Grew diary, 20 November 1937, Joseph Grew Papers, Houghton Library, Harvard University, Cambridge, Mass.; Grew to W. Cameron Forbes, 19 February 1940, Letters to W. Cameron Forbes file, Grew Papers.

9. Grew to W. Cameron Forbes, 19 February 1940, Letters to W. Cameron Forbes file, Grew Papers.

10. Dower, *Empire and Aftermath,* 204; and Michael A. Barnhart, *Japan Prepares for Total War: The Search for Economic Security, 1919–1941* (Ithaca: Cornell University Press, 1987), 91–114.

11. Joseph C. Grew, *Ten Years in Japan: A Contemporary Record Drawn from the Diaries and Private and Official Papers of Joseph C. Grew, United States Ambassador to Japan, 1932–1942* (New York: Simon and Schuster, 1944), 332–39.

12. F. C. Jones, *Japan's New Order in East Asia, Its Rise and Fall, 1937–1945* (London: Oxford University Press, 1954), 265–92; and James C. Thomson, Jr., "The Role of the Department of State" in Borg and Okamoto, eds., *Pearl Harbor as History,* 102–4.

13. See especially Grew speeches in *Department of State Bulletin,* 29 August 1942, 5 February, 3 April, and 3 July 1943.

14. Grew to G. William Gahagan, 11 December 1942, Grew Papers; *New York Herald-Tribune,* 15 September 1942; *Albany Knickerbocker News,* 18 September 1942, *Detroit Evening Times,* 8 February 1943; *New York Mirror,* 17 January 1943, Clipping Files, Grew Papers. Grew often referred to the danger of peace initiatives from former "liberal" statesmen as the "jiu-jitsu" peace trick.

15. Grew to Elmer Davis, 25 September 1942, and Joseph C. Grew, "Liberal Elements in Japan," n.d., ca. October 1942, Grew Papers.

16. *Department of State Bulletin,* 24 October 1942, 27 May 1943; Joseph C. Grew, *Report from Tokyo* (New York: Simon & Schuster, 1942), 68.

17. Grew to Francis Hickman, 8 May 1943, Grew Papers. "Steady jobs, business profits, a richer life for the American consumer," Grew told readers of the *Cotton Trade Journal* in May 1943, "all are possible by swelling the two rivers of import and export to a size this nation never yet has enjoyed. Full employment and maximum consumption after the war can be assured in this way and no other."

18. Gardiner to Grew, 12 March 1943, William Leahy Papers, Library of Congress, Washington, D.C.; Grew to Gardiner, 23 March, 3 May 1943, Grew Papers.

19. Grew to Leahy, 8 April 1943, Leahy Papers; Grew to Cordell Hull, 11 July 1943, Grew Papers.

20. *Department of State Bulletin,* 28 August 1943; *Common Sense,* March 1943, Clipping Files, Grew Papers. In a review of Grew's short *Report from Tokyo* published in 1942, Clarke Kawakami noted that the former ambassador "assumes that the Emperor Hirohito is a man of peace and that his subjects, or a large number of them did not want their country plunged into the holocaust . . . [Grew] bids us believe, by inference, that once the militarists are crushed by Allied might, the Japanese will take heart and build a peaceful nation with the throne as its rallying point."

21. Grew to Paul Rowland, 9 July 1943, Grew Papers.

22. Hugh Borton memorandum, 6 October 1943, T-381, Harley Notter Papers, Records of the Department of State, Record Group 59, National Archives, Washington, D.C. (hereafter cited as DOS, RG 59); Grew to Robert Fearey, 24 August, 30 November 1943; and Grew to Hornbeck, 30 September 1943, Grew Papers.

23. *Department of State Bulletin,* 1 January 1944.

24. Grew to B. I. Griffith, 28 December 1943, Grew Papers; Christopher Thorne, *Allies of a Kind: The United States, Britain, and the War Against Japan, 1941–1945* (New York: Oxford University Press, 1978), 173–78.

25. *Sacramento Bee,* 18 January 1944; *New York Times,* 2 January 1944, Clipping Files, Grew Papers.

26. Foreign Policy Association, *Bulletin,* 7 January 1944; *PM,* 24 April 1944, Clipping Files, Grew Papers.

27. Heinrichs, *American Ambassador,* 366. On the "peace party" see also Akira Iriye, *Power and Culture: The Japanese-American War, 1941–1945* (Cambridge: Harvard University Press, 1981), 168–83.

28. Grew to Quincy Howe, 31 January 1944, Grew Papers; *Baltimore News,* 28 January 1944, Clipping Files, Grew Papers; Grew, *Ten Years in Japan,* 63–71, 218–34, 300–12; and Heinrichs, *American Ambassador,* 368–69.

29. Gary May, *China Scapegoat: The Diplomatic Ordeal of John Carter Vincent* (Project Heights, Ill.: Waveland Press, 1979), 90–93; and Grew to Sir Robert Clive, 28 June 1944, Grew Papers.

30. "A New Far Eastern Policy? Japan versus China," *Amerasia,* 9 June 1944; see also the editorial "Are We 'Soft' Toward Japan's Rightists," *Des Moines Register,* 23 June 1944, Clipping Files, Grew Papers.

31. Department of State, *Foreign Relations of the United States, 1944* (Washington, D.C.: Government Printing Office, 1965), 5:1202 (hereafter cited as *FRUS,* with appropriate year, volume and page).

32. *FRUS,* 1944, 5:1213–14, 1230–35, 1257–60.

33. Hugh Borton memorandum PWC 116a, 24 April 1944, Notter Papers, DOS, RG 59.

34. Earle Dickover memorandum PWC 116a, 24 April 1944, Notter Papers, DOS, RG 59.

35. See chapter 3.

36. Grew to Cordell Hull, 26 April 1944 (PWC 146), Grew Papers.

37. *FRUS,* 1944, 5:1250–55.

38. *Congressional Record,* 78th Cong., 2d sess., 6 December 1944, 90:7:8900–8908.

39. *Department of State Bulletin,* 17 December 1944, and *Congressional Record,* 78th Cong., 2d sess., 19 December 1944, 90:7:9716.

40. Marlene J. Mayo, "American Wartime Planning for Occupied Japan: The Role of the Experts," in Robert Wolfe, ed., *Americans as Proconsuls, United States Military Government in Germany and Japan, 1944–1952* (Carbondale: Southern Illinois University Press, 1984), 37–39.

41. Brian L. Villa, "The U.S. Army, Unconditional Surrender, and the Potsdam Proclamation," *Journal of American History,* 63, 1 (June 1976): 77.

42. Grew to Stettinius, 3 January 1945, Grew Papers. For a fuller account of Grew's affinity with the military on the emperor question and unconditional surrender, see "Notes on Mr. Grew's Report of His Recent Visit to Pearl Harbor," Minutes, Inter-Divisional Area Committee on the Far East, 28 November 1944, Inter-Divisional Area Committee on the Far East Papers (microfilm), National Archives.

43. Grew, *Turbulent Era* 2:1420–21.

44. Villa, "The U.S. Army, Unconditional Surrender, and the Potsdam Proclamation," 86.

45. Heinrichs, *American Ambassador,* 373–74.

46. Dower, *Empire and Aftermath,* 259–65. This famous Konoye Memorial was prepared with the help of Yoshida Shigeru.

47. Gabriel Kolko, *Politics of War: The World and United States Foreign Policy, 1943–1945* (New York: Random House, 1968), 364–66; Grew, *Turbulent Era* 2:1445–46. Grew cites a private memorandum to himself dated 19 May 1945.

48. Grew to Forrestal, 12 May 1945, Grew Papers.

49. Memorandum of Conversation, 28 May 1945, Grew Papers.

50. Memorandum of Conversation, 29 May 1945, Grew Papers.

51. Barton Bernstein, "Roosevelt, Truman, and the Atomic Bomb, 1941–1945: A Reinterpretation," *Political Science Quarterly* 90, 1 (Spring 1975): 54–55; see also Henry L. Stimson and McGeorge Bundy, *On Active Service in Peace and War* (New York: Harper & Brothers, 1947), 629–32.

52. Makoto Iokibe, "American Policy towards Japan's 'Unconditional Surrender,'" *The Japanese Journal of American Studies* 1, 1(1981):42–53. Iokibe argues that despite his silence concerning the bomb, Grew feared the destructive force of the new weapon and hence decided the time had come to offer Japan surrender terms.

53. Grew to Truman, 13 June 1945, #740.00119 PS/6-1345, DOS, RG 59; Memorandum of Conversation, 18 June 1945, Grew Papers.

54. Martin Sherwin, *A World Destroyed: The Atomic Bomb and the Grand Alliance* (New York: Knopf, 1975), 225.

55. Iriye, *Power and Culture,* 253–54.

56. *FRUS, The Conference of Berlin (Potsdam Conference),* 1945, 1:895–97, 900–901.

57. Cordell Hull, *The Memoirs of Cordell Hull* (New York: Macmillan, 1948), 1593–94.

58. Bernstein, "Roosevelt, Truman, and the Atomic Bomb," 56–57.

59. Robert J. C. Butow, *Japan's Decision to Surrender* (Stanford: Stanford University Press, 1954), 142–209.

60. Heinrichs, *American Ambassador,* 377–78.

61. Grew to Castle, 5 September 1945, Grew Papers.

62. Grew to Dean Acheson, 16, 22 August 1945; Grew to Douglas MacArthur, 22 August 1945; and Grew to Nelson Newton, 9 September 1945, Grew Papers.

63. The theoretical principles of the China Crowd for handling of the Occupation were laid out in Lattimore, *Solution in Asia*. Just as influential as Lattimore's book amongst the China Crowd supporters was Andrew Roth, *Dilemma in Japan* (Boston: Little, Brown, 1945). Both Lattimore and Roth were attacked by the Japan Crowd as disciples of the leftist *Amerasia* magazine whose writings paralleled the Communist line.

64. James W. Morley, "The First Seven Weeks,"*Japan Interpreter* 6, 2 (September 1970): 151–54.

65. Moore, *Japanese Workers and the Struggle for Power*, 7–31. See also Theodore Cohen, *Remaking Japan: The American Occupation as New Deal*, ed. Herbert Passin, (New York: Free Press, 1987), 338–48.

66. Grew to Mr. and Mrs. Cecil B. Lyon, 30 September 1945, Grew Papers. Grew expressed amusement at the ouster of the "Japan Crowd" from the State Department for being in favor of a soft peace when "our plan [SWNCC 150] for the post-war treatment of Japan was a great deal more drastic than the plan [SWNCC 150/4/A] finally sent by Byrnes to MacArthur. [We] wanted to go a lot farther than was finally done. Among other things we recommended that the Emperor be deprived of all authority for the time being [i.e., military government] and placed in protective custody at Hayama. However things seem to be working out pretty well. . . ."

67. Mayo, "American Wartime Planning for Occupied Japan," 45–47; Jon Halliday, *A Political History of Japanese Capitalism* (New York: Pantheon Books, 1975), 168–69.

68. Minutes, SWNCC Sub-Committee on Far East, 3 October 1945, National Archives, Microfilm Publication T–1198; Mayo, "American Wartime Planning for Occupied Japan," 45–46.

69. Roger Buckley, *Occupation Diplomacy : Britain, the United States and Japan, 1945–1952* (Cambridge: Cambridge University Press, 1982), 62–63; see also Roger Buckley, "Britain and the Emperor: The Foreign Office and Constitutional Reform in Japan, 1945–1946," *Modern Asian Studies* 12, 4 (1978): 562.

70. Grew to Mrs. J. Borden Harriman, 9 September 1945; and Grew to William B. Wharton, 25 October 1945, Grew Papers.

71. Marlene Mayo, "American Economic Planning for Occupied Japan: The Issue of Zaibatsu Dissolution, 1942–1945," in Laurence H. Redford, ed., *The Occupation of Japan: Economic Policy and Reform* (Norfolk: MacArthur Memorial, 1980), 218–28.

72. Grew to Clayton, 13 January 1947, 740.0019 Control (Japan) 1–1347, DOS, RG 59. Grew attached a copy of an article by Burton Crane headlined "Pro-Allied Group is Cooler in Japan: Managerial Class is Doubtful of Recovery with Reparations and Widening Purges,"*New York Times,* 11 January 1947.

73. See chapter 5.

2 DOUGLAS MACARTHUR

1. D. Clayton James, *The Years of MacArthur: Triumph and Disaster, Volume III, 1945–1964* (Boston: Houghton Mifflin, 1985). For a major exception see Michael Schaller, "MacArthur's Japan: The View from Washington," *Diplomatic History* 10, 1 (Winter 1986): 1–23.

2. D. Clayton James, *The Years of MacArthur, Volume II, 1941–1945* (Boston: Houghton Mifflin, 1975), 776–78.

3. Douglas MacArthur, *Reminiscences* (New York: McGraw-Hill, 1964), 31–32.

4. D. Clayton James, *The Years of MacArthur, Volume I, 1880–1941* (Boston: Houghton Mifflin, 1970), 96–347.

5. Roger Daniels, *The Bonus March: An Episode of the Great Depression* (Westport, Conn.: Greenwood Press, 1971), 167–74.

6. Carol M. Petillo, *Douglas MacArthur: The Philippine Years* (Bloomington: Indiana University Press, 1981), 166–91.

7. Louis Morton, *The Fall of the Philippines* (Washington, D.C.: Office of the Chief of Military History, 1953), 77–97.

8. Lawrence Wittner, ed., *MacArthur* (Englewood Cliffs, N.J.: Prentice-Hall, 1971), 9.

9. Carolyn J. Mattern, "The Man on the Dark Horse: The Presidential Campaigns for General Douglas MacArthur, 1944 & 1948," (Ph.D diss., University of Wisconsin, 1976), 29–141; see also D. Clayton James, *Years of MacArthur 2:403–30*.

10. Ibid., 431–40.

11. James, *The Years of MacArthur* 2:534.

12. Petillo, *Douglas MacArthur: The Philippine Years*, 232–37.

13. Robert Eichelberger diary, 15 August 1945, Robert Eichelberger Papers, Perkins Library, Duke University, Durham, N.C.

14. Iriye, *Power and Culture*, 233–60.

15. W. Averell Harriman and Elie Abel, *Special Envoy to Churchill and Stalin, 1941–1946* (New York: Random House, 1975), 508–9.

16. Herbert Feis, *Contest Over Japan* (New York: Norton, 1967), 31–58; Harry S. Truman, *Memoirs: 1945 Year of Decisions* (Garden City, N.J.: Doubleday, 1955), 520.

17. Joyce and Gabriel Kolko, *The Limits of Power: The World and United States Foreign Policy, 1945–1954* (New York: Harper and Row, 1972), 304–5; Daniel Yergin, *Shattered Peace: The Origins of the Cold War and the National Security State* (Boston: Houghton Mifflin, 1977), 131–32, 149–50.

18. Feis, *Contest Over Japan*, 114–16.

19. Mark Gayn, *Japan Diary* (New York: William Sloane, 1948), 237; Douglas MacArthur to Frank McCoy, 13 April 1946, MacArthur Papers, MacArthur Memorial, Norfolk, Va.

20. Quoted in Feis, *Contest Over Japan*, 23.

21. SWNCC 150/4/A, The Initial Post-Surrender Policy for Japan, and JCS 1380/15 are most conveniently available in SCAP, Government Section, *Political Reorientation of Japan* (Washington, D.C.: Government Printing Office, 1949), 2:423–26, 428–39 (hereafter cited as *PRJ*). For the best discussion of the conflicts amongst wartime planners for the Occupation see Mayo, "American Wartime Planning for Japan: The Role of the Experts," 3–51.

22. *FRUS*, 1945, 6:715–17.

23. Quotations are from James, *The Years of MacArthur* 3:17–19; Schaller, "MacArthur's Japan: The View from Washington," 6.

24. Dean Acheson, *Present at the Creation: My Years in the State Department* (New York: Norton, 1969), 177–79; Harry S. Truman, *Memoirs: 1945 Year of Decisions*, 571.

25. James, *The Years of MacArthur* 3:19.

26. Eichelberger diary, 23 October 1945, Eichelberger Papers.

27. *FRUS*, 6, 837–38.

28. MacArthur to David Reed, 28 September 1945, and MacArthur to Walter Wolf, 28 September 1945, MacArthur Papers.

29. Harry Emerson Wildes, *Typhoon in Tokyo: The Occupation and Its Aftermath* (New York: Macmillan, 1954), 8–20.

30. Press Release by Hugh Baillie, President of United Press, 21 September 1945, Item 122–05, Justin Williams, Sr., Papers, East Asia Collection, McKeldin Library, University of Maryland, College Park, Md.

31. Howard to MacArthur, 20 November 1945; and Lloyd Lehrbas to MacArthur, 4 January 1946, MacArthur Papers.

32. James, *The Years of MacArthur* 2:409; Gallup, *The Gallup Poll* 1:584, 503–4, 605, 706.

33. *Economist* (London), 19 January 1946, 82–83.

34. Walter Millis, ed., *The Forrestal Diaries* (New York: Viking, 1951), 325.

35. Faubion Bowers, "Twenty-five Years Ago, How Japan Won the War," *New York Times Magazine*, 30 August 1970; *New Republic*, 30 September 1946.

36. U.S. Senate, Committee on Armed Services and the Committee on Foreign Relations, *Hearings to Conduct an Inquiry into the Military Situation in the Far East*, 82d Cong., 1st sess., 1951, 1:312.

37. George F. Kennan, *Memoirs, 1925–1950* (Boston: Little, Brown, 1967), 371.

38. Gallup, *The Gallup Poll* 1:533.

39. Theodore H. McNelly, "The Japanese Constitution: Child of the Cold War," *Political Science Quarterly* 74 (June 1959): 178–84.

40. *PRJ* 2:741.

41. Schaller, "MacArthur's Japan: The View From Washington," 7–8.

42. MacArthur, *Reminiscences*, 299–300.

43. *Life*, 22 October 1945, 40–41; MacArthur to War Department, 25 January 1946, 894.001 (Hirohito) 1–2546 DOS, RG 59.

44. *PRJ* 2:470.

45. Ibid., 2:489.

46. *Nation*, 19 January 1946, 57–58; *Time*, 14 January 1946, 25–26; *Reader's Digest*, January 1946, 23; *Life*, 2 December 1946, 105; *U.S. News*, 25 January 1946; and *Amerasia*, February 1946.

47. *Fortune*, January 1946, 221.

48. McNelly, "The Japanese Constitution: Child of the Cold War," 184; MacArthur, *Reminiscences*, 299–300.

49. McNelly, "The Japanese Constitution: Child of the Cold War," 184–85.

50. Ibid., 186–88.

51. Dower, *Empire and Aftermath*, 319–20; Courtney Whitney, *MacArthur: His Rendezvous with History* (New York: Knopf, 1956), 247–54.

52. Eiichi Shindo, "Divided Territories and the Origin of the Cold War in Asia," (unpublished paper, Amherst Conference on the Occupation of Japan, 1980), 29–30; "Pakenham Notes and Emperor's Message," in Harry F. Kern to William V. Pratt, 8 September 1950, William V. Pratt Papers, Naval War College Archives, Newport, R.I.; MacArthur, *Reminiscences*, 288.

53. *PRJ* 2:671.

54. Theodore H. McNelly, "The Renunciation of War in the Japanese Constitution," *Political Science Quarterly*, 77 (September 1972): 350–78; see also Yoshida Shigeru, *The Yoshida Memoirs* (London: William Heinemann, 1961), 137.

55. Justin Williams, "Chronology of SWNCC 228, SWNCC 228/1 and Subsequent Developments Leading to Preparation of Model Constitution by GHQ," 12 February 1966, Williams Papers.

56. *PRJ* 2:737; MacArthur to All University Memorial Service, n.d. [ca. October 1945], MacArthur Papers.

57. *PRJ* 2:747–48.

58. *Christian Century*, 17 April 1946, 487–88. For conservative praise of MacArthur's handling of the Constitution see *Time*, 18 March 1946, 30–31.

59. *Saturday Evening Post*, 25 May 1946, 48–51; *Nation*, 26 July 1947, 95–98.

60. Lawrence Taylor, *A Trial of Generals: Homma, Yamashita, MacArthur* (South Bend:

Icorns Press, 1981), 221–25.

61. Richard Minear, *Victor's Justice, The Tokyo War Crimes Trial* (Princeton: Princeton University Press, 1971), 20–33.

62. Yoshida Shigeru to MacArthur, 23 October 1946, Correspondence with Prime Minister of Japan, John Dower Collection. Professor Dower kindly allowed me the use of his vast collection of xeroxed materials on the Occupation.

63. *Newsweek*, 27 January 1947, 40.

64. MacArthur, *Reminiscences*, 298; Hans H. Baerwald, *The Purge of Japanese Leaders Under the Occupation* (Berkeley: University of California Press, 1959), 80; and John D. Montgomery, *Forced to be Free: The Artificial Revolutions in Germany and Japan* (Chicago: University of Chicago Press, 1957), 27.

65. Halliday, *A Political History of Japanese Capitalism,* 172–75.

66. McCloy to MacArthur, 19 November 1945; and S. J. Chamberlin to MacArthur, 18 July 1946, MacArthur Papers.

67. Harry S. Truman, *Memoirs, 1945 Year of Decisions,* 519; and SCAP, General Headquarters, Press Release on Japanese food situation, 6 May 1946, Item 127–12, Williams Papers.

68. Moore, *Japanese Workers and the Struggle for Power,* 41–70, 177–208.

69. Kazuo Kawai, *Japan's American Interlude* (Chicago: University of Chicago Press, 1960), 164–65.

70. Cohen, *Remaking Japan,* 289; see also *Time,* 24 March 1947, 30.

71. Cohen, *Remaking Japan,* 299.

72. *Free Trade Union News,* February 1949; *PRJ* 2:756.

73. Bisson, *Zaibatsu Dissolution in Japan,* 67–79.

74. Schonberger, "Zaibatsu Dissolution and the American Restoration of Japan," 16–20.

75. Bisson, *Zaibatsu Dissolution in Japan,* 140–41.

76. Ronald P. Dore, *Land Reform in Japan* (London: Oxford University Press, 1959), 131–48.

77. Al McCoy, "Land Reform as Counter-Revolution: U.S. Foreign Policy and the Tenant Farmers of Asia," *Bulletin of Concerned Asian Scholars,* 3, 1 (Winter-Spring 1971): 17–19.

78. MacArthur to O'Laughlin, 1 December 1946, John Callan O' Laughlin Papers, Library of Congress.

79. Dower, *Empire and Aftermath,* 331–32; and McCoy, "Land Reform as Counter Revolution," 19.

80. On education see Toshio Nishi, *Unconditional Democracy: Education and Politics in ∙ Occupied Japan, 1945–1952* (Stanford: Stanford University Press, 1982); on law enforcement and local government see Dower, *Empire and Aftermath,* 346–48; 356–61.

81. William K. Bunce, *Religions in Japan: Buddhism, Shinto, Christianity* (Rutland, Vt.: Charles Tuttle, 1955), 170.

82. Lawrence Wittner, "MacArthur and the Missionaries: God and Man in Occupied Japan," *Pacific Historical Review* 40 (February 1971): 81–82.

83. *PRJ* 2:770.

84. Wittner, "MacArthur and the Missionaries," 89–90.

85. Ibid., 97.

86. William J. Coughlan, *Conquered Press, The MacArthur Era in Japanese Journalism* (Palo Alto: Pacific Books, 1952), 111–16.

87. Ibid., 117–19.

88. Ibid., 120–22.

89. Gayn, *Japan Diary,* 344–45.

90. Coughlan, *Conquered Press,* 122–23.

91. MacArthur to O'Laughlin, 1 December 1946, O'Laughlin Papers.

92. See chapter 6.

93. MacArthur to Wood, 12 February 1947, Robert E. Wood Papers, Herbert Hoover Library, West Branch, Iowa.

94. Schonberger, "Zaibatsu Dissolution and the American Restoration of Japan," 26–27.

95. Coughlan, *Conquered Press,* 126–29. See editorial, "Free Speech a la Mac," in *Wisconsin State Journal,* 13 March 1948.

96. Coughlan, *Conquered Press, 135–40.*

97. *PRJ* 2:730–31; *New Republic,* 31 March 1947, 28.

98. See chapter 6 and Schaller, *The American Occupation of Japan,* 97–100.

99. Buckley, *Occupation Diplomacy,* 148–52.

100. *FRUS,* 1947, 6:536–43. The document was PPS/10, "Results of Planning Staff Study of Questions Involved in the Japanese Peace Settlement," 14 October 1947.

101. Howard Schonberger, "The General and the Presidency: Douglas MacArthur and the Election of 1948," *Wisconsin Magazine of History,* 57, 3 (Spring 1974): 205.

102. Eichelberger diary, 13 September 1947, Eichelberger Papers; MacArthur to MacNider, 14 October 1947, Hanford MacNider Papers, Herbert Hoover Library; and MacArthur to Wood, 15 October 1947, MacArthur Papers.

103. Harold Eastwood to MacNider, 21 November 1947, MacNider Papers; and Schonberger, "The General and the Presidency," 205–7. See also Mattern, "The Man on the Dark Horse," 157–64.

104. MacArthur to Wood, 16 November 1947, MacNider Papers.

105. William Draper to Gordon Gray, 14 December 1947, enclosure Memorandum of 12 December 1947, Under Secretary of the Army, General Correspondence August 1947–January 1949, SAOUS 004 Japan, Records of the Office of Secretary of the Army, RG 335, National Archives (hereafter cited as Draper/Japan File with appropriate number).

106. Eastwood to MacNider, 8 December 1947, MacNider Papers; and *PRJ* 2:778–79.

107. Eichelberger diary, 4, 26 July, 13 September 1947, 8 January, 30 April 1948, Eichelberger Papers.

108. Eichelberger diary, 13 September 1947, Eichelberger Papers; *New York Times,* 24 January 1948; and Eastwood to MacNider, 4 February 1948, MacNider Papers.

109. Schaller, *The American Occupation of Japan,* 117–18.

110. *FRUS,* 1948, 6:694–700; Kennan, *Memoirs, 1925–1950,* 395–410.

111. Sir Alvory Gascoigne Memo to Foreign Office, 6 April 1948 and 21 May 1948, Foreign Office Records 371/F5237/662/23 and F7999/662/23, Public Records Office, London (hereafter cited as FO with appropriate numbers).

112. *FRUS,* 1948, 6:706–9. See also chapter 5.

113. Donald Young, ed., *Adventures in Politics: The Memoirs of Philip La Follette* (New York: Holt, Rinehart, and Winston, 1970), 133–280; and Charles H. Backstrom, "The Progressive Party of Wisconsin, 1934–1946," (Ph.D. diss., University of Wisconsin, 1956).

114. Schonberger, "The General and the Presidency," 211–12.

115. Ibid., 213–14.

116. Ibid.

117. Ibid., 215–17.

118. *New York Times,* 29 March 1948, 1; Gallup, *The Gallup Poll* 1:725.

119. Schonberger, "The General and the Presidency," 217–18.

120. Ibid., 218–19. For a full account of the national campaign for MacArthur see Mattern, "The Man on the Dark Horse," 226–65.

121. Bisson, *Zaibatsu Dissolution in Japan,* 148–49.

122. *FRUS,* 1948, 6:819–23, 857–62.

123. See chapter 7.

124. See chapter 4.

125. *FRUS,* 1949, 7:601-3.

126. Nishi, *Unconditional Democracy,* 246-47.

127. Halliday, *A Political History of Japanese Capitalism,* 196.

128. *FRUS,* 1949, 7:811, 805-6, 809; John Allison to John Foster Dulles, 22 May 1950, 794.00/5-2250, DOS, RG 59; and Justin Williams, Sr., *Japan's Political Revolution Under MacArthur: A Participant's Account* (Athens: University of Georgia Press, 1979), 210-12.

129. *Newsweek,* 18 April 1949; and *Fortune,* April, October 1949; *FRUS,* 1949, 7: 674-78; and James, *The Years of MacArthur* 3:270.

130. James, *The Years of MacArthur* 3: 270-72.

131. *FRUS,* 1949, 7:808-12, 773-77.

132. Ibid., 870-73.

133. W. Walton Butterworth to Dean Acheson, 3 May 1950, 694.001/5-350, DOS, RG 59; and *FRUS,* 1949, 7:780-81, 803-7. In an exclusive interview appearing in the May 1950 issue of the Japanese edition of *Reader's Digest* MacArthur said Japan should be unarmed and "neutral for the same reason that Switzerland is neutral—no matter which side she might join she would inevitably be destroyed."

134. *FRUS,* 1949, 7:862-64; and Philip Jessup to W. Walton Butterworth, 10 January 1950, 694.001/1-1050, DOS, RG 59.

135. Beverly D. Spotswood, "The Memphis Reaction to the Occupation of Japan, 1945-1952," (Master's thesis, Memphis State University, 1977), 98-100.

136. *FRUS,* 1949, 7:656; and John Foster Dulles to Douglas MacArthur, 18 March 1951, John Foster Dulles Papers, Princeton University Library, Princeton, N.J.

137. *FRUS,* 1950, 7:161-65; Nancy B. Tucker, *Patterns in the Dust: Chinese-American Relations and the Recognition Controversy 1949-1950* (New York: Columbia University Press, 1983), 178-94; and Robert M. Blum, *Drawing the Line: The Origin of the American Containment Policy in East Asia* (New York: Norton, 1982), 193-97.

138. Stephen Ambrose, *Rise to Globalism: American Foreign Policy Since 1938,* 3d rev. ed. (New York: Penguin Books, 1983), 167-78.

139. Richard H. Rovere and Arthur Schlesinger, Jr., *The MacArthur Controversy and American Foreign Policy* (New York: Farrar, Strauss and Giroux, 1965), 165-75.

140. James, *The Years of MacArthur* 3:611-21.

141. Ibid., 621-40.

142. Ibid., 641-55.

143. MacArthur, *Reminiscences,* 303, 399-400; and James, *The Years of MacArthur* 3:369-70, 689-90.

3 T. A. BISSON

1. Yoshida, *The Yoshida Memoirs,* 43-55, 153-54.

2. Reischauer, *The United States and Japan,* 283-88; see also Sheila K. Johnson, *American Attitudes Toward Japan, 1941-1975,* (Washington, D.C.: American Enterprise Institute for Public Policy Research, 1975), 27.

3. T. A. Bisson and Faith Bisson interviews by author, Waterloo, Ontario, 2, 3 January 1978 (hereafter cited as Bisson interviews); Maxwell S. Stewart telephone interview by author, 12 November 1979.

4. T. A. Bisson, "The Nanking Government," *Foreign Policy Reports,* 30 October 1929; and

Warren I. Cohen, *America's Response to China: An Interpretive History of Sino-American Relations* (New York: John Wiley, 1971), 113–20.

5. T. A. Bisson, "East Asia Over Fifty Years: Selected Writings," (Typescript, 1976) preface, T. A. Bisson Papers, University of Maine, Orono, Maine. While in graduate school Bisson wrote three articles which were published in scholarly journals on China and had planned for his dissertation a translation of a mid–eighteenth century novel by Wu Ching-tzu, *Ju-lin wai-shik,* a satirical account of the empty formalism of the Confucian elite and of accepted customs of traditional China.

6. T. A. Bisson, *Japan in China* (New York: Macmillan, 1938); T. A. Bisson, *American Policy in the Far East, 1931–1940* (New York: International Secretariat, Institute of Pacific Relations, 1940); T. A. Bisson, *Yenan in June 1937: Talks with Communist Leaders* (Berkeley: Center for Chinese Studies, University of California, 1973); and the numerous articles in *Foreign Policy Reports* and the *Foreign Policy Bulletin,* 1929–41.

7. *China Today,* "8-Point Program of the Friends of the Chinese People," October 1934. See Philip J. Jaffe, "Introduction" to 1968 Greenwood Press reprint of *Amerasia.* Frederick Spencer, "Nanking Clasps Hands with Japan," *China Today,* October 1934; Frederick Spencer, "New Light on the Far Eastern 'Problem,' " *China Today,* March 1936. The use of the pseudonym was necessitated by the "non-partisan" restrictions imposed by the FPA.

8. T. A. Bisson, "Hemispheric Armaments and the Open Door," *Amerasia,* December 1938; T. A. Bisson, "What Kind of Peace in the Far East?," *Amerasia,* November 1939; T. A. Bisson, "The United States Can Block a Far Eastern Munich," *China Today,* November 1939. Bisson was one of the founders in 1938 of the American Committee for Non-Participation in Japanese Aggression.

9. Norman D. Markowitz, *The Rise and Fall of the People's Century: Henry A. Wallace and American Liberalism, 1941–1948* (New York: Free Press, 1973), 65–74; *New York Times,* 30 March 1942.

10. U.S. House of Representatives, Special Committee to Investigate Un-American Activities, *Hearings on Investigation of Un-American Propaganda Activities in the United States,* 78th Cong. 1st sess., 1943, 7:3472–79.

11. John N. Thomas, *The Institute of Pacific Relations: Asian Scholars and American Politics* (Seattle: University of Washington Press, 1974), 3–35.

12. Edward C. Carter to T. A. Bisson, 3 April 1943, Institute of Pacific Relations Papers, Columbia University, New York (hereafter cited as IPR Papers). After Bisson left the IPR, Faith Bisson wrote Carter that her husband's two years with IPR were "good years from every point of view—with time for two books, the great amount of academic freedom, and the warm staff friendships, the opportunities . . . opened up, our family life in this home which has been contented and happy." F. A. Bisson to Carter, 17 January 1946, IPR Papers.

13. T. A. Bisson, "China's Part in a Coalition War," *Far Eastern Survey,* 14 July 1943.

14. *FRUS, China,* 1943, 81–82; Thomas, *The Institute of Pacific Relations,* 37; *FRUS, China,* 1943, 149; Stanley K. Hornbeck to Carter, 1 August 1943, Stanley K. Hornbeck Papers, Hoover Institute on War, Revolution, and Peace, Stanford University, Stanford, Calif. Carter to Bisson, 29 July 1943, and Holland to Lattimore, 20 July 1943, IPR Papers.

15. Lattimore, *Solution in Asia,* and Roth, *Dilemma in Japan.* Roth, a Navy lieutenant during the war, organized a talk at City College of New York for Bisson in 1938 and afterwards wrote him a note of thanks. "Your reputation in your field is unsurpassed as far as we are concerned. Your articles and monographs are widely read here and much appreciated. . . . My personal admiration for your work is probably implicit in the above. You [were] largely responsible for making a Chinese major out of me. I believe I have read almost everything you have written." Board of Directors Meeting, *Minutes,* 16 March 1938, Foreign Policy Association Papers, Wis-

consin State Historical Society, Madison, Wis. Lattimore, who had been editor of *Pacific Affairs* from 1933 to 1941, maintained contact during the war with IPR officials, including Bisson, and refereed manuscripts and did book reviews for *Pacific Affairs*. See Carter to Bisson, 27 June 1945, IPR Papers.

16. T. A. Bisson, "Japan as a Political Organism," *Pacific Affairs,* December 1944, 417-20.

17. Ibid. See also T. A. Bisson, *America's Far Eastern Policy* (New York: International Secretariat, Institute of Pacific Relations, 1945), 152-54.

18. T. A. Bisson, *Japan's War Economy* (New York: Macmillan, 1945), vii-xi; see also T. A. Bisson, "The Price of Peace for Japan," *Pacific Affairs,* March 1944.

19. Bisson, "Japan as a Political Organism," 417-20. See also T. A. Bisson, "Ambassador Grew's Mission," *The Nation,* 3 June 1944.

20. T. A. Bisson, "Japan Can Be Democratic," *New Republic,* 8 October 1945, 473-74.

21. Ibid.

22. T. A. Bisson, "Reform Years in Japan 1945-47: An Occupation Memoir," (unpublished manuscript, ca. 1975), n.p., Bisson Papers. This manuscript is based primarily on a collection of over one hundred letters Bisson exchanged with his wife while in Japan. For quotes, see 38-45.

23. Ibid., 91.

24. Ibid., 130-45.

25. Ibid., 102.

26. Ibid., 291-95

27. Ibid. For an analysis of the constitution issue along lines similar to Bisson's see Dower, *Empire and Aftermath,* 318-29.

28. Ibid., 352-58.

29. Ibid.

30. Ibid.

31. Ibid., 364.

32. Theodore Cohen interview with Eiji Takemae, 25 December 1971 in Eiji Takemae, "The U.S. Occupation Policies for Japan," *Tokyo Metropolitan University Journal of Law and Politics* 14 (1973): 16-17 (hereafter cited as Cohen Interview); and T. A. Bisson, "An Occupation Memoir," 180-202.

33. Ibid., 208-11.

34. Bisson, *Prospects for Democracy in Japan,* 50-60; SCAP, Government Section Memorandum, "The Merits of the Electoral System Proposed by Mr. Yoshida," 17 March 1947, Box 2032, Records of the Supreme Commander for Allied Powers, Record Group 331, National Archives, Suitland, Maryland (hereafter cited as SCAP Records).

35. Willoughby to MacArthur, 7 June 1947, with enclosures, Charles Willoughby Papers, MacArthur Memorial. There is no study of the purge of "radicals" within SCAP though reference is made to it in Cohen, *Remaking Japan,* 92-96, and Wildes, *Typhoon in Tokyo,* 228, 276, 286.

36. Bisson to Holland, 22 September 1946; Holland to Bisson, 4 and 20 December 1946; and Bisson to Holland, 31 October 1946, IPR Papers.

37. Dower, "Occupied Japan as History and Occupation History as Politics," 485-504, reviews the conservative tradition of Occupation historiography; Bisson, *Prospects for Democracy in Japan,* 130-33.

38. Bisson, *Zaibatsu Dissolution in Japan,* 33-60.

39. Ibid., 202-3.

40. Ibid., 158-79, 204.

41. Ibid., 154-56, 205-6. See chapter 5.

42. Ibid., 208-13.

43. Ibid., 217–18.

44. Ibid., 51–57, 218.

45. On the loyalty oath controversy in California see Walton Bean, *California: An Interpretive History* 3d ed. (New York: McGraw-Hill, 1978), 474–76; on the national hysteria see, Lawrence S. Wittner, *Cold War America: From Hiroshima to Watergate* (New York: Praeger, 1974), 30–110; for a complacent study of IPR and the McCarren Hearings see Thomas, *The Institute of Pacific Relations*.

46. For Bisson's testimony see U.S. Senate, Committee on the Judiciary, Subcommittee on Internal Security, *Hearings on the Institute of Pacific Relations*, 82d Cong., 2d sess., 1951–52, 12:4159–4288 (hereafter cited as *IPR Hearings*).

47. Bisson interviews; James Earl Watson, "A History of Political Science at the University of California, 1875–1960," (Ph.D. diss., University of California, Berkeley, 1961), 325.

48. Bisson interviews.

49. Wesley R. Fishel and T. A. Bisson, *The United States and Vietnam: Two Views* (Public Affairs Pamphlet, 1966), No. 391. Bisson's piece was titled, "Why the United States Should Not Be in Vietnam." The defense of American policy in Vietnam was authored by Wesley R. Fishel, head of the Michigan State University group in Vietnam during the 1950s which was exposed later as a CIA operation. The *Western Round-Up* articles by Bisson were "Vietnam—Escalation or Negotiation in Viet-Nam?" (26 February 1965); "On Michael's Address" (10 December 1965); "The Geneva Conference and After" (28 January 1966); and "Why Not Support the Vietnam War?" (28 April 1967). These are all in Bisson, "Selected Writings,"chapter 6, Bisson Papers.

50. T. A. Bisson, "The American Japanese 'Co-Prosperity Sphere': Review of Halliday and McCormack, *Japanese Imperialism Today*," *Bulletin of Concerned Asian Scholars* 6, 1 (January–March 1974): 62.

51. Bisson, "Selected Writings," 370–71; Bisson interviews; and Faith Bisson to author, 26 September 1979.

52. Dower, *Origins of the Modern Japanese State*, 33–43.

53. Ibid. See also Richard Kagan, "McCarren's Legacy: The Association of Asian Studies," *Bulletin of Concerned Asian Scholars*, 1, 4 (May 1969): 18–22.

4 JAMES S. KILLEN

1. James C. Abegglen, *The Japanese Factory: Aspects of Its Social Organization* (Glencoe, Ill.: Free Press, 1958). This influential book established the dominant American conception of Japanese industrial relations.

2. Taishiro Shirai, ed. *Contemporary Industrial Relations in Japan* (Madison: University of Wisconsin Press, 1983), 90; see especially the chapters by Kazuo Koike, "Internal Labor Markets: Workers in Large Firms," and "Workers in Small Firms and Women in Industry." Koike cites figures for 1974 that of Japan's total labor force of 51.3 million, 70 percent were employees and 30 percent were self-employed. Of the employees' segment of the total labor force, 33 percent are women, 28 percent are male workers in large firms with more than 500 employees, including public corporations. The remaining 40 percent, the largest group, are male workers in medium and small firms. For estimates of current average wages see Andrew Gordon, *The Evolution of Labor Relations in Japan: Heavy Industry, 1853–1955* (Cambridge: Harvard University Press, 1985), 401–8.

3. Halliday, *A Political History of Japanese Capitalism*, 204–17.

4. The standard histories of the Occupation, monographs on Japanese labor history, and

studies of American labor's foreign policy treat this subject only cursorily or ignore it altogether. Among the most important monographs on Japanese labor during the Occupation are Farley, *Aspects of Japan's Labor Problems;* and Solomon B. Levine, *Industrial Relations in Postwar Japan* (Urbana: University of Illinois Press, 1958). A history of American labor's international activities is Ronald Radosh, *American Labor and United States Foreign Policy* (New York: Random House, 1969).

5. For background on Cohen and American labor's input into SWNCC 92/1 see Cohen Interview, 5–13, and Cohen, *Remaking Japan,* xii-xiii. SWNCC 92/1, "Treatment of Japanese Workers' Organizations," is in Combined Civil Affairs Committee, Geographic Series, Record Group 218, National Archives. For a more complete summary of labor policy planning for the Occupation see Eric H. Svensson, "The Military Occupation of Japan: The First Years Planning, Policy Formulation, and Reforms," (Ph.D. diss.; University of Denver, 1966), 48–49, 105–6, 255–58; Theodore Cohen to author, 25 June 1978.

6. Levine, *Industrial Relations in Postwar Japan,* 24, 60–67. Unlike American industrial and craft unions, Japanese enterprise unions tended to include production workers, white collar workers, and management with the exception of the president of the firm. Members of an enterprise union were confined to a single shop, establishment or enterprise. Such organization fostered intra-plant collaboration between workers and management and limited working-class consciousness.

7. Cohen to author, 25 June 1978. Prior to his work with SCAP and FEA, Cohen was an intelligence analyst with the Office of Strategic Services, an instructor of history at City College of New York, and a graduate student at Columbia University. He dates his antipathy to communism from 1936 while a student at City College.

8. Though differing in interpretation on Japanese government economic policy, Western sources are agreed that distribution of military stockpiles of food and materials to favored parties, the acceleration of note issues by the Bank of Japan, subsidies to nonproductive industries, tokenistic enforcement attempts against hoarding and black market operations, and other actions by the Japanese government wreaked inflationary havoc in Japan. According to Martin Bronfenbrenner the "main internal force for inflation came . . . from big business (Zaibatsu) firms which had had war contracts with the Japanese Government. Without substantial inflation most of Japan's war contracting companies and the banks which financed them would have failed like Confederate companies and banks after our own Civil War." Martin Bronfenbrenner, "The American Occupation of Japan: Economic Retrospect," in Grant K. Goodman, ed., *The American Occupation of Japan: A Restrospective View* (Lawrence: University of Kansas Press, 1968), 19. See also Joyce and Gabriel Kolko, *The Limits of Power,* 308. For an excellent contemporary analysis from a Japanese perspective see Shigeto Tsuru, *Essays on the Japanese Economy* (Tokyo: Kinokuniya Bookstore, 1958), 5–16.

9. SCAP, *Non-Military History of the Occupation of Japan, 1945–1951,* "Working Conditions," 29:126, SCAP Records.

10. SCAP, *Final Report of the Advisory Committee on Labor in Japan,* 29 July 1946, B-3, MacArthur Papers.

11. For Murphy's views see "Labor in Japan Today," *American Federationist,* (September 1946), 28.

12. For the importance of production control strikes and SCAP reaction see Farley, *Aspects of Japan's Labor Problems,* 92–95, and especially Moore, *Japanese Workers and the Struggle for Power,* 177–243.

13. Theodore Cohen, "Labor Democratization in Japan: The First Years," in Redford, *The Occupation of Japan: Economic Policy and Reform,* 162–73. The restrictive impact of the LRAL

is most clearly stated in Halliday, *A Political History of Japanese Capitalism*, 210. See also SCAP, *Final Report of the Advisory Committee on Labor in Japan*, 29 July 1946, 1, 123, B-3, MacArthur Papers.

14. Deverall to "Dear Folks," 15 January 1947, Richard Deverall Papers, Catholic University Archives, Washington, D.C.

15. On the structure of the early post-war Japanese trade union movement and its ties to political parties see Levine, *Industrial Relations in Postwar Japan*, 26, and Evelyn S. Colbert, *The Left Wing in Japanese Politics* (New York: Institute of Pacific Relations, 1952). The staunchly anti-Communist views of Deverall are the dominant theme of his voluminous correspondence and published writings. Following Sanbetsu's first convention, Deverall commented that "the opinion has come to be more here that [Sanbetsu] is not really interested in trade unionism, but is using the trade unions for political purposes." He noted that the speeches of Sanbetsu leaders sounded "like the carefully rehearsed phrases of a column in the *Daily Worker*." Deverall to "Dear Folks," n.d. (ca. 31 August 1946), Series 2, Letter No. 17, Deverall Papers.

16. *Free Trade Union News*, "Revival of Japanese Unions Will Require Aid," April 1946, 7. Leaders of the postwar Sodomei, like Matsuoka, were tainted by their wartime records. When the government dissolved Sodomei in 1940, Matsuoka not only supported the state-sponsored movement calling for cooperation between labor and industry but became a leader of the movement calling for Japanese industries to render service to the state. For more on the background of the anti-Communist leadership of Japanese unions see Fukuji Taguchi, "Leadership in the General Council of Japanese Labor Unions," *Journal of Social and Political Ideas in Japan* 3 (1965): 73–78.

17. *Free Trade Union News*, "Japanese Labor Weaving New Pattern," March 1947, 5. For Starr's biographical sketch see Gary M. Fink, ed., *Biographical Dictionary of American Labor Leaders*, (Westport, Conn.: Greenwood Press, 1974), 336–37; Woll to MacArthur, 11 December 1946, 24 January 1947, MacArthur Papers.

18. Farley, *Aspects of Japan's Labor Problems*, 44–50, 144–52, 248–49; see also the fascinating recollection of the politics of the strike in Cohen, *Remaking Japan*, 277–300.

19. Lewis Schwellenbach to Secretary of War, 9 May 1947, CIO Secretary Treasurer's Office Collection, Wayne State University Archives of Labor History, Detroit, Mich. (hereafter cited as CIO Papers). Schwellenbach was relaying the message of the Trade Union Advisory Committee on International Affairs of the Labor Department (TUAC) to have U.S. labor's role upgraded in Japan. On TUAC in 1947 were James B. Carey, Secretary-Treasurer, CIO; David Dubinsky, President, ILGWU; Clinton S. Golden, Vice-President, United Steel Workers; Thomas Harkins, Brotherhood of Locomotive Engineers; A. E. Lyon, Railway Labor Executives Association; George Meany, Secretary-Treasurer, AFL; Frank Rosenblum, Secretary-Treasurer, Amalgamated Clothing Workers; Michael Ross, Director, Department of International Affairs, CIO; Robert J. Watt, International Representative, AFL; and Matthew Woll, Vice-President, AFL. TUAC met regularly with not only the Labor Department but the State and War departments as well. Cohen recalls that in his contacts with TUAC "they demonstrated that their prime concern was to prevent Communist infiltration into both German and Japanese labor movements."

20. On the fundamentally conservative handling of the Japanese political situation during the 1947 election see Bisson, *Prospects for Democracy in Japan*, 50–74; Cohen interview, 35.

21. Telephone interview with Mrs. Marilyn Killen, 13 January 1985; telephone interview with Mrs. Rose Killen Reese, 16 February 1985; Rose Killen Reese to author, 16 February 1985.

22. For a discussion of the union and its leadership during the depression see Robert Zeiger, *Rebuilding the Pulp and Paper Workers' Union, 1933–1941* (Knoxville: University of Tennessee Press, 1984). On Burke's high regard for Killen see International Brotherhood of Pulp, Sulphite and Paper Mill Workers, *Report of the Proceedings of the 20th Convention, Toronto, Canada,*

October 9–13, 1944, 74–75, and *Pulp, Sulphite and Paper Mill Workers' Journal* 23, 1 (January-February 1939): 19.

23. International Brotherhood of Pulp, Sulphite and Paper Mill Workers, *Report of the Proceedings of the 18th Convention, St. Paul, Minnesota, March 14–17, 1939*, 43–44.

24. International Brotherhood of Pulp, Sulphite and Paper Mill Workers, *Report of the Proceedings of the 20th Convention, Toronto, Canada, October 9–13, 1944*, 75–81; telephone interview with Mrs. Rose Killen Reese, 16 February 1985.

25. Killen to Burke, 28 March and 7 April 1947, International Brotherhood of Pulp, Sulphite and Paper Mill Workers Papers, Microfilm P83–264, Wisconsin State Historical Society, Madison, Wis. (hereafter cited as IBPSPMW Papers); and Woll to MacArthur, 3 April 1947, MacArthur Papers.

26. Killen to Burke, 6 May and 4 June 1947, IBPSPMW Papers; and Memorandum of Conversation, "Japanese Labor Situation," 6 November 1947, 894.504/11–647, DOS, RG 59.

27. Killen to Burke, 6 May 1947, IBPSPMW Papers; SCAP, *History of the Non-Military Activities of the Occupation of Japan*, "Development of the Trade Union Movement," 28:64, SCAP Records; Levine, *Industrial Relations in Postwar Japan*, 28, 71–73; and Killen to William Green, 30 July 1947, IBPSPMW Papers.

28. Killen to Green, 30 July 1947, IBPSPMW Papers.

29. This document is contained in Paul L. Stanchfield to Killen, 27 May 1947, Labor Division Papers, SCAP Records.

30. Deverall to Chief ESS/LAB, Memorandum on Workers Education in Government Railway Workers Union, 10 April 1947; Deverall to "Dear Folks," Series 3, No. 9, ca. 31 October 1947, Deverall Papers; Deverall to Green 30 April 1948, Florence Thorne Papers, State Historical Society of Wisconsin, Madison, Wis. (hereafter cited as Thorne Papers).

31. SCAP, *History of the Non-Military Activities of the Occupation of Japan*, "Development of the Trade Union Movement," 28:103–11, SCAP Records.

32. Resolution No. 202, "Pledging Support to Japanese Workers" in 1947 Convention File, Thorne Papers; Minutes of Meeting of the International Labor Relations Committee, AFL, 11 November 1947, Thorne Papers. Present at this meeting were the top FTUC officials Matthew Woll, William Green, George Meany, David Dubinsky, Jay Lovestone, James Killen, and Florence Thorne. For the details of the dismay of the FTUC at the permission granted by the War Department for the visit of the WFTU mission see Woll to Patterson, 13 March 1947 and 2 April 1947; Patterson to Woll, 25 March 1947; and Lovestone to MacArthur, 19 March 1947, MacArthur Papers.

33. Killen to International Labor Relations Committee, AFL, "Observations and Suggestions Concerning the Development of Free Trade Unions in Japan," n.d. (ca. 1 November 1947); Deverall to Green, 30 June 1948, Thorne Papers. In an undated, unsigned report it was noted that in Japan the FTUC had "stepped up our efforts to strengthen the ranks of democratic trade unionists who have had to face a powerful and lavishly financed and unscrupulous Communist enemy. We have been working closely with the Democratic Leagues [and] also sending CARE parcels to needy trade unionists of Japan."

34. Matthew Woll to Florence Thorne, 9 May 1947 with enclosure "Confidential Report on Japan by James S. Killen," Thorne Papers. Woll requested Miss Thorne to mimeograph Killen's report because the "situation in Japan . . . is of vital concern to American labor and the nation as a whole."

35. Killen to Green, 30 July 1947, IBPSPMW Papers; and Killen to Green, 10 February 1948, Thorne Papers. For the difficulties of the Katayama Cabinet see Allan B. Cole, George O. Totten, and Cecil Uyehara, *Socialist Parties in Postwar Japan* (New Haven: Yale University Press, 1966), 16–22.

36. SCAP, *History of the Non-Military Activities of the Occupation of Japan*, "Working Conditions," 29:129, Appendices 1I, 1H, 1J, SCAP Records.

37. For a discussion of the shift in Washington policy towards Japan in 1947–48 see chapter 6. The NSC statement is from a draft of NSC 13 prepared under the direction of George F. Kennan in *FRUS*, 1948, 6:780. Draper's statement is in *Nippon Times*, 26 March 1948. William J. Sebald to Secretary of State, 13 February 1948, 894.504/2–1348, DOS, RG 59.

38. SCAP, *History of Non-Military Activities of the Occupation of Japan*, "Reorganization of Civil Service," 13, 39–47, SCAP Records.

39. Killen to Burke, 6 March and 24 April 1948, IBPSPMW Papers.

40. Marshall Green to John M. Allison, 9 September 1948, with enclosure "Mr. Killen's remarks on the denial of collective bargaining and strike rights of Japanese Government and public employees," 894.504/9–948, DOS, RG 59. Also see Cohen interview, 36–39, for Killen's view of Hoover.

41. Cohen, *Remaking Japan*, 385–90.

42. Ibid., 390–95.

43. Farley, *Aspects of Japan's Labor Problems*, 189–204.

44. Killen to Burke, 15 July 1948, IBPSPMW Papers.

45. *FRUS*, 1948, 6:838; *Pulp, Sulphite and Paper Mill Workers' Journal* 33, 1 (January–February 1949): 19; and telephone interview with Attorney Leonard Appel, 1 December 1984.

46. *Pulp, Sulphite and Paper Mill Workers' Journal* 33, 1 (January–February 1949): 19.

47. Meeting of the International Labor Committee, AFL, 9 September 1948, Thorne Papers; *Free Trade Union News*, "Japanese Labor and American Occupation Policies" and "A. F. of L. Urges Maximum Opportunity for Japanese Trade Unions," February 1949, 6. Killen and Burke were enthusiastic contributors to the newly formed Americans for Democratic Action. Killen thought the ADA "represents a philosophy which must be given great recognition both in America and in other places in the world if totalitarianism of one brand or the other is not to overrun the greater portion of the so-called civilized areas." See Killen to Burke, 6 March 1948, IBPSPMW Papers.

48. For TUAC views see John W. Gibson to James Forrestal, 16 September 1948, Department of Labor, Office of the Secretary, General Subject File, RG 174, National Archives. AFL pressure on the Army Department is found in Matthew Woll to James Forrestal, 14 September 1948, Thorne Papers.

49. For a small portion of the international criticism of the revised NPSL see *FRUS*, 1948, 6:866–70, 910–11, General G. L. Eberle to William Draper, 20 August 1948, Records of the Secretary of the Army, Civil Affairs Division File 014 Japan, Box 248 Record Group 165, National Archives (hereafter cited as CAD/Japan File with appropriate number); Farley, *Aspects of Japan's Labor Problems*, 205–6.

50. *Pulp, Sulphite and Paper Mill Workers' Journal* 34, 6 (November–December 1950): 8 and 37, 2 (March–April 1953): 2; telephone interview with Mrs. Marilyn Killen, 16 February 1985.

51. Max W. Bishop to W. Walton Butterworth, 13 April 1949, 894.504/4–1349, DOS, RG 659; Tracy Voorhees to General A. P. Fox, 30 March 1950, Tracy Voorhees Papers, Rutgers University Library, New Brunswick, N.J.; and CINCFE to Department of the Army, 23 April 1949, Labor Division Papers, SCAP Records.

52. Halliday, *A Political History of Japanese Capitalism*, 188–90.

53. Burati to Lovestone, 11 October 1949; Robert T. Amis to General William Marquat, 10 October 1949; and MacArthur to Joint Council for the Promotion of Affiliation with the New Free World Labor Conference, 8 November 1949, all in Labor Division Papers, SCAP Records.

54. Burati to Lovestone, 11 October 1949, Labor Division Papers, SCAP Records; Matsuoka Komakichi to William Green, 23 November 1949, Thorne Papers; and Levine, *Industrial Rela-*

tions in Postwar Japan, 74–76.

55. For more detail on the Struggle Committee see Farley, *Aspects of Japan's Labor Problems,* 233–39. The quotation is from Kikukawa Takeo to Green, 25 February 1950, Thorne Papers. On the secret abandonment of the general strike threat by the Struggle Committee leadership see Robert Amis to William Marquat, 11 February 1950, Labor Division Papers, SCAP Records.

56. For a distinctly anti-Communist analysis of the JCP during the Occupation see Arthur Swearingen and Paul Langer, *Red Flag in Japan: International Communism in Action, 1919–1951* (Cambridge: Harvard University Press, 1952), 87–252; Valery Burati to William Marquat, 29, 30 June 1950, Labor Division Papers, SCAP Records; Halliday, *A Political History of Japanese Capitalism,* 220.

57. Valery Burati, Memorandum on the General Council of Trade Unions of Japan, 13 March 1950, Office of the Chief, Economic and Scientific Section Papers, SCAP Records (hereafter cited as Chief/ESS Papers, SCAP Records); Marquat to MacArthur, 20 July 1950, Chief/ESS Papers, SCAP Records; and John W. Brophy to Anita Brophy, 17 July 1950, John W. Brophy Papers, Catholic University Archives, Washington, D.C.

58. *Free Labour World,* "Democratic Trade Unions of Japan Achieve Unity," July 1950, 7–10.

59. Ibid.; Levine, *Industrial Relations in Postwar Japan,* 74–79.

60. Cole, Totten, and Uyehara, *Socialist Parties in Postwar Japan,* 33–36; and Takano Minoru to William Green, 18 July 1951, Thorne Papers.

61. On Townsend see J. H. Oldenbroek to William Green, 20 February 1952, and Green to Oldenbroek, 23 February 1952, Thorne Papers; on Deverall see Deverall to Lovestone, 23 March 1952, and Deverall to Woll, 28 March 1952, Deverall Papers. The Lovestone quote is in Lovestone to Philip Pearl, 14 April 1952, Thorne Papers.

62. Lovestone to Deverall, 9 June 1953, Deverall Papers. For the growing split between FTUC and ICFTU over the proper tactics in dealing with Sohyo see ICFTU Executive Board, Report on Japan by Willard Townsend, 5 December 1952, Deverall Papers. By this time Deverall was almost certainly being financed indirectly through the CIA. In a 1971 interview Deverall recalled being in Lovestone's office and "a man would come in with a stack of crisp new hundred dollar bills." Lovestone would sign a receipt for them and then turn over most of the money "to support me in the field." Deverall later satisfied himself that the money came from the CIA. "Of course it's all pretty much common knowledge now, and I don't see anything wrong with it." See Joseph C. Goulden, *Meany* (New York: Atheneum, 1972), 130.

63. Press Release, CIO Viewpoint on "Neutralism" stated by President Walter P. Reuther in letter to Japanese General Council of Trade Unions, 15 June 1953, CIO Washington Office Records, CIO Papers. For the disarray and weakness of the Japanese labor movement in the immediate post-Occupation period see Levine, *Industrial Relations in Postwar Japan,* 79–84.

64. Halliday, *A Political History of Japanese Capitalism,* 220–34.

5   HARRY F. KERN

1. *New Republic,* 30 May 1949, 5–6.

2. Harvard University, *Harvard Nineteen Thirty-Five Class Album,* 154; *The Daily Yomiuri,* "Harry Kern's Story (1): Getting Interested in Japan," 1 September 1979; and Raymond Moley, *After Seven Years* (New York: Harper and Brothers, 1939), 278–81.

3. *The Daily Yomiuri,* "Harry Kern's Story (1): Getting Interested in Japan," 1 September 1979, 9. The prominence which Kern and his friends in Japan gave to Kern's role in organizing the ACJ was challenged by former Ambassador Shimanouchi Toshiro in the *Asahi Journal,* 30

March 1979, in an article titled "Kern Is Not a Big Shot." Shimanouchi emphasizes the critical importance of Eugene Dooman and his friend Kay Sugahara in the ACJ. I am currently doing research on these men.

4. *The Daily Yomiuri,* "Harry Kern's Story (1): Getting Interested in Japan," 1 September 1979, 9.

5. W. Averell Harriman to author, 22 January 1974. Although Harriman resigned from the board of directors of *Newsweek* in 1941, he remained one of its largest stockholders; his younger brother, E. Roland Harriman, was a member of the board in the postwar period. See *Who's Who in America, 1972–1973* 1:1334–35; *Newsweek,* 27 January 1947, 40.

6. Eleanor Hadley, *Antitrust in Japan,* (Princeton: Princeton University Press, 1970), 87–99; see also Baerwald, *The Purge of Japanese Leaders Under the Occupation,* 80.

7. MacArthur to Robert E. Wood, 12 February 1947, Robert E. Wood Papers, Herbert Hoover Library; *The Daily Yomiuri,* "Harry Kern's Story (2): Japan Surrendered Intact," 2 September 1979, 7; *Newsweek,* 10 February 1947. For MacArthur's views of the Zaibatsu see *Nippon Times,* 21, 23 February 1948.

8. *Newsweek,* 10 May 1947 and 23 June 1947.

9. *The Daily Yomiuri,* "Harry Kern's Story (2): Japan Surrendered Intact," 2 September 1979, 7.

10. *Newsweek,* 23 June 1947; *The Daily Yomiuri,* "Harry Kern's Story (2): Japan Surrendered Intact," 2 September 1979, 7.

11. Kern to Herbert Hoover, 27 June 1947; Hoover to Kern, 2 July 1947; and Hoover to Pratt, 26 June 1947, Hoover Papers, Herbert Hoover Library. For a discussion of Pratt's long official and unofficial relations with Hoover, his career with *Newsweek,* and his involvement in the American Council on Japan, see Gerald E. Wheeler, *Admiral William Veazie Pratt, U.S. Navy* (Washington, D.C.: Naval History Division, Department of the Navy, 1974). The leaked documents were Robert Patterson to Hoover, 5 April 1947, with enclosures of the Strike report on Japanese reparations of 24 February 1947, and the draft of a reparations policy approved by the State-War-Navy Coordinating Committee (SWNCC).

12. Kauffman to Eichelberger, 13 May 1949, Eichelberger Papers. Kauffman was selected by the Commerce Department's high-powered Business Advisory Council early in 1947 to serve on a proposed five member "economic cabinet" for MacArthur. MacArthur's rejection of the proposal began the long and bitter conflict between the general and Kauffman.

13. Hadley, *Antitrust in Japan,* 125–30, 495–514. This includes the complete text of FEC-230, which was first approved in 1946 as SWNCC 302 policy on the deconcentration of industry. SWNCC 302 was forwarded to the eleven nation Far Eastern Commission (FEC) for its approval and also sent to SCAP as an "interim" but operative directive.

14. James Lee Kauffman, "Report on Conditions in Japan as of September 6, 1947," enclosure in Kauffman to Eichelberger, 13 May 1949, Eichelberger Papers.

15. "Memorandum of Conversation: Report on Mr. Draper's Trip to Japan," 8 October 1947, Far Eastern Commission-U.S. Delegation, DOS, RG 43. For a full discussion of the background and impact of the Kauffman report, see Schonberger, "Zaibatsu Dissolution and the American Restoration of Japan," 16–31.

16. Charles L. Kades, "Memorandum for the Under-Secretary of the Army," undated but probably September 1947, in Postwar Financial History Project of the Okurasho (Japanese Ministry of Finance), Tokyo, Japan (hereafter cited as Okurasho Collection).

17. MacArthur to Department of the Army, 24 October 1947, Henry L. Stimson Papers, Yale University Library, New Haven, Conn.

18. Forrestal, "Memorandum for Mr. Royall," 1 November 1947, James V. Forrestal Papers, Princeton University Library, Princeton, N.J.; "Statement of U.S. Policy toward Economic

Recovery of Japan,'' November 1947, Stimson Papers. For the developing consensus on economic rehabilitation, see *FRUS,* 1947, 6:492–93, 541–42.

19. ''Memorandum for H. F. Kern,'' in Kern to Hoover, 22 April 1948, Hoover Papers; *Newsweek,* 1 December 1947, 36–37.

20. Bisson, *Zaibatsu Dissolution in Japan,* 140–41; Hadley, *Antitrust in Japan,* 144; and Kern to Eichelberger, 23 October 1949, Eichelberger Papers.

21. *FRUS,* 1947, 6:536; interview with Joseph Ballantine, 1961, Oral History Collection, Columbia University, New York. For a summary of the work of Kennan's Planning Staff in 1947 see Frederick S. Dunn, *Peace-making and the Settlement with Japan* (Princeton: Princeton University Press, 1963), 59–62.

22. Millis, *The Forrestal Diaries,* 328–29; *FRUS,* 1948, 6:694–700; see also Kennan, *Memoirs, 1925–1950,* 395–410.

23. ''Preliminary Report on the American Council on Japan,'' 31 July 1948, in Kern to Pratt, 4 August 1948, William V. Pratt Papers, Naval War College Archives, Newport, R.I.; see also *Newsweek,* 1 December 1947, 37, and 19 April 1948, 42.

24. Joyce and Gabriel Kolko, *The Limits of Power,* 518–21.

25. ''Memorandum from H. F. Kern,'' in Kern to Hoover, 22 April 1948, Hoover Papers.

26. Ibid.

27. ''Preliminary Report on the American Council on Japan,'' 31 July 1948, in Kern to Pratt, 4 August 1948, Pratt Papers. The founding members of the ACJ were Joseph W. Ballantine, William R. Castle, John Curtis, Eugene Dooman, Joseph C. Grew, Thomas C. Hart, James L. Kauffman, Harry F. Kern, Kenneth S. Latourette, Clarence C. Meyer, Compton Pakenham, William V. Pratt, Antonin Raymond, John W. B. Smith, Henry St. George Tucker, Langdon Warner, and Charles W. Wood. Kern claimed periodically that he was ''enrolling a good many new members on the Council.'' But the only names of members who were not founders of the ACJ that appear in the available record are George N. Coe, General W. Cary Crane, and Ivan F. Baker. See Kern to Pratt, 5 September 1949; and ''Minutes of Organization Meeting of Board of Directors of American Council on Japan, Inc., 17 May 1949,'' Pratt Papers. In the process of compiling the membership of the ACJ for use by Government Section, Charles Kades wrote that the chief of the State Department's Division of Northeast Asian Affairs, Max Bishop, although apparently not a member of the ACJ, ''works closely with the Council.'' See Kades, ''Memorandum for General Whitney,'' 12 July 1949, Williams Papers.

28. *New York Times,* 19 July 1948, 7.

29. On Grew and Dooman, see Heinrichs, Jr., *American Ambassador;* on Castle, see Robert H. Ferrell, *American Diplomacy in the Great Depression* (New Haven: Yale University Press, 1957), 30–42; on Meyer, see *Who Was Who in America* 4:657, and *Official Report of the Thirty-Third National Foreign Trade Convention,* New York, 1947; on Raymond, see *Who's Who in America, 1974–75* 2:2536; and on Ballantine, see interview with Joseph Ballantine, 1961, Oral History Collection, Columbia University.

30. Martin E. Weinstein, *Japan's Postwar Defense Policy, 1946–1968* (New York: Columbia University Press, 1971), 18–25. For Eichelberger's association with the Japan Lobby, see notes 36 and 37 below.

31. Kern to Eichelberger, 8 May, 5 September and 23 October 1949, Eichelberger Papers; see also notes 59 and 64 below.

32. Kern to Pratt, 15 November 1946 and 31 May 1950, Pratt Papers; Kiba Hirosuke, *Nomura Kichisaburo* (Osaka: 1961), x; James E. Auer, *The Postwar Rearmament of Japanese Maritime Forces, 1945–1971* (New York: Praeger, 1973), 70; and Wheeler, *Admiral William Veazie Pratt,* 386–412.

33. Auer, *The Postwar Rearmament of Japanese Maritime Forces,* 70–77; and Ivan M. Morris,

Nationalism and the Right Wing in Japan (London: Oxford University Press, 1960), 447.

34. "Preliminary Report on the American Council on Japan," 31 July 1948, in Kern to Pratt, 4 August 1948, Pratt Papers; Eichelberger diary, 29 June 1947, and "Memorandum for the Record," 5 May 1949, Eichelberger Papers.

35. In December 1948 Charles Kades was sent by MacArthur to Washington to keep an eye on the Japan Lobby, discredit the Kauffman report, and temper the reverse course, among other things. See Shukan Shincho Henshubu, ed., *MacArthur no Nihon* (Tokyo, 1970), 327–41, where Kades, in a rare interview, provides details on his failures in Washington and resignation from SCAP in May 1949. Several of the relevant memoranda obtained by Shukan Shincho are in the Okurasho Collection. See also Kades, "Memorandum for General Whitney," 1 March 1949, and Courtney Whitney to Charles Kades, 15 August 1949, Williams Papers.

36. Kern to Eichelberger, 21 October 1948, Eichelberger Papers; Kern to Pratt, 30 October 1948, Pratt Papers. On Eichelberger's military career, see Jay Luvaas, ed., *Dear Miss Em: General Eichelberger's War in the Pacific, 1942–1945* (Westport, Conn.: Greenwood Press, 1972).

37. Kern to Eichelberger, 30 October 1948; Eichelberger diary, 16 February 1949; and Voorhees to Eichelberger, 24 April 1950, Eichelberger Papers.

38. "American Policy toward Japan: A Statement for Private Circulation Prepared in Conjunction with members of the American Council on Japan by Harry F. Kern," n.d., in Kern to Pratt, 8 April 1949, Pratt Papers.

39. Ibid.

40. Ibid.; *New York Times,* 9 January 1950.

41. "American Policy toward Japan . . . ," in Kern to Pratt, 8 April 1949, Pratt Papers. See also Eichelberger diary, 16, 23 January 1947, 22 March and 14, 17 September 1948, Eichelberger Papers. These diary entries provide strong evidence that the military section of the ACJ report reflected Eichelberger's obsession with internal sabotage. Eichelberger emphasized his views to Draper, Kennan, George Marshall, and the Joint Chiefs of Staff during and after his tour of duty in Japan.

42. Kern to Eichelberger, 24 March 1949, Eichelberger Papers; *New York Times,* 16 February 1949; *Newsweek,* 18 April 1949, 45; *Fortune,* April 1949, 67–72. According to *Fortune,* most of the material for the article came from American businessmen, "who have tried to do business in Japan since the war and have seen SCAP in action."

43. Kern to Joseph Dodge, 24 January 1949, Joseph Dodge Papers, Detroit Public Library, Detroit, Mich.

44. Richard W. Barnett, "Office Memorandum: American Council on Japan Dinner for Mr. Royall's Mission," 23 February 1949, Okurasho Collection. Barnett prepared this memorandum for circulation within the State Department and included, in his own words, "a free-hand summary of what each of the participants of the meeting said—necessarily compressed of course." See also Charles Kades, "Memorandum for General Whitney," 1 March 1949, Williams Papers.

45. Kades, "Memorandum for General Whitney," 1 March 1949, Williams Papers.

46. Barnett, "Office Memorandum: American Council on Japan Dinner for Mr. Royall's Mission," 23 February 1949, Okurasho Collection.

47. Dunn, *Peace-making and the Settlement with Japan,* 77. For the complete text of NSC 13/2, see *FRUS,* 1948, 6:857–62.

48. Kern to Eichelberger, 24 March and 8 May 1949, Eichelberger Papers.

49. Kern to Pratt, 2 November 1949, Pratt Papers.

50. *IPR Hearings* 5:1676.

51. Ibid., 1677. See also Owen Lattimore, "Japan Is Nobody's Ally," *Atlantic Monthly,* April *1949, 54–58.*

52. U.S. Department of Defense, *United States-Vietnam Relations, 1945–1967* (Washington, D.C.: Government Printing Office, 1971), 239–42.

53. John W. Dower, "The Superdomino in Postwar Asia: Japan in and out of the Pentagon Papers," in Noam Chomsky and Howard Zinn, eds., *The Senator Gravel Edition: The Pentagon Papers* (Boston: Beacon Press, 1972), 5:105, 114–16; and Dower, "Occupied Japan and the American Lake, 1945–1950," 194.

54. Kern to Pratt, 23 April 1950, Pratt Papers.

55. "The Position of Japan in the Framework of American Policy toward the Far East," n.d., in Kern to Pratt, 22 March 1950, Pratt Papers. Kern also enclosed a copy of a detailed report written by Castle, Dooman, and Admiral Thomas Hart on "Japanese Shipping—Operation and Production," The ACJ lobbied Congress and the State Department to permit an enlarged Japanese merchant fleet in the final peace treaty proposal.

56. Evert J. Lewe van Aduard, *Japan: From Surrender to Peace* (The Hague: Martinus Nijhoff, 1953), 159.

57. Harry F. Kern to William V. Pratt, 8 September 1950, Pratt Papers; Yoshida, *The Yoshida Memoirs,* 249–50; Dunn, *Peace-making and the Settlement with Japan,* 98; and William J. Sebald and Russell Brines, *With MacArthur in Japan: A Personal History of the Occupation* (New York: Norton, 1965), 257.

58. Watanabe Takeshi, *Senryoka no Nihon Zaisei Oboegaki* (Tokyo: Nihon Keizai Shimbunsha, 1966), 290–97.

59. *Newsweek,* 3 July 1950, 25; Dower, *Empire and Aftermath,* 362–66; and Lewe van Aduard, *Japan: From Surrender to Peace,* 163–64.

60. Herbert P. Bix, "Japan: The Roots of Militarism," in Mark Selden, ed., *Remaking Asia: Essays on the American Uses of Power* (New York: Pantheon Books, 1974), 319–27; John W. Dower, "The Eye of the Beholder: Background Notes on the U.S.-Japan Military Relationship," *Bulletin of Concerned Asian Scholars* 2, 1 (October 1969): 21–22.

61. "Transcript of the Meeting of the Study Group on Japanese Peace Treaty Problem of the Council on Foreign Relations, October 23, 1950," John Foster Dulles Papers, Princeton University Library, Princeton, N.J.

62. Kern to Dulles, 19 August 1950, Dulles Papers; see also Kern to Pratt, 8 September 1950, Pratt Papers. Kern explained that the "day after the Korean war broke out, Matsudaira paid a visit to Pakenham. He said he had a message which he hoped Pakenham and I would deliver to Mr. Dulles. The message was from the Emperor. We duly delivered it, and I am told Mr. Dulles regards this message as the most important development of his trip . . . . The mere fact that the Palace would go as far as to by-pass SCAP . . . shows . . . how serious the situation is."

63. "Pakenham Notes and Emperor's Message," in Kern to Pratt, 8 September 1950, Pratt Papers.

64. Weinstein, *Japan's Postwar Defense Policy,* 59; *Newsweek,* December 1950, 30; Kern to Dulles, 19 January 1951, Dulles Papers.

65. Kern to Dulles, 15 January 1951, Dulles Papers; Robert D. Murphy, *Diplomat among Soldiers* (Garden City, N.Y.: Doubleday, 1964), 424–26.

66. *Newsweek,* 24 April 1950, 38; see also Ross Y. Koen, *The China Lobby in American Politics* (New York: Macmillan, 1960), 161–62; *IPR Hearings,* 3:703–54.

67. Dower, "The Eye of the Beholder: Background Notes on the U.S.-Japan Military Relationship," 22–23.

68. Quoted in Joyce and Gabriel Kolko, *The Limits of Power,* 533.

69. Kern to "Members of the American Council on Japan," 16 March 1952, Pratt Papers; see also Eugene Dooman, "Japan Revisited: 1942–1952" and "Supplement to Japan Revisited: 1942–1952," in Kern to Pratt, 25 November 1953, Pratt Papers. These lengthy reports were circulated to ACJ members in the spring and fall of 1953 and are the last available evidence of ACJ activity.

70. Carl Bernstein, "The CIA and the Media," *Rolling Stone,* 20 October 1977; *New York Times,* 27 December 1977, 63. Kern's close collaborator in the Japan Lobby, Eugene Dooman, did engage in clandestine operations for the CIA in the early 1950s. See Dooman to William Castle, 20, 21, 22 February 1955, and H. Alexander Smith to Castle, 14 March 1955, H. Alexander Smith Papers, Princeton University Library, Princeton, N.J.

71. On Kishi's background see George R. Packard, *Protest in Tokyo: The Security Treaty Crisis of 1960* (Princeton: Princeton University Press, 1966), 47–54; on the assistance of Kern and the Japan Lobby to Kishi see John Roberts, "The Rebirth of Japan's Zaibatsu," *Insight: Asia's Business Monthly,* July 1978; *Newsweek,* 13 June 1955,50; *Newsweek,* 5 September 1955, 30.

72. *The Daily Yomiuri,* "Harry Kern's Story," (5): 'Japan Failed to Take Advice Suggested About Middle East,' " 16 May 1979; *The Daily Yomiuri,* "Harry Kern's Story (9): Kishi's Comings and Goings," 15 September 1979. On the founding of Foreign Reports see Harvard University, *Harvard Class of 1935,* 726. On PR Japan see John Roberts, "Top Politicians Implicated in Grumman Hawkeye Payoff Scandal," *New Asia News,* 14 January 1959.

73. Kern to Kishi Nobusuke, 2 July 1956 in Kern to William Knowland, 5 July 1956, William Knowland Papers, Bancroft Library, Berkeley, Calif.

74. Kern to Allen Dulles, 3 June and 21 July 1955; Allen Dulles to Kern, 24 October 1962, Allen Dulles Papers, Princeton University Library, Princeton, N.J.; Kern to John Foster Dulles, 7 April and 10 December 1958; John Foster Dulles to Kern, 16 April and 18 November 1958, Dulles Papers; Kern to Knowland, 25 June, 7 August, 4 October 1956, and 9 April 1957, Knowland to Kern, 5, 16 July, 13 August 1956, and 16 April 1957, Knowland Papers.

75. *Far Eastern Economic Review,* 19 January 1979.

76. Grumman Corporation, Securities and Exchange Commission Form 8-K Current Report, 4 January 1979, 27–28.

77. *Asahi Shimbun,* 26 January 1979; *Japan Times,* 29 March 1979; and Ruth A. Cohen to John Roberts, 20 August 1980, in John Roberts to author, 25 September 1980.

78. Halliday and McCormick, *Japanese Imperialism Today;* Walter LaFeber, "Fifty-Year Flirtation: Our Illusory Affair with Japan," *The Nation,* 11 March 1968, 330–38; and John G. Roberts, "The Lockheed Affair," *Mainichi Daily News,* 11, 13, 15 March 1976.

6 WILLIAM H. DRAPER

1. Among the most important general histories of the Occupation focusing on "political reorientation" are Reischauer, *The United States and Japan,* and Kazuo Kawai, *Japan's American Interlude.* Important work on economic recovery and the "reverse course" in postwar Japan is that by Joyce and Gabriel Kolko, *The Limits of Power;* Dower, *Empire and Aftermath;* and Schaller, *The American Occupation of Japan.*

2. *Nippon Times,* 28 May 1948, 3; *New Republic,* 9 August 1948, 15; and *Newsweek,* 5 April 1948, 39.

3. U.S. House of Representatives, Committee on Appropriations, *Hearings on Foreign Aid Appropriations for 1949,* 80th Cong., 2d sess., 1948, 84; *Who's Who in America, 1948–49,* 680. See also the obituary in the *New York Times,* 27 December 1974.

4. Bruce Kuklick, *American Policy and the Division of Germany* (Ithaca: Cornell University Press, 1972), 187; see also John Gimbel, *The American Occupation of Germany: Politics and the Military 1945-1949* (Stanford: Stanford University Press, 1968).

5. Jerry N. Hess, *General William H. Draper, Jr., Oral History Interview* (transcript 11 January 1972), 47, Harry S. Truman Library, Independence, Mo. (hereafter cited as Draper Interview); and James Stewart Martin, *All Honorable Men* (Boston: Little, Brown, 1950), 176-77.

6. *New York Times,* 30 August 1947, 20 February 1949.

7. T. N. Dupuy Memo to General Lauris Norstad, "Report on Visit to Japan with Under Secretary of the Army," 6 October 1947, Draper/Japan File 091.

8. SWNCC 381, "Revival of the Japanese Economy, Study Presented by State Member, SWNCC," 22 July 1947, State-War-Navy Coordinating Committee Papers, Record Group 353, National Archives.

9. The importance of the European and Japanese recovery programs to the domestic, as well as to the foreign policy, objectives of American political and business leaders is amply documented in William A. Williams, *Tragedy of American Diplomacy,* rev. ed. (New York: Dell Publishing, 1962); Barton Bernstein, ed., *Politics and Policies of the Truman Administration* (Chicago: Quadrangle Books, 1970); Thomas G. Paterson, *Soviet-American Confrontation* (Baltimore: Johns Hopkins University Press, 1973); and Joyce and Gabriel Kolko, *The Limits of Power.*

10. Kenneth Royall Memo to William Draper, 24 September 1947, Records of the War Department and Special Staffs 014 Japan (1 September to 31 December 1947), Section 15, Record Group 165, National Archives (hereafter cited as WD, RG 165). The Zaibatsu dissolution problem Draper confronted grew out of the policy initiated by economic officers of the State Department, adopted as SWNCC 302 in 1946, and approved by the FEC in May 1947 as FEC-230. The controlling assumption behind FEC-230 was that the Zaibatsu system, not simply the ten major Zaibatsu families, was linked with the Japanese program of aggression and war. By dissolving the 67 holding companies and "deconcentrating" their 4,000 operating subsidiaries that exerted effective domination of 75 percent of Japanese business after the war, the proponents of FEC-230 hoped to create the conditions for a more competitive capitalism, allow for the growth of a middle class that would be the social base for democratic government, and thwart international price-fixing, output restrictions, and other cartel agreements. Bisson, *Zaibatsu Dissolution in Japan,* and Hadley, *Antitrust in Japan* are the major studies in English on the Zaibatsu dissolution question.

11. Draper Memo to Secretary Royall, 1 October 1947, Assistant Secretary of State Lot File, Box 3, DOS, RG 59 (hereafter A/S File with appropriate box number).

12. On Japan's reparations policy, see George H. Blakeslee, *The Far Eastern Commission,* State Department Publication 5138, Far Eastern Series 60 (Washington, D.C.: U.S. Government Printing Office, 1953); Jerome B. Cohen, *Japan's Postwar Economy* (Bloomington: Indiana University Press, 1958); and Bruce M. Brenn, "United States Reparations Policy toward Japan, September 1945 to May 1949," in Richard K. Beardsley, ed., *Studies in Japanese History and Politics* (Ann Arbor: University of Michigan, Center for Japanese Studies, 1967).

13. Charles Saltzman Memo to Robert A. Lovett, 5 February 1948, A/S File, Box 6, DOS, RG 59.

14. R. Burr Smith Memo to Charles Hodge, 17 October 1947, 740.00119PW, DOS, RG 59; Draper Memo to Secretary Royall, 1 October 1947, A/S File, Box 3, DOS, RG 59; and Dupuy Memo to General Norstad, "Report on Visit to Japan with Under Secretary of the Army," 6 October 1947, Draper/Japan File 091.

15. Draper Memo to Secretary Royall, 1 October 1947, A/S File, Box 3, DOS, RG 59; Draper Memo to MacArthur, 4 October 1947, Draper/Japan File 091.3.

16. Memorandum on SWNCC 381, 12 September 1947, A/S File, Box 6, DOS, RG 59; for a toned-down version of the Japanese government's contribution to inflation and the economic crisis see Edwin M. Martin, *The Allied Occupation of Japan* (Stanford: Stanford University Press, 1948), 96.

17. Charles E. Saltzman Memo to George C. Marshall, 9 October 1947 (draft not used), 894.50/10–947, DOS, RG 59; Whitman Memo to Charles L. Hodge, 20 October 1947, 740.00119PW/10–2047, DOS, RG 59. For Draper's influence in SWNCC, see Marshall Green Memo to John M. Allison, 3 May 1948, 740.00119PW/5–348, DOS, RG 59.

18. *FRUS,* 1947, 6:486–87.

19. John Lewis Gaddis, *Strategies of Containment: A Critical Appraisal of Postwar American National Security Policy,* (New York: Oxford University Press, 1982), 40. Kennan recalls in his memoirs that "as in the case of Europe, I did not suspect the Russians of any intention to launch an outright military attack [on Japan]. The greatest danger to the security of Japan lay, as I saw it, in the possibilities for intrigue, subversion and seizure of power by the Japanese Communists." Kennan, *Memoirs, 1925–1950,* 415.

20. Gaddis, *Strategies of Containment,* 34–51. Gaddis offers the most cogent exposition available of both the theory and implementation of the containment doctrine.

21. *FRUS,* 1947, 6:536–41.

22. Policy Planning Staff, Minutes, Meetings of 9, 10 September 1947, and Carlton Savage to Eugene Dooman, 8 September 1947, Policy Planning Staff Papers, Department of State Lot File 64D563, DOS, RG 59; *FRUS,* 1947, 6:542–43.

23. Minutes of Sixty-first Meeting, State-Army-Navy-Air Force Coordinating Committee, 23 October 1947, SWNCC Papers.

24. Roswell Whitman Memo to Emerson Ross, 11 March 1948, 894.50, DOS, RG 59; see also Far Eastern Subcommittee, SWNCC, *Interim Report on SWNCC 381 to Advisory Committee on Occupied Areas,* 12 September 1947, A/S File, Box 6, DOS, RG 59.

25. SCAP/ESS, *Economic Rehabilitation for Japan, South Korea, and the Ryukyu Islands,* 1947, Box 7692, Economic and Scientific Section Papers, SCAP Records (hereafter cited as ESS Papers, SCAP Records).

26. My understanding of the Eightieth Congress and foreign aid relies heavily on H. Bradford Westerfield, *Foreign Policy and Party Politics: Pearl Harbor to Korea* (New Haven: Yale University Press, 1955); Susan M. Hartmann, *Truman and the 80th Congress* (Columbia: University of Missouri Press, 1971); and Richard M. Freeland, *The Truman Doctrine and the Origins of McCarthyism: Foreign Policy, Domestic Politics, and Internal Security 1946–1948* (New York: Knopf, 1972).

27. William J. Sebald Memo to George Marshall, 10 February 1948, Box 2289, Tokyo Post Files, Record Group 84, National Archives Depository, Suitland, Md. (hereafter cited as Tokyo Post Files).

28. MacArthur to Department of the Army, 24 October 1947, Stimson Papers.

29. Millis, ed., *The Forrestal Diaries,* 328–29; James Forrestal, "Memorandum for Mr. Royall," 1 November 1947, James Forrestal Papers, Princeton University Library, Princeton, N.J.

30. Royall to MacArthur, 6 December 1947, CD 3-1-9, Records of the Office of the Secretary of Defense, Record Group 330, National Archives.

31. See chapter 5. There are several indications of the discreet collaboration between Kern and Draper. According to a summary of a letter dated 3 October 1948 from Kern to Draper regarding *Newsweek's* publication of an article on the Deconcentration Review Board, "Kern had decided to be guided by opinion of US/Army [that is, Under Secretary of the Army Draper] as to proper time to publish matter discussed w/ US/Army and would appreciate being advised when US/Army

Draper feels proper time has arrived." Office of the Under Secretary of the Army, Record Form, 3 October 1948, Draper/Japan File 010. Draper also lobbied in February 1949 for Army and State department officials to attend an ACJ sponsored dinner to discuss a report written by Kern that was highly critical of major aspects of the Occupation reform and economic policies. Despite appearing at the dinner as sharply offended by the Kern report, Draper privately considered it constructive. He described Kern as having "consistently supported our recovery program in Japan." Draper Memo to Royall, 10 February 1949, A/S File, Box 4, DOS, RG 59.

32. Rex E. Greaves, "Memorandum for File," 24 November 1947, Box 248, CAD/Japan File 014. Frank Wisner of the State Department and soon a close ally of Draper in establishing the covert action and foreign propaganda arm of the Central Intelligence Agency was in charge of coordinating a joint State Department/Pentagon response to the expected flurry of questioning upon the publication of the 1 December *Newsweek* article. Frank Wisner [?], Memorandum for the Files, 24 November 1947, 894.602/11-2447, DOS, RG 59.

33. *Newsweek*, 1 December 1947. (On the interaction of MacArthur's presidential ambitions with his handling of the FEC-230 controversy, see chapter 2); "Excerpts from Telephone Conversation between Honorable James Forrestal, Secretary of Defense and Mr. John Biggers," 5 December 1947, Draper/Japan File 091.3.

34. *Congressional Record*, 80th Cong., 1st sess., 19 December 1947, 93:9:11686–88. Kern maintained close ties with Knowland at least until 1955 and explained his role in providing FEC-230 to the senator in the memo from Kern to Eichelberger, 23 October 1949, Eichelberger Papers; see also Knowland Memo to Royall, 29 December 1947, enclosure in General Clark L. Ruffner Memo to Draper, 27 February 1948, Draper/Japan File 091.3.

35. *FRUS*, 1947, 6:435–37, 441–42; Edwin Martin Memo to Charles Saltzman, 30 October 1947, 740.00119 Control (Japan) 10–3047, DOS, RG 59; Lovett Memo to Draper, 13 January 1948, A/S File, Box 6, DOS, RG 59; and *FRUS*, 1949, 6:945–46.

36. Frank McCoy to Ross Whitman, 10 December 1947, Frank McCoy Papers, Library of Congress.

37. Royall's speech is reproduced in Jon Livingston, Joe Moore, and Felicia Oldfather, eds., *The Japan Reader, Postwar Japan, 1945 to the Present* (New York: Pantheon Books, 1973), 116–19.

38. Ibid.

39. *FRUS*, 1948, 6:654–56.

40. Frank Wisner Memo to Charles Saltzman, 2 February 1948; and Noel Hemmendinger Memo to Charles Saltzman, 9 February 1948, A/S File, Box 4, DOS, RG 59; Overseas Consultants Inc., "Report on Industrial Reparations Survey of Japan to the United States of America" (New York, typescript, 1948); see also Brenn, "United States Reparations Policy toward Japan," 91.

41. *PRJ* 2:778–79.

42. *Congressional Record*, 80th Cong., 2d sess., 19 January, 7 February 1948, 94:1:298–301, 1362–64; *PRJ* 2:783.

43. Bisson, *Zaibatsu Dissolution in Japan*, 142.

44. *FRUS*, 1948, 1:2:523–26; Kennan, *Memoirs, 1925–1950*, 401–2; and Wisner to Frank McCoy, 19 March 1948, 740.00119/3–1948, DOS, RG 59.

45. Schaller, *The American Occupation of Japan*, 173, 315–16.

46. *FRUS*, 1948, 6:697–706; Kennan, *Memoirs, 1925–1950*, 404–6.

47. *FRUS*, 1948, 6: 691–98.

48. Ibid. 727–36. This is a detailed critique of Kennan's report by Charles Saltzman, Assistant Secretary of State for Occupied Areas.

49. "Memorandum of Conversation," 13 February 1948, Miscellaneous Papers, Draper

/Japan File 010.

50. "Report of Conference on Mr. Strike's Visit to the Far East," 1 December 1947, Draper/Japan File 387.6; and "Memorandum of Conversation," 13 February 1948, Miscellaneous Papers, Draper/Japan File 010.

51. SCAP Memo to Department of Army, 24 February 1948, SCAP Records in Dower Collection; and Bisson, *Zaibatsu Dissolution in Japan,* 144. The members of the Review Board were Chairman Joseph V. Robinson, of the Robinson Connector Company, New York; Roy S. Campbell, president and general manager of the New York Shipbuilding Corporation; Edward J. Burger, vice-president of the Central Banking Company of Lorain, Ohio; Walter R. Hutchinson, former special assistant to the United States attorney general; and Bryon D. Woodside of the Securities and Exchange Commission.

52. Royall Memo to Robert Lovett, 18 December 1947, enclosure in Hugh Borton Memo to James Penfield, 26 February 1948, and Walton Butterworth Memo to Hugh Borton, 27 February 1948, 740.00119/2–2748, DOS, RG 59.

53. Freeland, *The Truman Doctrine and the Origins of McCarthyism,* 264–68.

54. House of Representatives, Committee on Appropriations, *Hearings on Foreign Aid Appropriations for 1949,* 80th Cong., 2d sess., 11 May 1948, 87.

55. Frank Wisner Memo to George Marshall, 16 March 1948, 740.00119 Control (Japan)/3–1648, DOS, RG 59.

56. Jerome B. Cohen, *Japan's Economy in War and Reconstruction* (Minneapolis: University of Minnesota Press, 1949), 479–92. Of Japan's $452 million total aid requirements from all sources in the first year of the Green Book plan, $231 million was for textile fibers, mostly cotton. Textile exports were expected to grow from about $200 million in FY 1949 (67 percent of total exports) to around $900 million in FY 1953 (57 percent of total exports). See William J. Sebald Memo to George Marshall, 10 February 1948, Tokyo Post Files.

57. Draper Memo to Edgar Nourse, 10 March 1948, Draper/Japan File 423.

58. William Jacobs Memo to Draper, 18, 27 October 1947; Scheuer Memo to William Draper, 13 February 1948, Draper/Japan File 423.

59. Ray J. Laux Memo to Lt. Col. Hartman, 8 March 1948; Alice G. Bests Memo to Draper, 5 March 1948 with enclosure; Scheuer Memo to Peter A. McDermott, 5 March 1948; and Scheuer Memo to William C. Baker, 8 March 1948, all from Draper/Japan File 423.

60. Paul Cleveland Memo to Daniel Noce, 12 September 1947, Box 5977, Chief/ESS Papers, SCAP Records; Daniel Noce Memo to Draper, 16 December 1947, Draper/Japan File 423. The Gold Pot was a cache of around $137 million of gold and other precious metals looted by the Japanese during the war and, by FEC decision, held in SCAP custody until returned to claimant nations as reparations.

61. Paul Cleveland Memo to Daniel Noce, 15 March 1948, Dower Collection.

62. "Memorandum of Conference," 7 May 1948, Box 5979, Chief/ESS Papers, SCAP Records. In addition to Eastland and Knowland, the other "cotton senators" were Burnet Maybank (D-SC), John Sparkman (D-AL), and James Kern (R-MO).

63. *Nippon Times,* 27 March 1948, 2; U.S. Senate, Committee on Agriculture and Forestry, *Providing a Revolving Fund for the Purchase of Agricultural Commodities and Raw Materials to Be Processed in Occupied Areas and Sold, Report 1099,* 80th Cong., 2d sess., 1948. This proposal called for a 2½ percent interest rate compared to 3½ percent demanded by the New York bankers in negotiations over the OJEIRF backed loan.

64. "Candidates for Economic Mission to Japan," n.d., Draper/Japan File 010; *New York Times,* 7 April 1948, 4; see Frank Wisner Memo to Lovett, 26 February 1948, 740.00119 control (Japan) and Robert F. Loree Memo to Lovett, 5 March 1948, 611.9431, DOS, RG 59; Report of Conference held in Draper's office, "Foreign Investments in Occupied Areas, Particularly

Japan," 10 August 1948, Draper/Japan File 004.

65. Draper Interview, 55.

66. Sir Alvory Gascoigne Memo to Foreign Office, 6 April, 21 May 1948, FO 371/F5237/662/23 and FO 371/F7999/662/23. For reactions to Draper by other SCAP officials see Cohen, *Remaking Japan*, 401-13.

67. Wisner Memo to George Marshall, 16 March 1948, 740.00119 (Control) Japan/3-1648, DOS, RG 59; *FRUS*, 1948, 6:706-9.

68. Dupuy Memo to Draper, 31 March 1948, Draper/Japan File 091; *New York Times*, 29 March 1948, 5; 11 April 1948, 22; and T. N. Dupuy, "Memorandum for Record, Conference between Under Secretary Draper and Prime Minister Ashida," 25 March 1948, Draper/Japan File 091.

69. Bisson, *Zaibatsu Dissolution in Japan*, 142-43; Charles Hodge Memo to Roswell Whitman, 1 April 1948, 740.00119PW/4-148, DOS, RG 59.

70. Percy Johnston et al., "Report on the Economic Position and Prospects of Japan and Korea and the Measures Required to Improve Them," Washington, D.C., 26 April 1948, 11, Dodge Papers (hereafter cited as Johnston Committee Report.)

71. *FRUS*, 1948, 6:710; Hodge Memo to Whitman, 1 April 1948, 740.00119PW/4-148, DOS, RG 59.

72. Johnston Committee Report, 14. The following table illustrates the extent of the reparations changes recommended by the Draper Mission:

Recommended Removals for Reparations
(In millions of 1939 yen)

	SWNCC 236/43 (April 1947)	Overseas Consultants (February 1948)	Johnston Committee (April 1948)
Industry total	990	172	102
Primary War Facilities	1,476	1,476	560
Grand Total	2,466	1,648	662

Source: Cohen, *Japan's Economy in War and Reconstruction*, 425. Cohen incorrectly identifies SWNCC 236/43 figures with those in the Pauley Report.

73. Dupuy, "Memorandum for the Record, Conference between Under Secretary Draper and Prime Minister Ashida," 25 March 1948, Draper/Japan File 091.

74. Draper Memo to MacArthur, 22 November 1948 (draft, not used), Draper/Japan File 091.3.

75. *Nippon Times*, 25 March 1948,1; Dupuy, "Memorandum for the Record, Conference between Under Secretary Draper and Prime Minister Ashida," 25 March 1948, Draper/Japan File 091; and Theodore Cohen, "Memorandum of Conference, Private Business and Investment in Japan," 30 March 1948, Box 5977, Chief/ESS Papers, SCAP Records.

76. Dupuy, "Memorandum for the Record, Conference between Under Secretary Draper and Prime Minister Ashida," 25 March 1948, Draper/Japan File 091.

77. Schaller, *The American Occupation of Japan*, 141-42.

78. Borden, *The Pacific Alliance*, 108-11. S. C. Brown, Memorandum on Economic Implementation of U.S. Policy with Respect to the Far East, 27 December 1948, 894.50/12-2748, DOS, RG 59.

79. Johnston Committee Report, 21-22.

80. *New York Times*, 27 March 1948, 6.

81. The almost unanimous international opposition to the "reverse course" policies initiated by Washington is seen in Dower, "Occupied Japan and the American Lake, 1945-1950," 183-92. The many reports in State Department records from China, Australia, and the Philippines in 1948 and 1949 attacking the rehabilitation of Japan are particularly bitter.

82. Department of the Army, "Record Form," 15 April 1948, Draper/Japan File 091.

83. Draper Memo to Knowland, 29 April 1948, Draper/Japan File 010; Draper Memo to MacArthur, 28 April 1948, Box 6721, ESS Papers, SCAP Records.

84. U.S. House of Representatives, Committee on Appropriations, *Hearings on Foreign Aid Appropriations for 1949*, 80th Cong., 2d sess., 11, 13 May 1948, 84-170.

85. Draper Memo to MacArthur, 12 May 1948, Box 6721, ESS Papers, SCAP Records; and U.S. House of Representatives, *Revision of Appropriation Language for the Civil Functions, Department of the Army*, 80th Cong., 2d sess., 19 May 1948, H. Doc. 659.

86. *New York Times*, 20 May 1948, 13; and William H. Draper, "Japan's Key Position in the Far East," 17 May 1948, Dower Collection.

87. *New York Times*, 4 June 1948; and U.S. Senate, Committee on Appropriations, *Hearings on Economic Cooperation Administration*, 80th Cong., 2d sess., 1948, 572-78.

88. Hubert A. Graves Memo to D. F. MacDermot, 25 June 1948, FO 371/F9139/1230/23. Graves carefully untangles the complex history of EROA legislation in the Eightieth Congress. For the overall aid program, see Westerfield, *Foreign Policy and Party Politics*, 287-90.

89. U.S. Senate, Committee on Appropriations, *Hearings on Foreign Aid Appropriation Bill, 1950*, 81st Cong., 1st sess., 29 June 1949, 789.

90. Dick K. Nanto, "The United States' Role in the Postwar Economic Recovery of Japan," (Ph.D. diss.; Harvard University, 1976), 45-89. The only published study on American aid to Japan during the Occupation is by William Adams Brown, Jr., and Redvers Opie, *American Foreign Assistance* (Washington, D.C.: Brookings Institute, 1953), chapter 12. It is useful but not reliable.

91. William P. Jacobs Memo to William Marquat, 17 April 1948, Box 5977, Chief/ESS Papers, SCAP Records.

92. U.S. Senate, Committee on Agriculture and Forestry, *Hearings on Revolving Fund for the Purchase of Agricultural Commodities*, 80th Cong., 2d sess. 1948; *Congressional Record*, 80th Cong., 2d sess., 22 April, 10 May 1948, 94:4:4739-43, 5551, 5553; and Abe Kojiro, *The Story of the Japanese Cotton Textile Industry* (Osaka: All Japan Cotton Spinners' Association, 1957), 8.

93. Daniel Noce Memo to MacArthur, 22 April 1948; Frank E. Pickelle Memo to William Marquat, 27 April 1948, Dower Collection.

94. Kojiro, *The Story of the Japanese Cotton Textile Industry*, 8; SCAP, *History of the Non-Military Activities of the Occupation*, "Textile Industries," 48:53, SCAP Records.

95. Draper Memo to Daniel Noce, 23 June 1948, WD, RG 165.

96. Draper Memo on PPS 28/2, n.d. ca. 1 June 1948, Draper/Japan File 091.3.

97. Bisson, *Zaibatsu Dissolution in Japan*, 147-48. There are many documents on the reparations deadlock in the State and Army departments' records. In summary, after much internal debate, the State Department refused to alter its support for SWNCC 236/43, despite pressure from Draper to adopt the Johnston Report's levels. But in June 1948 SCAP cabled him to support the Army's rather than the State Department's approach. When the State Department hedged on adopting the Army Department's retention levels for shipbuilding, iron and steel, and private munitions plants, the issue was sent to the National Security Council (NSC). At its October 1948 meeting the NSC threw the issue back to the State and Army departments. Kennan and Draper were appointed by their respective departments to reach a final compromise which took several more months. The final result was approved as NSC 13/3 on 6 May 1949 and read by General Frank McCoy to the FEC on 9 May 1949.

98. *FRUS*, 1948, 6:860. In his memoirs Kennan fails to mention Draper at all and focuses exclusively upon NSC 13/2. Kennan, *Memoirs, 1925–1950*, 381–93.

99. Roger Dingman, "Strategic Planning and the Policy Process: American Plans for War in East Asia, 1945–1950," *Naval War College Review* 32, 6 (November-December 1979): 11–13.

100. *FRUS*, 1948, 6:858–59.

101. "Program for a Self-Supporting Japanese Economy," November 1948, Box 8361, ESS Papers, SCAP Records.

102. Draper Memo to Yoshida Shigeru, 16 May 1950; and Draper Memo to MacArthur, 19 May 1950, in Dower Collection; Draper Memo to Ikeda Hayato, 24 October 1950; and Draper Memo to Marquat, 24 October 1950, Box 5977; and W. John Logan Memo to Marquat, 14 February 1950, Box 7502, in Chief/ESS Papers, SCAP Records.

103. William H. Draper, "The Rising Sun of Japan," Address to the Thirty-seventh Convention of the National Foreign Trade Council, 31 October 1950, Dower Collection.

7 JOSEPH M. DODGE

1. *Economist* (London), 16 April 1949, 709.

2. *New York Times*, 3 December 1964; and General Headquarters Far East Command, Public Information Office, Information Bulletin, "Biography: Joseph M. Dodge, Financial Advisor to SCAP with the personal rank of Minister," 31 January 1949, MacArthur Papers.

3. Ibid.

4. Dodge to MacArthur, 13 June 1949, MacArthur Papers.

5. Dodge to Nakashima Kumakichi, 30 April 1952, Dodge Papers. Dodge took special interest in promoting a major investment scheme for a Tokyo office building, hotel, and Japanese internal airline put forward by Juan Trippe, president of Pan American Airlines and a member, along with Dodge, of the board of directors of Chrysler Corporation. See Dodge to Marquat, 10 June 1949, Dodge Papers.

6. Dodge to Marquat, 29 May 1951, Matthew B. Ridgway Papers, U.S. Army Military History Institute, Carlisle Barracks, Pa.

7. Dodge to Marquat, 1 June 1949, MacArthur Papers; Dodge diary, 23 February 1949; Kano Hisaakira to Dodge, 25 April 1949; Dodge to Kano Hisaakira, 27 July 1950, 13 May 1952, all in Dodge Papers. For a sketch of Kano see Cohen, *Remaking Japan*, 182–83.

8. "Minutes of Budget Meeting with ESS," 14 March 1949, Dodge Papers; see Joyce and Gabriel Kolko, *The Limits of Power*, 522–24.

9. Dodge diary, 23 February 1949, Dodge Papers; and *Fortune*, "Mister Dodge," June 1948, 120.

10. Warren Hunsberger, *Japan and the United States in World Trade*, (New York: Harper and Row, 1964), 106.

11. William Borden, "International Trade Policy Under the Occupation," (unpublished seminar paper, University of Wisconsin, February 1974), 13.

12. Joseph Dodge, "The Role of Japan in our Relations With the Orient," July 1949, Dodge Papers. This speech was cleared by the State and Army departments and according to Dodge's assistant Ralph Reid, all "parties are enthusiastic as to value." See Reid to Dodge, 9 July 1949, Dodge Papers.

13. Cohen, *Japan's Economy in War and Reconstruction*, 418–48; and Martin Bronfenbrenner, "Four Positions on Japanese Finance," *Journal of Political Economy* 43, 4 (August 1950): 281–86.

14. Dower, *Empire and Aftermath,* 342.

15. Draper Memo to MacArthur, 22 November 1948 (draft not used), Draper/Japan File 091.3.

16. NAC meeting, 21 June 1948, Records of the National Advisory Council on International Financial and Monetary Affairs, National Archives (hereafter NAC Files).

17. Draper to MacArthur, 25 June 1948, Box 5981, Chief/ESS Papers, SCAP Records.

18. MacArthur to Draper, 29 June 1948, Draper/Japan Files 732. This message was prepared primarily by General Marquat. See Marquat to MacArthur, ca. 15 June 1945, Box 5981, Chief/ESS Files, SCAP Records.

19. NAC meeting, 28 June 1948, NAC Files.

20. Draper to MacArthur, 22 November 1948 (draft not used), Draper/Japan Files 091.3. Among those Draper asked to be financial advisor to SCAP were Allen Sproul, head of the FRB branch in New York, Warren R. Burgess, a member of the FRB from New York, and Thomas McCabe, president of Scott Paper Company.

21. Ralph W. E. Reid, Memorandum on Japanese Recovery Program, 23 November 1948, and Memorandum for Record, 15 November 1948, Draper/Japan Files 091.3.

22. NAC meeting, 3 December 1948, NAC Files.

23. The "Nine-Point Program" is most easily found in "Statement of the United States Government," 10 December 1948, *FRUS,* 1948, 6:1059–60. The nine points were: 1) Achieve a true balance in the consolidated budget; 2) Accelerate and strengthen the program of tax collection; 3) Assure rigorous limitation of credit extension to projects contributing to economic recovery; 4) Establish an effective program to achieve wage stability; 5) Strengthen the existing price control programs; 6) Improve the operation of foreign trade controls; 7) Improve the allocation and rationing system, particularly to the end of maximizing exports; 8) Increase production of all indigenous raw material and manufactured products; and 9) Improve efficiency of the food collection program. The directive also gave the target date for the establishment of a single exchange rate not later than three months after the initiation of the stabilization program.

24. *Fortune,* "Two Billion Dollar Failure," April 1949, 67.

25. Dodge, Memorandum to Cleveland Thurber, 13 December 1948, Dodge Papers.

26. Dodge to Draper, 3 January 1949, Draper/Japan Files 091.

27. Dodge, Notes on Conference of Dodge Mission with ESS, 9 February 1949, Dodge Papers.

28. Dodge, Memorandum of Meeting with Minister Ikeda, 15 April 1949, Dodge Papers; Tsuru, *Essays on the Japanese Economy,* 6; and Dodge, Diary of Trip, 26 February 1949, Dodge Papers.

29. Dodge to Tracy Voorhees, 23 March 1949, Dodge Papers; William Sebald to Dean Acheson, 26 March 1949, Box 7102, Tokyo Post Files. Dodge listed four reasons why the 1949 budget appeared so much larger than the 1948 budget when, in fact, it represented a "relative decrease in total expenditures": 1.) It was a consolidated budget; 2.) it was on a higher inflation level than in 1948; 3.) items appearing in the budget the first time were previously obscured in other government records; and 4.) it included many inter-account transfers, namely items appearing in the disbursement side of one account and the revenue side of another. See Dodge to Voorhees, 7 April 1949, Dodge Papers.

30. Nanto, "The United States' Role in the Postwar Economic Recovery of Japan," 225; *Oriental Economist,* 9 April 1949.

31. Chalmers Johnson, *Conspiracy at Matsukawa,* (Berkeley: University of California Press, 1972), 50–89; see also Farley, *Aspects of Japan's Labor Problems,* 229–30.

32. Nanto, "The United States' Role in the Postwar Recovery of Japan," 226; Benjamin C. Duke, *Japan's Militant Teachers: A History of the Left-Wing Teachers' Movement* (Honolulu:

East-West Center, University of Hawaii Press, 1973), 86.

33. Nanto, "The United States' Role in the Postwar Economic Recovery of Japan," 223.

34. *Nippon Times,* 21 February 1949, 2; Bronfenbrenner, "Four Positions on Japanese Finance," 284; and Dodge, Summary of Meeting with Finance Minister Ikeda, 25 March 1949, Dodge Papers.

35. Dodge to Marquat, 20 September 1949, Dodge Papers.

36. Marquat to Department of Army, 9 August 1949, Box 5981, Chief/ESS Papers, SCAP Records.

37. Nanto, "The United States' Role in Postwar Economic Recovery of Japan," 233–45.

38. Marquat to Department of Army, 9 August 1949, Box 5981, Chief/ESS Papers, SCAP Records.

39. Dodge, Memorandum on Foreign Exchange Rate, 30 March 1949, Dodge Papers.

40. Nanto, "The United States' Role in Postwar Economic Recovery of Japan," 255–57.

41. Department of State, Office of Intelligence Research, Report 4938 (pv), "Political Repercussions of the Economic Stabilization Program in Japan," 19 April 1949, DOS, RG 59.

42. W. Walton Butterworth, Memorandum on Political Situation in Japan, 20 June 1949, 894.00/6-2049, DOS, RG 59.

43. Dodge, Memorandum of Meeting with Finance Minister Ikeda, 25 March 1949, Dodge Papers.

44. Soong H. Kil, "The Dodge Line and the Japanese Conservative Party," (Ph.D. diss.; University of Michigan, 1977), 139.

45. Dodge, Memorandum of Meeting with Party Leaders, 26 March 1949; and Diary of Trip, 23 February 1949, Dodge Papers.

46. Dodge, Memorandum on Meeting with Budget Committee of the HOR of the Diet, 16 April 1949, Dodge Papers.

47. Cole, Totten, and Uyehara, *Socialist Parties in Postwar Japan,* 25–31; see also Department of State, Office of Intelligence Research, Report 4938 (pv), "Political Repercussions of the Economic Stabilization program in Japan," 19 April 1949, DOS, RG 59.

48. Robert Scalapino, *The Japanese Communist Movement, 1920–1966* (Berkeley: University of California Press, 1967), 72–73; and Colbert, *The Left Wing in Japanese Politics,* 286.

49. Dodge, Memorandum on Meeting with Budget Committee of the HOR of the Diet, 16 April 1949, Dodge Papers; and *Economist* (London), 16 April 1949, 709.

50. Dodge to Robert West, 13 April 1949; and Marquat to Dodge, 11 September 1949, Dodge Papers.

51. Duke, *Japan's Militant Teachers,* 86; and Joseph Dodge, Notes on Meeting with Budget Committee of House of Representatives of Diet, 16 April 1949, Dodge Papers.

52. *Nippon Times,* 16 April 1949, 1; see also Department of State, "Special Report on American Opinion, Japan and Korea," 22 April 1949, Eichelberger Papers.

53. *Nippon Times,* 18 April 1949, 2.

54. Dodge, Memorandum on Possible Post-Budget Problems, 21 April 1949; and Marquat to Dodge, 19 April 1949, Dodge Papers.

55. Dodge to Harold Moss, 16 August 1949, Dodge Papers; and Economic Stabilization Board, "Stabilization and Reconstruction," 9 March 1949, 7–27, Dower Collection.

56. Dodge to Harold Moss, 16 August 1949, Dodge Papers.

57. *Oriental Economist,* 2 April, 25 June, 27 August 1949.

58. Ralph Reid to Robert West, 22 June 1949, Dodge Papers. Dodge had edited this letter before it was sent.

59. Dick Nanto, "The Dodge Line: The Control of Inflation in Occupied Japan," (unpublished manuscript, 1974), 27. Dodge is quoted on inflation in Cohen, *Remaking of Japan,* 437.

60. Department of State, *Public Relations Aspects of the Economic Stabilization Program in Japan,* 13 June 1949, and Dodge to Ralph W. E. Reid, 31 August 1949, Dodge Papers.

61. Dodge to Hayato Ikeda, 9 August 1949, and Dodge to Marquat, 9 September 1949, Dodge Papers.

62. Blum, *Drawing the Line,* 214–20; Michael Schaller, "Securing the Great Crescent: Occupied Japan and the Origins of Containment in Southeast Asia," *Journal of American History* 69, 2 (September 1982): 393; and Dodge to Marquat, 29 June 1949, Dodge Papers.

63. SCAP, *History of the Nonmilitary Activities of the Occupation of Japan,* "Foreign Trade," 50:208, SCAP Records. This study includes a "chronology of U.S. Policies for Japanese Foreign Trade 1945–1951."

64. Borden, *The Pacific Alliance,* 95–98.

65. *New York Times,* 21 November 1949, 2; and *Oriental Economist,* 5 November 1949, 1079–80. Dodge's support at home also weakened. Under Secretary of the Army Tracy Voorhees thought that the stringent measures of the spring of 1949 might not be necessary. "I should like to see the economic patient returned to performance of useful duties . . . . I am not sure, however, that Joe [Dodge] is fully prepared to discharge his patient . . . putting him back to work for objectives . . . more important than the economy itself." Voorhees to MacArthur, 22 October 1949, Voorhees Papers.

66. Nanto, "The United States' Role in Postwar Economic Recovery of Japan," 92; and William Sebald to Dean Acheson, 28 November 1949, Tokyo Post Files.

67. Dodge, Statement before National Advisory Council Staff Committee, 12 January 1950; and Marquat to Dodge, 26 February 1950, Dodge Papers.

68. Tracy Voorhees, "Outline of Work as Under Secretary of the Army," unpublished manuscript, 22 March 1962, 61–69, Voorhees Papers; and Voorhees, "NSC Policy Paper on Asia," 10 January 1950, enclosure in NSC 61/1, "Coordination of U.S. Aid Programs for Far Eastern Areas," 16 May 1950, National Security Council Papers, National Archives; see also Schaller, "Securing the Great Crescent," 405–13.

69. Voorhees to MacArthur, 6 April 1950, Voorhees Papers.

70. Dodge to Hoffman, 25 February 1949, Draper/Japan Files 091; and Advisory Committee on Fiscal and Monetary Problems (to the Economic Cooperation Administration), Minutes of Meeting, 28 April 1950, Dodge Papers.

71. Bank of Japan, *Quarterly Review,* January-March 1950, 6–8; Economic Stabilization Board, "On the Promotion of Trade between Japan and Asia," 18 April 1950, Dower Collection; *Asahi* newspaper quote in Borden, *Pacific Alliance,* 99.

72. Department of State, Office of Intelligence Research, Report 5247, "Japanese Political Trends Affecting U.S. Position in Japan, 23 May 1950," DOS, RG 59.

73. *Nippon Times,* 5 March 1950.

74. Farley, *Aspects of Japan's Labor Problems,* 227–39.

75. Department of State, Office of Intelligence Research, Report 5247, "Japanese Political Trends Affecting U.S. Position in Japan, 23 May 1950," DOS, RG 59.

76. Dodge to Martin Bronfenbrenner, 12 June 1950, Dodge Papers.

77. *Oriental Economist,* "One Year of the Dodge Plan (1)," 6 May 1950, 404–6.

78. Edna E. Ehrlich and Frank M. Tamagna, "Japan," in Benjamin Berkhart, ed., *Banking Systems* (New York: Columbia University Press, 1954), 531–39.

79. Dodge, Memorandum of Meeting with Mr. Ichimada, Governor of Bank of Japan, 1 April 1949, and Dodge, Memorandum of Meeting with Mr. Ichimada, 12 April 1949, Dodge Papers.

80. Marquat to Dodge, 4 June 1950; and Dodge to Count Kano Hisaakira, 27 July 1950, Dodge Papers. Kano was chairman of the board of directors of the Hakodate Dock Company of Tokyo.

81. Redford, *The Occupation of Japan: Economic Policy and Reform,* 83.

82. Department of State, Office of Intelligence Research, Report 5247, "Japanese Political Trends Affecting U.S. Position in Japan, 23 May 1950," DOS, RG 59.

83. Tsuru, *Essays on Japanese Economy,* 45.

84. Dodge to Eva Alexander, 12 July 1950; and Dodge to Colonel S. L. A. Marshall, 29 August 1950, Dodge Papers.

85. Dodge to Marquat, 17 July 1950, Dodge Papers.

86. Ibid., 21 August 1950.

87. Dodge, Arrival Press Statement, 7 October 1950, Dodge Papers.

88. Dodge, Memorandum of Meeting with Mr. Ikeda, 25 October 1950, Dodge Papers.

89. Borden, *Pacific Alliance,* 148.

90. Dodge, Memorandum of Meeting with Mr. Ikeda, 25 October 1950, Dodge Papers.

91. Dodge, Conference, Joseph Dodge-Governor Ichimada, Bank of Japan, 30 November 1950, Dodge Papers; and Nanto, "The United States' Role in the Postwar Economic Recovery of Japan," 282.

92. Tsuru, *Essays on Japanese Economy,* 17–18; and Cohen, *Japan's Postwar Economy,* 89–94.

93. William Marquat to Department of the Army, 12 April 1951, Box 5983, Chief/ESS Papers, SCAP Records.

94. Borden, *Pacific Alliance,* 143–65; SCAP, ESS, Programs and Statistics Division, "Japan's Industrial Potential," 2, 20 February 1951, Dower Collection. This JIP report, as it was called, assumed that if Japan's sizable industrial capacity remained idle "by reason of exclusion from available military export markets, the probability of attractive offers by the Communist area after the peace treaty is not entirely remote. Under the capitalistic system the profit motive is difficult to control." JIP went on to argue that Japan "can produce ammunition of almost any type" from light machine guns to tanks at about the same cost as in the U.S. "Japan's chemical industry is outstanding in that it can produce virtually any type of material required in chemical warfare . . . there are facilities for producing war-ship hulls and engines."

95. Borden, *Pacific Alliance,* 154–55.

96. Dodge to Marquat, 13 July 1951, Dodge Papers; *Oriental Economist,* 29 March 1952.

97. Frank Pace, Jr., to Dodge, 16 July 1949, Dodge Papers.

98. Joseph Dodge to Marquat, 12 September 1951, with enclosure Dodge to Ikeda Hayato, n.d., Ridgway Papers.

99. Cited in Dower, *Empire and Aftermath,* 420.

100. Dodge to Kaufman T. Keller, 9 November 1951, Dodge Papers; and Joseph Dodge, Memorandum of Meeting with Foreign Exchange Control Board, 23 November 1951, Ridgway Papers.

101. William Marquat to Ridgway, 19 November 1951, enclosure "Japanese Security Force Issues in the JFY 1952–1953 Budget," Ridgway Papers.

102. Joseph Dodge, "Memorandum on Preliminary Meeting on JFY 1952 Budget," 22 November 1951, Ridgway Papers.

103. Ibid.

104. Joseph Dodge, Statement to Press, 27 November 1951, Ridgway Papers; and Dodge to Jerome Cohen, 8 January 1952, Dodge Papers.

105. Dodge, "Japan: Post-treaty Relationship," 17 January 1952, Dodge Papers.

106. Economic Stabilization Board, "Establishment of a Viable Economy and Promotion of Economic Cooperation," 12 February 1952, Dodge Papers.

107. SCAP, ESS, Programs and Statistics Division, "Japanese Industrial Potential," 3, 21 February 1952, Dower Collection.

108. Department of State, Office of Public Information, "Summary of Japanese Press Reaction to Appointment of Joseph Dodge as Consultant to Secretary of State," 24 August 1952, Dodge Papers; and Dower, "Occupied Japan as History and Occupation History as Politics," 63.

109. Cited in Borden, *Pacific Alliance,* 175.

110. *New York Times,* 3 December 1964.

111. Cited in Nanto, "The United States' Role in the Postwar Recovery of Japan," 293–94.

112. Borden, *Pacific Alliance,* 214–19.

8 JOHN FOSTER DULLES

1. U.S. Senate, Committee on Foreign Relations, *Hearings on Treaty of Mutual Cooperation and Security with Japan,* 86th Cong., 2d sess., 1960, 10. For Japanese criticism of original security treaty see Packard, *Protest in Tokyo,* 12–31.

2. Haruhiro Fukui, *Party in Power: The Japanese Liberal-Democrats and Policy-making* (Berkeley: University of California Press, 1970), 227–51.

3. Reischauer, *The United States and Japan,* 330–31; Ward, "The Legacy of the Occupation," in Herbert Passin, ed., *The United States and Japan,* (Englewood Cliffs, N.J.: Prentice-Hall, 1966), 51–54.

4. Dower, "The Eye of the Beholder: Background Notes on the U.S.-Japan Military Relationship," 15–31; and Michael Yoshitsu, *Japan and the San Francisco Peace Settlement* (New York: Columbia University Press, 1983), 67–100.

5. Ronald W. Pruessen, *John Foster Dulles: The Road to Power* (New York: Free Press, 1982), 1–177.

6. Yergin, *Shattered Peace,* 226–310.

7. Pruessen, *John Foster Dulles,* 355–403, 432–38.

8. Acheson, *Present at the Creation,* 344–45.

9. John Foster Dulles, *War or Peace* (New York: Macmillan, 1950), 224–32; Vandenberg to Acheson, 31 March 1950, Dulles Papers.

10. *FRUS,* 1949, 7:774–75.

11. Ibid., 775–77.

12. "Policy Planning Staff Comments on NSC 49" 28 June, 1949, Department of State Lot File 64D563, DOS, RG 59; see also Gaddis, *Strategies of Containment,* 77–79.

13. *FRUS,* 1949, 7:871–73.

14. Ibid.

15. "Draft Treaty of Peace with Japan," in Robert Fearey to John Allison, 14 October 1949, 740.0011 p.w. (peace)/10–1449, DOS, RG 59; and Schaller, *The American Occupation of Japan,* 171.

16. *FRUS,* 1949, 7:922–23.

17. Schaller, *The American Occupation of Japan,* 176; and Blum, *Drawing the Line,* 160–77.

18. Shinobu Seizaburo, "The Korean War as an Epoch of Contemporary History," *Developing Economics* 4 (March 1966): 26–27.

19. Weinstein, *Japan's Postwar Defense Policy,* 24–25; and Dower, *Empire and Aftermath,* 374.

20. *FRUS,* 1950, 6:1194–98.

21. Ibid., 1207–9.

22. Ibid., 1210–12.

23. Dulles memorandum, 18 May 1950, Dulles Papers. Dean Rusk presented this memorandum verbatim to Acheson on 30 May 1950. See *FRUS,* 1950, 6:349–50.

24. H. Alexander Smith diary, 24 May 1950, Smith Papers; *New York Times,* 22 June 1950, 18.

25. *New York Times,* 20 June 1950.

26. *FRUS,* 1950, 6:1213–21.

27. Sebald and Brines, *With MacArthur in Japan,* 252–53.

28. *FRUS,* 1950, 6:1227–28.

29. Joint Chiefs of Staff, "Memorandum for the Secretary of Defense," 1 March 1949, in NSC 44, "Limited Military Armament for Japan," National Security Council Papers, National Archives.

30. John B. Howard, "Memorandum for the Files: Max Bishop's Views on the Japanese Peace Treaty," 740.0011 pw (peace)/11–1449, DOS, RG 59; and "Address by John Foster Dulles at Luncheon of Tokyo American Chamber of Commerce, June 22, 1950," Dulles Papers.

31. *FRUS,* 1950, 6:1232; Yoshitsu, *Japan and the San Francisco Peace Settlement,* 41; and *FRUS,* 1950, 6:1232; Yoshida Shigeru interview, Dulles Oral History Project, Princeton University Library, Princeton, N.J. (hereafter cited as DOHP).

32. *FRUS,* 1950, 6:1232–33.

33. Ambrose, *Rise to Globalism,* 170–75; and John Allison, *Ambassador from the Prairie, or Allison Wonderland* (Boston: Houghton Mifflin, 1973), 139.

34. *FRUS,* 1950, 6:1259–61, and 1264–65.

35. Ibid., 1279–80, 1288–90, and 1293–96.

36. Ibid., 1304.

37. Ibid., 1293–96.

38. Ibid., 1231; and Dower, *Empire and Aftermath,* 365–66.

39. *FRUS,* 1950, 6:1263.

40. Dower, "The Eye of the Beholder: Background Notes on the U.S.-Japan Military Relationship," 21.

41. George F. Kennan interview, DOHP. Kennan quotes liberally in the interview from his diary for 17 and 18 July 1950.

42. Frank Kowalski, *Nihon Saigunbi* (Tokyo: Simul Press, 1969), 123. I am indebted to John Dower for a copy of the original English language version, *The Rearmament of Japan,* of Kowalski's important manuscript. Page citations are to that typed manuscript.

43. Ibid., 125–26, 143–44, and 156–61.

44. Auer, *The Postwar Rearmament of Japanese Maritime Forces,* 53–68.

45. Ibid., 76.

46. Allison, *Ambassador from the Prairie,* 151–52.

47. *FRUS,* 1950, 6:1333–34.

48. Dulles to Arthur Vandenberg, 30 November 1950, Dulles Papers; and *FRUS,* 1950, 6:162–164, 1359.

49. *FRUS,* 1950, 6:1385–92.

50. Ibid., 787–89.

51. *FRUS,* 1951, 6:781–83.

52. Ibid., 827–30, 832; and Weinstein, *Japan's Postwar Defense Policy,* 81.

53. Dower, *Empire and Aftermath,* 389–93; and Takeshi Igarashi, "Peace-Making and Party Politics: The Formation of the Domestic Foreign-Policy System in Postwar Japan," *Journal of Japanese Studies* 11, 2 (Summer 1985): 323–56.

54. *FRUS,* 1951, 6:833–34.

55. Yoshitsu, *Japan and the San Francisco Peace Settlement,* 57–66.

56. *FRUS,* 1951, 6:857–59.

57. "Memorandum for Record: Substance of remarks by Ambassador Dulles at conference

with Gen. Ridgway," 17 April 1951, Ridgway Papers. Dulles confided to Ridgway that "the point the United States wanted to be clear on [with the Japanese in February] was that we wanted the right to station these troops so long as we felt it was in our interest, but we wanted no obligation to so station them. . . . [It] wasn't any easy thing to get a nation to agree to such conditions. He [Dulles] had . . . some qualms as to whether or not we could get the Japanese to agree to it at all."

58. *FRUS*, 1951, 6:849–54.

59. Ibid., 856–57.

60. Ibid., 863.

61. Dulles statement, 10 February 1951, Dulles Papers.

62. *FRUS*, 1950, 6:20–21, 26–27, 53–54, 1412–16, 1157–59, and 1162–63.

63. Ibid., 121–22; and *FRUS*, 1951, 6:793.

64. "Memorandum for the Record: Substance of remarks by Ambassador Dulles at conference with Gen. Ridgway," 17 April 1951, Ridgway Papers; and *FRUS*, 1951, 6:931.

65. "Memorandum for the Record: Substance of remarks by Ambassador Dulles at conference with Gen. Ridgway," 17 April 1951, Ridgway Papers; and C. Stanton Babcock to Earl D. Johnson, 26 February 1951, CD 387 Japan 1951 Decimal Files, Secretary of Defense Papers, RG 330, National Archives.

66. Dunn, *Peace-Making and the Settlement with Japan,* 130–32; and Joseph M. Siracusa and Glen St. John Barclay, "Australia, the United States, and the Cold War, 1945–51: From V-J Day to ANZUS," *Diplomatic History* 5, 1 (Winter 1981): 49–52.

67. K. V. Kesavan, *Japan's Relations with Southeast Asia: 1952–1960* (Bombay: Somaiya Co., 1972), 32–34, 51–57.

68. *FRUS*, 1951, 6:819; and C. Stanton Babcock to Earl D. Johnson, 18 March 1951, CD 387 (Japan) 1951 Decimal Files, Secretary of Defense Papers, RG 330.

69. Roger Dingman, "Peacemaking in Asia: The Philippines' Experience, 1949–1951," (paper prepared for Conference of International Association of Historians of Asia, Manila, 21–25 November 1983).

70. Lewe van Aduard, *Japan: From Surrender to Peace,* 198, 205–13.

71. Acheson, *Present at the Creation,* 696; and Dower, "The Eye of the Beholder: Background Notes on the U.S.-Japan Military Relationship," 24.

72. Packard, *Protest in Tokyo, The Security Treaty Crisis in 1960,* 12–14; and *FRUS*, 1951, 6:1367–68.

73. Roger Dingman, "Reconsiderations: The United States-Japan Security Treaty," *Pacific Community* (July 1976): 478; and Lewe van Aduard, *Japan: From Surrender to Peace,* 232–33.

74. *FRUS*, 1951, 6:1282–84.

75. Ibid., 1289, 1345.

76. Ibid., 1378–79.

77. Ibid., 1380–81; and *New York Times,* 19 November 1951, 4.

78. *FRUS*, 1952, 14:2:1095–1115.

79. *FRUS*, 1952, 14:2:1105–1107, 1123; see also Yoshitsu, *Japan and the San Francisco Peace Settlement,* 90–94.

80. *FRUS*, 1952, 14:2:1125, 1198; see also Yoshitsu, *Japan and the San Francisco Peace Settlement,* 96–98.

81. *FRUS*, 1952, 14:2:1141–42, 1148, 1175–79, 1187–90, 1204; see also Yoshitsu, *Japan and the San Francisco Peace Treaty,* 86–90.

82. *FRUS*, 1952, 14:2:1142; *New York Times,* 14 January 1952.

83. *New York Times,* 3 March 1952, 3.

84. *FRUS*, 1952 6:1194–95, 1208.

85. Weinstein, *Japan Postwar Defense Policy,* 80–83, 110–11.

86. *New York Times,* 29 February 1952, 22; Lewe van Aduard, *Japan: From Surrender to Peace,* 236; and *FRUS,* 1952, 6:1208.

87. Howard Schonberger, "John Foster Dulles and the China Question in the Making of the Japanese Peace Treaty," in Thomas W. Burkman, ed., *The Occupation of Japan: The International Context,* (Norfolk: MacArthur Memorial, 1984), 236-38.

88. *FRUS,* 1951, 6:952-53; and *FRUS,* 1950, 6:1350.

89. Sir Oliver Franks to Foreign Office, 30 March 1951, FO 371/FJ1022/227; and *FRUS,* 1951, 6:964.

90. *FRUS,* 1951, 6:1050.

91. Sir Oliver Franks to Foreign Office, 30 March 1951, FO 371/FJ1022/192; C. H. Johnston to F. S. Tomlinson, 28 March 1951, FO 371/FJ1022/97; Cabinet Papers (51) 137, "Memorandum by Secretary of State for Foreign Affairs on Japanese Peace Treaty," 23 May 1951, Herbert Morrison to F. S. Tomlinson, 24 April 1951, FO 371/FJ1022/255; and *FRUS,* 1951, 6:1107-9.

92. Cabinet Minutes, CM 41 (51), 7 June 1951.

93. Cabinet Papers (51) 158, "Memorandum of Secretary of State for Foreign Affairs on Japanese Peace Treaty: Chinese Participation," 9 June 1951; and Cabinet Minutes 42 (51), 11 June 1951.

94. *FRUS,* 1951, 6:1134; and Notes on a Conversation with John Foster Dulles, 28 June 1951, Wellington Koo Papers, Columbia University Library, New York, N.Y.

95. Dulles to Herbert Morrison, 21 June 1951, FO 371/FJ1022/631; Walter Gifford to Morrison, 26 June 1951, FO 371/FJ1022/656; and Gifford to Morrison, 3 July 1951, FO 371/FJ1022/697.

96. Notes on a Conversation with Dulles, 3 July 1951, Koo Papers.

97. U.S. Department of State, Conference for the Conclusion and Signatures of the Treaty of Peace with Japan, *Record of Proceedings,* 1952, 305; and *FRUS,* 1951, 6:1315-16.

98. *FRUS,* 1951, 6:1343-44.

99. *New York Times,* 14 September 1951, 3.

100. *FRUS,* 1951, 6:1389.

101. *Foreign Affairs,* January 1951, 179; see also Dower, *Empire and Aftermath,* 384-414; Fukui, *Party in Power: The Japanese Liberal Democrats and Policy-making,* 227-51; and Notes on a Conversation with Dulles, 29 November 1951, Koo Papers.

102. *FRUS,* 1951, 6:1409-15.

103. "Record of Conversations this Date with Ambassador Dulles, December 10, 1951," Ridgway Papers.

104. *FRUS,* 1951, 6:1437-39.

105. "Memorandum of Conversation with Ambassador Dulles and Sebald and Senators Sparkman and Smith, December 14, 1951," Ridgway Papers.

106. *FRUS,* 1951, 6:1443-46.

107. *FRUS,* 1952, 14:2:1079, 1083-85; and Memorandum of Japan and China, 11 January 1952, Dulles Papers.

108. Anthony Eden to Foreign Office, 10 January 1952, FO 371/FJ10310/4; and Anthony Eden, *The Memoirs of Anthony Eden: Full Circle* (Cambridge; Houghton Mifflin, 1960), 20-22.

109. Sir Esler Dening to Foreign Office, 16 January 1952, FO 371/FJ10310/8.

110. Dulles to MacArthur, 25 February 1952, Dulles Papers; Sir Esler Dening to Foreign Office, 18 June 1952, FO 371/FJ10310/15; and Sir Esler Dening to R. H. Scott, 18 February 1952, FO 371/FJ10310/54.

111. *FRUS,* 1952, 14:2:1093, 1080.

112. U.S. Senate, Committee on Foreign Relations, *Hearings on Japanese Peace Treaty and*

Other Treaties Relating to Security in the Pacific, 82d Cong., 2d sess., 1952, 9–14, 49–50, 78–82, 155–56, 164–66.

113. Karl L. Rankin, *China Assessment* (Seattle: University of Washington Press, 1964), 116–17.

114. *Congressional Record,* 82d Cong., 2d sess., 1952, 98:2:2367, 2501–5, 2329, 2337, and 2452–53.

115. E. H. Jacobs-Larkson to Foreign Office, 7 May 1952, FO 371/FJ10310/79.

116. *FRUS,* 1952, 14:2:1247; Wang Yu-san, "Sino-Japanese Peace Making and Settlement," (Ph.D. diss., University of Pennsylvania, 1968), 214–18.

117. *FRUS,* 1951, 6:1467–70.

SELECT BIBLIOGRAPHY

Official Records

Great Britain

Public Record Office, London
 Foreign Office Records, FO 371
 Cabinet Minutes and Papers

Japan

Ministry of Finance (Okurasho), Tokyo
 Postwar Financial History Project Records

United States

Unless otherwise indicated, all records are located in the National Archives, Washington, D.C. Records obtained from the Washington National Records Center, Suitland, Md., are noted as WNRC.
 Allied Council for Japan, RG 43
 Department of Defense
  General Omar Bradley File, RG 218
  Army Civil Affairs Division, RG 165
  Joint Chiefs of Staff, RG 218
  Admiral William Leahy File, RG 218
  Office of the Secretary of the Army and Under Secretary, RG 335
  Office of the Secretary of Defense, RG 330
  Supreme Commander for the Allied Powers, RG 331, WNRC
  War Department and Special Staffs, RG 165

Department of Labor
   Office of the Secretary, RG 174
Department of State
   Assistant Secretary for Occupied Areas, RG 59
   Bureau of Intelligence and Research, RG 59
   Decimal Files, RG 59
   Far Eastern Commission-U.S. Delegation Papers, RG 43
   Harley Notter Papers, RG 59
   Inter-Divisional Area Committee on the Far East Papers, RG 59
   Policy Planning Staff, RG 59
   Tokyo Post Files, RG 84, WNRC
   U.S. Mission on Reparations, RG 59
National Advisory Council on International Financial and Monetary Affairs Papers
National Security Council Papers
State-War-Navy Coordinating Committee, RG 353

Manuscript Collections

Army War College, Carlisle, Pa.
   Matthew B. Ridgway Papers
   Charles Willoughby Papers
University of California, Berkeley, Calif.
   William Knowland Papers
University of California, San Diego, Calif.
   John Dower Collection
Catholic University, Washington, D.C.
   John Brophy Papers
   Richard Deverall Papers
Columbia University, New York, N.Y.
   Institute for Pacific Relations Papers
   Wellington Koo Papers
   Oral History of the Occupation of Japan
Detroit Public Library, Detroit, Mich.
   Joseph M. Dodge Papers
Duke University, Durham, N.C.
   Robert M. Eichelberger Papers
Harvard University, Cambridge, Mass.
   William C. Castle Diary
   Joseph C. Grew Papers
Herbert Hoover Library, West Branch, Iowa
   William C. Castle Papers
   Hanford MacNider Papers
   Robert Wood Papers
Library of Congress, Washington D.C.

William Leahy Papers
Frank McCoy Papers
John C. O'Laughlin Papers
MacArthur Memorial, Norfolk, Va.
    Douglas MacArthur Papers
    Charles Willoughby Papers
University of Maine, Orono, Maine
    T. A. Bisson Papers
University of Maryland, College Park, Md.
    Justin Williams, Sr., Papers
Naval War College, Newport, R.I.
    William V. Pratt Papers
Princeton University, Princeton, N.J.
    John Foster Dulles Papers
    James Forrestal Papers
    George F. Kennan Papers
    Karl L. Rankin Papers
    H. Alexander Smith Papers
Rutgers University, New Brunswick, N.J.
    Tracy Voorhees Papers
Stanford University, Stanford, Calif.
    Stanley K. Hornbeck Papers
Harry S. Truman Library, Independence, Mo.
    Harry S. Truman Papers
Wayne State University, Detroit, Mich.
    Congress of Industrial Organizations Papers
Wisconsin State Historical Society, Madison, Wis.
    Foreign Policy Association Papers
    International Brotherhood of Pulp, Sulphite and Paper Mill Workers Papers
    Florence Thorne Papers
Yale University, New Haven, Conn.
    Henry L. Stimson Papers

Government Documents

U.S. Congress. *Congressional Record*. 80th and 81st Cong. Washington, D.C.: Government Printing Office, 1948–1950.
U.S. Department of State. *Bulletin*. 1943–1951.
———. *Conference for the Conclusion and Signatures of the Treaty of Peace with Japan, September 4–8, 1951, Record of Proceedings*. Publication 4392, International Organization and Conference Series II, Far Eastern 3. Washington, D.C.: Government Printing Office, 1951.
U.S. Department of State. *Foreign Relations of the United States*. Volumes for 1944–52. Washington, D.C.: Government Printing Office, 1966–82.
U.S. House. Committee on Appropriations. *Hearings on Foreign Aid Appropriations*

for 1949. 80th Cong., 2d sess. Washington, D.C.: Government Printing Office, 1948.

U.S. Senate. Committee on Agriculture and Forestry. *Providing a Revolving Fund for the Purchase of Agricultural Commodities and Raw Materials to Be Processed in Occupied Areas and Sold, Report 1099.* 80th Cong., 2d sess. Washington, D.C.: Government Printing Office, 1948.

———. *Hearings on Revolving Fund for the Purchase of Agricultural Commodities.* 80th Cong., 2d sess. 1948. Washington, D.C.: Government Printing Office, 1948.

U.S. Senate. Committee on Armed Services and Committee on Foreign Relations. *Hearings to Conduct an Inquiry into the Military Situation in the Far East.* 82d Cong., 1st sess. 1951. Washington, D.C.: Government Printing Office, 1951.

U.S. Senate. Committee on Appropriations. *Hearings on Economic Cooperation Administration.* 80th Cong., 2d sess. 1948. Washington, D.C.: Government Printing Office, 1948.

U.S. Senate. Committee on Appropriations. *Hearings on Foreign Aid Appropriation Bill, 1950.* 81st Cong., 1st sess. 1949. Washington, D.C.: Government Printing Office, 1949.

U.S. Senate. Committee on Foreign Relations. *Hearings on Japanese Peace Treaty and Other Treaties Pertaining to Security in the Pacific.* 82d Cong., 2d sess. 1952. Washington, D.C.: Government Printing Office, 1952.

———. *Hearings on Treaty of Mutual Cooperation and Security with Japan.* 86th Cong., 2d sess. 1960. Washington, D.C.: Government Printing Office, 1960.

U.S. Senate. Committee on the Judiciary. Subcommittee to Investigate the Administration of the Internal Security Act and Other Internal Security Laws. *Hearings on the Institute of Pacific Relations.* 82d Cong. 2d sess. 1951-52. Washington, D.C.: Government Printing Office, 1951-52.

Supreme Commander for the Allied Powers. *The Political Reorientation of Japan, September 1945-September 1948, Report of the Government Section of SCAP.* 2 vols. Washington, D.C.: Government Printing Office, 1949.

Newspapers and Periodicals

Amerasia, 1938-46.
Bank of Japan Quarterly Review, 1947-51.
Economist (London), 1945-52.
Far Eastern Survey, 1943-51.
Foreign Policy Bulletin, 1929-41.
Foreign Policy Reports, 1929-41.
Free Trade Union News, 1946-52.
The Nation, 1944-52.
Newsweek, 1945-52.
New York Times, 1945-52.
Nippon Times, 1945-52.
Oriental Economist, 1949-51.
Pacific Affairs, 1944-52.

Books

Acheson, Dean. *Present at the Creation: My Years in the State Department.* New York: Norton, 1969.

Allison, John. *Ambassador from the Prairie, or Allison Wonderland.* Boston: Houghton Mifflin, 1973.

Ambrose, Stephen. *Rise to Globalism: American Foreign Policy Since 1938.* 3d ed. New York: Penguin Books, 1983.

Auer, James E. *The Postwar Rearmament of Japanese Maritime Forces, 1945–1971.* New York: Praeger, 1973.

Ball, W. MacMahon. *Japan: Enemy or Ally.* New York: John Day, 1949.

Baerwald, Hans H. *The Purge of Japanese Leaders Under the Occupation.* Berkeley: University of California Press, 1959.

Barnhart, Michael A. *Japan Prepares for Total War: The Search for Economic Security, 1919–1941.* Ithaca: Cornell University Press, 1987.

Bisson, Thomas A. *American Policy in the Far East, 1931–1940.* New York: Institute of Pacific Relations, 1940.

———. *Japan in China.* New York: Macmillan, 1938.

———. *Japan's War Economy.* New York: Macmillan, 1945.

———. *Prospects for Democracy in Japan.* New York: Macmillan, 1949.

———. *Yenan in June 1937: Talks with Communist Leaders.* Berkeley: Center for Chinese Studies, University of California, 1973.

———. *Zaibatsu Dissolution in Japan.* Berkeley: University of California Press, 1954.

Blakeslee, George. *The Far Eastern Commission.* Department of State Publication 5138. Far East Series 60. Washington, D.C., 1953.

Blum, Robert M. *Drawing the Line: The Origin of the American Containment Policy in East Asia.* New York: Norton, 1982.

Borden, William S. *The Pacific Alliance: United States Foreign Economic Policy and Japanese Trade Recovery, 1947–1955.* Madison: University of Wisconsin Press, 1984.

Borg, Dorothy, and Shumpei Okamoto, eds. *Pearl Harbor as History: Japanese-American Relations, 1931–1941.* New York: Columbia University Press, 1973.

Borg, Dorothy, and Waldo Heinrichs, eds., *Uncertain Years: Chinese-American Relations, 1947–1950.* New York: Columbia University Press, 1980.

Brown, W. Adams Jr., and Redvers Opie. *American Foreign Assistance.* Washington, D.C.: Brookings Institute, 1954.

Buckley, Roger. *Occupation Diplomacy: Britain, the United States and Japan, 1945–1952.* Cambridge: Cambridge University Press, 1982.

Burkman, Thomas W., ed. *The Occupation of Japan: The International Context.* Norfolk: MacArthur Memorial, 1984.

Butow, Robert J. C. *Japan's Decision to Surrender.* Stanford: Stanford University Press, 1954.

Cohen, Jerome B. *Japan's Economy in War and Reconstruction.* Minneapolis: University of Minnesota Press, 1949.

Cohen, Jerome. *Japan's Postwar Economy*. Bloomington: Indiana University Press, 1958.

Cohen, Theodore. *Remaking Japan: The American Occupation as New Deal*. Edited by Herbert Passin. New York: Free Press, 1987.

Cohen, Warren I., ed. *New Frontiers in American-East Asian Relations: Essays Presented to Dorothy Borg*. New York: Columbia University Press, 1983.

Cole, Allan B., George O. Totten, and Cecil Uyehara. *Socialist Parties in Postwar Japan*. New Haven: Yale University Press, 1966.

Coughlan, William J. *Conquered Press, The MacArthur Era in Japanese Journalism*. Palo Alto: Pacific Books, 1952.

Crowley, James. *Japan's Quest for Autonomy, National Security and Foreign Policy, 1930–1938*. Princeton: Princeton University Press, 1966.

Dore, Ronald P. *Land Reform in Japan*. London: Oxford University Press, 1959.

Dower, John W. *Empire and Aftermath: Yoshida Shigeru and the Japanese Experience, 1878–1954*. Cambridge: Harvard University Press, 1979.

———. *War Without Mercy: Race and Power in the Pacific War*. New York: Pantheon Books, 1986.

Dower, John W., ed., *Origins of the Modern Japanese State: Selected Writings of E. H. Norman*. New York: Pantheon Books, 1975.

Duke, Benjamin C. *Japan's Militant Teachers: A History of the Left-Wing Teachers' Movement*. Honolulu: University of Hawaii Press, 1973.

Dunn, Frederick S. *Peace-making and the Settlement with Japan*. Princeton: Princeton University Press, 1963.

Emmerson, John K. *The Japanese Thread: A Life in the U.S. Foreign Service*. New York: Holt, Rinehart and Winston, 1978.

Farley, Miriam. *Aspects of Japan's Labor Problem*. New York: John Day, 1950.

Feis, Herbert. *Contest Over Japan*. New York: Norton, 1967.

Freeland, Richard M. *The Truman Doctrine and the Origins of McCarthyism: Foreign Policy, Domestic Politics, and Internal Security, 1946–1948*. New York: Knopf, 1972.

Friedman, Edward, and Mark Selden, eds. *America's Asia: Dissenting Essays on Asian-American Relations*. New York: Pantheon Books, 1971.

Fukui, Haruhiro. *Party in Power: The Japanese Liberal-Democrats and Policy-making*. Berkeley: University of California Press, 1970.

Gaddis, John L. *Strategies of Containment: A Critical Appraisal of Postwar National Security Policy*. New York: Oxford University Press, 1982.

Gayn, Mark. *Japan Diary*. New York: William Sloane, 1948.

Goodman, Grant K., ed. *The American Occupation of Japan: A Retrospective View*. Lawrence: University of Kansas Press, 1968.

Gordon, Andrew. *The Evolution of Labor Relations in Japan: Heavy Industry, 1853–1955*. Cambridge: Harvard University Press, 1985.

Grew, Joseph C. *Turbulent Era, A Diplomatic Record of Forty Years, 1904–1945*. Boston: Houghton Mifflin, 1952.

———. *Ten Years in Japan: A Contemporary Record Drawn from the Diaries and Private and Official Papers of Joseph C. Grew, United States Ambassador to Japan,*

1932–1942. New York: Simon and Schuster, 1944.

Hadley, Eleanor. *Antitrust in Japan.* Princeton: Princeton University Press, 1970.

Halliday, Jon. *A Political History of Japanese Capitalism.* New York: Pantheon Books, 1975.

Halliday, Jon, and Gavan McCormick. *Japanese Imperialism Today.* New York: Monthly Review Press, 1973.

Harriman, W. Averell, and Elie Abel. *Special Envoy to Churchill and Stalin, 1941–1946.* New York: Random House, 1975.

Heinrichs, Waldo H., Jr. *American Ambassador: Joseph C. Grew and the Development of the United States Diplomatic Tradition.* Little, Brown, 1966.

Hunsberger, Warren. *Japan and the United States in World Trade.* New York: Harper and Row, 1964.

Iriye, Akira. *Power and Culture: The Japanese-American War, 1941–1945.* Cambridge: Harvard University Press, 1981.

James, D. Clayton. *The Years of MacArthur.* 3 vols. Boston: Houghton Mifflin, 1970–1985.

Johnson, Chalmers. *Conspiracy at Matsukawa.* Berkeley: University of California Press, 1972.

Kennan, George F. *Memoirs, 1925–1950.* Boston: Little, Brown, 1967.

Kolko, Gabriel. *Politics of War: The World and United States Foreign Policy, 1943–1945.* New York: Random House, 1968.

Kolko, Joyce, and Gabriel Kolko. *The Limits of Power: The World and United States Foreign Policy, 1945–1954.* New York: Harper and Row, 1972.

Kowalski, Frank. *Nihon Saigunbi.* Tokyo: Simul Press, 1969.

Lattimore, Owen. *Solution in Asia.* Boston: Little, Brown, 1945.

———. *The Situation in Asia.* Boston: Little, Brown, 1949.

Levine, Solomon B. *Industrial Relations in Postwar Japan.* Urbana: University of Illinois Press, 1958.

Lewe van Aduard, Evert J. *Japan: From Surrender to Peace.* The Hague: Martinus Nijhoff, 1953.

Livingston, Jon, Joe Moore, and Felicia Oldfather, eds. *The Japan Reader, Postwar Japan, 1945 to the Present.* New York: Pantheon Books, 1973.

MacArthur, Douglas. *Reminiscences.* New York: McGraw-Hill, 1964.

Martin, Edwin M. *The Allied Occupation of Japan.* Stanford: Stanford University Press, 1948.

May, Gary. *China Scapegoat: The Diplomatic Ordeal of John Carter Vincent.* Project Heights, Ill.: Waveland Press, 1979.

Millis, Walter, ed. *The Forrestal Diaries.* New York: Viking, 1951.

Minear, Richard. *Victor's Justice, The Tokyo War Crimes Trial.* Princeton: Princeton University Press, 1971.

Moore, Joe. *Japanese Workers and the Struggle for Power, 1945–1947.* Madison: University of Wisconsin Press, 1983.

Morris, Ivan. *Nationalism and the Right-Wing in Japan: A Study of Post-war Trends.* London: Oxford University Press, 1960.

Nagai, Yonosuke, and Akria Iriye, eds. *The Origins of the Cold War in Asia.* New

York: Columbia University Press, 1977.

Nishi Toshio. *Unconditional Democracy: Education and Politics in Occupied Japan, 1945–1952.* Stanford: Stanford University Press, 1982.

Packard, George R. *Protest in Tokyo: The Security Treaty Crisis of 1960.* Princeton: Princeton University Press, 1966.

Passin, Herbert, ed. *The United States and Japan.* Englewood Cliffs, N.J.: Prentice-Hall, 1966.

Petillo, Carol M. *Douglas MacArthur: The Philippine Years.* Bloomington: Indiana University Press, 1981.

Pruessen, Ronald W. *John Foster Dulles: The Road to Power.* New York: Free Press, 1982.

Radosh, Ronald. *American Labor and United States Foreign Policy.* New York: Random House, 1969.

Redford, Laurence H., ed. *The Occupation of Japan: Economic Policy and Reform.* Norfolk: MacArthur Memorial, 1980.

Reischauer, Edwin O. *The United States and Japan.* 3d rev. ed. Cambridge: Harvard University Press, 1965.

Roth, Andrew. *Dilemma in Japan.* Boston: Little, Brown, 1945.

Scalapino, Robert. *The Japanese Communist Movement, 1920–1966.* Berkeley: University of California Press, 1967.

Schaller, Michael. *The American Occupation of Japan: The Origins of the Cold War in Asia.* New York: Oxford University Press, 1985.

Sebald, William J., and Russell Brines. *With MacArthur in Japan: A Personal History of the Occupation.* New York: Norton, 1965.

Selden, Mark, ed. *Remaking Asia: Essays on the American Uses of Power.* New York: Pantheon Books, 1974.

Sherwin, Martin. *A World Destroyed: The Atomic Bomb and the Grand Alliance.* New York: Knopf, 1975.

Stueck, William W. *The Road to Confrontation: American Policy Toward China and Korea, 1947–1950.* Chapel Hill: University of North Carolina Press, 1981.

Swearingen, Rodger, and Paul Langer. *Red Flag in Japan: International Communism in Action, 1919–1951.* Cambridge: Harvard University Press, 1952.

Thomas, John N. *The Institute of Pacific Relations: Asian Scholars and American Politics.* Seattle: University of Washington Press, 1974.

Thorne, Christopher. *Allies of a Kind: The United States, Britain, and the War Against Japan, 1941–1945.* New York: Oxford University Press, 1978.

Truman, Harry S. *Memoirs.* 2 vols. Garden City, N.J.: Doubleday, 1955–56.

Tsuru, Shigeto. *Essays on the Japanese Economy.* Tokyo: Kinokuniya Bookstore, 1958.

Tucker, Nancy B. *Patterns in the Dust: Chinese-American Relations and the Recognition Controversy, 1949–1950.* New York: Columbia University Press, 1983.

Ward, Robert E., and Frank J. Shulman, eds. *The Allied Occupation of Japan, 1945–1952: An Annotated Bibliography of Western-Language Materials.* Chicago: American Library Association, 1974.

Weinstein, Martin E. *Japan's Postwar Defense Policy, 1946–1968.* New York: Columbia University Press, 1971.

Westerfield, H. Bradford. *Foreign Policy and Party Politics: Pearl Harbor to Korea.* New Haven: Yale University Press, 1955.

Whitney, Courtney. *MacArthur: His Rendezvous with History.* New York: Knopf, 1956.

Wightman, David. *Toward Economic Cooperation in Asia: The Economic Commission for Asia and the Far East.* New Haven: Yale University Press, 1963.

Wildes, Harry E. *Typhoon in Tokyo: The Occupation and Its Aftermath.* New York: Macmillan, 1954.

Williams, William A. *Tragedy of American Diplomacy.* Rev. ed. New York: Dell Publishing, 1962.

Willoughby, Charles A., and John Chamberlain. *MacArthur, 1941-1951.* New York: McGraw-Hill, 1954.

Wittner, Lawrence S. *Cold War America: From Hiroshima to Watergate.* New York: Praeger, 1974.

Wolfe, Robert, ed. *Americans as Proconsuls, United States Military Government in Germany and Japan, 1944-1952.* Carbondale: Southern Illinois University Press, 1984.

Yamamura, Kozo. *Economic Policy in Postwar Japan: Growth Versus Economic Democracy.* Berkeley: University of California Press, 1967.

Yanaga, Chitoshi. *Big Business in Japanese Politics.* New Haven: Yale University Press, 1968.

Yergin, Daniel. *Shattered Peace: The Origins of the Cold War and the National Security State.* Boston: Houghton Mifflin, 1977.

Yoshida, Shigeru. *The Yoshida Memoirs.* London: William Heinemann, 1961.

Yoshitsu, Michael. *Japan and the San Francisco Peace Settlement.* New York: Columbia University Press, 1983.

Articles

Bernstein, Barton. "Roosevelt, Truman, and the Atomic Bomb, 1941-1945: A Reinterpretation." *Political Science Quarterly* 90, no. 1 (Spring 1975): 23-69.

Bronfenbrenner, Martin. "Four Positions on Japanese Finance." *Journal of Political Economy* 58, no. 4 (August 1950): 281-88.

Buckley, Roger. "Britain and the Emperor: The Foreign Office and Constitutional Reform in Japan, 1945-1946." *Modern Asian Studies* 12, no. 4 (1978): 553-70.

Dingman, Roger. "Reconsiderations: The United States-Japan Security Treaty." *Pacific Community* 7, no. 4 (July 1976): 472-93.

Dingman, Roger. "Strategic Planning and the Policy Process: American Plans for War in East Asia, 1945-50." *Naval War College Review* 32, no. 6 (November-December 1979): 4-21.

Dower, John W. "The Eye of the Beholder: Background Notes on the U.S. Military Relationship." *Bulletin of Concerned Asian Scholars* 2, no. 1 (October 1969): 15-31.

———. "Occupied Japan as History and Occupation History as Politics." *Journal of*

Asian Studies 34, no. 2 (February 1975): 485–504.

Igarashi, Takeshi. "Peace-Making and Party Politics: The Formation of the Domestic-Foreign Policy System in Postwar Japan." *Journal of Japanese Studies* 11, no. 2 (Summer 1985): 323–56.

Iokibe, Makoto. "American Policy towards Japan's 'Unconditional Surrender.' " *The Japanese Journal of American Studies* 1, 1(1981): 19–53.

Kagan, Richard. "McCarren's Legacy: The Association of Asian Studies." *Bulletin of Concerned Asian Scholars* 1, no. 2 (May 1969): 18–22.

McCoy, Al. "Land Reform as Counter-Revolution: U.S. Foreign Policy and the Tenant Farmers of Asia." *Bulletin of Concerned Asian Scholars* 3, no. 1 (Winter-Spring 1971): 14–49.

McNelly, Theodore. "The Japanese Constitution: Child of the Cold War." *Political Science Quarterly* 74, no. 2 (June 1959): 176–95.

–––––. "The Renunciation of War in the Japanese Constitution." *Political Science Quarterly* 77, no. 3 (September 1962): 350–78.

Morley, James W. "The First Seven Weeks." *The Japan Interpreter* 6, no. 2 (September 1970): 151–64.

Schaller, Michael. "MacArthur's Japan: The View from Washington." *Diplomatic History* 10, no. 1 (Winter 1986): 1–23.

–––––. "Securing the Great Crescent: Occupied Japan and the Origins of Containment in Southeast Asia." *Journal of American History* 69, no. 2 (September 1982): 392–414.

Schonberger, Howard. "American Labor's Cold War in Occupied Japan." *Diplomatic History* 3, no. 3 (Summer 1979): 249–72.

–––––. "The Japan Lobby in American Diplomacy, 1947–1952." *Pacific Historical Review* 46, no. 3 (August 1977): 327–59.

–––––. "Peacemaking in Asia: The United States, Great Britain, and Japan's Decision to Recognize Nationalist China." *Diplomatic History* 10, no. 1 (January 1986): 59–73.

–––––. "Zaibatsu Dissolution and the American Restoration of Japan." *Bulletin of Concerned Asian Scholars* 5, no. 2 (September 1973): 16–31.

Shinobu Seizaburo. "The Korean War as an Epoch of Contemporary History." *Developing Economics* 4 (March 1966): 20–36.

Takemae, Eiji. "The U.S. Occupation Policies for Japan." *Tokyo Metropolitam University Journal of Law and Politics* 14 (1973): 1–39.

Villa, Brian L. "The U.S. Army, Unconditional Surrender, and the Potsdam Proclamation." *Journal of American History* 63, no. 1 (June 1976): 66–92.

Wittner, Lawrence S. "MacArthur and the Missionaries: God and Man in Occupied Japan." *Pacific Historical Review* 40 (February 1971): 77–98.

Unpublished Doctoral Dissertations

Kil, Soong H. "The Dodge Line and the Japanese Conservative Party." Ph.D. diss., University of Michigan, 1977.

Mattern, Carolyn. "The Man on the Dark Horse: The Presidential Campaigns for

General Douglas MacArthur, 1944 & 1948.'' Ph.D. diss., University of Wisconsin, 1976.

Nanto, Dick K. ''The United States' Role in the Postwar Economic Recovery of Japan.'' Ph.D. diss., Harvard University, 1976.

Svensson, Eric H. ''The Military Occupation of Japan: The First Years Planning, Policy Formulation, and Reform.'' Ph.D. diss., University of Denver, 1966.

Wang, Yu-san, ''Sino-Japanese Peace Making and Settlement.'' Ph.D. diss., University of Pennsylvania, 1968.

INDEX